Kant and the Transformation
of Natural History

Kant and the Transformation of Natural History

ANDREW COOPER

OXFORD
UNIVERSITY PRESS

OXFORD
UNIVERSITY PRESS

Great Clarendon Street, Oxford, OX2 6DP,
United Kingdom

Oxford University Press is a department of the University of Oxford.
It furthers the University's objective of excellence in research, scholarship,
and education by publishing worldwide. Oxford is a registered trade mark of
Oxford University Press in the UK and in certain other countries

Published in the United States of America by Oxford University Press
198 Madison Avenue, New York, NY 10016, United States of America

British Library Cataloguing in Publication Data
Data available

Library of Congress Control Number: 2023903275

ISBN 978-0-19-286978-4

DOI: 10.1093/oso/9780192869784.001.0001

Printed and bound by
CPI Group (UK) Ltd, Croydon, CR0 4YY

Contents

Preface

When we think of the revolutions that have changed the course of modern science, Copernicus' heliocentric model of the heavens and Darwin's theory of evolution by natural selection come to mind as two important examples. There is, however, another revolution that often goes overlooked, one that links the Copernican and Darwinian revolutions together: the addition of *time* to the frame in which explanations are required, sought, and justified in natural science. In this study, I examine this revolution as the *transformation of natural history*, a seismic shift whereby scientific knowledge ceased to be understood as a logical practice of taxonomy and was reconceived as the physical explanation of things as a temporal process (the cover image, a plate taken from the Second Discours of Buffon's *Histoire Naturelle*, reworks Michelangelo's *The Creation of Adam* to offer a provocative illustration of the latter, physical conception of nature). The transformation of natural history was catalysed by new phenomena made available by the technologies that followed Galileo's telescope, including the air pump, the microscope, the seafaring chronometer, and the dissection theatre. Against the backdrop of colonial expansion, natural philosophers on the continent were guaranteed a steady influx of new specimens into their gardens and display cabinets. On the frontier, the human body offered a pressing object of inquiry, as the global movement of military personnel, missionaries, indentured labourers, and chattel slaves raised new anxieties about the porosity of the body when relocated to foreign lands. These phenomena sparked an expansive programme of research into the mutability of material things in the system of nature—a programme that was framed by, and undertaken in the service of, colonial power. One of my aims in this study is to explore the extent to which natural history's transformation challenged—and reinforced—the prejudice of European superiority. There is still much work to be done to deconstruct the constellations of power at play in the Enlightenment, especially in the work of its canonical figures. I hope to contribute to this end by examining the writings and lectures of one philosopher whose life was thoroughly enmeshed in the tensions confronting natural historians in the eighteenth century: Immanuel Kant.

Kant and the Transformation of Natural History is the centrepiece of an Early Career Fellowship generously funded by the Leverhulme Trust in partnership with the Departments of Philosophy at University College London and the University of Warwick (ECF–2017–035). It has benefitted enormously from the help and encouragement of colleagues around the world, who have either read sections of the book or refined its contents through conversation. In no particular order, these include Ido Geiger, Robert Richards, Andy Jones, Angela Breitenbach, Alix

Cohen, Yarran Hominh, Nathan Lyons, Christopher Mayes, Lorenzo Spagnesi, Huaping Lu-Adler, Sebastian Gardner, John Zammito, Peter Anstey, Ina Goy, Naomi Fisher, Peter McLaughlin, Rachel Zuckert, Eric Watkins, Clinton Tolley, Lucy Allais, Michael Hardimon, Phillip Sloan, Cinzia Ferrini, Thomas Khurana, and Sabina Vaccarino Bremner. I also thank David Barnes for incisive editorial suggestions, and my anonymous reviewers, whose perceptive criticisms were immensely helpful as I revised the text. Naturally, all remaining errors are my own.

This project benefitted immensely from the hospitality of several lively academic communities, including the Department of Philosophy at the University of California, San Diego, The Stevanovich Institute on the Formation of Knowledge at the University of Chicago, and the Master and Fellows of Corpus Christi College, Cambridge. Portions of the book have been greatly improved through early trials in various international forums, including The Sydney Centre for the Foundations of Science (Sydney University), The History of Philosophy Roundtable (University of California, San Diego), The Morris Fishbein Center for the History of Science and Medicine (University of Chicago), The Chicago-area Consortium for German Philosophy (Loyola University), Kant's Scots (University of Edinburgh / University of St Andrews), the Joint Session (Durham University), and the Centre for Post-Kantian Philosophy (Universität Potsdam).

I thank the staff members of several libraries for helpful advice and support, including The British Library, Niedersächsische Staats- und Universitätsbibliothek Göttingen, The UCL Library, The University of Chicago Library, The Geisel Library, Cambridge University Library, and The University of Warwick Library. I am grateful for Werner Stark's momentous achievement to transcribe the student notes from Kant's lectures on physical geography, which are scattered across the globe in private collections and public libraries. The transcriptions have recently been published as vols. 26.1, 26.2.1, and 26.2.2 of *Kants gesammelte Schriften*.

It has been a pleasure to work with Peter Momtchiloff, my editor at OUP, who believed in the project and masterfully guided it through the various stages to publication. Some of the research in this book draws on and develops ideas that have been published in earlier papers, and I am grateful to Elsevier for granting permission to reproduce them here. The account of Kant's early cosmogony in Chapter 3 was first presented in "Kant's Universal Conception of Natural History," *Studies in History and Philosophy of Science* 79 (2020): 77–87. The examination of Kant's lectures on physical geography in §§4.1 and 4.2 builds on "Living Natural Products in Kant's Physical Geography," *Studies in History and Philosophy of Biological and Biomedical Sciences* 78(1) (December 2019, online publication): Doi:10.1016/j.shpsc.2019.101191. And the account of hypotheses in §5.4 draws on research first presented in "Hypotheses in Kant's Philosophy of Science," *Studies in History and Philosophy of Science* (May 2022, online publication): Doi:10.1016/j.shpsa.2022.04.007.

Finally, I am deeply indebted to the community at The Vicarage, Tufnell Park, including Alexandra, Michael, Buki, Pete, and Ed. Throughout my labours on this book, our experiments in hospitality have oriented me to the world with openness and joy.

Tufnell Park, London

Note on Citations

With two exceptions, citations of Kant's works refer to the volume and page number of *Kants gesammelte Schriften* (AA), edited by the Königlich Preußischen Akademie der Wissenschaften, later the Deutschen Akademie der Wissenschaften zu Berlin (Walter de Gruyter (and predecessors), 1902–). Citations of *Critique of Pure Reason* refer to the pagination of the 1781 (A) and 1787 (B) editions. Citations of *Hechsel Logic*, which is not included in the Akademie Ausgabe, refer to the original pagination (reproduced by Meiner Verlag). Where available, I have used translations from the Cambridge University Press editions. Modifications are noted in the footnotes, except for the following: *Kraft* is translated consistently as *force*; *Zweck* as *purpose*; the classificatory terms *Gattung, Art*, and *Stamm* as *species, kind*, and *stem*. For the student lecture notes that are unavailable in English, translations are my own. Citations to Kant's works are given in-text, using the abbreviations listed below.

Citations to other texts are by page number, except in cases where the cited paragraph or chapter would be more useful. Unless otherwise noted, translations of non-English texts are my own.

Works Published during Kant's Lifetime

A/B   *Kritik der reinen Vernunft, Critique of Pure Reason*, translated by Paul Guyer and Allan Wood (Cambridge: Cambridge University Press, 1999).

Anth   *Anthropologie in pragmatischer Hinsicht* (AA 7:117–333), *Anthropology from a Pragmatic Point of View*. In *Anthropology, History, and Education*, edited by Gunter Zöller and Robert Louden, translated by Robert Louden (Cambridge: Cambridge University Press, 2007), 227–429.

BBMR   *Bestimmung des Begriffs einer Menschenrace* (AA 8:89–106), "Determination of the Concept of a Human Race." In *Anthropology, History, and Education*, edited by Günter Zöller and Robert Louden, translated by Holly Wilson and Gunter Zöller (Cambridge: Cambridge University Press, 2007), 145–59.

BDG   *Der einzig mögliche Beweisgrund zu einer Demonstration des Daseins Gottes* (AA 2:63–163), *The Only Possible Argument in Support of a Demonstration of the Existence of God*. In *Theoretical Philosophy*,

	1755-1770, edited and translated by David Walford (Cambridge: Cambridge University Press, 1992), 107–201.
BGSE	*Beobachtungen über das Gefühl des Schönen und Erhabenen* (AA 2:205–56), *Observations on the Feeling of the Beautiful and the Sublime*. In *Anthropology, History, and Education*, edited by Günter Zöller and Robert Louden, translated by Paul Guyer (Cambridge: Cambridge University Press, 2007), 18–62.
EACG	*Entwurf und Ankündigung eines Collegii der physischen Geographie* (AA 2:1–12), "Plan and Announcement of a Series of Lectures on Physical Geography." In *Natural Science*, edited by Eric Watkins, translated by Olaf Reinhardt (Cambridge: Cambridge University Press, 2012), 386–95.
GMS	*Grundlegung zur Metaphysik der Sitten* (AA 4:385–463). *Metaphysics of Morals*, edited by Lara Denis, translated by Mary Gregor (Cambridge: Cambridge University Press, 2017).
GSK	*Gedanken von der wahren Schätzung der lebendigen Kräfte* (AA 1:1–181), *Thoughts on the True Estimation of Living Forces*. In *Natural Science*, edited by Eric Watkins, translated by Jeffrey Edwards and Martin Schönfeld (Cambridge: Cambridge University Press, 2012), 1–155.
IaG	*Idee zu einer allgemeinen Geschichte in weltbürgerlicher Absicht* (AA 8:17–31), "Idea for a Universal History with a Cosmopolitan Aim." In *Anthropology, History, and Education*, edited by Günter Zöller and Robert Louden, translated by Allen W. Wood (Cambridge: Cambridge University Press, 2007), 107–20.
KpV	*Kritik der praktischen Vernunft* (AA 5:1–163), *Critique of Practical Reason*, translated by Mary Gregor (Cambridge: Cambridge University Press, 2015).
KU	*Kritik der Urteilskraft* (AA 5:165–485), *Critique of the Power of Judgment*, translated by Paul Guyer (Cambridge: Cambridge University Press, 2000).
Log	*Logik* (AA 9:1–150), *Jäsche Logic*. In *Lectures on Logic*, edited and translated by J. Michael Young (Cambridge, Cambridge University Press, 1992), 521–642.
MAM	*Muthmaßlicher Anfang der Menschengeschichte* (AA 8:107–23), "Conjectural Beginning of Human History." In *Anthropology, History, and Education*, edited by Gunter Zöller and Robert Louden, translated by Allan W. Wood (Cambridge: Cambridge University Press, 2007), 163–75.
MAN	*Metaphysische Anfangsgründe der Naturwissenschaften* (AA 4:465–565), *Metaphysical Foundations of Natural Science*, edited and translated by Michael Friedman (Cambridge: Cambridge University Press, 2004).

MSI   *De mundi sensibilis atque intelligibilis forma et principiis* (AA
            2:385–419), *On the Form and Principles of the Sensible and
            the Intelligible World [Inaugural Dissertation]*. In *Theoretical
            Philosophy, 1755–1770*, edited and translated by David Walford
            (Cambridge: Cambridge University Press, 1992), 373–416.

NEV   *Nachricht von der Einrichtung seiner Vorlesungen in dem
            Winterhalbenjahre von 1765–1766* (AA 2:303–314), "M. Immanuel
            Kant's Announcement of the Programme of his Lectures for the
            Winter Semester 1765-1766." In *Theoretical Philosophy, 1755–1770*,
            edited and translated by David Walford (Cambridge: Cambridge
            University Press, 1992), 287–300.

NTH   *Allgemeine Naturgeschichte und Theorie des Himmels* (AA 1:215–368),
            Universal Natural History and Theory of the Heavens. In *Natural
            Science*, edited by Eric Watkins, translated by Olaf Reinhardt
            (Cambridge: Cambridge University Press, 2012), 182–308.

PG   *Physische Geographie* (AA 9:151–436), *Physical Geography*. In *Natural
            Science*, edited by Eric Watkins, translated by Olaf Reinhardt
            (Cambridge: Cambridge University Press, 2012), 441–682.

PND   *Principiorum primorum cognitionis metaphysicae nova dilucidatio*
            (AA 1:385–416), *A New Elucidation of the First Principles of
            Metaphysical Cognition*. In *Theoretical Philosophy, 1755–1770*,
            edited and translated by David Walford (Cambridge: Cambridge
            University Press, 1992), 1–46.

Prol   *Prolegomena zu einer jeden künftigen Metaphysik* (AA 4:253–383),
            Prolegomena to Any Future Metaphysics, edited and translated by
            Gary Hatfield (Cambridge: Cambridge University Press, 2004).

RezHerder   *Recensionen von J. G. Herders Ideen zur Philosophie der Geschichte der
            Menschheit* (AA 8:43–106), "Reviews of Herder's Ideas on the
            Philosophy of the History of Mankind." In *Anthropology, History,
            and Education*, edited by Günter Zöller and Robert Louden,
            translated by Allen W. Wood (Cambridge: Cambridge University
            Press, 2007), 124–42.

TG   *Träume eines Geistersehers, erläutert durch die Träume der Metaphysik*
            (AA 2:315–73), *Dreams of a Spirit Seer Elucidated by Dreams of
            Metaphysics*. In *Theoretical Philosophy, 1755–1770*, edited and
            translated by David Walford (Cambridge: Cambridge University
            Press, 1992), 301–60.

ÜGTP   *Über den Gebrauch teleologischer Principien in der Philosophie* (AA
            8:157–84), "On the Use of Teleological Principles in Philosophy." In
            Anthropology, History, and Education, edited by Gunter Zöller and
            Robert Louden, translated by Gunter Zöller (Cambridge: Cambridge
            University Press, 2007), 195–218.

VM   *Über die Vulkane im Monde* (AA 2: 67–76), "On the Volcanoes on the Moon." In *Natural Science*, edited by Eric Watkins, translated by Olaf Reinhardt (Cambridge: Cambridge University Press, 2012), 418–25.

VvRM75   *Von den verschiedenen Racen der Menschen zur Ankündigung der Vorlesungen der physischen Geographie im Sommerhalbenjahe 1775 von Immanuel Kant der Log. und Met. ordentl. Prof.* (AA 2:427–43 / *Werke* VI:3–26), "Of the Different Races of Human Beings to Announce the Lectures on Physical Geography of Immanuel Kant, Professor Ordinarius of Logic and Metaphysics." In *Kant and the Concept of Race*, edited and translated by Jon Mikkelsen (Albany, NY: State University of New York Press, 2013), 41–54.

VvRM77   *Von den verschiedenen Racen der Menschen* (AA 2:427–43), "Of the Different Races of Human Beings." In *Anthropology, History, and Education*, edited by Günter Zöller and Robert Louden, translated by Holly Wilson and Gunter Zöller (Cambridge: Cambridge University Press, 2007), 82–97.

Nachlass

Br   *Briefe* (AA 10–13), *Correspondence*, edited and translated by Arnulf Zweig (Cambridge: Cambridge University Press, 1999).

EEKU   *Erste Einleitung in die Kritik der Urteilskraft* (AA 20:193–251), "First Introduction to the *Critique of the Power of Judgment*." In *Critique of the Power of Judgment*, translated by Paul Guyer (Cambridge: Cambridge University Press, 2000), 1–52.

OP   *Opus postumum* (AA 21–2), *Opus postumum*, edited by Eckart Förster, translated by Eckart Förster and Michael Rosen (Cambridge: Cambridge University Press, 1993).

V-Geo/Dohna   *Vorlesungen über Physische Geographie, Ms Dohna.* In *Vorlesungen über die Physische Geographie*, vol. 26.2.2 of *Kant's gesammelte Schriften*, edited by Werner Stark (Berlin: Walter de Gruyter, 2020), 1117–43.

V-Geo/Dönhoff   *Vorlesungen über Physische Geographie, Ms Dönhoff.* In *Vorlesungen über die Physische Geographie*, vol. 26.2.2 of *Kant's gesammelte Schriften*, edited by Werner Stark (Berlin: Walter de Gruyter, 2020), 743–1092.

V-Geo/Hesse   *Vorlesungen über Physische Geographie, Ms Hesse.* In *Vorlesungen über die Physische Geographie*, vol. 26.2.1 of *Kant's gesammelte Schriften*, edited by Werner Stark (Berlin: Walter de Gruyter, 2020), 1–296.

V-Geo/Holstein   *Vorlesungen über Physische Geographie, Ms Holstein*. In *Vorlesungen über die Physische Geographie*, vol. 26.1 of *Kant's gesammelte Schriften*, edited by Werner Stark (Berlin: Walter de Gruyter, 2009), 7–320.

V-Geo/Kaehler   *Vorlesungen über Physische Geographie, Ms Kaehler*. In *Vorlesungen über die Physische Geographie*, vol. 26.2.1 of *Kant's gesammelte Schriften*, edited by Werner Stark (Berlin: Walter de Gruyter, 2020), 297–616.

V-Lo/Blomberg   *Logik Blomberg* (AA 24:7–301), *Blomberg Logic*. In *Lectures on Logic*, edited and translated by J. Michael Young (Cambridge, Cambridge University Press, 1992), 5–250.

V-Lo/Dohna   *Logik Dohna-Wundlacken* (AA 24:676–784), *Dohna-Wunlacken Logic*. In *Lectures on Logic*, edited and translated by J. Michael Young (Cambridge, Cambridge University Press, 1992), 431–520.

V-Lo/Hechsel   *Logik Hechsel* (Meiner Verlag, 269–500), *Hechsel Logic*. In *Lectures on Logic*, edited and translated by J. Michael Young (Cambridge, Cambridge University Press, 1992), 381–430.

V-Lo/Vienna   *Logik Vienna* (AA 24:787–940), *Vienna Logic*. In *Lectures on Logic*, edited and translated by J. Michael Young (Cambridge, Cambridge University Press, 1992), 251–380.

V-Met/Herder   *Metaphysik Herder, 1762–1764*. In *Vorlesungen über Metaphysik*, vols. 28.1 and 28.1.1 of *Kant's gesammelte Schriften*, edited by Gerhard Lehmann (Berlin: Walter de Gruyter, 1968/70), 1–524, 525–987.

V-Met/Mron   *Metaphysik Mrongovius, 1782–1783*. In *Vorlesungen über Metaphysik*, vol. 29.2 of *Kant's gesammelte Schriften*, edited by Gerhard Lehmann (Berlin: Walter de Gruyter, 1983), 747–940.

It is clear that the cognition of natural things as they *are now* always leaves us desirous of the cognition of that which they once *were* and of the series of changes they underwent to arrive at each place in their present state. *Natural history*, which we still lack almost entirely, would teach us about the changes in the shape of the earth, likewise that of its creatures (plants and animals) that they have undergone through natural migrations and the resultant degeneration from the archetype of the stem species. It would presumably trace a great many of seemingly different kinds to races of the same species and would transform the sprawling school system of natural description into a physical system of the understanding.

Immanuel Kant, "Of the Different Races of Human Beings"

Each may well hope from our instauration that it claims nothing infinite, and nothing beyond what is mortal; for in truth it prescribes only the end of infinite errors, and this is a legitimate end.

Immanuel Kant, *Critique of Pure Reason*, citing
Francis Bacon's *Instauratio Magna*

Introduction

Immanuel Kant spent his life in awe of nature's immense complexity and the potentially infinite number of material things, which exceeds anything we could expect in advance. He was captivated by the human capacity to orient ourselves in the face of such vast empirical diversity, and, by recognizing our finite standpoint within the causal process of nature, to seek affinities between objects, to craft empirical concepts that pick out their defining qualities, and to classify the variety of things in the system of nature. To this extent Erich Adickes is right to portray him as a *Naturforscher*: Kant denied that logical possibility can tell us what is really possible, and anchored scientific knowledge in what is actual.[1] Nowhere is Kant's admiration for the diversity of material things more obvious, and his fascination for the response it evokes in the human understanding more apparent, than in his extensive writings and lectures on natural history. While he was famously reluctant to leave his beloved Königsberg, Kant devoured the latest travel writings and natural histories pouring into Europe from the rapidly growing trade routes and the unbridled expansion of the colonial frontier. Over his lengthy career, he never ceased from lecturing on current debates in natural history, or from discerning what those debates reveal about human knowledge.

This book undertakes a contextual and systematic study of Kant's account of natural history. It has two major aims. The first is to reconstruct Kant's writings and lectures on classification within the methodological debates unfolding in the eighteenth century concerning the extension of Newtonian science from mathematical physics to the generation of material things. While recent scholarship frames Kant's work on natural history within the human origins debate unfolding in Prussian periodicals during the 1770s and 80s,[2] or the development of a

---

[1] In *Kant als Naturforscher*, Adickes challenges two predominant readings in the early twentieth-century scholarship: Kant as natural scientist (*Naturwissenschaftler*) and Kant as philosopher of nature (*Naturphilosoph*). Taking Kant's work as a whole, including the unpublished lecture notes, remarks, and letters, Adickes argues that Kant is better understood as a *Naturforscher*, an investigator of nature's empirical, philosophical, and metaphysical dimensions. Throughout the study I stress the nascent meaning of "natural science" in eighteenth-century philosophy, which Kant ambitiously sought to define according to the structure of rational thought. Natural science did not have a stable meaning until well into the nineteenth century, and the term "natural scientist" did not exist during Kant's lifetime. I thus avoid using the terms "scientist" and "natural scientist" in the study, and favour "natural philosopher" as a more accurate rendering of *Naturforscher*. Adickes, *Kant als Naturforscher*, I 1–7. See Ross, "*Scientist*," 67–8; Toulmin and Goodfield, *The Discovery of Time*, 241.

[2] Eze, "The Color of Reason"; Serequeberhan, "Eurocentrism in Philosophy"; Bernasconi, "Who Invented the Concept of Race?"; McNulty, "A Science for Gods, a Science for Humans."

Kant and the Transformation of Natural History. Andrew Cooper, Oxford University Press. © Andrew Cooper 2023.
DOI: 10.1093/oso/9780192869784.003.0001

biological science at the close of the century,[3] I argue that it must first be understood in the context of earlier attempts to reconceive of the logical categories *genus, species,* and *variety* as physical concepts that represent causal connections in a self-producing, mechanical system if Kant's significance in the history of science is to be fully appreciated.

Building on this contextual reconstruction, the second aim of this book is to present a new interpretation of the place of natural history in Kant's theory of science, and to show how this interpretation can enhance our understanding of the difficult and sometimes perplexing account of reason's regulative use in his critical philosophy. Scholars generally accept that while Kant's early work advanced a radical, explanatory conception of natural history (*Naturgeschichte*) in the vein of Georges-Louis Leclerc Comte de Buffon's *Histoire naturelle* (1749), his critical turn in the 1770s and 80s staged a "*historical* retreat" to something much closer to the descriptive project (*Naturbeschreibung*) presented in Carl Linnaeus' *Systema naturae* (1735).[4] In contrast, I argue that while Kant's critical philosophy separates natural history from proper science, it does not follow that natural history is limited to a logical procedure of classification. Drawing from both Kant's writings on natural history and his critical epistemology, I contend that Kant aimed to present and surpass a dialectic between the logical and physical conceptions of the natural system represented by the Linnaean and Buffonian schools of taxonomy, which, in his view, continued to stifle the progress of natural history in the late eighteenth century. Kant's transcendental vindication of Newtonian mechanics demonstrated that natural historians are required to judge the generation of material things in accordance with mechanical laws and provides the standard of demonstration to which they must aspire. It is this requirement and standard of demonstration that enabled him to discern the problem that *living* material things pose to the historian of nature, for such things require the introduction of final causes into the field of research if the mechanical ideal of explanation is to be applied to their function and form. Kant's attempt to resolve the problem methodologically, and the historical significance of his solution, will be the focus of this study.

Experimental and Historical Science

The motivation behind this book lies in the fact that, despite the recent flood of research on the experimental and historical sciences in Kant's philosophy, commentators continue to hold a comparatively negative view of the place of natural

---

[3] Lenoir, *The Strategy of Life*; Lagier, *Les Races humaines selon Kant*; Fisher, "Kant's Explanatory Natural History"; Zammito, *The Gestation of German Biology*.

[4] Zammito, "Teleology Then and Now," 749. See also Sloan, "Kant on the History of Nature," 629; Lagier, *Les Races humaines selon Kant*, 140.

history in his system of natural science.[5] Previous scholarship on Kant's theory of natural science focused on the constructive parts of *Critique of Pure Reason*, including the Transcendental Aesthetic and Analytic, and the *Metaphysical Foundations of Natural Science*.[6] Over the past two decades, however, scholars have developed a broader conception of Kantian science in which the experimental and historical sciences participate in science as such.[7] This development has led to ground-breaking work on previously overlooked themes in Kant's writings and lectures, including his novel conception of experimental science,[8] his pioneering work on anthropology,[9] and his necessitarian account of empirical laws.[10] Moreover, it has demonstrated how these neglected aspects of Kant's writings and lectures help us to better understand his critical philosophy.[11]

When it comes to natural history, however, scholars tend to revert to the older and more restrictive conception of Kantian science.[12] John Zammito speaks

[5] For several monographs representative of this flood of research, see Frierson, *Freedom and Anthropology in Kant's Moral Philosophy*; Zammito, *Kant, Herder and the Birth of Anthropology*; Zuckert, *Kant on Beauty and Biology*; Cohen, *Kant and the Human Sciences*; Breitenbach, *Die Analogie von Vernunft und Natur*; van den Berg, *Kant on Proper Science*.

[6] This view spans from Kant's early reviewers to the neo-Kantians, and to the bourgeoning field of Kant scholarship in the latter part of the twentieth century. For a sample of representative works, see Fichte, *Science of Knowledge*; Hegel, *Science of Logic*; Cohen, *Kants Theorie der Erfahrung*; Brittan, *Kant's Theory of Science*; Kemp-Smith, *A Commentary on Kant's Critique of Pure Reason*; Friedman, *Kant and the Exact Sciences*; Ellis, *Scientific Essentialism*.

[7] For instance, van den Berg offers a thorough treatment of how Kant's account of proper science in *Metaphysical Foundations* shapes his account of a biological science and its distinctive methodology. Van den Berg, *Kant on Proper Science*. Breitenbach proposes the idea of "normative science" in which proper science projects a standard of demonstration to which other sciences aspire but may or may not reach. Breitenbach, "Kant's Normative Conception of Science."

[8] Vanzo, "Kant on Experiment"; McNulty, "Rehabilitating the Regulative Use of Reason"; Cooper, "Kant and Experimental Philosophy."

[9] Wilson, *Kant's Pragmatic Anthropology*; Clewis, "Kant's Natural Teleology?"; Cohen, *Kant's Lectures on Anthropology*.

[10] Watkins, *Kant and the Metaphysics of Causality*; Kreines, "Kant on the Laws of Nature"; Stang, *Kant's Modal Metaphysics*; Massimi, "Grounds, Modality, and Nomic Necessity in the Critical Kant"; Messina, "Kant's Necessitation Account of Laws and the Nature of Natures"; Engelhard, "The Problem of Grounding Natural Modality"; Cooper, "Hypotheses in Kant's Philosophy of Science"; Geiger, *Kant and the Claims of the Empirical World*.

[11] For instance, Louden and Frierson argue that Kant's anthropology and history vindicate the "empirical part" of ethics (GMS 4:388) that remains undeveloped in the critical philosophy. Louden, *Kant's Impure Ethics*, 3–30; Frierson, *Freedom and Anthropology in Kant's Moral Philosophy*, 5. Others including Cohen, van den Berg, McNulty, and Breitenbach argue that Kant's writings on experimental philosophy vindicate a broad conception of natural science that is underdeveloped in *Metaphysical Foundations*, yet shapes Kant's account of empirical knowledge in the Transcendental Dialectic and the third *Critique*. Cohen, *Kant and the Human Sciences*; van den Berg, *Kant on Proper Science*; McNulty, "Rehabilitating the Regulative Use of Reason"; Breitenbach, "Laws and Ideal Unity." Mensch and Sloan contend that Kant's account of generation informs his critical epistemology. Mensch, *Kant's Organicism*; Sloan, "Preforming the Categories."

[12] While natural history is discussed in the above-mentioned literature, studies tend to consider Kant's understanding of the subject with other concerns in mind: his pre-critical cosmology (Massimi, "Kant's Dynamical Theory of Matter"), his concept of race (Sandford, "Kant, Race, and Natural History"), his work on human origins (Zammito, *The Genesis of Kant's Critique of Judgment*), and his theory of biology (van den Berg, *Kant on Proper Science*). Sloan offers the most extensive treatment of Kant's natural history in "Kant on the History of Nature," which McNulty develops in "A Science for Gods, a Science for Humans." Fisher offers several reasons for the neglect of natural history in Kant scholarship in "Kant's Explanatory Natural History," 101.

for many commentators when he argues that "*Critique of Judgment* (1790) essentially proposed the reduction of life science to a kind of pre-scientific descriptivism, doomed *never* to attain authentic scientificity."[13] This interpretation was initially proposed in opposition to an optimistic reading of Kant's influence in the development of biology, in which scholars argued that Kant's transcendental account of organic structure anticipated Darwin's comparative anatomy.[14] To quell the recurring image of Kant as a proto-Darwinian biologist, critics point to the schema of natural science presented in *Metaphysical Foundations*, in which natural history is supposedly denied the status of a "proper natural science" and classified instead under the "historical doctrine of nature" (MAN 4:468). In contrast to proper natural science, which "treats its object wholly according to *a priori* principles," the historical doctrine of nature begins with experience and works towards the "systematic presentation of natural things at various times and places" (MAN 4:468). "Systematic" is taken to refer to the logical ordering of cognitions, disconnected from the apodictic system of natural laws.[15] Several commentators have gone as far as to claim that Kant's strict view of proper science was crafted to curb the development of a science of life, ensuring that organic form is metaphysically distinct from the material dynamics of nature.[16]

This negative take on Kant's account of natural history is compounded by the fact that his writings and lectures on the subject confront us with a dimension of his work that has recently caused a great deal of discomfort to Kant scholars: Kant's concept of race, and, more pointedly, his racism.[17] Kant argued that a physical conception of the natural system requires a new set of class concepts that capture causal connections between extended things through time and in space. While *race* is a general classificatory concept that refers to a physical line of descent in which members of a common species have, in response to changes in

---

[13] Zammito, "Should Kant have Abandoned the 'Daring Adventure of Reason'?," 135.

[14] This reading has appeared periodically since the consolidation of biology in the mid- to late nineteenth century. Stadler presented an early iteration of the reading in 1874, arguing that the transcendental principle of purposiveness presented in the third *Critique* presages the inductive reasoning of Darwin's comparative anatomy. Stadler, *Kants Teleologie und ihre erkenntnistheoretische Bedeutung*, 113. The reading rose to such prominence that in his 1910 essay, "Kant and Evolution," Lovejoy describes the view of Kant as a precursor to Darwin as one of the "generally accepted legends of the history of science." Lovejoy, "Kant and Evolution," 538. In 1922, Ungerer argued that Kant's reflective account of organic unity in the third *Critique* enables the inductive reasoning practiced by biologists in the early twentieth century. Ungerer, *Die Teleologie Kants*. Despite heavy resistance in the mid-nineteenth century, it found new life in the work of Lenoir, which presents Kant as the founder of nineteenth-century morphology. Lenoir, *The Strategy of Life*, 2.

[15] Pratt, "System-Building in the Eighteenth Century," 429–30. See also Koselleck, "Vergangene Zukunft der frühen Neuzeit," 546–66.

[16] Zammito, "Teleology Then and Now," 755; Richards, "Kant and Blumenbach on the *Bildungstrieb*," 229; van den Berg, "Kant and the Scope of Analogy in the Life Sciences," 75.

[17] In this study I use the term "racism" to refer to judgments about variation in the human species that employ what Hardimon terms a *racialized* concept of race, a concept of race that is (1) essentialist and (2) hierarchical. A racialized concept of race is one that justifies racial divisions according to normative biological features, such as intelligence and moral character, which can be used to rank the races as inferior and superior. See Hardimon, *Rethinking Race*, 2.

environment, altered in form, his most sophisticated treatment occurs in the context of a public debate concerning human origins in the 1770s and 80s. In a series of public essays dubbed his *Racenschriften*, Kant deploys the framework of his critical philosophy to define skin colour as the primary marker of a human race, and illustrates a fourfold taxonomy with pernicious claims about the enduring moral and temperamental characteristics of non-white races.[18] While scholars formerly passed over Kant's racism as an unfortunate product of its time,[19] new research pioneered by Emmanuel Eze, Charles Mills, and Robert Bernasconi contends that Kant was in fact the pioneer of a "scientific" conception of race that assisted white Europeans to clothe their felt sense of cultural superiority in the garb of Enlightened knowledge.[20] Thus framed, Kant's theory of race is not— as he states in the 1775 course announcement to his lectures on physical geography—a mere "game" played alongside the "deep inquiry" of philosophy (VvRM75 2:429/6:3).[21] It both anticipates and is enabled by his critical project, which establishes the conditions of scientificity. More seriously, it threatens to undermine the universal moral and political theory Kant developed during the 1780s, for his claim that certain races have acquired temperamental profiles that are unsuited to industry and culture entails that members of those races do not merit full consideration as moral persons.[22] Given the weight of this threat, it

---

[18] Consider an example from "On the Use of Teleological Principles in Philosophy" (1788), where Kant reports on the travel writings of Spanish naval officer Don Antonio de Ulloa. He concludes from Ulloa's testimony that members of the Amerindian race are "too weak for hard labor, too indifferent for industry and incapable of any culture" (ÜGTP 8:176). Taken on its own, this remark could be considered as a repetition of widely held views, and thus a product of its times. Yet Kant is not content with Ulloa's observations. Rather, he seeks to *explain* them: "hardly another reason can be given" for such indolence other than that "their natural disposition [*Naturanlagen*] did not achieve a *perfect* suitability for any climate" (ÜGTP 8:175). Kant's explanation serves to justify his hierarchical inference that the Amerindian race "ranks still far below even the Negro, who stands on the lowest of all the other steps that we have named as differences of the races" (ÜGTP 8:176).

[19] Mills characterizes this view as the prevailing position in Kant scholarship, which he describes as follows: "Ok, Kant was a racist, but that doesn't affect his theories." Mills, "Kant and Race, Redux," 2. For some examples of the view, see Louden, *Kant's Impure Ethics*, 105; Hill and Boxill, "Kant and Race," 449.

[20] Bernasconi describes Kant as "the inventor of the concept of race," by which he means "the one who gave the concept sufficient definition for subsequent users to believe that they were addressing something whose scientific status could at least be debated." Bernasconi, "Who Invented the Concept of Race?," 11. For overviews of the recent literature, see Mikkelsen, "Recent Work on Kant's Race Theory"; and Sloan, "The Essence of Race." Readers should also consult Lu-Adler's *Kant, Race, and Racism*, which became available to me only as this book went through its final proofs.

[21] Citations of the 1775 version of "Of the Different Races of Human Beings" include references to both the Akademie Ausgabe and Kant's *Werke*, separated by a forward slash. The Akademie Ausgabe does not clearly distinguish between the 1775 announcement for Kant's lectures on physical geography and the 1777 version published in *Der Philosoph für die Welt*, which obscures the fact that Kant dropped the disclaimer that his theory of race is simply a "game" when he published the essay (see §4.4). The 1775 version has been reproduced in Kant, *Werke*, VI 3–26, allowing the reader to follow Kant's revisions in the 1777 version. Both versions are translated in Mikkelsen, *Kant and the Concept of Race*, 41–72.

[22] Eze, "The Color of Reason"; Serequeberhan, "Eurocentrism in Philosophy"; Mills, "Kant's *Untermenschen*"; Bernasconi, "Kant as an Unfamiliar Source of Racism." Cf. Hill and Boxill, "Kant and Race"; Allais, "Kant's Racism"; Kleingeld, "Kant's Second Thoughts on Race." For an overview of the various positions that have consolidated in the literature, see Frierson, *What Is the Human Being?*,

would surely be good news to Kant scholars if his account of natural history were *not* scientific.[23]

While united by a negative take on Kant's account of natural history, the existing literature is divided. Scholars working on the history of biology tend to argue that Kant denied natural history the status of a science. Those working on his concept of race tend to claim that his physical system of nature pioneers a distinctly scientific natural history. Noting this predicament, Phillip Sloan contends that we are yet to fully appreciate the connection between Kant's classificatory categories and the regulative principles prescribed by reason in the first and third *Critiques*. Further work is needed "before we can assess the full importance of the race treatises for Kant's larger project."[24]

With this need in mind, my approach in this study is to investigate Kant's writings and lectures on natural history in the context of his broader philosophical development. My central claim is that the relation between Kant's general theory of natural science and his particular account of natural history has been misunderstood. To drive a wedge between natural history and natural science, or to conflate the two entirely, is to misinterpret how his theory of science informs the particular domains of research that fall under it. In this study, I hope to shift the parameters of debate by drawing scholarship on Kant's account of natural history into conversation with recent work on his broader conception of science. The debate's current framing, I argue, does not sufficiently contextualize Kant's account of scientific knowledge within the contested landscape of Newtonian science, leading scholars on both sides to overlook his decisive contribution to one of the most significant shifts in eighteenth-century natural philosophy: the inclusion of *time* as the methodological frame in which explanations are required, sought after, and justified in natural history.[25] Kant's critical reflection on the method of classification can be viewed as a culminating moment in what I term *the transformation of natural history*, a seismic shift occurring in eighteenth-century philosophy whereby natural history ceased to be understood as the logical practice of classification and was reconceived as the presentation of a physical process. In the midst of the epistemic and metaphysical problems raised by this transformation, Kant aspired to determine the scientific character of historical claims.

101–18. Recent work has also argued that Kant's concept of race plays a greater role in his critical epistemology than many Kant scholars are comfortable to acknowledge. See Lagier, *Les Races humaines selon Kant*; Mensch, *Kant's Organicism*; Sandford, "Kant, Race, and Natural History."

[23] To grasp the implications of the threat, see the debate between Banton and Bernasconi in *Ethnicities*. Banton, "The Vertical and Horizontal Dimensions of the Word *Race*"; Bernasconi, "Defining Race Scientifically."

[24] Sloan, "The Essence of Race," 194.

[25] Sloan and Lyon argue that, while often overlooked, this transformation was "as great an intellectual event as the scientific revolution of the seventeenth century." Sloan and Lyon, "Introduction," 3. A similar claim can be found in Gould, *Time's Arrow, Time's Cycle*, 1–2. While most scholars point to the Copernican and Darwinian revolutions as the two defining moments in the development of modern science, Gould argues that the discovery of "deep time" links them together.

His answer had significant implications for his critical account of reason's regulative use, I claim, and raises a challenge for the logic of historical reasoning today.

An upshot of this claim is that Kant's concept of race is indeed part of a scientific conception of natural history. While the moral and political implications of Kant's race concept lie beyond the scope of this study, I aim to show that his theory of science encompasses a broader set of concepts and laws than those that can be established with certainty and completeness. Kant's broad conception of science, I contend, entails that his opinions about racial characteristics are contestable, prone to error, and subject to ongoing revision. This by no means saves Kant from the charge of racism. Indeed, it will enable us to better discern the workings of racism in the formation of his opinions. What it does do, however, is loosen the connection between Kant's racism and his theory of natural science (though it will not entirely disconnect them). Kant's account of empirical knowledge replaces the natural historian's hope that a logical system will somehow converge with nature's pre-established order with a procedure by which historical claims can be genuinely contested. Opinions—including Kant's opinions about racial characteristics—are "scientific" to the extent that they can be evaluated against (a) possible experience (synthetic *a priori* knowledge), (b) actual experience (the available evidence), and (c) their adequacy to explain the given consequents (see Chapter 5). By shifting historical knowledge from the frame of convergence to an intersubjective sphere in which claims are contested against a standard of communicability, Kant's method invites his readers to critically examine the reasoning found in his historical texts. I argue that when judged against this standard, his opinions about racial characteristics lack the justification required to merit the positive epistemic attitude he adopts towards them, revealing several of his failings as a *Naturforscher*. To understand Kant's misplaced credence, I follow Huaping Lu-Adler's contention that we should neither elevate Kant as an irreproachable figure in the history of philosophy nor to look down on him on account of his racist views. The challenge of reading Kant today is rather to examine his work within its historical context and ask "whether he still has something worthwhile to offer."[26] My hope is that this approach will aid us to gain a clearer grasp of both the power and the limitations of Kant's theory of science.

Chapter Overview

I have written this book with two audiences in mind. It is first of all a work of Kant scholarship, and aspires to contribute to the growing body of literature on the experimental and historical sciences in Kant's philosophy. However, it does so by situating his account of natural history within the broader transformation

---

[26] Lu-Adler, *Kant, Race, and Racism*, 336.

considered in this study, and thus also seeks to extend the growing body of work on the role of Newtonianism in the early development of biology.[27] The dual focus of the study may, of course, fail to satisfy readers whose interest lies solely in one of these bodies of work. Yet my aim is to show that a constructive dialogue between Kant scholarship and the history of science can raise provocative questions for scholars working in both fields. The conviction guiding this study is that our understanding of Kant's account of scientific knowledge can be enhanced by a broader investigation of the contribution he attempted to make to natural history's transformation. As recent work by John Zammito and Joan Steigerwald has shown, this transformation did not occur as a discontinuous *snap* in the history of science, as if a developmental conception of nature could suddenly replace a static, logical schema of natural history.[28] For the established community of natural philosophers to accept a new programme of research that investigates natural objects as products of a physical process, a deep epistemological and metaphysical shift would have to occur.[29] In terms of epistemology, it would require a change in the foundation of empirical knowledge that could overcome the scepticism held by natural philosophers in regards to our knowledge of processes that lie beyond the reach of experience, such as changes undergone in the earth's history. This change would have to permit certain forms of speculative reasoning about events that occurred long ago, and define a new standard of epistemic justification for historical claims. In terms of metaphysics, it would require the integration of the formative principles of organic development into the natural order, such that living beings could be understood as products of natural forces. Thus conceived, the fit between organic function and environment would no longer be understood according to the causality of a designer but rather as the consequence of a developmental process that occurred over a long period of time, such that living

---

[27] See Hall, "On Biological Analogs of Newtonian Paradigms"; Schlanger, *Les Metaphors de l'organisme*; Wolfe, "On the Role of Newtonian Analogies"; Zammito, *The Gestation of German Biology*; McLaughlin, "The Impact of Newton on Biology.

[28] Narratives in which the atemporal conception of natural order assumed by natural historians is eclipsed by the developmental system of biology at the turn of the nineteenth century prevail in the literature. For instance, Mayr argues that natural theology enshrined natural history as the science of living beings, meaning that "biology was basically dormant until the nineteenth and twentieth centuries." Mayr, *This Is Biology*, 29. While Foucault presents an alternative genealogy, it has a similar result: before the advent of biology in the early nineteenth century, "life itself did not exist. Only living beings existed, which were viewed through a grid of knowledge constituted by *natural history*." Foucault, *Les Mots et les choses*, 139. In the past few years, a number of scholars have taken Foucault's claim as an investigative challenge to interrogate the supposed dichotomy between natural history and biology at the turn of the nineteenth century. See Zammito, *The Gestation of German Biology*, 1; and Steigerwald, *Experimenting at the Boundaries of Life*, 15–16. While I am indebted to these studies, my investigation will not focus on the biological writings that emerged around 1800 but rather on the century leading up to this period.

[29] See Sloan and Lyon, "Introduction," 18. Russo identifies four dimensions of this shift, yet they ultimately boil down to a metaphysical dimension, concerning generation and development, and an epistemological dimension, concerning how we attain knowledge of changes that occurred in the past. Russo, "Théologie naturelle et secularisation de la science au XVIII siècle," 43.

things are considered as products formed in dynamic relation to the broader changes undergone in the earth's history, including geophysical morphology, climactic variation, and the activities of other living beings.

In Part I of the study, I argue that the key to this epistemological and metaphysical shift lies in the extension of Newtonian science from the movement of material bodies to the generation of natural products, thereby broadening the scope of natural philosophy to include geology, geography, botany, and zoology. I begin in Chapter 1 by arguing that the intensive practice of natural history during the Renaissance raised a problem for the Aristotelean tradition of natural interpretation taught in the schools, for it became increasingly apparent that the properties used to classify individuals under a group are, at least in part, arbitrarily selected by the student of nature. I characterize this problem in terms of a gap that opened between the order of names and the order of things. Starting with Francis Bacon's attempt to replace Aristotle's *Organon* with a new method for interpreting nature, I show how the experimental turn in natural philosophy placed natural history at the foundation of a new hierarchy of learning. I explore the implications of this turn in the following generation of British natural philosophers, including Robert Boyle, Isaac Newton, and John Locke, who drew from Bacon's *Novum organum* to separate two kinds of classificatory project: the presentation of the natural system, which captures essential divisions between natural things, and the construction of an artificial system, which arranges the manifold of nature according to human interests. I conclude with Carl Linnaeus' *Systema naturae*, which proposes a method by which artificial classification can track natural boundaries.

In Chapter 2, I argue that the epistemological and metaphysical changes required to establish a physical conception of the natural system, understood as a presentation of the changes undergone by nature through time, were made possible by the extension of Newtonian science to events and processes that are not strictly amenable to mathematical demonstration. If Newtonian science upholds Newton's official claim that the possibility of material motion is unknown, then its explanatory power lies simply in the ability to describe the movements of material bodies on a geometrical plane according to attractive and repulsive forces. On this "mechanical" interpretation of Newtonianism, such as that found in Stephen Hales' plant physiology, the natural philosopher applies the Newtonian forces to the unfolding of natural products understood as pre-existing machines. Yet if Newtonian science could move beyond Newton's epistemic reservations and vindicate metaphysical knowledge of fundamental forces, then material bodies would not simply follow Newtonian laws; they would also be constituted by them. Generation—what Aristotle understood as *motion towards form*—could thus be studied as a physical process.[30] On this "materialist"

---

[30] Here I extend beyond the conventional focus on theories of generation (preformation, epigenesis, etc.) to include the interpretations of Newtonianism that constrain the hypotheses about generation

interpretation of Newtonianism, pioneered by Émilie du Châtelet, Pierre Louis Maupertuis, and Georges Buffon, the possibility of the mechanical system lies in nature's material conditions. Theoretically at least, the initial state of Newtonian mechanics could be explained by attractive and repulsive forces, meaning that the order of nature could be studied as a physical achievement. Thus understood, a natural history would not simply describe and catalogue the manifold of natural objects according to logical affinities, but also reconstruct the physical connections between extended things in space and time. Yet several links in this universal conception of natural history, including the original formation of organized beings and variation within species, continued to resist explanation, leading the materialist Newtonians to fill the gaps with speculative hypotheses. Sceptical of such hypotheses, Albrecht von Haller developed an "analogical" interpretation of Newtonianism, according to which the natural philosopher examines recalcitrant phenomena through an analogy with Newton's deduction of the law of universal gravitation without needing to speculate about their cause.

In Parts II and III, I argue that in both his early and his mature work, Kant aspired to make a decisive contribution to the transformation of natural history. In Part II, I begin by providing evidence to show that Kant's early account of natural history extends the materialist interpretation of Newton championed by Maupertuis at the Berlin Academy. Scholars tend to interpret Kant's Newtonianism in direct relation to Newton's *Principia*, overlooking the developments in Newtonian science that occurred in the first half of the eighteenth century.[31] This has led to considerable misunderstanding of Kant's relation to Newton, for it remains unclear why he would frame his early defence of Newtonian physics in the form of a natural history. In Chapter 3, I argue that Kant's *Universal Natural History* (1755) extends Buffon's physical account of knowledge, in which a universal natural history recounts the generation of the entire system of natural phenomena from just a few natural laws, thereby reducing the contingent appearance of design to material necessity. Thus conceived, nature is no longer a divinely ordered system of bodies on a geometrical plane but a self-actualizing process that generates its own spatial and temporal conditions. History

that one can legitimately entertain. To examine the various theories of generation without this background can lead to misinterpretations regarding the decisive points of disagreement. See Wolfe, "Why Was There No Controversy Over Life in the Scientific Revolution?," 209–10.

[31] There are notable exceptions to this neglect. Zammito for instance identifies several different ways of applying Newton's method under the banner of Schofield's "experimental" Newtonianism. However, by collecting natural philosophers as diverse as Hales, Haller, and Kant under a single framework, his presentation oversimplifies the diversity of positions. Zammito, *The Gestation of German Biology*, 37–8. Massimi has made some headway in recognizing the influence of the materialist interpretation of Newtonianism on the pre-critical Kant. Yet she also relies on Schofield's topology, which has been improved in recent literature. Massimi, "Kant's Dynamical Theory of Matter," 533. I draw from Wolfe's topology of eighteenth-century Newtonianisms to provide an alternative account. Wolfe, "On the Role of Newtonian Analogies," 226–7. For a similar position, see Sloan, "Life Science and *Naturphilosophie*," 99.

is no longer a description of natural order but a narrative of the changes that explain nature's present state.

Kant's extension of materialism clarified the problem that *living* natural products pose to a universal natural history. Living natural products can only be examined as developing through time if natural historians assume the operation of a generative force by which members of a species adapt to changes in climate, landscape, and other living beings. In Chapter 4, I consider a tension emerging in the student notes from Kant's lectures on physical geography between living natural products and the mechanical-teleological system presented in *Universal Natural History*. While Kant structured his physical geography according to Buffon's distinction between a general theory of the earth and the history of particular natural products, I suggest that during the 1760s he recognized an error in Buffon's materialist account of generation. The error occurs when natural historians speculate about unobservable phenomena on the assumption that nature's objective conditions reflect the subjective conditions of the intellect. The implications of Kant's diagnosis of the error can be seen in his 1777 essay on race, which presents a physical procedure of classification based on projected casual connections between individuals in a line of descent. I argue that the structure for Kant's concept of race is drawn from Buffon's article "On the Degeneration of Animals" (1766), which grounds racial boundaries on the distinction between the accidental and necessary variation of a stem species. Yet to avoid Buffon's error, and thus to resolve the tension between living natural products and the mechanical-teleological system, Kant develops a second, pragmatic tier of natural history situated within the formal conditions of nature. In contrast to Buffon, Kant's concept of race is "real" to the extent that it captures an enduring line of descent, whose defining characteristics become fixed. I argue that Kant's 1777 essay presents a *racialized* concept of race, which enables him to formulate several of his unwarranted assumptions as (racist) opinions. One of the questions to be considered in the remaining chapters is whether Kant's critical philosophy bolsters or resists those opinions.

In Part III, I argue that Kant's ongoing engagement with epistemic problems arising in the practice of natural history played an important and yet underappreciated role in the development of his critical philosophy. In Chapter 5, I suggest that Kant's attempt to vindicate a regulative use of reason's ideas in *Critique of Pure Reason* can be understood against the backdrop of the methodological questions concerning the use of hypotheses in natural philosophy considered in Parts I and II of this study. I argue that following his recognition of the error that plagues historical reasoning, Kant no longer grounds natural history in matter understood as extended substance, the possibility of which lies in a divine mind. Kant amends his position in the *Critique* by grounding historical knowledge in the universal laws that govern material substance, the possibility of which lies in the understanding. Turning to the Transcendental Dialectic, I argue that Kant's examination of the synthetic application of reason to the understanding in the context of empirical research reflects two conflicting demands on natural historians. The first demand is to recognize the limits of finite, human cognition. As Bacon established in *Novum organum*, natural historians must discipline the human tendency to conflate the logical system represented in the mind with the system of nature if we are to make genuine progress in our understanding of nature. The second demand is to *seek* connections within the natural system, which requires that we *assume* that natural things are arranged in a way that can be discovered by minds like ours. Both the sceptical natural historian, who accepts the artificial nature of their system, and the radical natural historian, who seeks to construct a natural system, presuppose that nature is arranged in a determinate way. Neither takes the first demand—the recognition of cognitive limits—to its conclusion by reconceiving the presupposition of determinate, rational order as an idea that is immanent to inquiry. Moved by the first demand, Kant restricts cognition to the finite conditions of the understanding. Moved by the second demand, he anchors historical reasoning in reason's hypothetical use, which prescribes the relations between appearances and their conditions for which the understanding must seek. Kant thus combines the metaphysical question of nature's systematicity with the epistemological question of cognitive limits, thereby removing the illusory influence of metaphysics from natural history and providing an immanent standard for assessing historical claims.

While Kant vindicated the immanent use of reason in *Critique of Pure Reason* by establishing that we are rationally required to seek the material conditions of our cognitions, he did not resolve the question of *living* natural products, which manifest a temporal structure that is at odds with the understanding's linear time determination. The issue was thrust into Kant's attention in the mid-1780s, when two young naturalists (Johann Gottfried Herder and Georg Forster) attacked his concept of race and argued that his account of natural history entails a speculative history of origins. In Chapter 6, I consider Kant's response as a case study in how reason's principles, under the discipline of critique, are applied to the practice of nature history. I argue that in the course of responding to Herder and Forster, Kant identified a new kind of analogy that enables natural historians to reflect on the whole-to-part dynamics of organized beings by transposing the form of their own purposiveness as practical agents into the field of empirical inquiry. This new kind of analogy requires the operation of judgment without the aid of the understanding, such that judgment prepares the field for the application of empirical concepts to living natural products. An upshot of this move, I suggest, is that the fixity built into Kant's racialized concept of race loosens, exposing several pernicious assumptions that motivate his racist views.

In Chapter 7, I examine *Critique of the Power of Judgment* as a culminating moment in Kant's work on natural history, for it demonstrates how the competing theories of generation are natural for a discursive cognition like ours as it enters more deeply into the demands of empirical nature. Kant interprets these theories as different responses to an antinomy that arises between two maxims, mechanical and teleological, that guide our investigation of the material generation of objects and their form. Commentators often overlook the fact that the antinomy does not arise from the empirical underdetermination of organized form, as if there were causal processes in nature that could not be judged mechanistically. Rather, it arises when we discover that to judge the material generation of some natural products, it is necessary to adopt an *additional* principle, thereby introducing *too much* determinacy to our investigation. This interpretation of the antinomy has several implications for how we understand the resolution Kant proposes in §§77–8. In contrast to commentators who claim that Kant's critical portrayal of reason's "daring adventure" (the search for an undetermined genus of organized beings) deflates natural history to mere description, I argue that the resolution of the antinomy does not curtail the explanatory power of natural history but rather clarifies its epistemic status. Kant's claim, I suggest, is that if we refrain from locating the conflict in nature and consider it instead as one that arises from the peculiar character of discursive cognition when confronted with the demands of empirical nature, we can develop a logically consistent method for natural history that *retains* the conflict between the two maxims while removing its power to deceive. According to this method, nature summons us to search for an undetermined genus, up to the limit of an original organization, yet the viability of this search remains an empirical problem. An upshot of this interpretation is that the existence of a stable subspecies in natural history—such as a fixed race—is not required by reason but a matter of empirical testing.

In sum, this study aims to extend the recent literature on Kant's theory of science by demonstrating that his extensive work on natural history plays a greater role in his transcendental justification of Newtonianism than has hitherto been acknowledged. My contention is that Kant's *a priori* conception of proper science was not a foil to biology, as if the field we know today were gestating in the work of his opponents.[32] Neither was his account of natural purposiveness a proto-Darwinian theory of morphological change.[33] Kant's account of natural science features within a series of attempts made by natural philosophers in the eighteenth

---

[32] In this study, I avoid using the term "biology" to refer to various attempts to account for the generation of living things during the seventeenth and eighteenth centuries. While biology was first used to refer to an independent domain of scientific inquiry in France and Germany during the 1790s, with a few scattered uses in the preceding decades, a working definition did not emerge until around 1802. There are several earlier texts that identify biology as a distinct region of scientific knowledge, such as Roose's *Grundzüge de Lehre von der Lebenskraft* (1797). However, most studies identify its first use to define a unified field of inquiry in Treviranus' *Biologie, oder Philosophie der lebenden Natur für Naturforscher und Aerzte* (1802). See Jahn, *Grundzüge der Biologiegeschichte*, 258, 275, 298; Lepenies, *Das Ende der Naturgeschichte*, 29–30; Ballauff, *Die Wissenschaft vom Leben*, 326; Lenoir, *The Strategy of Life*, 1; Gambarotto, *Vital Forces, Teleology and Organization*, xv.

[33] My argument charts a position between Lenoir's biological Kant and Zammito's reaction against it. Thus, it is fundamentally indebted to the pioneering work of both scholars.

century to anchor the historical examination of natural products in a defensible metaphysics of nature. These attempts continued to face theoretical problems, for they were unable to reconcile Newton's mathematical account of force with either a physical-mechanical conception of the natural system or the material generation of living things. Kant's critical philosophy alters the field, for by anchoring natural science in the structure of rational thought it removes the reconstruction of past events from the domain of cognition and places it instead in an intersubjective sphere of historical knowledge.

While Kant denies that the reconstruction of past events can appear as an object of cognition, it does not follow that historical speculation is fictional. In this study, I argue that Kant's account of natural history constitutes a third kind of system that stands between the apodictic system of natural science and the logical system of reason. Natural history for Kant is a physical system of empirical concepts that can, given the right method, merit our assent. While natural history is an exercise in reason's hypothetical use, for natural historians work back from actual objects to projected alterations that occurred long in the past, it nevertheless presents a *physical* system, for historical reasoning is guided by and judged against the standard of rational physics. In this sense Kant's physical system is not dissimilar to what contemporary philosophers of science describe as a model, raising a similar set of epistemological and metaphysical questions regarding how we ought to judge its truth.[34] For Kant, the difference between natural science and natural history is that while the propositions of natural science are certain and thus non-revisable, the propositions of natural history are adjudicated by our consciousness of the reasons we have for *judging* them to be true. The formal structure of historical claims can be held with certainty, yet their content remains open to revision as new regions of knowledge become available to empirical investigation. The attentive reader of Kant's critical philosophy is thus invited to evaluate the opinions expressed in his writings on natural history—such as his opinions about racial characteristics—against this method, to discern whether those opinions are warranted. I argue that Kant's opinions about racial charac teristics are not warranted, and betray serious failings as a *Naturforscher*. I conclude that Kant's contribution to the immense shift occurring in eighteenth-century natural philosophy is to show how the achievements made in Newtonian science can furnish natural history with a method that determines how natural historians ought to proceed and which opinions they are licensed to adopt. He thus identifies a standard by which natural historians can genuinely dispute historical claims and potentially come to consensus, which, I contend, was a ground-breaking achievement in eighteenth-century natural philosophy.

---

[34] For an insightful comparison of Kant's account of empirical knowledge and the use of models in contemporary science, see Massimi, "From Data to Phenomena," 110–11.

PART I
THE TRANSFORMATION OF NATURAL HISTORY

1

Nature and Art

Natural history exploded in the sixteenth century. At the height of the
Renaissance, natural philosophers across Europe—including Conrad Gessner in
Zürich, Ulisses Aldrovandi in Bologna, Guillaume Rondelet in Montpellier, and
Pierre Belon in Paris—embarked on a massive project of taxonomy. Their labours
were motivated by an immense social and economic shift that opened routine
voyages to India and China and across the Atlantic, ensuring a steady influx of
animal, mineral, and vegetable specimens unknown to European collectors. The
nascent colonial project simultaneously destabilized, energized, and bolstered the
scholastic tradition of natural philosophy. Naturalists on the frontier required a
practical system of collection that could be easily learned by memory. Collectors
on the continent required a new classificatory scheme to accommodate the
enormous range of foreign specimens. To amalgamate and extend existing histories, Renaissance natural historians searched for resources in neglected classical
texts that celebrated empirical investigation, including Aristotle's *Historia animalium*, Theophrastus' *De plantis*, and Pliny the Elder's *Naturalis historia*. Yet as we
find in Gessner's *Historia animalium* (1551–8), which consists of five volumes and
spans over 4,500 pages, they did not blindly reproduce the work of the ancients.
They used the ancient sources as models, inspiring new classifications.

Historians of science tend to present natural history as a homogenous body of
inquiry that persisted undisturbed from the Renaissance to the late eighteenth
century, marked by a logical and atemporal conception of the natural system and
an "obsession" with taxonomy.[1] In this chapter, I lay the foundations for an
alternative account. By examining the methodological debates that accompanied
the natural histories produced in the seventeenth and eighteenth centuries, I argue
that natural history was already perceived to be a malleable and contested field
that raised deeper epistemological and metaphysical questions concerning the
relation between words and things. These questions provide the background
against which natural philosophers began to separate two kinds of system: a

[1] Pratt, "System-Building in the Eighteenth Century," 429–30. See also Koselleck, "Vergangene
Zukunft der frühen Neuzeit," 546–66. While Foucault identifies a gap between "words and things" that
opened during the Renaissance, he presents a static conception of natural history that lacked a dynamic
conception of life. Foucault, *Les Mots et les choses*, 140–4. Focusing on the writings and correspondences of naturalists in the eighteenth century, Terrall offers an alternative account in which "natural
philosophy and experimental physics both entered crucially into natural history." See Terrall, *Catching
Nature in the Act*, 5.

Kant and the Transformation of Natural History. Andrew Cooper, Oxford University Press. © Andrew Cooper 2023.
DOI: 10.1093/oso/9780192869784.003.0002

natural system, which presents the essential divisions between things, and an artificial system, in which things are pragmatically arranged according to human interests. "Natural" and "artificial" came to denote two distinct projects, the former concerned with truth and the latter with practical intelligibility.

In Section 1.1, I examine Francis Bacon's attempt to replace the scholastic system of logic with a new account of learning grounded in the practice of natural history. In Section 1.2, I suggest that while Bacon's reform did not have the immediate impact he intended, his distinction between speculative and experimental philosophy provided a framework for the following generation of British natural philosophers (including Boyle and Newton) to develop a new standard of explanation that begins with natural history. According to this standard, to understand what something is is not to be able to name its essential qualities but to be able to explain the physical process by which its essential qualities came to be. In Section 1.3, I then consider the implications of this standard of explanation for the practical task of classification in John Locke's analysis of human understanding. I argue that Locke's distinction between nominal and real essence can be interpreted in two ways, one that accepts the arbitrary nature of classificatory categories and the other in which classificatory categories are held to be real. While Locke's distinction clarified the fact that the divisions made by natural historians do not necessarily track the essential properties of natural kinds, in Section 1.4, I examine the work of Carl Linnaeus to show how it also gave expression to a new conception of the natural system as a reconstruction of the connections between extended things in time and space. Linnaeus established the natural system as an open research question, which, I suggest in Part II of this study, framed Kant's early work on natural history.

1.1 The Nursing Mother of Natural Philosophy

Renaissance natural history developed outside the universities, which did not encourage the study of plants and animals as a distinct branch of knowledge.[2] The scholastic system of knowledge taught in the schools differentiated between the causal investigation of *philosophia* and the descriptive field of *historia*, and placed greater epistemological merit with the former. Aristotle's historical books were not a prominent feature of the arts curriculum, and the history of animals, minerals, and vegetables was studied more closely in the new medical faculties established in the sixteenth century. In the preface to the opening volume of *Historia animalium*, Gessner explains that he first came to the study of living things through his medical training in therapeutics.[3] While he hopes that the work

---

[2] Findlen, "Courting Nature," 57–71.   [3] Gessner, *Historia animalium*, I α2r.

will make a contribution to medicine, he states that it will also be of interest to people of many different livelihoods, including cooks, tanners, farmers, and breeders.[4] His goal is to provide a practical lexicon for the sprawling array of specimens entering European collections.

As the title suggests, the primary inspiration for Gessner's *Historia animalium* comes from Aristotle. In the *Organon* (Aristotle's collected texts on logic and scientific method), Aristotle presents the goal of scientific inquiry as a hierarchically organized system of concepts, in which any individual can be classified under an interlaced cascade of general concepts of varying scope (species, genus, family, etc.) according to the essential properties it shares with other members of each class. In *Posterior Analytics*, for instance, he states that scientific understanding displays the "reason why" any member of a kind has this property, which is to say that knowing the cause of an individual is the same as knowing its essential qualities (what it really is).[5] How this method applies to living things, however, is a complex matter, for natural historians must avoid classification by non-essential qualities. Natural historians could divide animals according to *light coloured* and *dark coloured*, and those kinds into *footed* and *footless*, but they would not be tracking natural divisions. In *Parts of Animals*, Aristotle explains that the classification of animals proceeds by appealing to the form of an individual, which is the goal for the sake of which its parts exist. Natural historians should not begin with the parts, for the parts do not necessitate an animal's form. It is the form that necessitates the generation of the parts that are necessary for the animal to be the kind of thing that it is. Genera such as *bird* and *fish* are the names for kinds "with common natures, and forms not very far apart."[6] The difference is that animals that fall under *bird* differ by degree (one bird has light coloured feathers, the other has dark coloured feathers), whereas an animal that falls under *bird* differs from an animal that falls under *fish* by analogy (feathers are to *bird* as scales are to *fish*). The task of a *Historia animalium*, then, is to present the variety of living things in such a way that the reader can come to understand these kinds, that is, know why the members falling under that kind share essential properties.

Gessner followed Aristotle's framework for deciding which properties are essential, arranging each volume according to the five genetic divisions established in Aristotle's *Historia* (viviparous quadrupeds, oviparous quadrupeds, birds, fish, and snakes). However, many of the specimens he examined had no precedent in Aristotle, nor in any of the ancients. Indeed, Gessner actively sought out anomalies, monsters, and recalcitrant items that resisted Aristotelean divisions, and his descriptions show little interest in identifying features that could lead to scientific understanding. Aristotle had assumed the "naturalness" of the kinds that he identified, yet he provided very little clarification of the common natures shared

---

[4] Gessner, *Historia animalium*, I a2v.   [5] Aristotle, *Posterior Analytics*, 89b23–91a11.
[6] Aristotle, *Parts of Animals*, 644b2–3.

by members of a group and how further classificatory divisions might be made. Gessner recognized that before commencing a system of classification, one had to decide on which features to prioritize, and even to create new divisions and subdivisions to arrange the growing inventory of available specimens in a workable schema. He was less concerned with the naturalness of his divisions than he was with achieving an exhaustive collection.

Francis Bacon discovered in Gessner's generation of natural historians a new model of learning that, in contrast to the schools, did not take the ancients as a standard to be reproduced but as inspiration for new discoveries. Yet he was unsatisfied by their endless collections, which did little to advance the understanding of natural things. In *The Advancement of Learning* (1605), Bacon argues that natural history has the potential to expose certain idols that "garrison the human intellect" by enticing natural philosophers to worship a system in the mind.[7] He pins the problem on Aristotle, who did not derive his axioms from experience but instead made "experience a slave to his fancies."[8] If natural philosophy is to progress beyond the endless metaphysical debates staged in the schools, the student of nature must discard Aristotle's method of anticipation, which aims to satisfy the mind, and adopt a new manner of learning rooted in the natural ordering of the faculties. Bacon identifies three parts of learning, each of which have their origin in "the three partes of Mans vnderstanding...: HISTORY to his MEMORY, POESIE to his IMAGINATION, and PHILOSOPHIE to his REASON."[9] When dissected along its *"lines and veins,"* we find that the three parts of the understanding do not share an equal level of primacy.[10] Memory and imagination are concerned with particular things, events, and facts; memory with real particulars, imagination with feigned particulars. Reason is concerned with general concepts and laws. Thus, if philosophy is to cease imposing arbitrary categories onto the facts of experience and align itself with the natural ordering of the understanding, natural history must become its "primary matter" and "nursing mother", presenting the facts with which reason must begin.[11]

Despite the clear divisions in Bacon's anatomy of the mind, the line between fact collection and the search for general concepts is not, in practice, cleanly cut. This is particularly evident in his examination of the concept of *variety*, a concept that falls under *species* and is supposed to arrange particular substances according to their essential qualities. The study of variety cannot be restricted to physics, Bacon explains, for it is "but as a GLOS or PARAPHRASE that attendeth vpon the Text of NATURAL HISTORY."[12] Natural history is not devoid of discriminations, for the basic presentation of the facts given by memory requires a general schema to organize them into a useful collection. In *Historia Naturalis et Experimentalis*

[7] Bacon, *Oxford Francis Bacon*, XI 79.   [8] Bacon, *Oxford Francis Bacon*, IV 26.
[9] Bacon, *Oxford Francis Bacon*, IV 62.   [10] Bacon, *Oxford Francis Bacon*, IV 93.
[11] Bacon, *Oxford Francis Bacon*, IV 105.   [12] Bacon, *Oxford Francis Bacon*, IV 83.

(1622), Bacon states that natural history involves the comparison, reflection, and differentiation of individuals as the historian seeks a general concept:

> For the images of individuals are taken up by the sense and fixed in the memory.... The mind recalls and reflects on them, and, exercising its true function, puts together and divides their portions. For single individuals have something in common with each other and, on the other hand, something distinct and manifold. Now this composition and division takes place either according to the mind's own way of acting or according as we find it in things. If it take place according to the mind's own way and those portions are transformed at will into some similitude of an individual, it is the work of the imagination which, constrained by no law and necessity of nature or matter, can join together objects which do not at all come together in nature, and tear apart things which are never found apart.[13]

Bacon opens this passage with the claim that experience gives only individuals. He then identifies two kinds of classification, one that arbitrarily imposes its own categories onto those individuals, and one that is capable of grouping these individual records under a species on the basis of the "likeness of natural things."[14] The challenge facing natural historians is to practice discipline, such that their minds do not leap to satisfying conclusions in the imagination but instead discern within the facts of memory the *natural* likeness of individuals. In *Novum organum* (1620), Bacon explains that if they are to discern natural likenesses, natural historians must not "fly up immediately from the sense and particulars to the highest generalisations" but instead discipline their minds by grounding reason in memory:[15]

> we are surely looking for a class of experiments much more subtle and simple than those which we just bump into. For I am unearthing and adumbrating many things which no one who was not pressing forward on a certain and direct road to the discovery of causes would have thought to investigate ... but stand in the same relation to things and works as the letters of the alphabet do to speech and words which, though useless in themselves, are still the fundamental elements of all discourse.[16]

Bacon contends that experiment enables natural historians to identify similarities in nature as one might study the letters in a foreign alphabet. If one seeks a proper account of the arrangement of the letters in a foreign word, one must refrain from imposing the grammatical form of one's own language onto the phenomena and

---

[13] Bacon, *Oxford Francis Bacon*, VI 97–9.   [14] Bacon, *Oxford Francis Bacon*, VI 101.
[15] Bacon, *Oxford Francis Bacon*, XI 31.   [16] Bacon, *Oxford Francis Bacon*, XI 41.

instead conform the mind to a system that is manifest only in instances of its use. The logic of experiment is thus not one of application but of discovery. Natural historians must suspend the tendency to apply what is already known and instead search for classificatory markers in the natural items themselves.

1.2 Mechanical Generation and Classification

René Descartes was also a fierce opponent of the Aristotelian method of natural interpretation, and attempted to replace the scholastic programme with a monistic account of material substance that privileges mechanical explanations. If one follows Aristotle, the generation of a substance is explained by appealing to its form, the *for the sake of which* each part necessarily comes into being. A mechanical explanation, in contrast, describes the process by which the parts of a material composite push against each other to manifest an effect, just as the inner mechanisms of a clock produce the visible movement of its hands. In a provocative work entitled *The World* (1629–33), Descartes attempts to demonstrate the superiority of mechanical explanations by sketching a developmental history of nature in which every feature can be explained in mechanical terms. He invites his readers to place the biblical creation narrative in suspension, according to which the Creator breathes form onto an initial dispersion of matter that is *tohu wa-bohu* ("without form, and void"). Instead, he asks them to imagine an Epicurean narrative in which the world begins with formless matter alone. Such a world "does not have the form of earth, fire, or air, or any more specific form, like that of wood, stone, or metal."[17] It has no secondary qualities such as "being hot or cold, dry or moist, heavy or light." In consists simply of a diffuse cloud of inert particles and a few natural laws instated by the Creator. These laws were arranged

> In such a marvellous way that even if we suppose that He creates nothing more than what I have said, and even if He does not pose any order or proportion on it but...the laws of nature are sufficient to cause the parts of this chaos to disentangle themselves and arrange themselves in such a good order that they will have the form of a most perfect world, a world in which one will be able to see not only light, but all the other things as well, both general and particular, that appear in the actual world.[18]

Descartes presents a world in which the qualities of particular things can be explained by the mechanical process of generation from an initial state. To

---

[17] Descartes, *The World*, 22.   [18] Descartes, *The World*, 23.

know what something is is to be able to explain how it came to acquire its defining properties within the mechanism of the world. Clearly Descartes could see that a universal explanation of natural phenomena was likely to create a scandal. Following the Inquisition of 1633, in which Galileo was condemned for expounding the doctrine of the earth's movement, he decided not to publish the text. Yet even in the unpublished version he does not present his narrative as a true series of events but simply as a "fable."[19] Descartes' contention is that his fable makes the world "more intelligible" than both the Aristotelians, who remain befuddled by their speculations about inner essences, and the physicotheologians, who dogmatically adhere to a literal reading of the biblical narrative.[20] Descartes rejects both systems on the grounds that his fable makes more sense of the available phenomena. Without appealing to hyperphysical causes, his account of the world can explain how the particles of inert matter interacted with each other by means of physical forces (collision and direct pressure) and began to swirl into vortex shapes, just like eddies in a river. The particles came to form solid masses along the gradient of the vortex, eventually becoming the solar system we see today.

There are gaping holes in Descartes' fable. If matter is inert, how can one piece cause the motion in another? It would have to have an essential quality that precedes the formation of the system. And if teleological causes are banished from such an account, whence the existence of living things? Descartes anticipated such objections in *Principles of Philosophy* (1644), where he managed to insert the hypothesis of a mechanical world system as a subsidiary remark. Once more he reminds readers that his fable is not meant to describe the actual world but rather to provide "a better explanation for the things found in nature."[21] Of course, one *could* postulate that the Creator formed a full-grown man and woman in a particular garden, for past events are hidden from finite minds. Yet he asks his readers whether it would be any more speculative to imagine a beginning in which "basic principles" or "seeds" explain the way that living things came into being: "For although we know for sure that they never did arise in this way, we shall be able to provide a much better explanation of their nature by this method than if we merely described them as they are now."[22] Descartes calls for a new horizon of intelligibility in which mechanical causes account for the present state of phenomena more simply than hidden powers and teleological causes, even if it leaves many things unexplained. Instead of appealing to his readers' ignorance, asking them to accept an unknown cause as a matter of faith, he appeals to their understanding, inviting them to accept an explanation based on principles that any mind can reach through experience.

The mechanical conception of philosophy promoted by Descartes and his followers had a profound effect on the founders of the Royal Society in London,

---

[19] Descartes, *The World*, 21.   [20] Descartes, *The World*, 26.
[21] Descartes, *Principles of Philosophy*, 256.   [22] Descartes, *Principles of Philosophy*, 256.

including Robert Boyle, Robert Hooke, and John Woodward. They discovered in Descartes' writings a new system of explanation that made the explanations offered by the scholastic philosophers seem facile. Yet they ultimately rejected Descartes as the figurehead for the new movement of natural philosophy. His hypothetical account of basic particles, which provide the foundation of his mechanical world system, is not anchored in memory but appeals directly to the intellect.[23] Cartesian philosophy thus remained tethered to the speculative method of the scholastics, rushing to intellectually satisfying conclusions in the imagination that bypass experience. The founders of the Royal Society called on Bacon as an alternative figurehead for the new conception of natural philosophy, for his hierarchy of learning anchored reason in the facts of natural history.[24] Inspired by Bacon's *Novum organum*, they distinguished between two parts of natural philosophy, speculative and experimental, and placed greater epistemological merit with the latter.[25] As William Wotton explains in his manifesto for the Society, experimental philosophers "avoid making general Conclusions, till they have Collected a great number of Experiments or Observations upon the Thing in hand; and as new Light comes in, the old hypotheses fall without any Noise or Stir."[26]

Wotton presents a new kind of natural philosophy that rejects essential qualities as the basis for discerning individual differences between things and instead examines natural objects as different arrangements of a single, homogeneous substance. In *The Origin of Forms and Qualities* (1666), Boyle rejects the irreducible elements of classical and Renaissance chemistry and advocates a monistic account of physical particles in which the elements of nature can be reduced to their physical properties. In contrast to Aristotle's hylomorphism, Boyle proposes a "corpuscular" philosophy in which all matter is understood as a single substance.[27] His strategy is to convince his readers that the Aristotelian explanation of motion is childish in contrast to mechanical explanations. If one asks "how snow comes to dazzle the eyes, they [the school philosophers] will answer,

---

[23] In Descartes' Twelfth Rule, for instance, we see a very different picture of the relation between memory, imagination, and intellect to that presented by Bacon. For Descartes, intellectual clarity and distinctness is the primary source of knowledge. Descartes, *Rules for the Direction of the Mind*, 39–51.

[24] For recent work on the importance of Bacon's hierarchy of learning in the formation of the Royal Society, see Findlen, "Francis Bacon and the Reform of Natural History in the Seventeenth Century," 251; Anstey, "Francis Bacon and the Classification of Natural History," 29–31; Jalobeanu, *The Art of Experimental Natural History*, 117.

[25] While this distinction does not strictly feature in Bacon's works (Bacon separates speculative from operative philosophy), it was nonetheless *presented* as Baconian by the founders of the Royal Society. Anstey explains that the distinction between experimental and speculative philosophy "is adumbrated in some form by Francis Bacon" but "none of Bacon's distinctions is co-extensive with the experimental/speculative distinction." Anstey, "Experimental Versus Speculative Natural Philosophy," 216–17.

[26] Wotton, *Reflections upon Ancient and Modern Learning*, 348.

[27] Boyle, *Works*, II 451. Anstey contends that one of Boyle's key strategies in *Forms and Qualities* is to package and promote the new theory of matter proposed by members of the Royal Society. Anstey, *The Philosophy of Robert Boyle*, 2.

that it is by a quality of whiteness that is in it which makes all very white bodies produce the same effects."[28] If you probe further they continue to point to "a real entity, which they call a quality."[29] In contrast, corpuscular philosophy aims to determine "how [qualities] are generated" by offering a model of perception as the result of contact senses, such as touch. Boyle's chief goal is

> to make it probable to you by experiments...that almost all sorts of qualities, most of which have been by the schools either left unexplained, or generally referred to I know not what incomprehensible substantial forms, may be produced mechanically; I mean by such corporeal agents, as do not appear either to work otherwise than by virtue of the motion, size, figure, and contrivance, of their own parts (which attributes I call the mechanical affections of matter, because to them men willingly refer the various operations of mechanical engines): or to produce the new qualities, exhibited by those bodies their action changes, by any other way than by changing the texture, or motion, or some other mechanical affection, of the body wrought upon.[30]

By exorcizing form and quality from matter, Boyle removes volition and appetite from the constituent parts of nature. Mechanical affection exists between extended things, which can be understood in terms of contact forces. Once the scholastic categories have been cast aside, one can begin to reframe the natural system in mechanical terms; substance can be rethought in terms of divisibility, the quality of hardness in terms of resistance, and the quality of colour in terms of light and elasticity.

Boyle's corpuscular theory has clear resonances with Descartes' mechanical philosophy. It rejects the appeal to hidden qualities as a legitimate way of explaining corporeal movement, and searches instead for mechanical explanations that account for the generation of those qualities. Yet in contrast to Descartes, Boyle maintains that corpuscularism is strictly a hypothesis that is not confirmed by the intellect but is "made probable...by experiments." Boyle contends that a theory of matter should not connect diverse phenomena in an intellectual system but lead to new experiments and observations that will convince the reader that it is probable that physical phenomena are the result of microscopic particles and their interactions.

Isaac Newton's demonstration of the inverse square law of gravity confirmed and extended the experimental method of philosophy promoted by the Royal Society. By uniting Kepler's laws of planetary motion with Galileo's laws of terrestrial movement, Newton demonstrated how experimental reasoning can achieve the certainty of mathematics. In *Mathematical Principles of Natural*

---

[28] Boyle, *Works*, II 459.   [29] Boyle, *Works*, II 459.   [30] Boyle, *Works*, II 459.

Philosophy (1687), he followed Boyle by distancing natural philosophy from speculation about hidden properties. The "whole problem of philosophy," he states in the preface, is "to discover the forces of nature from the phenomena of motions and then to demonstrate the other phenomenon from these forces."[31] To solve the problem, the natural philosopher must refrain from speculating about the properties that cause fundamental particles to move each other and instead examine the consequences of attractions between spheres according to a function of the distance between them. The result is a mathematical account of force for which the means by which distant bodies seemingly act on each other is unimportant for the proof. By assuming the corpuscular hypothesis (that matter consists of a single substance arranged on a geometrical plane), one can demonstrate how the tendency of particles to move towards each other can be accounted by a single force and described mathematically. If the equation succeeds, and is applicable to all such cases without fail, the discovery becomes a theoretical principle and can then be used to explain other phenomena. The result is an exclusively "mathematical notion of those forces," which does not consider "their physical causes and seats."[32] In the General Scholium, Newton explains that we have "explained the phenomena of the heavens and of our sea by the power of gravity, but have not yet assigned the cause of this power."[33] In words that became a mantra for experimental philosophers, he states that

> I have not been able to discover the cause of those properties of gravity from phenomena, and I frame no hypotheses; for whatever is not deduced from the phenomena is to be called an hypothesis; and hypotheses, whether metaphysical or physical, whether of occult qualities or mechanical, have no place in experimental philosophy.[34]

Newton claimed to have established a new kind of natural philosophy capable of achieving mathematical certainty, such that the movement of all material things—from falling apples to planetary motions—can be explained by a single principle. He contrasts the mathematical procedure of experimental philosophy with the method of the school philosophers:

> These Principles I consider, not as occult Qualities, supposed to result from the specific Forms of Things, but as general Laws of Nature, by which the Things themselves are form'd; their Truth appearing to us by Phaenomena, though their Causes be not yet discover'd. For these are manifest qualities, and their Causes only are occult.[35]

---

[31] Newton, *Mathematical Principles*, I xviii.   [32] Newton, *Mathematical Principles*, I 5.
[33] Newton, *Mathematical Principles*, II 547.   [34] Newton, *Mathematical Principles*, II 546–7.
[35] Newton, *Opticks*, 401.

Newton fashioned a style of natural philosophy characterized by extreme epistemic modesty. To explain the particular qualities of an object, the natural philosopher banishes all reference to occult qualities and searches instead for a mathematical demonstration of the force responsible for manifest effects. The upshot, however, is that while experimental philosophy can provide a mathematical demonstration of the inverse square law of gravity, it cannot explain *why* the particles of matter behave as they do. To extend beyond the phenomena to hidden qualities is to hypothesize, satisfying the intellect and yet bypassing the procedure of deduction from phenomena. For many of his early followers, a commitment to Newton's method entails that the inner structure of objects is hidden from us. Things that lie beyond the reach of experiment and observation, including their generation, must be left in their proper place: the mind of the Creator. For others, however, Newton's demonstration of gravity was in fact the *revival* of an occult force—an essential quality of attraction—and cried out for a material explanation.[36]

1.3 Locke on Convergence

In *An Essay Concerning Human Understanding* (1689), Locke considers the implications of corpuscularism for the traditional objects of natural philosophy. The implication that concerns us here is Locke's practical critique of essentialism. If the only aspect of material objects available to experience is the motion, figure, bulk, and geometrical arrangement of insensible corpuscular particles, then what we can know of this reality takes the shape of subjective experiences. Subjective experiences are causally connected to the object through the activity of matter on our senses. The impression of a sensation on the mind causes what Locke terms a "simple Idea," an appearance that the mind has in its view. By means of association, the mind is able to generate a "complex Idea," which "consists of a determinate number of certain simple or less complex Ideas, joyn'd in such a proportion and situation, as the Mind has before its view."[37] Locke's account of simple and complex ideas entails that secondary qualities do not inhere in the object but are brought to experience by the human understanding.

Locke became acquainted with Boyle in Oxford in the 1660s, where he built up an extensive collection of plants in his personal herbarium. The specimens in his collection indicate that he was fascinated by species divisions, hybrids, and mutations, in keeping with the latest debates in botany regarding the classification

---

[36] For instance, in the Fourth Paper of his correspondence with Clarke, Leibniz argues that Newton's claim that bodies should attract one another at a distance, without intermediate means, is to invoke supernatural and miraculous powers. Leibniz, "Mr. Leibniz' Fourth Paper," §45. I explore the implications of Leibniz' critique of Newton in Section 2.3.

[37] Locke, *An Essay Concerning Human Understanding*, "Epistle to the Reader," 7.

of newly discovered species.[38] He stressed the artificial nature of classification, which stems from the imprecision of nature itself:

> Wherein then, would I gladly know, consists the precise and *unmovable Boundaries of* that *Species*? 'Tis plain, if we examine, there is *no* such thing *made by Nature*, and established by Her amongst Men.... So uncertain are the Boundaries of *Species* of Animals to us, who have no other Measures than the complex *Ideas* of our own collecting: And so far are we from certainly knowing what a Man is; though, perhaps; it will be judged great Ignorance to make any doubt about it. And yet, I think, I may say, that the certain Boundaries of the *Species*, are so far from being determined, and the precise number of simple *Ideas* which make the nominal essence so far from settled, and perfectly known, that very material Doubts may still arise from it.[39]

Locke's fascination with the plasticity of living things, combined with his associationist account of understanding, led him to doubt whether our categories could ever capture nature's order. His notion of simple and complex ideas frames the construction of categories in relation to cognition rather than to nature, which seems to ground an artificial conception of class distinctions. Locke's famous claim that "the sorting of Things, is the Workmanship of the Understanding" expresses a radically subjective account of classification, leading many commentators to portray him as a nominalist.[40]

Locke's claim, however, is not that the mind determines which classes there are in nature, but rather that our search for affinities and the naming of classes is an intellectual activity. In Book III he distinguishes "nominal" from "real" essence, for the nominal character of our ideas only becomes apparent when contrasted with inner features beyond our reach. Real essences are the "unknown constitution of Things, whereon their discoverable Qualities depend."[41] They are "a real, but unknown Constitution of their insensible Parts, from which flow those sensible qualities."[42] Nominal essences, in contrast, are clusters of Ideas that are caused by the sensible qualities of the members of a given species. The problem of classification for Locke is not that there are no natural kinds to be found. The problem is that, given that we lack access to the real essences of things, we must work from sensible qualities to complex ideas, with no guarantee that these secondary qualities track natural qualities.

---

[38] For example, see Locke's discussion of the bat, seal, and flying fish in *An Essay Concerning Human Understanding*, III vi, 23–30.

[39] Locke, *An Essay Concerning Human Understanding*, III vi 27, 290.

[40] Locke, *An Essay Concerning Human Understanding*, III iii 12, 265.

[41] Locke, *An Essay Concerning Human Understanding*, III iii 15, 266. Locke states that it is "past doubt, there must be some real Constitution, on which any Collection of simple *Ideas* co-existing, must depend."

[42] Locke, *An Essay Concerning Human Understanding*, III vi 17, 266.

Far from defending a metaphysical form of nominalism, Locke's distinction between nominal and real essence assumes a metaphysical form of *realism*. The nominal status of class categories is established in relation to inner features that determine membership within a species.[43] Nominalism is thus a matter of practice. Metaphysical realism places what Peter Anstey terms a "constraint" on the process of classification.[44] For Locke, there are naturally occurring clusters of properties that are grounded in the real essences (or corpuscular structures) of objectively existing kinds. These clusters of properties *cause* clusters of ideas in us (nominal essences), which are then formed by the understanding into a single complex idea and given a general name. The actual properties put constraints upon the nominal properties that can be instantiated in an individual, thus removing the possibility of arbitrary or ad hoc clusters of ideas. The problem of classification is that we do not have the means to distinguish which ideas are essential to a species and which are merely accidental.

The idea that nominal properties track actual properties (constraint) gives rise to the methodological ideal of convergence. The discovery of new properties enables increasingly fine-grained essences to be assembled as we move closer to knowledge of real constitution. Yet even if the knowledge of real constitution were possible, Locke questions whether it would be desirable. Knowledge of real constitution would consist merely of the particles on which qualities such as colour, shape, and form depend.[45] Such knowledge would surely disrupt the way that God had intended the human species to function. At the very least, to arrive at a finished natural system would take more work than could be imagined:

> It were therefore to be wished, That Men, versed in physical Enquiries, and acquainted with the several sorts of natural Bodies, would set down those simple *Ideas*, wherein they observe the Individuals of each sort constantly to agree. This would remedy a great deal of that confusion, which comes from several Persons, applying the same Name to a Collection of a smaller, or greater number of sensible Qualities, proportionably as they have been more or less acquainted with, or accurate in examining the Qualities of any sort of Things, which come under one denomination. But a Dictionary of this sort, containing, as it were, a Natural History, requires too many hands, as well as too much time, cost, pains, and sagacity, ever to be hoped for.[46]

The ideal of convergence entails that one can trust that nominal essences picked out by various natural historians will gradually align as they come to track real

---

[43] Mensch, *Kant's Organicism*, 27.   [44] Anstey, *John Locke and Natural Philosophy*, 209.
[45] Consider, for example, Locke's discussion of the microscope. Locke, *An Essay Concerning Human Understanding*, II xxiii 11, 301–2.
[46] Locke, *An Essay Concerning Human Understanding*, III xi 25, 329–30.

essences. Yet a truly natural system remains beyond our reach, for we have no way of determining whether the distinctions made on the basis of nominal essences corresponded to those that delimit real essences. Even the greatest level of agreement can only suggest that a nominal essence *probably* picks out the real essence.[47] Our taxonomical divisions cannot be certain, for classification is not a matter of deduction but analogy:

> There remains that other sort [of probability], *concerning* which men entertain opinions with variety of assent, though the *things* be such *that falling not under the reach of our senses, they are not capable of testimony.* Such are, 1.... the existence of material beings which, either for their smallness in themselves or remoteness from us, our senses cannot take notice of—as, whether there be any plants, animals and intelligent inhabitants in the planets, and other mansions of the vast universe. 2. Concerning the manner of operation in most parts of the works of nature: wherein, though we see the sensible effects, yet their causes are unknown.... These and the like effects we see and know: but the causes that operate, and the manner they are produced in, we can only guess and probably conjecture.... *Analogy* in these matters is the only help we have, and it is from that alone we draw all our grounds of probability.[48]

Locke notes that when the testimony of the senses fails us, we determine the strength of our assent to a hypothesis according to a calculus of probability. The appropriate form of reasoning for such phenomena is analogical, by which we judge that the causes of two distinct phenomena are sufficiently similar to transpose the cause of something we *do* know from experience (for example, that "the bare rubbing of two Bodies violently one upon the other, produces heat") to elucidate something that lies beyond experience (that heat "consists in a violent agitation of the imperceptible minute parts of the burning matter").[49] The strength of the analogy is a function of the degree of likeness between the characteristics. One of the examples he provides for (2), the "manner of operation" or "causes" that are to us unknown, is the generation of living things, the causality of a substance that is "produced in the ordinary course of Nature, by an internal Principle, but set on work by, and received from some external Agent, or Cause, and working by insensible ways, which we perceive not."[50] *How* the generation of a living thing (in this case, a single plant) took place once the internal principle is active, for Locke, is unknown:

[47] Sloan, "John Locke, John Ray, and the Problem of Natural System," 24.
[48] Locke, *An Essay Concerning Human Understanding*, IV xvi 12, 432.
[49] Locke, *An Essay Concerning Human Understanding*, IV xvi 12, 432.
[50] Locke, *An Essay Concerning Human Understanding*, II xxvi 2, 201.

For this Organization being at any one instant in any one collection of *Matter*, is in that particular concrete distinguished from all others, and is that individual Life, which existing constantly from that moment both forwards and backwards in the same continuity of insensibly succeeding Parts united to the living Body of the Plant, it has that Identity, which makes the same Plant, and all the parts of it, parts of the same Plant, during all the time that they exist united in that continued Organization, which is fit to convey that Common Life to all the Parts so united.[51]

While Locke identifies the convergence of classificatory categories with the inner constitution of things, he does not provide a conclusive answer to the question of whether the division between species exists simply in the mind or is the result of a physical process of individuation. Boyle had argued for the latter on the grounds that the Creator had contrived some portions of "matter into seminal rudiments or principles, lodged in convenient receptacles (and, as it were, wombs), and others into the bodies of plants and animals."[52] For Boyle, the effects of these seminal principles could be examined in experience, and yet he could not explain how they were consistent with the mechanical properties of matter, which apply universally in time and space.

By inserting a calculus of probability between our categories of classification and the real structure of an object, Locke's presentation of experimental philosophy has a twofold effect. On the one hand, the probability that a classificatory category tracks a natural category depends on there being a natural category. On the other hand, the probabilistic status of the category means that taxonomy is not in the business of capturing nature's boundaries but in constructing a practical artifice. In the following section, I show how the ambiguity within Locke's idea of convergence can be seen to open *two* classificatory projects that are made explicit in Linnaeus' *Systema naturae*: an artificial system, in which the commitment to metaphysical realism requires that the truth of classificatory divisions is held in suspension, and a natural system, in which classificatory categories are real to the extent that they depict physical connections in time and space.

1.4 Linnaeus and the Two Systems

Scholars concur that Linnaeus' binomial system was the first to explicitly accommodate an operative distinction between natural and artificial divisions. Yet the system itself has been interpreted in vastly different ways, most of which are negative. For his original opponents such as Georges Buffon, Linnaeus' system was

---

[51] Locke, *An Essay Concerning Human Understanding*, II xxvii 4, 206.
[52] Boyle, *Works*, II 483.

"arbitrary" and "non-scientific," for it accepts that many of the markers used in classification are dependent on the natural historian's choice.[53] For contemporary historians of biology, Linnaeus' commitment to the immutability of species marks him as an "essentialist," "scholastic," or even "Thomist" natural historian.[54] While each interpretation highlights an important feature in the Linnaean system, both overlook the practical register of his taxonomy. In this final section, I argue that Linnaeus' extensive fieldwork led him to a pragmatic settlement in which natural historians operate with simple markers to build a system that can be easily shared among an increasingly international community of naturalist philosophers. Yet his close engagement with new developments in Newtonian physiology led him to introduce a criterion by which natural historians could distinguish real from nominal essence: physical relations manifest in the process of generation. Linnaeus thereby established the natural system as what Staffan Müller-Wille describes as an "open research problem" that could only be confronted by "complex practices of collection, comparison and inscription."[55] In Part II of this study we will see that this research problem defined Kant's early work on natural history, whether he interpreted Linnaeus correctly or not.

In the course of his early fieldwork in Lapland, followed by his curation of George's Clifford's garden in Hartekamp, Linnaeus' identified several problems with the prevailing systems of classification advanced by John Ray, August Rivinus, and Joseph Pitton de Tournefort.[56] Their systems were ill equipped to handle his rapidly growing collection of local and foreign specimens in a single taxonomical programme, for they selected a range of arbitrary features to identify divisions between plants.[57] Shortly after completing his doctoral thesis at Harderwijk University, Linnaeus published *Systema naturae* (1735), a twelve-page outline of the general system he hoped would bring order to the study of natural history. The text advances a system of classification that acknowledges the role of natural historians in selecting the structural markers used to draw divisions between genus, species, and variety, and yet retains the metaphysical assumption that there are natural divisions to be found. Consider the following observation.

No natural system of plants, though one or the other approaches it quite closely, has so far been constructed; nor do I contend that this system is really natural

---

[53] Buffon, *Histoire naturelle*, I 51–2.

[54] Larson, *Interpreting Nature*, 18; Mayr, *The Growth of Biological Thought*, 173; Ereshefsky, *The Poverty of the Linnaean Hierarchy*, 1–6.

[55] Müller-Wille, "Collection and Collation," 542.

[56] Clifford was a director of the Dutch East India Company, and his garden and greenhouses contained specimens from across the globe. At the peak of his career, Linnaeus had cultivated around 2,000 plant species in his garden at Uppsala, and, with the help of his students, accumulated over 16,000 specimens in his herbarium. Müller-Wille, "Walnut-Trees at Hudson Bay, Coral Reefs in Gotland," 34.

[57] In an undated letter to Haller (presumably written in 1737), Linnaeus says of Ray: "What was he? Undoubtedly an indefatigable man in collecting, describing, &c.; but in the knowledge of genetic principles, less than nothing." Linnaeus, "Letter to Haller," in *A selection of the correspondence*, II 281. For a discussion of Ray's influence on Linnaeus, see Raven, *John Ray, Naturalist*, 306–7.

(perhaps some other time I may issue fragments of one); nor can it become a natural system before all details in connection with our system will be known. In the meantime, however, as long as a natural system is lacking, artificial systems will definitely be needed.[58]

Linnaeus recognized that the properties used in classification capture only a partial set of the divisions in nature that are selected in advance by natural historians. While he accepted a broadly Lockean epistemology, according to which our ideas capture only secondary qualities of objects, he claimed that one could potentially discover the essential divisions by observing physical relations under controlled conditions. In the domain of botany, Linnaeus proposed that these essential divisions could be discerned in the reproductive organs of plants. This allowed him to sketch a hierarchical system that arranged plants into twenty-four classes according to the number and position of their stamens (male parts), breaking the classes down into sixty-five orders based on the number and position of the pistils (female parts).[59] The sexual method of classification recasts the logical categories according to physical relations, introducing an intensive experimental method into the classification of plants.

In the methodological preface to *Systema naturae*, Linnaeus begins with a series of observations that capture the importance of generation to his taxonomical project. Consider the first three:

1. If we observe God's works, it becomes more than sufficiently evident to everybody, that each living being is propagated from an egg and that every egg produces an offspring closely resembling the parent. Hence no new species are produced nowadays.
2. Individuals multiply by generation. Hence at present the number of individuals in each species is greater than it was at first.
3. If we count backwards this multiplication of individuals in each species, in the same way as we multiplied forward (2), the series ends up in one single *parent*, whether that parent consists of *one single* hermaphrodite (as commonly in plants) or of a double, viz. a male and a female (as in most animals).[60]

It is not difficult to see from where the essentialist reading of Linnaean classification draws its evidence.[61] Yet it is vital to note that while (1) presupposes a pre-existing order, (2) and (3) introduce two interrelated concepts that reflect Linnaeus' attempt to ground classificatory divisions in physical relations:

---

[58] Linnaeus, *Systema Naturae*, 23.   [59] Farber, *Finding Order in Nature*, 9.
[60] Linnaeus, *Systema Naturae*, 18.
[61] Noting the fundamental role of divine creativity in the Linnaean system, Jahn describes Linnaeus as a "typical proponent of a religiously motivated program of natural research." Jahn, *Grundzüge der Biologiegeschichte*, 234.

generation, understood as a temporal process, and historical lines of descent, which trace back to a single parent or set of parents. To identify generation as a fundamental consideration in classification was, in 1735, a novel venture, for the connections between higher and lower concepts were still understood by most natural historians as logical affinities. The idea of historical lines of descent that branch out *through* generation is even more original, for it entails that natural historians can use experimental techniques to distinguish essential from merely accidental properties, which separate membership of a variety from membership of a species. If two distinct specimens relocated to a controlled garden manifest the same characteristics, natural historians can tell that the original difference was the result of an accidental change undergone by an original parent in response to a change in environment. If the two specimens remain distinct, then the different characteristics are essential and define the boundary between two species. In *Ratio operis* (1737), Linnaeus goes as far as to state that originally created species "afterwards produce more, but always similar forms according to inherent laws of generation."[62] The notion that generation follows determinate *laws*, which become a matter of debate following Stephen Hales' *Vegetable staticks* (1727) (see Section 2.2), had never before been used for classificatory purposes.

The sequence of observations outlined in *Systema naturae* offers a framework for natural historians to examine living beings as the products of original forms created by divine action. It is "necessary to attribute this progenitorial unity to some Omnipotent or Omniscient Being," Linnaeus states, lest the variation we find explode into an infinite collection of individuals.[63] Once an original taxon is created, each of its members will, by necessity, also have the essential properties of that taxon. Variation *within* a taxon is a result of the accidental modification of original forms in time. As the original set of living beings spread over the earth, they encountered varying physical conditions, which occasioned modifications that warrant the subdivision of variety under species. In *Fundamenta botanica*, Linnaeus defines variation as follows: "Varietas est planta mutata a causa accidentali" (a variety is a plant that mutated due to accidental causes).[64] Accidental causes consist of external influences, including climate, soil, and temperature. Time and environment account for variation, deformation, abnormalities, and monsters but not for the enduing qualities of a species. Species and variety can thus be separated by discovering which qualities are essential and which are accidental: a species is marked by the shared possession of invariable or fixed heritable characteristics (following Aristotle, physiology and anatomy are the

---

[62] Müller-Wille and Reeds, "A Translation of Carl Linnaeus's Introduction to *Genera Plantarum* (1737)," 565.

[63] Linnaeus, *Systema Naturae*, 18.

[64] Linnaeus, *Fundamenta botanica*, 18. In *Philosophia botanica*, a re-edition of *Fundamenta botanica* with further comments and examples, he states that "A variety is a plant changed by accidental cause: by climate, soil, heat, wind etc." Linnaeus, *Philosophia botanica*, §158.

primary candidates), a variety is a subclass of species marked by accidental alterations (size, colour, shape, etc.).

In Linnaean taxonomy, the division between fixed and accidental traits does not deny the possibility that new species are formed through hybridization.[65] In his prizewinning essay, Linnaeus considered the production of hybrids as evidence of plant sexuality, for it demonstrated that seeds develop only when pollen comes into contact with the stigma.[66] He considers plants discovered in the wild that exhibit characters of two known species. While he refers to such plants as new species, Linnaeus concludes that the two parent species belonging to the one genus must have been, in the beginning, a single species, which entails that the variants appeared through hybridization. Once the plants are cultivated in the controlled conditions of the botanist's garden, the enduring characteristics of each original species can be discerned experimentally. In "Metamorphoses of Plants" (1755), he explains how botanical gardens can reverse the history of variation by "reducing varieties to their species."[67] This reductive method operates on the assumption that a genus is the base stem of a plant that developed from a single mother and various fathers. The task of natural history is thus to identify the base stem from which the subsequent species groups were produced through a law of generation. Linnaeus defines the criteria for this differentiation as follows: "Certainty in species, to be distinguished from varieties, is detected by: cultivation in different and various soils; attentive examination to all parts of the plant."[68] Natural historians can thus differentiate the contingent features of a variety from the necessary and enduring characteristics of a species by conducting an experiment that reveals which specimens return to their original form and which exhibit an enduring change.

Linnaeus applied his principle of variation to the study of animals, and to human beings in particular, resulting in a system of classification that captures generative lines of descent. Given the importance of Linnaeus' schema of human classification for Kant's writings on race, it is worth noting its basic features here. The original edition of *Systema naturae* included a schema in which four varieties are classified under the taxon *Homo* (*Americanus, Asiaticus, Africanus,* and *Europeanus*), each marked by a distinct skin colour (*rufus, luridis, niger,* and *albus*). In the 1758 edition, Linnaeus speculated about the cause of variation by appealing to the Hippocratic-Galenic theory of humours. Following Hippocrates, Galen posited a correspondence between the four elements of nature (air, water,

---

[65] In contrast to many commentators, Richards argues that Linnaeus did not view species, understood as a set of defining essential traits, as fixed. Rather, he held that species taxa could alter through union with other species. It is fair to say, however, that taxa for Linnaeus do not develop over time. His point is rather that their expression is contingent on environmental factors. See Richards, *The Species Problem*, 57–8.

[66] Linnaeus, "Nya bevis för sexualitet hos växterna," 119–26.

[67] Linnaeus, "Metamorphoses plantarum," 380.   [68] Linnaeus, *Philosophia botanica,* §283.

fire, and earth) and the four humours composing the body (blood, phlegm, yellow bile, and black bile), establishing a dynamic proportionality between body and environment.[69] The humoral framework was widely deployed in European colonialism to address growing concerns associated with relocating human bodies to unknown places, especially in response to high rates of mortality among soldiers in distant territories. Galen's texts provided a standard for early colonial science, and the first travelogues of the New World, such as those by Gonzalo Fernández de Oviedo (1535) and José de Acosta (1590), included detailed descriptions of geographical conditions to enable future expeditions to maintain bodily health in new locations.[70] The success of colonial exploration depended on accurate reports, for Galenic medicine entails that the environment not only determines the body's health but also shapes its physical appearance and moral temperament. The travelogues thus played a vital role in consolidating what Mary Floyd-Wilson describes as "early modern geohumoralism": the idea that climate, temperament, external conditions, and inner constitution are causally contiguous in the process of human variation.[71]

The travelogues available to Linnaeus were thus composed of broad-ranging descriptions of foreign environments and the peoples encountered therein, interweaving physical, cultural, and moral peculiarities to encourage future exploration and, in many cases, to reflect and reaffirm the exclusionary laws enforced by the colonial administration.[72] Yet Linnaeus saw that these descriptions lacked the systematic form of the emerging experimental sciences. His fourfold schema was thus intended to extend early modern geohumoralism into the terrain of eighteenth-century experimental philosophy. The physical and temperamental qualities that define each variety of human being reflect a preponderance of one of the four humours, triggered by the unique geographical conditions found on the four continents as the original seeds scattered by the Creator sprouted and began to grow. The four varieties can thereby be defined by distinct temperamental profiles, one specific to each corner of the earth (Amerindians are choleric, Asians melancholic, Africans phlegmatic, and Europeans sanguine). The purpose of Linnaeus' schema was not to define the actual diversity of human life; he was

---

[69] In *On the Nature of Man*, a treatise attributed to Hippocrates, the humoralist theory is defined as follows: "The Human body contains blood, phlegm, yellow bile, and black bile. These are the things that make up its constitution and cause its pains and health. Health is primarily that state in which these constituent substances are in the correct proportion to each other, both in strength and quantity, and are well mixed. Pain occurs when one of the substances presents either a deficiency or an excess, or is separated in the body and not mixed with others." Hippocrates, *Hippocratic Writings*, 262. In *On Temperaments*, Galen argues that an ideal temperament involves a proportionally balanced mixture of the four qualities, and that different proportions among the humours have implications for moral character.

[70] Struik, "Early colonial science in North America and Mexico," 25–54.

[71] Floyd-Wilson, *English Ethnicity and Race in Early Modern Drama*, 2.

[72] For an account of the travel writings available to Linnaeus, see Mazzolini, "Inter-Racial Crossing and Social Structure (1770–1835)."

well aware that human skin colour and other distinctive features vary extensively across the globe. It was rather to look *through* the present diversity to its roots, providing natural historians with a working tool for making precise taxonomical distinctions within the four continents. The result is arguably the first taxonomy of the human species according to *race*, where race serves as a stable subclass that falls under a species.[73] For Linnaeus, the function of judgments about race is not to correspond with a real object but rather to anchor further judgments, enabling natural historians to discern the systematic connections behind the present manifold of human variety.

Linnaeus responded to the potential endlessness of variation by developing a system of classification that was explicitly artificial. Yet he refused to discard the ideal of a natural system. While the reproductive parts of plants and the colour of human skin do not tell the entire story of descent from an original parent, and thus provide a merely artificial marker for natural historians, they nevertheless provide some insight into the divisions originally made by the Creator. Linnaeus extended the scope of his system with enormous observational detail over his lengthy career, but he never felt that he had arrived at a truly natural system. The question raised by his work was *how* the natural system might be reconstructed according to physical connections. Or in practical terms, how observation and experiment could enable the community of natural historians to agree on which system is natural.

---

[73] Linnaeus never used the French term *race* but rather *varietas* in Latin and *slag* in Swedish, the latter being a term used by gardeners and breeders. Müller-Wille notes that while the use of race beyond the French language had not yet reached Swedish (it first appears in 1765), *varietas* and *slag* play the functional role that race would come to take in the mid- to late 1700s. See Müller-Wille, "Linnaeus and the Four Corners of the World," 194.

2

Charting *Terra Incognita*

In this chapter, I argue that the epistemological and metaphysical changes required to establish a developmental conception of nature as an acceptable programme of research occurred through the extension of Newtonian science to events and processes that are not strictly amenable to mathematical demonstration. The fable sketched by Descartes in *The World* offered a frame in which the generation of natural products could be examined according to mechanical laws. For the growing number of natural philosophers committed to Newton's method, however, Descartes' fable was yet another sky castle, a fanciful construction in which each hypothesis simply follows from a higher hypothesis. Linnaeus added some credibility to the idea of a developmental history, for he proposed a method for classifying plant specimens according to the inner constitution of natural groupings discerned though close examination of the generative organs. He added laws to Locke's notion of generation, introducing the idea that essential properties are inherited without fail despite changes in environment. Yet he did not offer a method by which those laws were forthcoming.

For the nascent community of experimental philosophers to accept a new programme of research that investigates natural objects as products of a physical process, a new conception of matter would be required that could enable the student of nature to anticipate properties of objects that lie beyond the testimony of the senses, such as events that occurred long in the past or those inaccessible to the human eye. The problem confronting experimental philosophers is that hypotheses are easy to come by, and any branch of natural philosophy has many to choose from. One of the fundamental tasks of experimental philosophy is thus to define and justify the constraints on *valid* hypotheses. If the fundamental properties of material bodies could be demonstrated metaphysically, then analogical reasoning about the generation of those bodies would not be entirely speculative. *Something* would be known; namely, that the generation of material bodies follows the same laws that can be deduced from experience. The field of known laws would provide a standard to adjudicate competing hypotheses, even those that purport to explain the origin of the natural system, such as the biblical creation narrative or Descartes' fable.

In Section 2.1, I begin with a brief sketch of Newton's ambiguous legacy, which left several unanswered questions regarding the metaphysical implications of his mathematical conception of force. While many experimental philosophers adhered to Locke's associationist account of Newton's achievement, which results

Kant and the Transformation of Natural History. Andrew Cooper, Oxford University Press. © Andrew Cooper 2023.
DOI: 10.1093/oso/9780192869784.003.0003

in a radical scepticism about empirical knowledge, the undeniable progress made by those who dared to extend Newton's method beyond celestial mechanics led others to search for a more expansive interpretation of Newtonianism. In the following sections, I identify three such interpretations, each of which advanced a distinct framework for extending Newton's method to plant and animal physiology. In Section 2.2, I examine Stephen Hales' *Vegetable staticks* (1727) as a *mechanical* interpretation of Newtonianism, which applies attraction and repulsion to the movement of fluids throughout the plant conceived of as a hydraulic machine. In Section 2.3, I consider the first three volumes of Georges Buffon's *Histoire naturelle, générale et particulière* (1749) as a *materialist* interpretation of Newtonianism, which attempts to explain the generative process on the assumption of organic forces resident in matter itself. And in Section 2.4, I examine Albrecht von Haller's classification of muscle fibres in *De partibus corporis humani sensibilibus et irritabilibus* (1753) as an *analogical* interpretation of Newtonianism. Haller's work stands between the epistemic modesty of Hales' plant physiology and Buffon's daring theory of generation, opening a science of animal movement that retains Newton's refusal to speculate about hidden causes. My selection of texts is not disinterested. In the following chapters, I argue that each has a vital role to play in Kant's early conception of natural history. Nevertheless, my examination aims to provide further insight into the eighteenth-century debate concerning the meaning of Newtonianism, which is a growing matter of scholarly interest.[1]

Before we begin, I want to address a possible objection to my use of Newtonianism as the guiding frame of the chapter. As we will see, Buffon's conception of physical truth builds on a Leibnizian conception of space and time, and Haller's notion of physiology draws from Galen's theory of living faculties. Why examine these proposals as Newtonian? Some historians constrain Newtonian science to Newton's self-proclaimed mathematical standard, such that Haller's physiology is only Newtonian in part and Buffon's speculation about organic matter is not Newtonian at all.[2] I reject this approach, for it overlooks the way in which Newtonianism provided a standard against which natural philosophers could propose and contest experiments despite significant geographical, institutional, and even metaphysical differences. In contrast, I follow Judith Schlanger's observation that when it comes to understanding the establishment of physiology in the eighteenth century, the issue at stake is "not what Newton said but what he enabled people to say."[3] Newtonianism, as I use it in this chapter,

---

[1] For a summary of the field, see Shrank, *The Newton Wars and the Beginning of the French Enlightenment*, 1–36.

[2] Hoquet for instance argues against the interpretation of Buffon as a Newtonian on the grounds that *Histoire naturelle* is a non-mathematical *physique*. Hoquet, "History without Time," 39. What interests me here is Buffon's presentation of his theory of generation through an analogy with Newton's discovery of gravity. It is in this methodological sense that I take Buffon to be Newtonian.

[3] Schlanger, *Les Métaphores de l'organisme*, 100.

consists of three relatively loose commitments: (1) a historical commitment to a programme of research continuous with Newton, (2) an epistemological commitment to experiment and observation as the ground of scientific claims, and (3) a methodological commitment to analogical reasoning for the examination of phenomena that are not strictly amenable to the application of mathematics.[4] By expressing a historical, epistemic, and methodological commitment to Newtonianism, eighteenth-century natural philosophers were able to signal their intention to participate in a collective project of natural philosophy understood as an experimental science.

2.1 Newton's Ambiguous Legacy

The impact of Newton's method on the European scientific community is difficult to exaggerate. Natural philosophers across the continent recognized that *Principia* opened a new standard of demonstration that works from phenomena to a law in such a way that can convince anyone familiar with mathematics. Yet it was unclear what should be done with his philosophy. As we saw in Chapter 1, Newton's argument in *Principia* did not provide a physical explanation of the movement of celestial bodies, but rather a mathematical demonstration of the inverse square law of universal gravitation. Without speculating about the cause of gravitational attraction, Newton proved that universal gravity accurately describes planetary motion. The key to his defence was not so much the content of his argument as the way he was able to deliver his results; Newton's provocative claim is that natural philosophy must be redefined methodologically.

Yet Newton's early critics, eager to see a new era of natural philosophy built on his success, complained that the initial presentation of his deductive method did not explain how it could be extended beyond celestial mechanics. In response, Newton included a section entitled "Rules for Reasoning in Philosophy" in the second edition of *Principia* (1713), which he formulated during the early 1690s while in close contact with Locke.[5] The numerous revisions of these rules in his manuscripts between the second and third editions indicate the seriousness with which he refined the presentation of his method.[6] By the third edition (1726), the

---

[4] While studies of eighteenth-century physiology tend to focus on the various hypotheses used to explain the process of animal generation, I extend my focus to include the methodological presuppositions that both constrain and enable the formation of such hypotheses. See Roe, *Matter, Life, and Generation*, 45–88; Roger, *The Life Sciences in Eighteenth-Century French Thought*, 259–367; Mensch, *Kant's Organicism*, 1–50; Goy, *Kants Theorie der Biologie*, 288–385; Cohen, "Kant on Epigenesis, Monogenesis and Human Nature," 676–81; Bowler, "Bonnet and Buffon," 259–81.

[5] Smith, "The Methodology of the *Principia*," 161.

[6] For instance, Koyré notes six revisions of rule two between the second and third editions, and five revisions of rule four before it was included in the third edition. Koyré, *Newtonian Studies*, 265–71.

section consisted of four methodological rules for handling unknown phenomena and working towards their explanation. Consider the first two rules:

Rule 1. We are to admit no more causes of natural things than such as are both true and sufficient to explain their appearances.

Rule 2. Therefore to the same natural effects we must, as far as possible, assign the same causes.[7]

The first rule instructs that we should "explain" or "explicate" (*explicandis*) nature in the simplest way without sacrificing experimental truth for the sake of theory. This is to say that we should only differentiate causes when the experimental data forces us to do so; theory construction must be limited to experiments and observations. The second rule is presented as a consequence of the first, instructing us to assign the same cause to the same phenomena. That is, it instructs us to make inferences about natural effects by following the model of mathematical analogies, which take the form of a quantitative relation between four variables $(X : Y = A : B)$. In mathematics, we can discover a fourth unknown variable when three variables are known and one unknown, provided that we draw an inference between the quantitative relation of the two pairs. In philosophy, we can discover a fourth unknown variable when three variables are known and one unknown, provided that we draw an inference between the qualitative relation of the two pairs. Newton invokes rules one and two when he classifies the acceleration of the moon and the centripetal accelerations of the planets as the same kind of acceleration.[8] Once we have inferred that the qualitative relation between the revolution of the moon around the earth and the circumsolar planets around the sun is of the same kind, the second rule instructs us to undertake a mathematical demonstration of planetary acceleration.

The third rule is often described as Newton's "argument from phenomena," and runs as follows:

Rule 3: The quality of bodies, which admit neither intensification nor remission of degrees, and which are found to belong to all bodies within the reach of our experiments, are to be esteemed the universal qualities of bodies whatsoever.[9]

If a property satisfies a certain empirical criterion—being a constant property of all bodies within the reach of our experiments—this rule instructs us to "esteem" or

---

[7] Newton, *Mathematical Principles*, II 398.

[8] In Proposition 5, Newton states that the revolutions of the circumjovial planets around Jupiter, the circumsaturnal planets around Saturn, and the circumsolar planets around the sun, are "appearances of the same sort with the revolution of the moon about the earth; and therefore, by Rule 2, must be owing to the same sort of causes." Newton, *Mathematical Principles*, II 410.

[9] Newton, *Mathematical Principles*, II 398.

"take" that property to be universal. Without rule three, Newton could not assert that *all* bodies near planets gravitate to those planets in the same way that observed bodies do. Building on the second rule, the third rule states that if we are able to demonstrate the quality of a body through experiment, we are to extend that quality to all instances of that body, based on an inference between the pairs. Newton illustrates the rule with the quality of hardness. Because all the bodies we encounter in experience are hard, we generate a principle to account for the phenomena—the hardness of a whole arises from the hardness of the parts—and "therefore justly infer the hardness of the undivided particles not only of the bodies we feel but of all others."[10] The inference from phenomena to a principle does not reach knowledge of the essential qualities of particles. Newton is clear that we must cast aside all "dreams and vein fictions of our own devising," for the only access we have to the qualities of bodies is their manifest expression. Rather, the inference is guided by the rule, which instructs us to extend the knowledge we have gained through experiment to phenomena that lies beyond the bounds of experience.

The fourth rule guides the conduct of the natural philosopher:

Rule 4. In experimental philosophy we are to look upon propositions inferred by general induction from phenomena as accurately or very nearly true, notwithstanding any contrary hypothesis that may be imagined, till such time as other phenomena occur, by which they may either be made more accurate, or liable to exceptions.[11]

In the following sections we will see that this rule has several implications that were of vital importance to Newton's followers. First, the rule shows that the inductive procedure may not be "evaded by hypotheses"; induction from phenomena overrides all other kinds of theory. Second, Newton's claim that the propositions gathered by the rules of reasoning should be considered as "accurately or very nearly true" instructs us to model the world through idealizations, or as George Smith puts it, "approximation[s] that would hold exactly in certain specifiable circumstances."[12] The final clause of the rule suggests that the task of natural philosophy is to continually make ever improving idealizations. Recalcitrant phenomena must be addressed in a new idealization that better approximates the world.

Newton restricts the scope of reasoning in philosophy to phenomena that could *potentially* be demonstrated mathematically. The application of the rules in *Principia*, for instance, extend from Newton's deduction that the accelerations of bodies are proportional to the inverse square of the distance from their centres

---

[10] Newton, *Mathematical Principles*, II 399.   [11] Newton, *Mathematical Principles*, II 400.
[12] Smith, "The Methodology of the *Principia*," 157.

of orbit. However, it was not difficult for his followers to find examples where Newton had extended his reasoning to phenomena that were not strictly amenable to mathematical demonstration. In *Opticks*, for instance, Newton attempted to explain the properties of light through "reason and experiments."[13] In contrast to the cumulative argument developed in *Principia*, *Opticks* consists of a loosely joined sequence of experiments to examine the fundamental thesis that an attractive force is responsible for all the phenomena in nature. Newton presents the results of quantitative experiments that explore a range of optical effects, including the cause of the rainbow, the formation of rings in sunlight, and the colours produced by plates of varying thickness. In applying his method to phenomena related to light, he takes a more liberal approach to analogical reasoning than the methodological reservations expressed in his General Scholium seem to allow. This was especially evident in the queries appended to Book III of *Opticks*, which outline propositions about which he was still undecided.[14] By the fourth edition of 1730, Newton had included thirty-one queries, several of which had become long essays. In Query 31, which was cited by his followers almost as often as the General Scholium, he begins by explaining that natural philosophy strictly adheres to an inductive procedure that draws only from experiments and observations. Yet he then states that this initial groundwork enables natural philosophers to "proceed from Compounds to Ingredients, and from Motions to the Forces producing them; and in general, from Effects to their Causes, and from particular Causes to more general ones, till the Argument end in the most general."[15] To reason backward from motion to force—from effect to cause—is to proceed further than the inductive procedure of the four rules seems to allow, at least as exemplified in *Principia*. This method is not restricted to the mathematical proof of a law but includes a corresponding *physical* proof of the cause of the effect. The movement from mathematical to physical proof entails a synthetic dimension by which the discovered cause, once established as a principle, can be used for "explaining the Phaenomena proceeding from them, and proving the Explanations."[16] In *Principia*, Newton did not show that the motion of the planets is *acted on* by physical forces. He merely showed that the forces acting on a planet are directed towards the centre, varying inversely as the square of the distance.[17] Yet in the methodological reflections of Query 31, he intends to move from mathematics *to* the physical properties of causes, and furthermore, to causes that are "both true and sufficient to explain the phenomena."

[13] Newton, *Opticks*, 1.
[14] In the second edition of *Opticks* (1706), Newton added seven new queries, covering a range of issues central to eighteenth-century experimental philosophy. In the 1717 edition he inserts eight new queries between those written for the first and second editions. Here he introduces his notoriously ambiguous notion of the aether.
[15] Newton, *Opticks*, 380.   [16] Newton, *Opticks*, 380–1.
[17] See Cohen, *The Newtonian Revolution*, 29.

The speculations found in *Opticks* were sufficiently broad to warrant multiple interpretations of Newtonian method. Noting the ambiguity of Newton's language, Robert Schofield identifies two interpretations that formed during the eighteenth century, which he describes as "mechanism" and "materialism."[18] Mechanical Newtonians held "that causation for all the phenomena of nature was ultimately to be sought in the primary particles, their motions, and the forces of attraction and repulsion between them which determine these motions."[19] To examine the qualities of objects more specific than attraction and repulsion, one must assume that natural objects are analogous to machines, in which manifest properties are caused by the action of attractive and repulsive on the functional parts of a whole. In contrast, materialist Newtonians held "that the causes of phenomena inhere in unique substances, each possessing an essential property the power to convey, in proportion to its quantity, some characteristic quality."[20] If Newtonianism permitted the reflection on basic particles as substances endowed with inner forces, then the principle of analogy could be extended with confidence.

Schofield's claim is that *both* interpretations appealed to Newton for authority; the mechanists appealed to Newton's mathematical deductive system as presented in *Principia*, and the materialists appealed to Newton's account of the aether, the active substance which opposed the passivity of other substances.[21] Despite their differences, proponents of each interpretation agreed that by combining mathematical reasoning with observation and experiment, Newton demonstrated that some forms of speculation are valid in experimental reasoning.

2.2 Mechanical Newtonianism

In 1733, Stephen Hales published a series of essays on the movement of air through plants. He prefaced the essays with a citation from Peter Browne's *The Procedure, Extent, and Limits of Human Understanding* (1729), which affirms Locke's denial of the knowability of real essences and seeks to clarify the application of Newton's rules for reasoning in natural philosophy. The danger confronting the natural philosopher, Browne contends, is to mistake metaphor, which feigns an identity between the idea and the thing in itself, with analogy, which accepts the incommensurability of idea and thing:

---

[18] Schofield, *Mechanism and Materialism*, 15. See also Wolfe, "On the Role of Newtonian Analogies in Eighteenth-Century Life Science," 226.

[19] Schofield, *Mechanism and Materialism*, 15.

[20] Schofield, *Mechanism and Materialism*, 15–16.

[21] Hall and Hall note that Newton's letters to Boyle and his early work *De Aere et Aethere* also provided a foundation for the materialist interpretation of Newtonianism during the eighteenth century. Hall and Hall, *Unpublished Scientific Papers of Isaac Newton*, 203.

all the real true Knowledge we have of Nature is entirely *Experimental*; insomuch that, how strange soever the Assertion seems, we may lay this down as the first fundamental Rule in Physics, *That it is not within the compass of human Understanding to assign a purely speculative Reason for any one Phenomenon in Nature*; as why Grass is green, or Snow is white; why Fire burns, or Cold congeals?...We find indeed, by Observation and Experience, that such and such Effects *Are* produced; but when we attempt to think of the Reason *Why*, and the *Manner How* the Causes work those Effects, then we are at a stand; and all our reasoning is precarious, or at best but probable conjecture.[22]

To establish rapport with the community of experimental philosophers, Hales begins by affirming Browne's epistemic reservations. The experimental philosopher must refrain from speculation, lest they take their idea for the thing itself, and instead restrict their inquiry to manifest effects. Yet in the very next sentence he moves beyond Browne's reservations to identify a legitimate twilight zone in which conjecture can lead to further discoveries:

Yet it seems not unreasonable on the other hand, tho' not far to indulge, yet to carry our Reasonings a little farther than the plain Evidence of Experiments will warrant; for since at the utmost Boundaries of those Things which we clearly know, there is a kind of Twilight cast from what we know, on the adjoining Borders of *Terra incognita*, it seems therefore reasonable in some degree to indulge Conjecture there; otherwise we should make but very slow advances in future Discoveries, either by Experiments or Reasoning.[23]

Hales was interested in developing a procedure that would allow experimental philosophers to ground their inquiry in what can be known with certainty, and yet to venture into the land of ignorance where conjecture can lead to small advances in understanding. The key to this incursion, he contends, lies in the extension of Newton's method from bodies in motion to the movement of pneumatic and static phenomena.

In 1727, Hales presented a series of experiments to the Royal Society that quickly became a landmark for those wanting to make a cautious incursion into *terra incognita*. The experiments were constructed to pursue a set of questions that were fundamental to the idea of a "plant physics," or a physiology of plants. The subtitle of the published version, "towards a Natural History of Vegetation," reflects Hales' ambition to overturn the arbitrary classifications found in extant natural histories with a schema that identifies the various parts of a plant

---

[22] Hales, *Statical essays*, xii–xiii, citing Browne, *The Procedure, Extent, and Limits of Human Understanding*, 205–6.
[23] Hales, *Statical essays*, xiii–xiv.

according to their functions within the plant machine, such as growth and maintenance. His aim was to examine the movement of moisture through the capillary tubes, the forces governing such movement, and, most importantly, the "chymico-statical" relation between plants and air, as the effects of attractive and repulsive forces operating between primary particles within the functional constraints of the plant machine.[24] Hales' plant machine is not made up of cogs, springs, and pendula, which require intelligent direction and constant winding up. It consists rather of pneumatic devises powered by combustion, pressure, and release, which explain how the function of each part operates undirected. While Hales carefully lays out his findings in the grammar of Newton's *Principia*, expressing his reluctance to speculate about the cause of plant movement and instead to present a detailed account of experiments, the inspiration for his extension of Newtonian principles to the movement of plants cannot be found exclusively in *Principia*. His experiments provide a model for how the natural philosopher can build on the speculations about air found in Query 31 of *Opticks*, where Newton explained fermentation and putrefaction through the application of attractive and repulsive forces to the movement of corpuscles.

Hales justifies the extension of Newtonian physics into the twilight of vegetable dynamics by means of a methodological rule. Mathematics can be applied to *any* alteration in nature, he states, for the "wise Creator has observed the most exact proportions, *of number, weight and measure*."[25] Hales calls upon this rule to extend the properties identified by Newton's demonstration of planetary movement according to "their common centers of motion and gravity" to the movement of fluids throughout the plant via fermentation.[26] Physiology provides "the most considerable and rational accounts" of the economy of living things by undertaking the "statical examination of their fluids," using attractive and repulsive forces to account for the movement of fluids through the proper channels. The task is to devise an experiment by which the movement of fluids could be tested against the rule. By proposing that the leaves of a plant act as the "lungs of the plant," Hales constructed an experimental device that enabled him to quantify the movement of fluids through various organic substances. This device consisted of a retort connected to a glass vessel with a small hole, and immersed in water.[27] By placing various kinds of animal, vegetable, and mineral substances in the retort, and by setting it on a stove, Hales was able to observe the effects of combustion, and to measure the quantity of air absorbed or released via fermentation by observing the changing level of water passing through the hole. The aim was to demonstrate Newton's claim in Query 31 that "true permanent Air arises by fermentation or heat, from those bodies which the chymists called fixed, whose particles adhere by a strong attraction, and are not therefore separated and rarified

---

[24] Hales, *Vegetable staticks*, viv.   [25] Hales, *Vegetable staticks*, 1.
[26] Hales, *Vegetable staticks*, 2.   [27] Hales, *Vegetable staticks*, 185–6.

without fermentation."[28] Hales claims that by making air elastic, combustion is the cause of repulsion in plant respiration. The attractive properties in "fixed air" form the solid parts of the plant, and the repulsive force of "elastick air" promote plant growth.[29]

Hales then employs his pneumatic chemistry to explain the generation of plants, in which a pre-existing miniature in the seed expands through pneumatic forces. The elasticity of air explains how pollen could reach the seeds that are tightly encased within the pistil to provide the nourishment that begins the generative process.[30] Air is thus appointed by the Creator to "convey nourishment to the embrio fruit and seeds," thereby invigorating the plant and creating an "unhatched tree":

> But as soon as the *Calix* is formed into a small fruit, now impregnated with its minute seminal tree, furnished with its Secondine, *Corion* and *Amnion*, (which new set fruit may in that state be looked upon as a compleat egg of the tree, containing its young unhatched tree, yet in embrio) then the blossom falls off, leaving this new formed egg, or first set fruit in this infant state, to imbibe nourishment sufficient for it self, and the Foetus with which it is impregnated.[31]

By applying his pneumatic chemistry to plant reproduction, Hales pioneered a mechanical explanation of the generative process. He concludes that if Newton's fluid dynamics can be successfully applied to the circulation of fluids through the plant, we have grounds to extend the analogy to animals as well: "as in vegetables, so doubtless in animals."[32] The qualities of the material, vegetable, and animal spheres are sufficiently alike to extend the discoveries made in one domain as guides for further research into the unknown properties of another:

> since in vegetables, the growth and the preservation of their vegetable life is promoted and maintained as in animals, by the very plentiful and regular motion of their fluids, which are the vehicles ordained by nature, to carry proper nourishment to every part, it is therefore reasonable to hope, that in them also, by the same method of inquiry, considerable discoveries may in time be made, there being, in many respects, a great analogy between plants and animals.[33]

---

[28] Hales, *Vegetable staticks*, 94–5, citing Newton, *Opticks*, 396.
[29] Hales, *Vegetable staticks*, 165–6, 300.
[30] Following Roger, I separate "pre-existence" from "pre-formation" to maintain the important distinction between the pre-formation of parts from the pre-existence of the complete embryo in miniature. See Roger, *The Life Sciences in Eighteenth-Century French Thought*, 259–60.
[31] Hales, *Vegetable staticks*, 355–6.   [32] Hales, *Vegetable staticks*, 192.
[33] Hales, *Vegetable staticks*, 3.

Hales' analogy between the generative laws of the plant and animal kingdoms had significant implications for Newtonian science in the mid-eighteenth century. In 1735, the young Buffon published a French translation of *Vegetable staticks* in which he praises Hales for presenting a method for the study of physiological movement that consists "only of experiment and observation," thereby extending "the method...of the great Newton" to the plant kingdom.[34] Buffon's translation brought Hales' plant physiology to the attention of natural philosophers on the continent. Once Hales had established that Newtonian laws could be fruitfully applied to the physiological processes of plants, a precedent was established in the rapidly growing community of Newtonians, permitting the extension of those laws to the animal kingdom as well.

2.3 Materialist Newtonianism

Buffon's praise of Hales' theory of generation suggests that, in 1735, he accepted the idea that the egg pre-exists the tree it is to become. Hales' study is worthy of emulation, he declares, for it is only those works "based on experiment" that merit "real confidence."[35] Yet Buffon evidently saw more in Hales' study than Hales had himself expressed. In his optimistic plea for a new epoch of inquiry inspired by *Vegetable staticks*, Buffon echoes Query 31 of Newton's *Opticks*, proclaiming that "the knowledge of effects will lead us imperceptibly to that of causes, and we shall no longer fall into the absurdities which seem to characterize all systems."[36] By the end of the 1730s, however, Buffon had concluded that Hales' mechanical Newtonianism did not strictly permit the discovery of causes from physiological effects. For discovery to arrive at the knowledge of causes, one must be committed to the prior assumption of the intelligibility of physical relations, a view that shares more in common with Leibniz' necessitarian metaphysics than Locke's associationism. Recall the epistemic constraints of Newton's third rule: we cannot with certainty assume that the qualities of bodies are the same beyond that which we have experienced. Analogical reasoning is provisional and serves merely to guide further inquiry. For Buffon, the success of Newton's celestial mechanics demonstrates that the analogy holds in regards to general physics. Hales' extension of Newton's method to the vegetable kingdom demonstrates that the analogy also holds in other domains of inquiry.

Buffon's departure from Hales' mechanical Newtonianism reflects a broader movement in French natural philosophy during the late 1730s, seen in the work of Voltaire, Émilie du Châtelet, and Pierre Louis Maupertuis. In *Foundations of Physics* (1740), Du Châtelet claimed that Newtonian physics both requires and

---

[34] Buffon, "Preface of the Translator," 37–8.   [35] Buffon, "Preface of the Translator," 37.
[36] Buffon, "Preface of the Translator," 38.

vindicates a metaphysical foundation for the investigation of nature. The reasons for her claim are particularly evident in chapter 4, "On Hypotheses," which provides a practical defence of speculative propositions in experimental science. Du Châtelet begins by attacking the Cartesians for tainting hypothetical reasoning. Their undisciplined use of hypotheses to explain everything according to causal mechanisms extends beyond the data of experience, and thus hampers the progress of science. Yet she then claims that our knowledge of nature cannot advance by the wholesale rejection of hypotheses. What we require is a prior determination of what counts as a valid hypothesis. To determine the validity of a hypothesis requires a clear distinction between possibility and actuality:

> It is necessary to distinguish between the possible and the actual. You have seen before that all that does not imply contradiction is possible, but is not actual. It is possible, for example, that this square table might become round, but this will perhaps never happen. Thus, all that exists being necessarily possible, one can conclude possibility from existence, but not existence from possibility.[37]

Possibility tells us what could be the case, Du Châtelet explains, but is it insufficient to determine existence. Actuality, in contrast, entails possibility. The asymmetry between possibility and actuality demonstrates that hypothetical propositions are not assertoric claims but state what *could* be the case. A valid hypothesis, then, is a statement that describes what is possibly true. Metaphysics is fundamental to experimental science to the extent that it determines the modal space in which to adjudicate whether a hypothesis can be legitimately entertained. The first principle of physics is thus the principle of sufficient reason. Boyle's corpuscles, which consist of extended bodies acted on by external forces, must be replaced with ultimate "simple beings [*êtres simples*]," fundamental bodies constituted by a perpetually acting force: "The principle that contains the sufficient reason for the actuality of any action is called *force*; for the simple power or ability to act [*faculté d'agir*] is only a possibility of action or of passion in beings, which requires a sufficient reason for its actuality."[38] Du Châtelet's account of force entails a materialist account of nature in practice, though not in theory.[39] The materialism of Descartes or Boyle requires that explanations can refer only to the extension, shape, or density of corpuscles. In contrast, Du Châtelet proposes a *phenomenal* materialism according to which material dynamics is determined by an underlying substance. The result is a unique field of material possibility in

---

[37] Du Châtelet, *Institutions de physique*, 26/131. Citations of Du Châtelet's *Institutions* include both the original and Bour and Zinsser's English translation, separated by a forward slash.

[38] Du Châtelet, *Institutions de physique*, 137/168.

[39] Sloan describes Du Châtelet's position as a "*dynamic* 'phenomenal' materialism," for it is not the extension, shape, or density of the atoms that give rise to phenomena but rather the underlying substance. Sloan, "Metaphysics and 'Vital' Materialism," 55.

which a valid hypothesis presents a candidate force that stands as the sufficient reason for a material movement. A valid hypothesis is not a generalization from experience, describing how things tend to happen. If one proposed that the planets *tend* to orbit the sun, then neither an instance confirming the proposition nor a counterfactual could shed light on the proposal's truth. To test a natural motion against a hypothetical force, that force must stand as the sufficient reason for the motion.

Once we have determined whether a hypothesis is materially possible, we can then undertake an experimental procedure to determine whether it is actual. This can be established by its capacity to account for the effects encountered in observation and experience:

> When certain things are used to explain what has been observed, and though the truth of what has been supposed is impossible to demonstrate, one is making a hypothesis. Thus, philosophers frame hypotheses to explain the phenomena, the cause of which cannot be discovered either by experiment or by demonstration.[40]

Du Châtelet's contention is that while Newton is right to reject hypotheses that cannot be deduced from phenomena, he was mistaken to reject hypotheses altogether. One is not necessarily a speculative system builder if one proposes hypotheses. Indeed, hypotheses *must* be deployed in experimental philosophy if we are to extend our knowledge beyond what is given into *terra incognita*. To vindicate her claim, Du Châtelet works through the great discoveries made of Copernicus, Kepler, and Newton to demonstrate how the formulation of hypotheses is neither detached from the knowledge of nature nor limited to it. She concludes that hypotheses are

> probable propositions that have a greater or lesser degree of certainty, depending on whether they satisfy a more or less great number of circumstances attendant upon the phenomenon that one wants to explain by their means. And, as a very great degree of probability gains our assent, and has on us almost the same effect as certainty, hypotheses finally become truths when their probability increases to such a point that one can morally present them as a certainty; this is what happened with Copernicus's system of the world, and with M. Huygens's on the ring of Saturn.[41]

While theoretical propositions are either true or false, hypothetical propositions are adjudicated according to degrees of probability. This does not mean, however, that they are banished from the realm of knowledge. Following Newton's third

---

[40] Du Châtelet, *Institutions de physique*, 76/148.
[41] Du Châtelet, *Institutions de physique*, 86–7/154.

rule, Du Châtelet explains that we can accept a hypothesis as true when there is no reasonable doubt that a practical agent could seriously entertain.

Du Châtelet's phenomenal materialism provides the background against which we can understand the theories of generation developed by Maupertuis and Buffon in the 1740s. In 1745, Maupertuis anonymously published *Vénus physique*, in which he presents a new defence of William Harvey's joint inheritance theory of generation. Harvey's theory states that organic parts do not expand from a pre-existing embryo but are progressively generated from an originally undifferentiated, homogenous material that comes from both parents.[42] The universal laws of Newtonian physics cannot account for the organizing process, Maupertuis claimed, for "Uniform and blind attraction diffused in all the particles of matter, would not be able to explain how these particles arrange themselves to form the organization of the simplest body."[43] To explain how a contribution from two parents could give rise to a single embryo, Maupertuis proposed the existence of organic particles (*molecules organiques*) which are acted on by secondary forces.

Maupertuis' organic particles extend the scope of Du Châtelet's simple beings, for they are substances imbued with "something resembling what we call desire, aversion, memory."[44] His reasoning is analogical: as simple beings are imbued with dynamic forces, so organic particles possess secondary forces that act like memories, governing the interaction of organic particles by a dialectical movement between desire and aversion.[45] Maupertuis presents his theory of secondary forces as a hypothesis that awaits empirical verification. Yet he contends that such a hypothesis is more plausible than one that accounts for animal movement according to primary forces acting on hidden mechanisms, for it does not presuppose an initial state of design but explains how unformed matter is integrated into a living body by means of growth, development, and repair. If Newtonian physics had already found it necessary to depart from a strictly mechanical framework by introducing attraction and repulsion as the fundamental forces of matter, then Newtonian physiology must likewise introduce inner forces of organic matter to account for plant and animal movement:

> The Astronomers were the first to feel the need for a new principle to explain the movements of the celestial bodies and thought they had discovered it in these very movements. Since then chemistry has felt the same necessity of adopting this concept, and the most famous Chemists admit Attraction and extend its

---

[42] In *Exercitationes de generatione animalium* (1651), Harvey proposed a theory of generation that located the genesis and development of the chick within the natural order: "The structure of these animals commences from some one part as its nucleus and origin, by the instrumentality of which the rest of the limbs are joined on, and this we say takes place by the method of epigenesis, namely, by degrees, part after part; and this is, in preference to the other mode [metamorphosis, wherein the form comes after the bulk], generation properly so called." Harvey, *The Works of William Harvey*, 335.

[43] Maupertuis, *Systéme de la nature*, 146–7.   [44] Maupertuis, *Systéme de la nature*, 147.

[45] Roger, *The Life Sciences in Eighteenth-Century French Thought*, 385.

function farther than had been done by the Astronomers. Why should not a cohesive force, if it exists in Nature, have a role in the formation of animal bodies? If there are, in each of the seminal seeds, particles predetermined to form the heart, the head, the entrails, the arms and the legs, if these particular particles had a special attraction for those which are to be their immediate neighbors in the animal body, this would lead to the formation of the fetus.[46]

Despite the speculative nature of his proposal, Maupertuis claims to uphold Newton's fourth rule (that the inductive procedure may not be "evaded by hypotheses") more consistently than the mechanical Newtonians. He does not, however, remove the need for design altogether, for his secondary forces are neither creative nor plastic but follow pre-given constraints (memories) that guide the generative process. Nevertheless, by locating these forces *in* nature, Maupertuis provided essential groundwork for a physical account of animal generation, for the forces responsible for the formative process are attributed to organic matter:

> It is true that when we say that the embryo is formed by the mixture of the two seminal fluids, we are far from having explained its creation. But the remaining obscurity must not be attributed to our reasoning. He who desires to know too remote an object and who registers only a blurry image of it, is more successful than he who sees objects that are not the only one in question more distinctly.[47]

While the hypothesis of joint inheritance does not explain the embryo's creation, Maupertuis claims that vague gestures towards a physical account are preferable to hypotheses in which pre-existing mechanisms explain the generative process. Joint inheritance directs inquiry to the phenomena rather than holding the question of generation in suspension.

Buffon set out to provide an experimental basis for Maupertuis' materialist account of generation. His experimental work began in collaboration with John Turberville Needham, who joined Buffon in Paris in the mid-1740s at the recommendation of Martin Folkes, president of the Royal Society.[48] With Buffon, Needham offered vivid descriptions of the regeneration and production of microscopic beings from decomposing materials, providing experimental evidence that matter may well possess properties denied to it by the mechanists.[49] In "A Summary of Some Late Observations upon the Generation, Composition,

---

[46] Maupertuis, *The Earthly Venus*, 56.   [47] Maupertuis, *The Earthly Venus*, 53.

[48] Roe, "John Turberville Needham and the Generation of Living Organisms," 161.

[49] Needham records that it was Buffon "who first engaged me in this Enquiry, by his ingenious System, which he has been pleas'd to read to me, and at the same time expressed his Desire I should pursue it, before I had myself any thoughts of it, or any one Experiment had been try'd." Needham, "A Summary of Some Late Observations," 633.

and Decomposition of Animal and Vegetable Substances" (1749), he claims that his experiments on plants and animals render the hypothesis of pre-existing germs "as unnatural, and as unphilosophical, as it is disagreeable to Observation."[50] In contrast, Needham speculates that God must have placed forces in nature that unify matter in a consistent form, such that "a small number of principles differently combined will yield an inconceivable variety, sufficient to produce them all."[51] Together with Needham, Buffon conducted a series of investigations in joint infusion to provide an experimental basis for a materialist account of generation in which the chance combination of organic particles give rise to microscopic structures that develop into mature adults. The result of these efforts—the opening three volumes of *Histoire naturelle*, published in 1749—has been described by historians as the "most important publication in natural history of the eighteenth century,"[52] for it "made it possible to conceive a strictly materialistic explanation... of the generation of living beings."[53] In this beguiling text, Buffon does not simply provide a natural explanation for some of the most contested points of natural history. He offers a new conception of natural philosophy, one that is continuous with Newton and yet transforms the Baconian tradition of natural history into a form of developmental reasoning.

Buffon announces this transformation in the Premier Discours, entitled "How to Study and Treat Natural History." He opens with a critique of system building that situates his account of natural history squarely within the experimental tradition. "Systems are built on uncertain facts [*des faits incertains*] that have never been examined," he explains, "which only serve to show the human penchant for wanting to find the resemblance between the most disparate objects, regularity where only variety reigns, and the order of things perceived with confusion."[54] In contrast to the systematic drive of speculative science, "the only true science is the knowledge of facts [*la connoissance des faits*]."[55] Yet facts for Buffon are not bare items abstracted from causal relations. Buffon aims to navigate two equally dangerous positions: "the first, to have no method at all, and the second, to try to bring everything into a particular system."[56] To move natural history beyond endless description and mere speculation, he proposes an anthropological method in which it is "more useful to consider the things in relation to us than from any other point of view."[57]

Buffon's anthropological method radicalizes Du Châtelet's defence of hypotheses, for it entails that analogical reasoning can reach a level of probability that, from a practical point of view ("in relation to us"), is *equal* to certainty. This

[50] Needham, "A Summary of Some Late Observations," 12.
[51] Needham, "A Summary of Some Late Observations," 12.
[52] Zammito, *The Gestation of German Biology*, 107.
[53] Schmitt, "Buffon's Theories of Generation," 43.   [54] Buffon, *Histoire naturelle*, I 10.
[55] Buffon, *Histoire naturelle*, I 28.   [56] Buffon, *Histoire naturelle*, I 22–3.
[57] Buffon, *Histoire naturelle*, I 34.

enables him to collapse the Baconian distinction between natural history, under-stood as an inventory of singulars, and natural philosophy, understood as the determination of laws, into a single programme of research called "general natural history [*histoire naturelle générale*]." General natural history, Buffon declares, is "a new method to guide the mind." It is not the method of Linnaeus, "which only serves to arrange words arbitrarily," but "a method that sustains the very order of things."[58] At first glance, Buffon's critique of Linnaeus seems unfair. Linnaeus presented his artificial system as an expression of epistemic humility, and his theory of generation made considerable progress towards establishing natural history as an experimental science. Yet Buffon aims to show that by maintaining the artificial nature of his divisions, Linnaeus presupposed a stable, logical order beneath the manifold of things, and thereby established truth as the consilience of artificial divisions with the mind of God. Under Buffon's curatorship, the Jardin du Roi was not arranged to reflect God's original order but as a laboratory in which natural historians could compel various specimens to reveal their physical connections. In contrast to Linnaean generation, according to which essential properties are passed on through an enduring line of descent, Buffonian gener-ation is more robust, for the branches within a line of descent are marked by the acquisition of traits that *become* heritable for subsequent generations. Natural historians should not settle for logical divisions but should seek the real divisions of nature's vast operations:

> in the study of natural history, one must ... raise oneself to something greater and still more worthy of our efforts: the combination of our observations, the generalization of facts, linking them together by the power of analogies, and the effort to arrive at a high degree of knowledge from which we can judge that particular effects depend upon more general ones, from which we can compare nature with herself in her vast operations.[59]

Buffon explains that analogical reasoning allows us to extend beyond is simply given, making us "capable of grasping distant relationships, bringing them together, and making out of them a body of reasoned ideas."[60] In contrast to mathematical reasoning, which presents "the truths of definition," analogical reasoning opens us to physical truths, which "are by no means arbitrary, and do not depend on us."[61] In contrast to mathematical truths, physical truths "depend on facts; a sequence of similar facts, or, if you will, a frequent repetition and an uninterrupted succession of the same events." Buffon thus inverts the scholastic hierarchy of truth by decoupling physics from the standard of mathematics: "what is called physical truth is thus only a probability, but a probability so great that it

---

[58] Buffon, *Histoire naturelle*, I 51–2.   [59] Buffon, *Histoire naturelle*, I 50–1.
[60] Buffon, *Histoire naturelle*, I 51.   [61] Buffon, *Histoire naturelle*, I 53–4.

amounts to a certainty. In mathematics, one supposes. In physics, one poses and then establishes. There, one has definitions, here, one has facts."[62] To free natural history from the mathematical standard of demonstrability, Buffon echoes Du Châtelet's defence of hypotheses. Yet once more he radicalizes her argument, replacing the mathematical standard of truth with an internalist standard of justification based solely on probability. While his denigration of mathematical truth might seem to be at odds with Newtonianism, Buffon claims that if Newtonianism consists in total commitment to an experimental, immanent conception of force, then Hales' plant mechanics, which examines the movement of fluids through a pre-structured machine, is not Newtonian enough. It does not consider the power to *give* structure—the generation of the plant machine—as a natural process.

While Buffon's general natural history is more radical than Du Châtelet's natural philosophy, it can nevertheless be understood in continuity with her attempt to fuse Leibnizian necessitarianism with the experimental procedure of Newtonian philosophy.[63] In contrast to the mechanical Newtonians, who privileged Newton's abstract idea of space and time, the materialist Newtonians endorsed Leibniz's critique of Newton, according to which abstraction is dependent on the actual.[64] For Leibniz, time and space are orders of things observed as existing together.[65] If they are grounded in the empirical relations or ordered succession of bodies, then the history of the world cannot be separated from spatial and temporal relations. The extension of time and space requires the extension of the world of created beings, meaning that instances without things would be nothing at all; time consists "only in the successive order of things."[66] Christian Wolff added to Leibniz' idea of the successive order the notion of a continuous series, arguing that "apart from the successive existence in a continual series, time does not exist."[67] For Wolff, time simply *is* the continuous series of the successive existence of beings. Du Châtelet argued that the Leibnizian-Wolffian conception of time is a requisite foundation for experimental science, for "there is no time without true, successive beings arranged in a continuous sequence, and there is time as soon as such beings exist."[68] Buffon too recognized that the Leibnizian account of time granted an epistemic distinction between two orders, one abstract and ideal and the other immanent and real. Temporality understood as historicity is thus exclusively associated with the immanent and real order.

---

[62] Buffon, *Histoire naturelle*, I 55.

[63] For an account of the influence of Leibniz in Buffon's intellectual development during the 1740s, see Sloan and Lyon, "Introduction," 20.

[64] See Sloan's account of physical and abstract knowledge in "The Historical Interpretation of Biological Species," 113–15.

[65] Leibniz, "Leibniz's Fifth Paper," §27.   [66] Leibniz, "Leibniz's Third Paper," §6.

[67] Wolff, *Philosophia prima sive ontologia*, cited in Sloan, "The Historical Interpretation of Biological Species," 114.

[68] Du Châtelet, *Institutions de physique*, 119/158.

The implications of the Leibnizian-Wolffian conception of time for general natural history are evident in the three discourses to follow the opening discourse: "History and Theory of the Earth," "Formation of Planets," and "Generation of Animals." In "History and Theory of the Earth," Buffon rejects the various attempts made by physicotheologians to account for the development of the earth through a series of discontinuous ruptures, for they remove our capacity to reason about the causal series of nature's development. General natural history demands instead a conception of natural order as the product of constant motions, completing Descartes' radical project in *The World* with the tools of Newtonian science.[69] The constancy of natural motion is especially important in the fourth discourse, "Generation of Animals," where Buffon rejects the Linnaean system in which there is no difference between the categories used in mineralogy, botany, or any other domain of natural history. For Buffon, a "real" category marks out a physical identity with determinate physical effects. The family *animal* is marked by the part-whole relation manifest in generation, growth, and reproduction. The genera that fall under *animal* are marked by the various modes of locomotion and reproduction originally defined by Aristotle. And the category of species, which falls under genus, is "nothing more than a constant succession of like individuals who reproduce one another."[70] Leibniz had made a similar point in *New Essays on the Human Understanding* when he claimed that, in the case of organic bodies, "we define species by *generation*, so that two similar individuals belong to the same species if they did or could have come from the same origin or seed."[71] Yet Buffon's internalist epistemology redefines succession as the essence of *physical* truth, for it concerns a logic of relations as natural events. We find Buffon's most extended account of the concept of species in his article "The Ass," published in the fourth volume of *Histoire naturelle* (1753):

> An individual is a being set apart, isolated, detached, and has nothing in common with other beings, except that he resembles or differs from them. All the similar individuals which exist on the surface of the earth are regarded as composing the species of these individuals. However, it is neither the number nor the collection of similar individuals which constitute the species, it is the constant succession and uninterrupted renewal of these individuals which forms it. For a creature which would last forever would not comprise a species, no more than would a million similar creatures which would last forever. The species is thus an abstract and general word, for which the thing exists only in considering Nature in the succession of time and in the constant destruction and just as constant renewal of

---

[69] The cover image for this book, a plate introducing Buffon's Second Discours "History and Theory of the Earth," illustrates the seamless formation of the cosmos. Note how the plate reworks Michelangelo's fresco painting *The Creation of Adam* in the Sistine Chapel; God does not imbue the spark of life into Adam, who reflects God's image, but into the nebula of matter, which generates increasingly complex form through a physical sequence.

[70] Buffon, *Histoire naturelle*, IV 356.

[71] Leibniz, *New Essays on Human Understanding*, VI, vi, 309.

creatures. It is in comparing Nature today to that of another time, and existing individuals to those past that we have drawn a clear idea of what is called a species, for the comparison of the number of the resemblances of these individuals is only an accessory idea, and often independent of the first.[72]

Buffon argues that membership within a class is arbitrary only when a specimen is understood as an individual in abstraction from the causes that connect it to other natural items in time and space. Natural history can be transformed into a general science of nature only if we reject the assumption that individuals are *educts* (substances that were once in another substances), and instead examine them as *products* (new members of a kind that are generated for the first time). In a general natural history, space *and* time are essential to the delineation of a species according to physical connections.

Yet what is the nature of this "constant succession" that unites individuals as members of a species? Like Maupertuis, Buffon claimed that the generation of animals could not be explained exclusively by reference to the causal sequence of inanimate nature. To explain the generative process, including the process by which species split off into varieties, he proposes a provisional explanatory concept in the grammatical form of Du Châtelet's "probable proposition":

> In the same manner we make moulds by which we can give the external parts of bodies whatever figure we please, let us suppose that nature can form moulds by which she gives to bodies not only an external figure, but also an interior form; would not this be one method by which reproduction could operate?[73]

Buffon presents his account of generation as a possible physical explanation of the mechanism by which members of a species are connected through time. Echoing Maupertuis' defence of a Newtonian physiology, he states that we "know that bodies possess internal qualities, some of which are general, like gravity."[74] Newtonian method is precisely the study of the *effects* of internal qualities: "we can compare their effects, and may draw analogies from them, in order to account for the effects of qualities of the same genre."[75] Thus we can infer that just as nature endows bodies with gravity, which "penetrates every particle of matter," so nature endows *living* bodies with *interior* moulds, which penetrate organic particles.[76] This analogy enables natural historians to group individuals under a concept that represents a physical succession through time. The

---

[72] Buffon, *Histoire naturelle*, IV 355–6.   [73] Buffon, *Histoire naturelle*, I 13.
[74] Buffon, *Histoire naturelle*, I 13.   [75] Buffon, *Histoire naturelle*, I 13.
[76] Roger traces the origins of the idea of inner moulds to the Swiss naturalist Louis Borguet. By comparing the generative process to the formation of crystals, Borguet grounded Leibniz's metaphysical account of germs in the physical order. Roger, *The Life Sciences in Eighteenth-Century French Thought*, 300–3. See also Schmitt, "Buffon's Theories of Generation," 29.

hypothesis of interior moulds guides natural historians as they reflect on the positioning of organic particles. To conceptualize the positioning of the particles, they must assume a non-mechanical force that moves certain organic particles into the part of the mould for which they are needed. While attraction and repulsion act two-dimensionally in brute matter, the penetrating force acts in three dimensions, integrating organic molecules into the living substance of organs.

The implications of Buffon's theory of generation are evident in the final article of the third volume of *Histoire naturelle*, "Varieties in the Human Species." This article aims to replace Linnaeus' geohumoralism with a physical account of variation. In other words, Buffon's aim is to arrange the physical, cultural, and moral particularities recorded in the available travelogues within the framework of general natural history.[77] To do so, he proposes a hypothetical original human stem from which various branches spread across the earth, acquiring new physical and moral characteristics through processes that Buffon attempts to define. Part way though the study, he identifies

> three causes as jointly productive of the varieties which we have remarked in the different peoples of the earth. The first is the influence of the climate; the second, which is very important to the first, is nutrition; and the third, which is perhaps still more important to the first, is the mores [*les mœurs*].[78]

In Buffon's classification, migration causes the body to come into contact with a new set of climactic conditions, altering patterns of nutrition and social behaviour. The three causes are responsible for the primary mark of a "variety" or "race" (Buffon uses the terms interchangeably): skin colour, which is passed on to the following generation. Buffon's guiding assumption that the primary human colour is "white," "the primitive colour of nature, which climate, nutrition, and mores alter, and even change into yellow, brown, or black."[79] This assumption is purportedly justified by the phenomenon of albinism, which occurs sometimes in black races but never in white.[80]

Buffon's theory of generation immediately came under fire. As an early reviewer pointed out, Buffon's mould hypothesis is unable to explain how an offspring could vary from its parent, or how, once acquired, a variation could be passed on to the following generation.[81] Buffon responded by including an entry

---

[77] For a critical analysis of the travelogues used by Buffon, see Mazzolini, "Inter-Racial Crossing and Social Structure (1770–1835)."

[78] Buffon, *Histoire naturelle*, III 447–8.   [79] Buffon, *Historie naturelle*, III 502.

[80] White is the "primitive colour of nature," Buffon claims, for "in certain circumstances [it] reappears; though by no means equal to its original whiteness, on account of its corruption from the causes here mentioned." Buffon, *Historie naturelle*, III 502. In Section 4.4, I consider the impact of this argument on Kant's formulation of a racialized concept of race.

[81] In 1751, Haller published a review of Buffon's theory of generation in Paris and Geneva, arguing that moulds could not account for the variation between the parents and a child. Haller, *Réflexions sur le système de la gérération de M. de Buffon*. I discuss Haller's review in Section 2.4.

in the fourteenth volume of *Historie naturelle* entitled "On the Degeneration of Animals" (1766), which extends his account of generation to include *degeneration*, a variation that *becomes* enduring for a future generation. The motivation behind the article is to explain why acquired characteristics, such as dark skin colour, do not change when relocated to new climactic conditions (unsurprisingly, his examples are drawn from chattel slavery). Because human beings seem to alter much more slowly than the lower animals, Buffon considers the same phenomenon within species of quadruped found in both the Old World (Europe) and the New World (the Americas). On the assumption that the present variety of quadrupeds has resulted from natural causes, he states that "the two hundred species we have given the history of, may be reduced to a small number of families, or principal stems [*souches principals*], from which it is not impossible all the others have derived their origin."[82] Consider the following example from his study of hares:

> one cannot therefore imagine with any foundation that the climate of America has so far changed the nature of our hares to so great a degree as to make them tapetis or apereas, which have no tail; or agoutis with pointed muzzles, and short round ears; or pacos, with a large head, short ears, and a coarse hair marked with white stripes.[83]

Buffon suggests that the variation within the species of hare across the continents is too excessive to be considered as an accidental modification, triggered by contingent environmental conditions. Yet he does not conclude that there are different species of hare originally created in different locations, as would Linnaeus. Degeneration marks a different kind of connection between generations, whereby a descendent inherits a characteristic that is gradually acquired across a population. It creates a new branch from a principal stem that Buffon defines as a *race*, which is now distinct from the Linnaean category of *variety*. It is not entirely clear in the essay whether or not race captures a real division, for degeneration does not involve a change in the principle stem. Having defined species according to reproductive capacity, Buffon explains that "This is the most fixed point that we have in natural history; all other resemblances and differences that we can grasp in the comparison of beings are neither so constant, real or certain."[84] Because the principle stem remains unaltered, he concedes that a race could potentially return to its original form.[85]

---

[82] Buffon, *Historie naturelle*, XIV 358.   [83] Buffon, *Historie naturelle*, XIV 371–2.
[84] Buffon, *Historie naturelle*, XIV 385–6.
[85] Buffon proposes an experiment to test this phenomenon, in which he recommends relocating a group of Senegalese to Denmark, keeping them in isolation to find out how long it takes their skin to return to white. Buffon, *Historie naturelle*, XIV 314.

Like the memories proposed by Maupertuis, Buffon's moulds do not explain the initial organization of organic particles. A mould is simply the structure of the organism itself, meaning that organic particles "must enter [the mould] in an order relative to this form, and consequently cannot alter its figure, but only augment its dimensions."[86] His hypothetical account of the generative process moves only one step towards a general natural history. While he demonstrated how natural historians can view class distinctions in terms of physical relations, Buffon did not think that either the moulds or the penetrative force could be explained mechanically. In his article "The Ox" (1753), he states that the moulds are implanted by God at the start of history.[87] In "On the Degeneration of Animals," he explains that morphological change is an effect of a change in organic molecules ingested though nutrition, leaving the mould unaltered.[88]

2.4 Analogical Newtonianism

In 1750, Barthold Joachim Zink and Abraham Gotthelf Kästner published a German translation of the first two volumes of *Histoire naturelle*, entitled *Allgemeine Historie der Natur nach allen ihren besondern Theilen abgehandelt* (*Universal History of Nature, Dealt with According to All Its Particular Parts*). Anticipating the negative reception of Buffon's materialism in the German speaking states, Kästner commissioned the help of the most trusted natural philosopher in Europe to write an introductory preface: Albrecht von Haller. While Haller expresses serious reservations about Buffon's speculations, he nevertheless calls the German readers to read the text with an open mind. What Buffon's audacious project demonstrates to the scientific community, Haller declares, is that the extension of Newtonian science *requires* the uses of hypotheses. The first task of natural philosophy is thus to determine their legitimate use. Haller's defence of hypotheses has clear resonances with Du Châtelet's argument in *Foundations*:

> After a Newton, no one will ever be completely ashamed to propose something which is not completely demonstrable. If such a respectable intellectual has used the probable as currency, then it cannot be entirely without value.... Without such an arbitrary currency we must remain silent on almost all of natural philosophy. All the parts of human science would become nothing but *fragments*

---

[86] Buffon, *Histoire naturelle*, I 17. As Bowler explains, the moulds can "be regarded as limits defining those combinations of organic particles which have a reasonable degree of stability." Bowler, "Bonnet and Buffon," 271.

[87] "God, in creating the first individuals of each species of animals and vegetables, has not only given form to the dust of the earth, but also gave it animation, by inclosing in each individual a greater or lesser quantity of active principles, organs, living molecules, incapable of being destroyed, and common to all organized beings." Buffon, *Histoire naturelle*, IV 437.

[88] Buffon, *Histoire naturelle*, XIV 311–74.

and independent pieces without connection and unification, if we did not fill in the missing parts with probabilities, the construction of a building instead of a ruin.... Thus I come to the true utility of hypotheses, which are, to be sure, still not the truth, but which lead to it.[89]

Haller's preface offers a backhanded endorsement of Buffon's project in *Histoire naturelle*. The value of a work in natural philosophy should not simply be judged according its truth. It should also be judged by its potential to open productive lines of inquiry that could *lead to* the truth. Like Buffon, Haller felt that *Vegetable staticks* demonstrated that the analogy between plants and celestial dynamics warranted a far greater extension of Newtonian science than Hales had attempted. Yet he remained sceptical that Buffon's materialist account of generation could advance the study of natural history.

Haller's scepticism was in part due to the medical education he received at Leiden under the supervision of Herman Boerhaave, professor of medicine, botany, and chemistry. Boerhaave was one of the first natural philosophers to bring Newtonianism to the continent, and developed the use of mechanical explanations in medicine on the assumption that bodily functions are "all performed by mechanical laws."[90] This involved a spermatist version of pre-existence, in which a new generation is thought to unfold from a miniature encapsulated in the head of the spermatozoa. In 1736, Haller accepted a professorship in the newly founded faculty of medicine at Göttingen, where he set out to develop a Newtonian physiology. Yet his extensive studies in animal movement led him to question Boerhaave's mechanical interpretation of Newtonianism. Haller recognized that the regenerative capacities of Abraham Trembley's polyp and Charles Bonnet's freshwater worms provided empirical evidence that refutes the ovist and spermaticist theories of pre-existence.[91] During his early years at Göttingen, he developed an epigenetic theory of generation in which unorganized fluid develops into an animal according to localized, mechanical forces. Within a few years of research, he boldly announced, "one will find that animals and, by consequence, vegetables are engendered from a fluid that thickens and organizes itself little by little, following laws that for us are unknown but that the eternal wisdom has rendered invariable."[92]

The idea that different kinds of matter operate according to distinct rules was entirely absent in Hales' plant physiology. It displays a closer proximity to

---

[89]   Haller, "Preface to the German Translation of *Histoire Naturelle*," 301.
[90]   Boerhaave, *Dr. Boerhaave's Academical Lectures on the Theory of Physic*, I 81.
[91]   In a review of Bonnet's discovery, Haller claimed that "One is forced to avow, after the observations made on the polyp, that several animals form themselves from heads, from arms, from organs of all species at the place they are cut off, where one would never have expected a miniature to have existed." Haller, "Review of *Traité d'Insectologie*, by Charles Bonnet," 188.
[92]   Haller, "Review of *Traité d'Insectologie*, by Charles Bonnet," 188–9.

Maupertuis and Buffon's materialist programme of research. Yet Haller refused to speculate about organic particles, and proposed instead to examine physiological movement in terms of "faculties" or "powers."[93] In the opening line of his textbook for physiology, he proposed an analogy by which to consider physiological properties as geometrical unknowns: "Fibra enim physiologo id est, quod linea geometræ" (the fibre is to physiology what the line is to geometry).[94] The analogy with geometry opens a method by which the physiologist can measure the relation between known points in a single space, enabling the discovery of new points within the nexus of relations. In an entry to the Swiss edition of Diderot and d'Alembert's *Encyclopédie* entitled "Faculté vitale," Haller develops the analogy by describing faculties as temporary place-holders:

> Every time we see effects, the mechanical cause of which is unknown to us, we can refer to this cause as a *faculty*, like we refer to an unknown quantity as x. If luminous experiments or perfected anatomy discover the mechanism which produces this effect, we would then erase the *place-holder* [nom d'attente], as one erases the character marking an unknown quantity.[95]

Recent scholarship on eighteenth-century Newtonianism has classified Haller's method as a distinct "analogical" interpretation of Newton's method.[96] Haller's proposal is that when we are unable to explain a known effect by a mechanical cause, we ought not jump to speculative particles but instead seek to understand the relation between cause and effect by introducing what Thomas Hall describes as "provisionally inexplicable explicative devices" or "physiological unknowns."[97] Following Newton's postulation of a physical unknown, which enabled him to consider celestial movement as the function of a geometrical equation, Haller extends the analogy to physiological movement, enabling the classification of different fibres in the body according to how they respond to stimulation. Haller was especially concerned with the problem of involuntary animal motion, in particular, the problem of the heart's constant movement. In the seventeenth

[93] Sloan notes that Haller's method invokes the Galenic notion of faculties. In *De facultatibus naturalibus*, Galen proposed a method for physiology that bears an uncanny similarity with Newton's use of unknown explicative devices: "so long as we are ignorant of the true essence [*ousia*] of the cause which is operating, we call it a *faculty* [dynamis]....If, therefore, we are to investigate methodically the number and kinds of faculties, we must begin with the effects; for each of these effects comes from a certain activity, and each of these again is preceded by a cause." Galen, *De facultatibus naturalibus*, I IV 17. Galen's method is based on a threefold distinction between effects, actions (motions productive of effects), and the causes of such actions (the faculties that permit them). See Sloan, "Life Science and *Naturphilosophie*," 99.
[94] Haller, *Elementa physiologiæ*, I 2.
[95] Haller, "Faculté vitale," translated in Wolfe, "On the Role of Newtonian Analogies in Eighteenth-Century Life Science," 241.
[96] Wolfe, "On the Role of Newtonian Analogies in Eighteenth-Century Life Science," 223.
[97] Hall, "On Biological Analogs of Newtonian Paradigms," 6; Hall, *Ideas of Life and Matter*, II 73.

century, several natural philosophers had shown that the heart could continue beating when removed from some organisms, or made to beat again by stimulation once removed.[98] This brought into question any spiritual faculty that would animate the body, and called for a local explanation. To account for such phenomena, Descartes proposed a mechanical theory of animal spirits, Borelli and Willis offered a partly mechanical fermentation-combustion model, and, in the early eighteenth century, Stahl accounted for living functions according to an immaterial soul.[99]

In a series of two papers presented to the Royal Society of Sciences at Göttingen in 1752, published the following year as *De partibus corporis humani sensibilibus et irritabilibus*, Haller presented a novel solution by classifying kinds of muscle fibre according to two faculties responsible for physiological movement: irritability and sensibility.[100] Irritability had already been explored as a property of animal fibres in Francis Gibson's *De rachidite* (1650), and in *Treatise on the Soul* (1745) La Mettrie identified sensibility as the proper faculty studied in physiology.[101] Yet Haller claimed that both Gibson and La Mettrie had mistakenly taken the properties of animal fibres for explanatory devices, meaning that they failed to advance physiology as an experimental science. "I am persuaded that the greatest source of error in physic," he declares, "has been owing to physicians, at least a great part of them, making few or no experiments, and substituting analogy instead of them."[102] Analogy is not a substitute for explanation, Haller stipulates, but a guide for experiments. Through an ordered presentation of these experiments, he defines irritability and sensibility as a new way of classifying the human body according to experimentally demonstrable concepts:

> I call that part of the human body irritable, which becomes shorter upon being touched.... I call that a sensible part of the human body, which upon being touched transmits the impression of it to the soul; and in brutes, in whom the existence of a soul is not so clear, I call those parts sensible, the Irritation of which occasions evident signs of pain and disquiet in the animal.[103]

Haller proposes to expose the parts of the animal's body to the touch of a needle, air, heat, or various chemicals to discover which are irritable, and, of those, which

---

[98] La Mettrie provides a survey of such cases in *L'Homme machine* (1747). See La Mettrie, *Machine Man*, 26–7.

[99] For further discussion of this debate, see Kardel, "Willis and Steno on Muscles," 100–7; and Kardel, "Function and Structure in Early Modern Muscle Mechanics," 61–70.

[100] The lectures quickly became the focus of debate across the European medical community. In 1755, Haller's friend Simon André Tissot, a Swiss physician, translated the text into French together with a short paper on the movement of the heart, also by Haller. An anonymous English text appeared in the same year, titled "A Dissertation on the Sensible and Irritable Parts of Animals."

[101] Gibson, *De rachidite, sive morbo puerili tractatus*; La Mettrie, *Traité de l'âme*, 153.

[102] Haller, "A Dissertation on the Sensible and Irritable Parts of Animals," 658.

[103] Haller, "A Dissertation on the Sensible and Irritable Parts of Animals," 658–9.

are properly sensible. The analogy with geometry enabled him to attribute irritability as a property of muscle fibre and sensibility as a property of nerves. By separating muscles from nerves, Haller demonstrated that muscular contraction is not caused by the soul but by a property inherent to fibres, the existence of which "Experiments have taught us." The reason *why* some parts of the body are endowed with irritability and sensibility, and others not, "lies beyond the reach of the knife and the microscope, beyond which I do not chuse to hazard any conjectures, as I have no desire of teaching what I am ignorant of myself."[104]

Haller's study rejects Gibson's analysis of irritability as the property of all animal fibres, and defines it instead as the exclusive property of muscle fibres. It discards La Mettrie's account of sensibility as a ubiquitous property of organic matter, for it demonstrates that sensibility is a property of a *specific* muscle fibre (nerves). Furthermore, it denies Stahl's thesis that life is dependent on the regulation of all physiological processes by the soul. If Stahl is right, then the soul, which is sensible of touch, "contracts the fibers that are touched, and pulls them back, to prevent them being injured."[105] Experiment, however, points to an alternative conclusion, for it demonstrates that "Irritability differs entirely from sensibility, and the most irritable parts are these, which are not subject to the command of the soul, which ought to be quite the reverse if the soul was the principle of Irritability."[106] Moreover, irritability continues after death, and in parts that have been separated from the body, which therefore cannot be sensible. Haller's critique of Gibson, La Mettrie, and Stahl is only secondarily about the nature of the soul. Primarily it concerns the role of experiment and observation in physiology. A properly experimental physiology does not treat irritability and sensibility as causes but rather as methodological instruments that enable the natural philosopher to classify muscle fibres according to the principles of their movement.[107]

Many readers interpreted Haller's demonstration of physiological forces as a victory for epigenesis, for it provided evidence for the existence of secondary forces resident in specific kinds of organic fibre. Yet Haller played a mixed role in the generation debate. While he had proposed an epigenetic theory of generation in the 1740s, Haller changed his position after leaving Göttingen and returning to Bern in 1753. This change seems to have been prompted by Buffon's theory of generation, which Haller reviewed in his preface to the third volume of Buffon's

---

[104] Haller, "A Dissertation on the Sensible and Irritable Parts of Animals," 658.
[105] Haller, "A Dissertation on the Sensible and Irritable Parts of Animals," 691.
[106] Haller, "A Dissertation on the Sensible and Irritable Parts of Animals," 691.
[107] Haller seems to adopt a speculative mode of presentation when he claims that irritability can be granted as "a property of the animal *gluten*, the same as we acknowledge attraction and gravity to be properties of matter in general, without being able to determine the causes of them." Yet he held that the concept of gluten referred to a fundamental chemical form of organic matter, and was thus analogous with the ether in Newton's celestial mechanics. Haller, "A Dissertation on the Sensible and Irritable Parts of Animals," 692.

Allgemeine Historie der Natur in 1752.[108] There Haller argued that Buffon's theory of moulds could not account for the variation between parents and their offspring. Given that offspring are clearly not copies of their parents, the idea of a blind, penetrating force is inadequate to explain the perfect formation of each body.[109] Haller concludes that "Mr. Buffon needs a force which has foresight, which can make a choice, which has a goal, which, against all the laws of blind combination, always and unfailingly brings about the same end."[110]

Haller sought to resolve this issue in his major embryological work, *On the Formation of the Heart in the Chicken* (1758), in which he presents an ovist version of pre-existence. Through detailed description of the chicken embryo at various stages of gestation, he claimed that the issues associated with epigenesis "are so difficult, and my experiments on the egg are so numerous, that I am proposing with less repugnance the contrary opinion, which is beginning to appear to me the more probable."[111] Throughout the study, Haller employs irritability and sensibility to explain the unfolding of the chick through mechanical laws that act on a pre-existing embryo. The heart, which already exists in miniature, is stimulated during the process of fertilization. Because of its inherent irritability as the greatest muscle of the body, it begins to beat, thus pumping blood through the folded vessels of the embryo and directing the development of the organized being. The structures increase in solidity, become progressively opaque, and shift in rates of expansion, transforming the embryo into the mature animal. These movements, Haller proposes, can be explained according to mechanical processes. The *possibility* of organization, however, lies beyond the scope of experimental inquiry.

While Haller continued to reject Boerhaave's spermaticist theory of pre-existence, he replaced it with the theory of a pre-existing egg. In *Elementa physiologiae* (1766), he outlines the generative process as follows:

> In the first rudiment the fetus is in the mother, if it has been built in the egg, and has been completed to such a point that it needs only to receive nourishment to grow from this, the greatest difficulty in building this most artistic structure from brute matter is solved. In this hypothesis, the Creator himself, for whom nothing is difficult, has built this structure: He has arranged at one time, or at least before the male force approaches, the brute matter according to foreseen ends and according to a model preformed by his Wisdom.[112]

Haller accounts for his return to pre-existence as a recognition of the experimental limits of physiology, which alerted him to the impossibility of explaining how

---

[108] The preface reproduces an essay on Buffon's theory of generation that Haller had published anonymously in French in 1751.
[109] Haller, "Reflections on the Theory of Generation of Mr Buffon," 318–24.
[110] Haller, "Reflections on the Theory of Generation of Mr Buffon," 320.
[111] Haller, *Sur la formation du coeur dans le poulet*, II 172.
[112] Haller, *Elementa physiologiae*, translated by Roe in "*Anatomia Animata*," 286.

irritable and sensible fibres come into existence. His words self-consciously echo Newton, who wrote in the General Scholium that "blind metaphysical necessity" cannot produce a variety of things.[113] The rich diversity of natural products, which are perfectly crafted for their environmental conditions, "could arise from nothing but the ideas and will of a Being necessarily existing."

Haller's return to pre-existence reflects the ongoing problems that continued to trouble the materialist Newtonians, who sought to explain the generative process by means of secondary forces. While Haller's religious commitments were certainly important to his change of mind, they were by no means disconnected from his dedication to experimentation and observation as the foundation of natural philosophy.[114] Sensibility and irritability are principles of movement, and while they can tell us about the generation of a pre-existing embryo into an adult, they tell us nothing about the generation of the muscle and nerve fibres themselves. What the two forces allow, however, is a much more sophisticated pre-existence theory than his predecessors had been able to provide. In contrast to Malebranche's use of the germ analogy to describe pre-existence as encasement (*embôitment*), Haller's germs are responsive, and can regulate the expression of component parts in response to environmental conditions.[115] In short, Haller demonstrated that pre-existence had several virtues that should not be given up lightly. When living form is said to lie pre-formed in the egg, generation is limited to those laws whose effects are observable, protecting the natural philosopher from confusing their methodological use of secondary causes with causal explanation.

The wide range of hypotheses notwithstanding, by expressing a historical, epistemological, and methodological commitment to Newtonianism, natural philosophers were able to form a shared standard of inquiry according to which the scope of experimental philosophy could be extended to plant and animal physiology. In the following chapters, I suggest that the conceptual tensions opened by Hales' application of attractive and repulsive forces to living nature, Buffon's extension of Hales' method to animal generation, and Haller's analogical method had a deep impact on Kant's thinking during the 1750s and 60s. Kant recognized that in their work, the dividing lines between classificatory concepts are no longer determined by logical analysis. It is the actual plants and animals that determine the boundaries in nature. The logical categories of variety, species, and genera can thus be considered as natural units, such that the natural system acquires an immanent, physical meaning.

---

[113] Newton, *Mathematical Principles*, II 546.

[114] Roe, *Matter, Life, and Generation*, 110–11. See Zammito's discussion of Haller's private and public religiosity in *The Gestation of German Biology*, 94–6.

[115] Malebranche claimed that "It does not even seem unreasonable to think that there are infinite trees in a single germ, since it does not contain only the tree which is the seed, but also a very great number of other seeds, which are all enclosed in those of the new tree." Malebranche, *Recherche de la vérité*, 82, translated in Roe, *Matter, Life, and Generation*, 5.

PART II
KANT'S PHYSICAL SYSTEM
OF NATURE

3

Universal Natural History

Kant finished his undergraduate studies at Königsberg in 1748, a year before the publication of Buffon's *Histoire naturelle*. Having recently lost his father, Kant had no means of his own and took up employment as a private teacher (*Hofmeister*), first with the reformed preacher Andersch in Judtschen, then in Groß-Arnsdorf with the estate von Hülsen, and finally with the Count Keryserlingk.[1] He returned to Königsberg in the spring of 1754 at the age of 30. Little is known about Kant's intellectual development during his time as a private teacher. What is clear, however, is that his return to Königsberg was marked by a considerable drive to undertake an academic career. In July 1755 he received the academic degree of *doctoris seu magistri philosophiae*, and in the same year he published *Universal Natural History and Theory of the Heavens* and *A New Elucidation of the First Principles of Metaphysical Cognition*, followed by *Physical Monodology* in 1756. These publications earned him the privilege of teaching in the Faculty of Philosophy at Königsberg during the winter semester of 1755/6.[2]

In this chapter, I examine Kant's early work on natural history, beginning with his second book, *Universal Natural History*. Scholars often draw attention to the idiosyncratic and progressive character of this text, separating it from both Kant's predecessors and his subsequent work.[3] While it received little more than a review following its initial publication, more than sixty years later Samuel Taylor Coleridge described Kant's early essay as an "astonishing *prophetic work*."[4] Coleridge presents *Universal Natural History* as a maverick text that, in contrast to most works in natural philosophy during the eighteenth century, collapses the boundary between natural history and natural philosophy. This reading remains standard in the contemporary literature. Martin Schönfeld goes as far as to claim

---

[1] Ritzel, *Immanuel Kant*, 9.　　[2] Kuehn, *Kant*, 98.

[3] For instance, Toulmin and Goodfield describe *Universal Natural History* as "the first systematic attempt to give an evolutionary account of cosmic history," claiming that "no one before Kant had talked so publicly and seriously of a *past* comprising of 'millions of years and centuries'." Toulmin and Goodfield, *The Discovery of Time*, 159, 163.

[4] Coleridge, *Collected Letters of Samuel Taylor Coleridge*, IV 808. *Universal Natural History* received a single early review, and the text was not widely read. This was principally due to the fact that the press was impounded for bankruptcy shortly after its publication, which included the initial print run of Kant's book. See Kuehn, *Kant*, 104–5. A portion of the text was published in 1791 by Kant's friend and colleague J. F. Gensichen, along with the German translation of three texts by Herschel, as *Über den Bau des Himmels*. The striking similarities with the cosmologies of Johann Lambert and Pierre-Simon Laplace brought renewed attention to Kant's book in the early nineteenth century. Yet its obscurity meant that Lambert and Laplace were probably not aware of it.

Kant and the Transformation of Natural History. Andrew Cooper, Oxford University Press. © Andrew Cooper 2023.
DOI: 10.1093/oso/9780192869784.003.0004

that several of Kant's theoretical innovations, including the connection between force and space and the nebular hypothesis of cosmological formation, have been confirmed by modern physics.[5] Kant brilliantly combines debates over the onto-logical status of force with a descriptive cosmology to develop a law-governed account of planetary movements that anticipated several key discoveries in the twentieth century.

What these interpretations overlook, however, is that *Universal Natural History* builds on several transformations that occurred in natural philosophy during the seventeenth and early eighteenth centuries.[6] As we saw in Chapter 1, at the close of the seventeenth century a number of fundamental epistemological assumptions had been established, including the fundamental role of natural history in pro-viding the factual basis for natural philosophy and the primacy of mathematics in the study of nature. Within this framework, natural history did not have a theoretical function of its own. Through careful description of the works of nature it served to provide what Bacon called a "storehouse of facts" for natural philoso-phy. In the Preface to his *New Experiments Touching the Spring of the Air* (1660), Boyle explains that the point of natural history is not

> to establish Theories and Principles, but to devise Experiments, and to enrich the History of Nature with Observations faithfully made and deliver'd; that by these, and the like Contributions made by others, men may in time be furnish'd with a sufficient stock of Experiments to ground *Hypotheses* and *Theorys* on.[7]

In the early eighteenth century, John Harris defined natural history in his influential *Lexicon Technicum* in the following way: "*Natural History* is a Description of any of the Natural Products of the Earth, Water or Air, such as Beasts, Birds, Fishes, Metals, Minerals, Fossils, together with such *Phaenomena* as at any time appear in the material world; such as Meteors &c."[8] The prevailing view of natural history before Hales' *Vegetable staticks* still consisted of a descrip-tive practice that provides natural philosophy with a storehouse of facts. Kant's *Universal Natural History*, in contrast, accounts for the present diversity of nature as the result of a single developmental process. It presents a hypothetical account of matter as the basis of a cosmogony that explains nature's development from a

---

[5] Schönfeld, "Kant's Early Cosmology," 47.

[6] An exception here is Massimi, who argues that the dynamical parts of Kant's cosmology, which Schönfeld attributes to Kant's Leibnizian-Wolffian metaphysics, can be attributed to the materialist interpretation of Newtonianism. Yet like Schönfeld, Massimi fails to identify the sense in which Kant's essay is a work of natural history, that is, why a theory of matter should feature within a historical account of nature rather than a straightforward work of philosophy or speculative physics. This obscures the full significance of Kant's achievement, which, I argue, is to shift the meaning of natural history from a logical system of classification to a physical explanation of the diversity of things. Massimi, "Kant's Dynamical Theory of Matter in 1755," 533.

[7] Boyle, *Works*, III 12.

[8] Harris, *Lexicon technicum*, cited in Sloan and Lyon, "Introduction," 2.

chaotic nebula to the highly structured system we see today exclusively through attractive and repulsive forces (recall the text's subtitle: *Essay on the Constitution and the Mechanical Origin of the Whole Universe according to Newtonian Principles*).

The complex reception of Newton's philosophy in the eighteenth century has led to considerable confusion in regards to Kant's Newtonianism. While most commentators view *Universal Natural History* as a manifesto for Kant's "conversion to Newton" on the grounds that it marks a shift from the Leibnizian account of force developed in his first published work, *Thoughts on the True Estimation of Living Forces* (1747), there is no consensus on the sense in which it is Newtonian.[9] To frame one's conversion to Newton in a work of natural history, one that draws physics together with a hypothetical cosmogony, is entirely at odds with the mathematical argument of *Principia*, and bears no obvious relationship with Newton's application of this method to the qualities of light in *Opticks*. Schönfeld examines *Universal Natural History* as an attempt to revise the gaps in Newton's system that arise due to his voluntarism by extending Newton's mathematical method to the domain of physics.[10] Michael Friedman claims that Kant's aim is to silence those who maintain "metaphysical doubts about Newtonian attraction" by showing its compatibility with "Leibnizian-Wolffian" metaphysics.[11] Yet as we saw in Chapter 2, philosophical reconsiderations of Newtonian physics were not uncommon in the early to mid-eighteenth century, and Newtonianism had become a dynamic programme well before Kant's essay. By searching for a direct link between Kant and the mathematical procedure of Newton's *Principia*, Schönfeld and Friedman fail to identify the sense in which Kant's essay is a work of *natural history*, that is, why a hypothesis about matter should feature within a historical account of nature rather than a work of philosophy or speculative physics.

In this chapter, I argue that *Universal Natural History* must be situated against the backdrop of the fierce debate regarding the extension of Newtonian method if we are to appreciate its full significance, for both Kant's philosophical development and the broader transformation of natural history considered in this study. In contrast to the standard readings of the book, I reject the idea that it marks a personal conversion to Newtonianism, as if praising Newton were incompatible with the Leibnizian account of matter Kant developed in his first published work. Further, I deny that it signals a radical break from the natural history of his time.

---

[9] Schönfeld presents the early Kant as Newtonian to the extent that he is committed to mechanical laws. Schönfeld, *The Philosophy of the Young Kant*, ch 4. Massimi argues that Kant's use of repulsion demonstrates his proximity to the materialist interpretation of Newtonianism. Massimi, "Kant's Dynamical Theory of Matter in 1755," 533. Watkins challenges the mainstream view of the early Kant as a straightforward Newtonian by drawing attention to his many criticisms of Newton. Watkins, "The Early Kant's (Anti-)Newtonianism," 429–30.

[10] Schönfeld, *The Philosophy of the Young Kant*, 97.

[11] Friedman, *Kant and the Exact Sciences*, 18–19, 10.

Alternatively, I claim that Kant builds on the materialist interpretation of Newtonianism advanced by Maupertuis and Buffon to elevate natural history to the status of an exhaustive, physical science capable of explaining the present diversity of things. His conception of natural history is "universal" to the extent that it grounds the mathematical principles of Newtonianism in quasi-Leibnizian material forces, thereby situating the diversity of natural products within a single causal nexus that traces back to the original diffusion of matter.

In Section 3.1, I locate Kant's argument in *Universal Natural History* within the materialist interpretation of Newtonianism, which transposes Leibniz's *vis viva* onto a physical plane. In Section 3.2, I provide evidence to show that Kant's conception of natural history draws heavily on the Second Discours of Buffon's *Histoire naturelle*, "History and Theory of the Earth" (1749), which accounts for the present diversity of things according to a hypothetical account of origins. Yet I argue that Kant's reading of Buffon is mediated through Haller's methodological preface to the first volume of Kästner's translation of *Histoire naturelle*, where Haller prescribes a legitimate use of hypotheses in Newtonian science.[12] In Section 3.3, I argue that Kant recognized the fragmentary and incomplete character of Buffon's system, which left the idea of universal natural history vulnerable to attack from the theologians. For these attacks to be rebuffed, a truly universal natural history requires a strategy of harmonizing the world system with teleology. In Section 3.4, I show how Kant finds a way forward in Thomas Wright's theory of the Milky Way, which accounts for *our* view of the stars, including their manifest order and beauty, as the result of a developmental history.

3.1 Kant's Newtonianism

There is no scholarly consensus on how *Universal Natural History* should be regarded as a Newtonian text. The difficulty begins with Kant's endorsement of Newton in the opening lines of the essay. Kant praises Newton for resolving "the true constitution of the universe on the large scale, the laws of motion, and the internal mechanism of the orbits of all the planets" (NTH 1:229). Yet in contrast to Newton's mechanics, which describes the movement of the celestial

---

[12] There is no concrete evidence that Kant worked with the German translation of *Histoire naturelle*, nor is there a record of any version of the text in Kant's library. Kant regularly cites from French editions of various works that were readily available in German. For instance, in *Universal Natural History* he cites the original French of Maupertuis' *Discours sur la figure des Astres* (NTH 1:254), and in the Rink lecture notes on physical geography Kant is recorded as citing Montesquieu and Ulloa in French (PG 1757/9 9:317). Nevertheless, the title of the book, Kant's choice of terminology, and the close parallels between his understanding of natural history and the methodological preface Haller wrote for the first volume suggest that Kant was working with Kästner's German translation; possibly it was available to him at one of the wealthy estates at which he worked as a private teacher. For similar views, see Stark, "La Géographie physique d'Immanuel Kant," 172; and Schmitt, "From Paris to Moscow via Leipzig (1749–1787)," 43.

bodies within a functioning system, Kant sets out to explain how the "ordering and arrangement of the universes [*Weltgebäude*]" are the result of a store of fundamental material that has developed "gradually in a temporal sequence" (NTH 1:310). Kant is not merely concerned with the forces resident in primordial matter, but also with the "mechanical consequences of the general laws of resistance," which explain the generation of heavenly bodies (NTH 1:267). Resistance, he explains, is the product of two counterbalancing forces, attraction and repulsion, which caused the fine matter to whirl into vortices. Kant's radical claim is that the general elements of the observable universe, including the formation and regular motion of the sun, planets, their moons, comets, and even the other solar systems of the Milky Way, can be explained by three assumptions: (1) an initial state of chaos, in which basic particles were distributed in various nebulae, (2) two Newtonian principles, attraction and repulsion, and (3) the motions initiated by these matters and the states they would come to take entirely according to mechanical principles.[13]

The most striking difference between Kant's *Universal Natural History* and Newton's *Principia* is methodological. While Newton presents his study as a work of mathematics, Kant presents his natural history "in the form of a hypothesis" (NTH 1:263). Newton of course rejected the use of hypotheses in natural philosophy, at least in the General Scholium, and crafted the fourth rule of reasoning to inhibit speculation (the inductive procedure may not be "evaded by hypotheses"). Yet in Kant's view, Newton failed on his own terms. His refusal to speculate about material forces left the *form* of celestial mechanics entirely contingent, requiring a hyperphysical cause—an intervening God—to explain the possibility of the celestial system and its ongoing maintenance. Echoing the materialist interpretation of Newtonianism advanced by Du Châtelet, Maupertuis, and Buffon, Kant claims that the only way to avoid the hyperphysical detritus of Newton's physics is to propose a material cause of celestial mechanics by transposing Leibniz's *vis viva*, which preserves a body in internal motion, onto a physical plane. His goal is to work from the present arrangement of the universe to its past through no presuppositions other than a hypothetical account of basic particles endowed with attractive and repulsive forces. This chain of reasoning is analogical, for it extends Newtonian principles to events that lie outside the reach of experience. Yet the analogy is warranted, for matter simply is the activity of force.

Kant recognized that analogical reasoning played a fundamental role in Newton's *Principia*. The second rule of reasoning (*same effect, same cause*) authorizes inferences in the form $X : Y = A : B$, instructing natural philosophers to account for a wide range of effects by the minimum number of forces. By

---

[13] See Watkins's reconstruction in "The Early Kant's (Anti-)Newtonianism," 430.

following this rule, Newton was able to consider the acceleration of the moon and the centripetal accelerations of the planets as the same kind of force. The fact that the acceleration of the moon and the centripetal accelerations of the planets are effects of the same force is not established via analogy, for the connection is, at first, simply one of likeness. The analogy guides natural philosophers to seek a possible mathematical proof of X's value. If the value of X can be demonstrated mathematically, then, following the third rule, they are instructed to consider that force as a universal property of bodies. Echoing the materialist Newtonians, Kant held that Newton's deduction of the inverse square law did not simply offer mathematical proof of universal gravitation. It provided a corresponding physical proof of attraction as a property of matter, which can be extended to natural bodies that lie beyond the reach of experiment and observation.

The hypothesis presented in *Universal Natural History* bares several similarities with Descartes' fable in *The World*. Yet in contrast to Descartes's fable, which stands merely as an intelligible fiction, Kant claims that his hypothetical account of the mechanical formation of the heavenly bodies can be established with certainty, for it fills in the explanatory gaps left by previous hypotheses with physical causes (NTH 1:255). The reader is invited to watch the hypothetical scene as matter unfolds into increasing levels of organization. The protagonist is the mass of subtle particles originally diffused across celestial space, "which offers infinitely little resistance and limits their motions as little in one direction as it does in the other" (NTH 1:336). Attraction lumps the primordial fine matter together into planets and stars, and yet attraction by itself is insufficient to explain the formation of heavenly bodies from primordial matter. A repulsive force is required, which serves to counterbalance attraction, making the fine matter take the whirling shape of vortices. Repulsion explains how matter did not come together into one big lump, but instead whirled in vortices of different densities that became the different planets and stars we observe today. In contrast to Descartes' fable, in which the vortex mechanism served as a physical account of gravity, Kant accounts for the generation of vortex structures from the counterbalancing of attraction and repulsion, which provides the organizing principle of his cosmogony.

Several commentators have criticized Kant's hypothetical method for the reason that it fails to reach the deductive standard of Newtonian science. Erich Adickes suggests that Kant's mathematical abilities were simply too limited, meaning that a quantitative procedure was possible but simply beyond Kant's reach.[14] Fritz Krafft blames the available empirical data, suggesting that there were insufficient resources in the mid-eighteenth century to conduct the qualitative kind of study of the universe's formation Newton had conducted in *Principia*.[15]

---

[14] Adickes, *Kant als Naturforscher*, I 55–6.
[15] Krafft, "Analogie—Theodizee—Akualismus," 179–95.

Yet Kant seems to be unperturbed by his chosen methodology, and entertained a high estimation of what analogical reasoning can achieve. In fact, he goes as far as to claim that the "presumptions in which analogy and observation corres-pond to support each other completely have the same value as formal proofs" (NTH 1:255).

Kant's essay fails as a work of Newtonian science only if it is judged against the mechanical interpretation of Newtonianism defended by members of the Royal Society. Mechanical Newtonianism assumes a voluntarist metaphysics, which entails that analogical reasoning remains problematic until it can be given a mathematical proof.[16] To extend inquiry beyond experiment and observation is to hypothesize, falling prey to the errors of Cartesian philosophy. Newtonianism thus entails that the past is hidden from us, just as the cause of gravity is hidden from celestial mechanics. This is why Newton's *Principia* outlines a mechanics of the present, and refrains from speculating about how the system came to be. When force is understood as external to bodies, nature has an entropic tendency. Without the constant intervention of God, Newton explains, "the Bodies of the Earth, Planets, Comets, Sun, and all things in them would grow cold and freeze, and become inactive Masses."[17] The fact that the universe exists at all is a result of God's choice: "God in the beginning formed Matter in solid, massy, hard, impenetrable, movable Particles, of such Sizes and Figures, and with such other Properties, and in such Proportion to Space, as most conducted to the End for which he form'd them."[18] In a cosmos that exists in a state of diminution, periodically propped up by an intervening God, speculation about events that lie outside the domain of experience is epistemologically unjustified. For the mechanical Newtonians, it is mere fiction to speculate on the origins and devel-opmental histories of natural phenomena. Descartes and Leibniz were the primary culprits.[19]

While the prospects of a hypothetical account of unobservable phenomena is contrary to the epistemic reservations Newton expressed in *Principia*, Kant's attempt to extend Newton's principles to the world system does not break from Newtonianism. Rather, it builds on the materialist interpretation of Newtonianism developed by Du Châtelet, Maupertuis, and Buffon. In the Premier Discours, Buffon acknowledged that many Newtonians held to a form

---

[16] See Schofield, *Mechanism and Materialism*, 15–16. For example, in 1734 Pieter van Musschenbroek claimed that the idea of a fixed law is accessible only though empirical induction, and thus can never be established with certainty. Musschenbroek, *The Elements of Natural Philosophy*, I 5.

[17] Newton, *Mathematical Principles*, II 399–400.   [18] Newton, *Mathematical Principles*, II 400.

[19] Descartes for example uses natural laws derived from God's perfection to show how, "in consequence of those laws, the greater part of the chaos had to become disposed and arranged in a certain way which made it resemble our heavens, and how at the same time, some of its parts had to form an earth, some planets and comets, and others a sun and fixed stars." Yet he does not explain *how* the planets, comets, and sun came to be. Descartes, *Discourse on Method*, 132.

of voluntarism that entails a radical scepticism about hypotheses.[20] Yet this form of Newtonianism is unsustainable, Buffon claimed, for by confining natural philosophy to Newton's mathematical account of force it assumes the efficacy of far more spurious forces. In contrast, Buffon set out to establish an analogical method for the study of physical nature that makes us "capable of grasping distant relationships, bringing them together, and making out of them a body of reasoned ideas."[21]

In the following sections, I argue that Kant's understanding of universal natural history can be understood against the background of Buffon's *Histoire naturelle*, so it is worth restating a few of its key elements here. In the Second Discours, "History and Theory of the Earth" (see cover image for the plate included at the start of this section), Buffon separates two kinds of natural history: the "general history of the earth," which provides a physical account of the formation of the solar system and the development of the earth's terrain, and the "particular history of the productions, and the details of the singular facts of life and the mores of the animals."[22] The general section ought to precede the particular, Buffon explains, for the particular natural facts are made up of materials and formed by processes studied in the first part. The theory of these processes can be described as the "primary science [*première science*] upon which the knowledge of particular phenomena solely depends," which Buffon names "physics."[23] His radical proposal is that "all of physics, where system is excluded, is part of the history of Nature."[24] By starting with physics, the categories used in classification are not taken from the sphere of logic and applied to the products of nature from the top down. They are derived from the bottom up, and represent causal connections that persist through time. The reason that a *physical* theory of the universe has not yet been established is that so much of it lies beyond our experience, tempting reason to fill in the void with fanciful hypotheses. Nevertheless, Buffon proposes that his physical procedure will aid the reader to distinguish between two kinds of hypothesis, one that "consists only of probabilities" and one "supported by facts."[25] By taking up the "hypothetical manner" of physics, Buffon claims to provide "a physical history of its [i.e. nature's] real condition." An early reviewer of *Histoire naturelle* writing for *Bibliothèque raisonée* was aghast at such a proposal, and offered an apt summary of Buffon's scandalous project: "Nature

---

[20] Buffon's stated intention in the Premier Discours is to assist the reader to "more readily specify the great difference that exists between a hypothesis, in which there is nothing but possibilities, and a theory based on facts." While his own theory is hypothetical, it proceeds via a probabilistic method in which speculative claims can be proved beyond reasonable doubt.

[21] Buffon, *Histoire naturelle*, I 52.   [22] Buffon, *Histoire naturelle*, I 65–6.
[23] Buffon, *Histoire naturelle*, I 66.   [24] Buffon, *Histoire naturelle*, I 66.
[25] Buffon, *Histoire naturelle*, I 129.

enjoys the right of forming herself, of organizing herself, and of passing freely from the inanimate state to that of a plant, or that of an animal."[26]

3.2 Haller and Hypotheses

Kant was clearly impressed by Buffon's arguments in favour of a general natural history, which, before turning to the task of classification, could demonstrate that the present diversity is the result of a physical process. Yet as we will see, he nevertheless found significant gaps in Buffon's account, which had been exploited by Buffon's theologically motivated reviewers. In this section, and in the section to follow, I provide textual evidence to show that Kant found a productive way to read Buffon's proposal via Haller's methodological preface to the first volume of Kästner's translation, which aimed to soften those who were sceptical of Buffon for epistemological and theological reasons. While Haller warns the reader that Buffon "always goes somewhat further than his information, experiments, and insight," and thus that extreme caution should be exercised in accepting his views, his aim is ultimately to vindicate the use of hypotheses in Newtonian science.[27] The true merit of Buffon's project, Haller postulates, lies in its capacity to open new and uncharted terrain for experimental philosophy.[28]

Haller's call to cautiously weigh up the merits of Buffon's project, combined with Zink and Kästner's rendering of *Histoire naturelle* as an *Allgemeine Historie der Natur*, invited Buffon's German readers to consider his radical project as an extension of Newtonian science. In Haller's overview of the text, Buffon grounds the descriptive part of natural history in a universal theory of nature understood as a physical system, thereby applying to physics what Newton had done for mathematics. Buffon originally framed his hypothesis as follows:

> Could one not imagine with some sort of probability that a comet, falling on to the surface of the sun, could have displaced that star, and that several small parts of it would have been separated, to which would have been communicated a movement of impulsion in the same direction by the same impact, so that the planets would have belonged formerly to the body of the sun, and been detached from it by a force of impulsion common to them all, a force which they conserve to this day?[29]

---

[26] Anon., "Review of Buffon's *Histoire Naturelle*, January–March 1751," 270. The reviewer is correct. In "Comparison of Animals, Vegetables and Minerals," for instance, Buffon defines the difference between plants, animals, and humans in terms of gradations in complexity. He concludes with a stunning line: "animation, or the principle of life, instead of a metaphysical step in the scale of being, is a physical property common to all matter." Buffon, *Histoire naturelle*, II 17.

[27] Haller, "Preface to the German Translation of *Histoire Naturelle*," 307.

[28] Haller, "Preface to the German Translation of *Histoire Naturelle*," 306.

[29] Buffon, *Histoire naturelle*, I 133.

As evidenced by its early reviews, the initial readers of *Histoire naturelle* found this hypothesis scandalous. How could such a blatantly speculative thesis find experimental vindication? Anticipating such an attack, Buffon spent considerable time in "Proofs of the Theory of the Earth" criticizing natural theologians such as William Whiston, Thomas Burnet, and John Woodward, who aimed to use mechanistic physics to defend the biblical creation narrative. In *The Natural History of the Earth* (1726), for example, Woodward insisted on "the exact Agreement betwixt Nature and Holy Writ from Observations, and Facts at this time demonstrable in the whole terraquous Globe."[30] Having reduced Whiston's cosmology to a physical absurdity, Buffon closes with the following remark:

> every time that one is so presumptuous as to attempt a physical explanation of theological truths, that one allows oneself to interpret the sacred texts from purely human views, that one reasons concerning the will of the Deity, and the execution of his decrees; one falls necessarily into the darkness and the chaos where the author of this system has fallen, who has, nevertheless, been received with great applaud.[31]

Buffon defends his general natural history by appeal to Newton's fourth rule (arguments from phenomena cannot be "evaded by hypotheses"). In contrast to the physical hypothesis presented in "History and Theory of the Earth," Whiston's hypotheses evoke physical causes within a hyperphysical system that renders those very causes unintelligible. Indeed, the natural theologians were not primarily concerned with providing a cosmology in keeping with Newton's rules but with showing how the new science was theologically orthodox. Buffon places his own history in proximity to Leibniz' celestial dynamics by fusing Newtonian mechanics with a dynamical theory of matter, according to which the world has been autonomous since it first began with the chance collision of a comet and the sun. As Phillip Sloan explains, the autonomy of this dynamical system enabled Buffon to extend Newton's mechanics to moments of world-time outside possible experience, thereby utilizing "a Newtonian methodological principle with greater consistency than Newton himself had done."[32] Newton's third rule, for instance, ensures that properties discovered to hold between bodies available to observation are attributed to *all* bodies, including those extant at the beginning of time. On the basis of this rule, Buffon claims that Leibniz' account of the origins of the planets would have been "more comprehensive, and more consonant to probability," if he

---

[30] Woodward, *The Natural History of the Earth*, 29.   [31] Buffon, *Histoire naturelle*, I 178–9.
[32] Sloan, "The 'Second Discourse' and 'Proofs of the Theory of the Earth' from Buffon's *Histoire Naturelle* (1749)," 131. Buffon presents this theory in "On the Formation of the Planets." See Buffon, *Histoire naturelle*, I 127–67.

had provided a causal account of how they originally split from the sun, rather than merely positing that they were themselves formerly suns.[33]

While Buffon extends Leibniz' cosmology to remove the need for divine tinkering in the Newtonian system, his universal natural history nevertheless presents a degenerating and ultimately dying system. The cost of removing God's direct role, it would seem, is a universe with an accidental beginning and without a teleological structure. For this reason the reviewer for *Nouvelles ecclésiastiques* attacked *Histoire naturelle* as a work filled with "venom" that expounds a "pernicious system."[34] Buffon's comet hypothesis replaces the theoretical certainty guaranteed by a purposeful Creator with a probabilistic calculus, thereby introducing scepticism into both "religion and all the human sciences" and surrendering human knowledge to "incertitude."[35] Moreover, the reviewer found *Histoire naturelle* to be deeply unscriptural, for it not only places humans on the same level as the animals but its account of geological formation, which involves the formation of landmasses and mountains from the sea, implies "a world far older than Moses made it out to be."[36]

Haller was aware that Buffon's use of hypothetical reasoning departed from the portrait of natural philosophy Newton had painted in the General Scholium. Combined with his attack on natural theology, this had earned Buffon a public reprimand from the Sorbonne's Faculty of Theology.[37] Yet Haller saw that the Sorbonne theologians articulated a position that was equally, if not more, damaging to natural philosophy. The "practice of rejecting all hypothesis," he states, "can become more detrimental to mankind than the dreams of the philosophers of the schools could ever have been."[38] Echoing Du Châtelet, Haller notes that not even Newton, the "destroyer of arbitrary conjectures," could do without hypotheses: "Was his ether the medium of light, sound, sensation and elasticity, not a hypothesis?"[39] Haller's reference to Newton's aether is illuminating, for it shows that the Newtonian context in which he seeks to defend Buffon consisted of a much broader view of Newton's work than *Principia*. His proposal is that Newton's work, taken as a whole, paves the way for the *valid* use of hypotheses.

---

[33] Buffon, *Histoire naturelle*, I 133.

[34] I assume that the review was written by the editor, Fontaine de la Roche. Roche, "Review of Buffon's *Histoire Naturelle*, February 1750," 237–8.

[35] Roche, "Review of Buffon's *Histoire Naturelle*, February 1750," 241.

[36] Roche, "Review of Buffon's *Histoire Naturelle*, February 1750," 243.

[37] In 1751, the Faculty of Theology at the Sorbonne charged Buffon for establishing "principles and maxims which are not in conformity with those of religion," and laid down fourteen "propositions extracted from a work entitled *Histoire naturelle* which have appeared reprehensible." The most important for our present purposes is Proposition IX: "Mathematical evidence and physical certitude are, then, the only two aspects under which we ought to consider truth. Insofar as it is distanced from one or the other, it is no more than verisimilitude and probability." The Deputies and Syndic of the Faculty of Theology of Paris, "Letter of the Deputies and Syndic of the Faculty of Theology of Paris to M. Buffon, January 17 1751," 285–7.

[38] Haller, "Preface to the German Translation of *Histoire Naturelle*," 298.

[39] Haller, "Preface to the German Translation of *Histoire Naturelle*," 299.

So little of nature is known to us that without the use of hypotheses—without trading with "the probable as currency"—"we must remain silent on almost all of natural philosophy."[40] Rather than constructing an aggregate of independent facts without connection, hypotheses allow us to "construct a building instead of a ruin."[41] Haller clarifies the epistemic status of hypotheses as dynamic guiding principles: truth should not be the initial register we use for evaluating a hypothesis, but rather its capacity to lead to the truth. Buffon's conjectures thus deserve a hearing.

3.3 A Universal Natural History

Kant's *Universal Natural History* reflects Haller's backhanded endorsement of *Histoire naturelle* in several important ways. Like Haller, Kant recognized the significance of Buffon's attempt to complete the Newtonian project by providing an exhaustive, physical system of nature. Kant seems to have fashioned the title of his book after Kästner's rendering of *Histoire naturelle* as *Allgemeine Historie der Natur*, indicating his intention to follow Buffon in providing a universal history of nature. However, while Kant agreed with Haller that Buffon's hypotheses opened a new and potentially ground-breaking field of inquiry, he also recognized that it consists of fragmentary reflections. The fragmentation begins with the comet hypothesis. If the planetary system began with a comet colliding with the sun, how did such heavenly bodies emerge from the chaotic nebula?[42] And how did this accidental collision result in the well-ordered system we see today? To complete the physical system opened by Buffon, Kant attempts to harmonize planetary physics with teleology. This requires a new theory of matter capable of grounding a truly universal programme of natural history. Kant acknowledges his debt to Buffon in the following way:

> what shows the natural formation of the heavenly spheres out of the basic material that was originally dispersed in the space of the heavens that are now empty as clearly as anything else is the correspondence I borrow from Herr von Buffon which, however, in his theory does not have by far the usefulness that it has in ours.   (NTH 1:345)

---

[40] Haller, "Preface to the German Translation of *Histoire Naturelle*," 299.
[41] Haller, "Preface to the German Translation of *Histoire Naturelle*," 299.
[42] Kant offers a similar criticism of Buffon thirty years later in "On the Volcanoes on the Moon," suggesting that his views on cosmology remained fairly consistent throughout his career (VM 8:74). What is new in the volcano essay is that Kant adopts Crawford's theory of heat, which provides a chemical explanation of the basic properties of matter that precedes and grounds the principles of mechanism. As we will see in Chapter 7, while teleology remains indispensable for mechanical inquiry, it takes on a regulative status. For a study of the continuities across Kant's pre-critical and critical cosmology, see Ferrini, "Heavenly Bodies, Crystals and Organisms."

In Kant's view, the basic problem with Buffon's cosmogony is not so much the comet thesis (Kant after all praised Buffon's idea of a physical origin) as the attribution of the ordered arrangements of the planetary masses to chance. It is no wonder that *Histoire naturelle* caught the critical eye of the Sorbonne theologians! Anticipating a similar response from the Königsberg theologians, Kant begins with greater caution than Buffon. Rather than attacking the natural theologians head on, his strategy is to beat them at their own game. In words that echo Haller's anticipatory remarks in the preface, Kant begins the essay by identifying two kinds of sceptics: the theologians, for whom the attempt to explain the origin of the universe and its subsequent formation by natural laws is a dangerous form of atheism; and the mechanical Newtonians, who saw such an attempt as a pernicious form of speculation. He formulates the theological objection as follows:

> If the universe [*Weltbau*] with all its order and beauty is merely an effect of matter left to its general laws of motion, if the blind mechanism of the powers of nature knows how to develop so magnificently and to such perfection all of its own accord: then the proof of the divine Author, which one derives from the sight of the beauty of the universe, is entirely stripped of its power, nature is sufficient in itself, divine government is superfluous.   (NTH 1:222)

Kant's notion of "blind mechanism" is the key to his portrayal of the theological objection. The materialist Newtonians remove purpose from nature, and with it the connection between our experience of beauty and a divine architect. This caricature was certainly true of Buffon. Yet for Kant, the objection does not add any credence to the notion of a "designed" mechanism. Kant was strongly opposed to those who attempted to save theology from the encroachment of natural philosophy by finding evidence of design in every trace of usefulness in nature's products. Christian Wolff, who located design in any natural phenomenon that bears the least hint of finality, was the worst offender. In *German Teleology* (1724), Wolff accounts for the existence of all kinds of natural products according to their role as final means: the placement of stars is explained by their role in enabling nocturnal navigation, and the sun by the aid it provides to human industry.[43] For Kant, Wolff's physicotheology inhibits natural science from discovering the mechanical laws that render nature's order necessary, for it provides hyperphysical explanations for the apparently contingent structural features of the system. In contrast to both the theologians and the sceptics, Kant attempts to fuse mechanism and teleology in a single framework, resulting in a *mechanical* teleology. Final means must be congruous with the physical processes of nature,

---

[43] Wolff, *Vernünfftige Gedancken von den Absichten der natürlichen Dinge*, §33, §47.

which entails that structural features of the system appear to be contingent only because we are ignorant of their mechanical etiology.

Kant had already opposed the idea of divine interference in his early essays on mechanics. In *Thoughts on the True Estimation of Living Forces* (1747), he presented a metaphysical account of force in which he affirms Leibniz's account of bodies as possessive of an essential, active force (*vis activa*). He begins by criticizing the experimental philosophers who claim to "look no further than the senses teach" (GSK 1:17). This goal changes what it means to give an explanation from Aristotelian entelechy, which accounts for force as an internal and goal-oriented principle of change, to a mathematically demonstrable theorem, which accounts for movement according to blind forces operating upon inert matter. Observation, Kant states, yields an account of "force as something communicated solely and entirely from the outside, something the body does not have when it is at rest" (GSK 1:17). The result is an entropic system in which God must constantly add motion to prevent its store from being depleted with time, thus maintaining the universe in its present state.

Kant claims that in contrast to the mechanical Newtonians (and "luckily" for reason), Leibniz properly understood Aristotle's notion of entelechy, allowing him "to teach that an essential force inheres in a body and belongs to it even prior to extension" (GSK 1:17). Since force is prior to extension, matter and space are not primitive but emerge through active processes. Yet Kant was critical of Leibniz's pre-established harmony, which accounts for interaction as an emergent property rather than as an intrinsic part of nature. As he later explains in *New Elucidation of the First Principles of Metaphysical Cognition* (1755), while Leibniz rightly acknowledges the agreement between substances he does not allow for "their reciprocal dependency on each other" (PND 1:415). In this sense Kant was closer to Martin Knutzen's theory of physical influx, which accepts a physical transfer of properties between substances. Yet Kant also found problems with his former teacher's position. Physical influx removes the harmony of forces, and thus begs the question of teleological order. To maintain Leibniz's conception of a harmonious system, and yet provide an explanation of harmony in terms of physical properties, he accounts for the action of primitive forces as affecting other forces. As Schönfeld explains, Kant's early theory of forces is "dynamic" to the extent that it begins with force as original presence, which would not exist if it did not act.[44] When a force acts it "spreads its self out [*ausbreiten*]," thereby becoming "outstretching" or "extended [*Ausdehnung*]" (PND 1:24). Kant expounds as follows: "It is easy to show that there would be no space and no extension if substances had

---

[44] My account of *New Elucidation* draws from Schönfeld's reconstruction in "Kant's Early Dynamics," 37.

no force to act external to themselves. For without this force there is no connection, without connection, no order, and, finally, without order, no space" (PND 1:23). The activity of force extends space, and by doing so it generates order and connection. From this dynamical account of matter, Kant reasons that force creates the world, and thus all of the natural products within it. Citing Wolff, he defines a world as a *nexus rerum*, "the series of all simultaneously and successively existing contingent things that are connected with each other" (PND 1:23). The idea is that relations are constitutive of a referential frame, and create the possibility of there being locations within it. Space and time themselves are dependent on the activity of the basic particles that constitute nature.

Kant's dynamical account of space is radically opposed to the empty space of the mechanical Newtonians. Empty space is an abstraction from the present state of the universe, for it claims priority over the external operation of force upon matter. Thus conceived, the orbits of the planets are simply "a consequence of the agreement they all must have had with the material cause by which they were set into motion" (NTH 1:261–2). Kant saw that the priority of space over force meant that Newton could not envisage a material cause for the arrangement of the planetary system, and thus had no alternative but to appeal to "the direct hand of God" (NTH 1:262). Here Kant seems to be referring to the General Scholium, where Newton states that "it is not to be conceived that mere mechanical causes could give birth to so many regular motions."[45] In contrast to a universally mechanical system, Newton claims that

This most beautiful system of the sun, planets, and comets, could only proceed from the counsel and dominion of an intelligent and powerful Being. And if the fixed stars are the centres of other like systems, these, being formed by the like wise counsel, must be all subject to the dominion of One ... and lest the systems of the fixed stars should, by their gravity, fall on each other, he hath placed those systems at immense distances from one another.[46]

Newton's claim is that the present diversity of things, and the harmony between qualities and environment, could not arise apart from the "ideas and will of a Being necessarily existing."[47] In *Opticks*, he similarly conceded that the elliptical movement of the planets is inexplicable according to natural philosophy. If universal gravitation were the only law responsible for the arrangement of the planetary orbits, then the orbits would be random. However, they are clustered

---

[45] Newton, *Mathematical Principles*, II 544.   [46] Newton, *Mathematical Principles*, II 544.
[47] Newton, *Mathematical Principles*, II 546. He states that while the planets and comets "continue in their orbits by the mere laws of gravity, they could by no means have at first derived the regular position of the orbits themselves from those laws" (II 543).

around one plane, and orbit the sun in the same direction. Because he could not envisage a mechanical cause for this pattern, Newton concluded that "such a wonderful Uniformity in the Planetary System must be allowed the Effect of Choice."[48]

Kant recognized that *both* Newton and Buffon call on arbitrary causes (choice and chance) to account for the origin of the universe. While Buffon rejected teleology altogether, Newton's teleology is external to the mechanical order and even works against it by occasionally redirecting events according to God's will. For Kant, both conclusions are a form of despair at the power of reason to live up to its vocation. In response, he argues that the very same difficulty that "deprived Newton of hope of understanding the orbital forces imparted to the heavenly bodies . . . is the source of the doctrine we have presented" (NTH 1:339). What Newton could achieve only in mathematics, Kant, following and yet superseding Buffon, proposes to do in physics, thereby bringing to physical science the "completeness to which Newton raised its mathematical half" (NTH 1:230). This project takes the form of a universal natural history, which presents the generation of the world system.

Kant's history of nature's self-organization entails a radically different conception of creation to that proposed by the theologians. The theologians separate the laws of motion, which constitute the world system, from the action of an omnipotent God. Alternatively, Kant claims that creation "is not the work of one moment" (NTH 1:314). After the creative process "has made a beginning with the production of an infinity of substances and matter," he explains, "it is effective throughout the entire sequence of eternity with ever increasing degrees of fruitfulness" (NTH 1:314). Historical development is thus maximally robust, constituting the ongoing creation of the universe. God does not create *in* time and space at a single moment, as Newton claimed. Time and space are rather the properties of matter that unfold in unbroken connection. Attraction "is precisely that universal relationship that unites the parts of nature in one space," connecting all particles together in "the great chain of all nature [*die große Kette der gesammten Natur*]" (NTH 1:308). Kant boldly claims that, given the system advanced in *Universal Natural History*, we can "now reconcile a mechanical doctrine with the teaching of intentions in such a way that what the highest wisdom itself designed has been delegated for implementation to coarse matter and the regiment of providence to nature left to its own devices" (NTH 1:363). The highest wisdom is not directly responsible for the design we discover in nature. Rather, it is responsible for an even more awe-inspiring act of creativity: the creation of formless matter capable of giving form to itself.

---

[48] Newton, *Opticks*, 402.

3.4 Wright and Physical Teleology

Kant's attempt to integrate continuous alteration into the static system of eighteenth-century celestial mechanics opens the problem of development. If the natural system is ordained by God, then it must be perfect. Yet any true alteration implies a contingent departure from perfection; contingent in the sense that one state comes after a different, antecedent state, such that the latter is not possible by itself (i.e. it is not necessary).[49] To protect God's perfection from the contingency of the world order, the mechanical Newtonians maintained a hard distinction between celestial mechanics and divine creativity. How then could perfection be maintained in a developmental system that generates its own conditions? In this final section, I argue that in contrast to the mechanical Newtonians, who held teleology separate from created matter, and in contrast to Buffon, who rejected teleology altogether, Kant followed Thomas Wright by differentiating between the finite standpoint of the human observer and the intellectual standpoint of universal natural history. While development cannot be reconciled with the stability of the universal order from the finite standpoint of the human observer, it can be reconciled from an abstract, disinterested standpoint that reconstructs a God-like view of the whole from which there is no difference between mechanism and teleology. Getting a clear grasp of this standpoint will be important for later chapters, where we will find that it reappears in Kant's philosophy not as a positive standpoint that is genuinely available to the natural philosopher but as the negative representation of an intuitive intellect for whom there is no contingency in nature (see Section 7.3).

In the preface to *Universal Natural History*, Kant explains that his idea of cosmological development builds on the insights of Wright's "An Original Theory or New Hypothesis of the Universe" (1750), a report of which appeared in German in the Hamburg journal *Freye Urtheile und Nachrichten* in January 1751.[50] In this essay, Wright described the celestial formations in terms of "shells" of stars, systems that were each organized around a divine centre of attraction. The stars of each shell orbit around the centre in a vortex formation through a combination of attractive and repulsive forces. The apparent chaos of stars we call the Milky Way could then be explained according to the effect of the observer looking from within our shell along one of its tangent planes.[51] Wright emphasized the developmental aspects of cosmology, and attributed

---

[49] For a discussion of the theological dimensions of Kant and Wright's speculations about the nebular origins of the universe, see Schaffer, "The Phoenix of Nature," 180.

[50] Schaffer notes that Wright's essay was reported quite badly, leading Kant to interpret Wright as suggesting that the Milky Way was an effect of an observer looking along the line of a thin layer of stars orbiting a centre on a single axis. This is in fact closer to Maupertuis' elliptical account of starry nebulae. See Schaffer, "The Phoenix of Nature," 189.

[51] Schaffer, "The Phoenix of Nature," 181.

changes in the system to the activity of fire, which implies constant change *and* self-maintenance.

While he did not suggest that the universe's structure evolved from a more primitive state, Wright broke from standard cosmologies of his time by locating the activity that forms and replenishes the cosmos with matter. The divine presence, Wright argued, is manifest through God's power and wisdom, meaning that one does not require miracles or intervention to account for God's ongoing role in creation. From our finite vantage on earth it might *seem* that change, perturbation, and decay signal a system in entropy. Thus we conclude that God *must* intervene to prevent the otherwise inevitable collapse. Yet Wright insists that the problem does not lie in creation but in our understanding. Just as the chaos of stars we call the Milky Way becomes a perfect, self-maintaining system when rightly understood (though it remains chaotic when we look through a telescope), so does the universe become a self-organizing whole when we correctly grasp the principles of its development (though its products still appear to us as contingent). In this sense Wright aims to rationalize development and decay as part of a perfect world. He thus criticizes Newton's *Principia* for failing to infer the divine attributes from the perfection of the world system. Newton had "contented him self with enumerating some of the principle Divine Attributes and leaving us in all things else to be lost in a kind of infinite common wealth of nature."[52]

Kant recalls that it was Wright's claim that originally gave him "cause to regard the fixed stars not as a scattered milling mass without any visible order" but rather as "a systematic constitution" (NTH 1:231). The key to Wright's discovery, on Kant's reading, lies in the shape of the Milky Way, which guides a thought experiment about the role of attractive and repulsive forces in the formation of vortices. The apparent chaos of the Milky Way is simply an effect of viewing a disk-shaped vortex along the plane of the disk. Kant generalizes beyond Wright's Milky Way hypothesis to claim that other nebulae are also similar disk-shaped galaxies viewed at different angles, building on Maupertuis' account of the starry nebula in *Discours sur les différentes figures des astres* (1742). The mechanical account of creation advanced by Descartes relied on the theory of vortices in which celestial movement supposedly follows stratified bands of secondary or primary matter left over from the fracture of larger elements.[53] This theory had been emphatically rejected by the mechanical Newtonians, for it is impossible to verify experimentally. Even Wright, at least in his 1750 essay, refrained from generalizing from his mechanical account of vortices to a speculative thesis concerning their role in creation.[54] Wright continually stressed the limits of

---

[52] Wright, *Second or Singular Thoughts upon the Theory of the Universe*, 18.

[53] See Descartes, *Principles of Philosophy*, 153–4.

[54] In his 1755 essay *Second or Singular Thoughts upon the Theory of the Universe*, Wright uses fire as the basis for God's action, which conserves as it also transforms the cosmos.

natural philosophy: "how the heavenly bodies were made, when they were made, and what they are made of, . . . seems to our present sight not to be within the reach of human philosophy."[55]

Dismissing Wright's hesitancy, the youthful Kant claimed that his Milky Way hypothesis could help locate the original formation of the vortices in the single causal sequence of nature. Kant explains that while he has "imitated" Wright's model, he has also "explained it further," combining Wright's self-organizing shells with Maupertuis' account of galaxies as open ellipses to describe the hierarchical order of the entire cosmos (NTH 1:232). The key is a physical account of the formation of vortices, which employs attraction to explain the initial condensation of the galactic cloud and repulsion to set it spinning (NTH 1:250). What seems to us as an expansive chaos of the heavens is, when reconstructed from a standpoint *outside* the Milky Way, the self-organization of a series of clustered galaxies, united as systems within a system. Development is permitted in a perfect order of things so long as the unity of the system as a whole is preserved. Systematic order can emerge from mechanical principles alone, provided one begins with the right theory of matter.

With Wright's account of the self-maintaining system of the Milky Way, Kant claims that he is able to explain the "distinct characteristics of transience" within a perfect physical world (NTH 1:326). As Hales' experiments had proved in *Vegetable staticks*, "all flames always devour much air and there is no doubt that the elastic force of the liquid element of air that surrounds the Sun must suffer over time a not inconsiderable disadvantage thereby" (NTH 1:326).[56] Kant notes that what "Hales has confirmed through careful experiments about the action of flame in our atmosphere" entails that the elasticity of the sun's atmosphere must eventually be destroyed. And if the sun were to extinguish itself, the earth would become uninhabitable for human life. While the apparent transience of the solar system drove the mechanical Newtonians to postulate the intervention of divine maintenance, Kant contends that the physical system of the universe "bears within itself the seed of renewal even in being conjoined with chaos" (NTH 1:327). The implosion of the sun would only lead to new forms of organization and life. Even in "the most loathsome state of its disorder," Kant extols, the destruction and chaos of the cosmos "brings about the beauty of the world and the benefit of the creatures" (NTH 1:328).

To grasp destruction and chaos as the means of beauty and benefit, Kant calls his readers to adopt Wright's abstract and disinterested standpoint, from which the Milky Way is a disk-shaped vortex consisting of thousands of stars, just one of

---

[55] Wright, *The Universe and the Stars*, 12.
[56] By observing the duration of a candle flame in various densities of air, Hales rejected the idea that a flame maintains its state due to a vivifying spirit. He argues instead that the elasticity of the air is consumed by the flame's activity. Kant extends Hales' experiments with candles and brimstone to make a general claim about the diminution of *all* fiery bodies. Hales, *Vegetable staticks*, 272ff.

which is our sun. Our first response to the sheer magnitude and infinite diversity of creation is "silent astonishment," for it causes us to feel our insignificance in the vastness of nature. Once we accept our insignificance, however, we discover a deeper, intellectual pleasure that "captures our understanding when it contemplates how so much splendour, so much grandeur flows from a single universal rule with an eternal and right order" (NTH 1:306). The delight of understanding vindicates the apparent transience of natural products—even those that threaten our very existence, such as the diminishing sun—for it results from the cognition of a purpose beyond ourselves: the great system of nature. Kant concludes in exhortation at the sheer exuberance of creation, which includes and even vindicates destruction:

> Nature shows its bounty in a kind of extravagance, which, while some parts pay their tribute to transience, maintains itself regardless through countless new creations in the whole extent of its perfections. What countless mass of flowers and insects does not a single cold day destroy; but how little do we miss them even though they are splendid artworks of nature and proofs of divine omnipotence!   (NTH 1:318)

Kant's account of nature's self-maintenance through destruction is vividly captured by his metaphor of the "phoenix of nature" (NTH 1:321). In stark contrast to the mechanical Newtonians, who called on divine tinkering to ensure the continuity of order, Kant insists that nature is *bound* to perfection, which means that it "must necessarily bring forth beautiful combinations" (NTH 1:228). Kant returns to this argument in chapter 8, where he offers a general proof for his mechanical doctrine of the universe. Once more he examines the two extremes identified in the preface, the theologians and the mechanical Newtonians. Yet here he shows that both positions are essentially the same, for each accepts the "almost universal prejudice" that nature is unable "to produce anything orderly through its universal laws just as though it would be disputing God's governance of the world if one were to seek original formations in the forces of nature" (NTH 1:332). To separate order from universal law is profoundly unscientific, Kant argues, for "any useful correspondences that shine forth in the constitution of nature points to the direct hand of God," thereby turning "the whole of nature into miracles" (NTH 1:332–3). The preponderance of miracles destroys nature as a continuous causal nexus, replacing it with "a god in the machine bringing about the changes in the world" (NTH 1:333).

Kant's summation and proof of his hypothesis aims to show that a universal natural history provides a sure foundation for physics without destroying teleology. If one considers how nature could produce so much beauty and order if left to itself, "then nature will appear to us more dignified than it is commonly regarded and one will expect from its unfolding nothing but correspondence, nothing but order" (NTH 1:332). God is no longer required to keep nature in operation, yet natural order continues to elicit our respect for a cosmic engineer. Kant's strategy is thus to remove the flaws from Buffon's universal conception of natural history by means of a Leibnizian view of the present arrangement as the best of all possible worlds. The result is profoundly unique. Leibniz ascribed mechanics to phenomena in the shape of law, and teleology to the substances in terms of entelechies. Kant advances an immanent teleology that collapses Leibniz' separation of the two orders of nature into a universal, physical domain manifest in tireless activity.

4
Physical Geography

In *Universal Natural History*, Kant outlined the general conditions of natural products by means of a hypothetical account of nature's building blocks. These blocks are not passive corpuscles but dynamic particles infused with attractive and repulsive forces. The particles necessarily whirl into vortices and, over long periods of time, give rise to all conceivable natural products, including suns, planets, terrestrial formations, and local climates. Yet Kant recognized that the immense complexity of living natural products poses an explanatory challenge to a universal natural history, for the structure of even the simplest form of life is more complex than the cosmos itself (NTH 1:230). While all that one requires to explain the arrangement of the cosmos is the right theory of matter ("Give me matter and I will build you a world out of it"), Kant asks whether one can also say, "Give me matter and I will show you how a worm can be created? Don't we get stuck at the first step due to ignorance about the true inner nature of the object and the complexity of the diversity contained within it?" (NTH 1:230). Kant concedes that his hypothetical account of matter does not explain the generation of living natural products. We require experience before we would ever expect nature to give rise to discrete objects that actively maintain their state of organization. Yet his reference to "inner nature" and "complexity" suggests that the difficulty is not so much a matter of kind as one of degree.[1] Kant's constant fusion of mechanical and organic analogies, along with the curious appendix "On the inhabitants of the planets," implies that the presence of organized beings could, in principle, be explained within a mechanistic framework. The mechanical development of the cosmos leads to ever increasing levels of organization, including

---

[1] McLaughlin argues that Kant's answer to the question of generation in 1755 remains unchanged throughout his career, linking *Universal Natural History* with Kant's denial of a biological Newton in *Critique of the Power of Judgment*. McLaughlin, "Kants Organismusbegriff in der *Kritik der Urteilskraft*," 102. Ginsborg concurs, conflating Kant's denial that we can *in practice* explain the generation of a worm with his denial *in principle*. Ginsborg, "Two Kinds of Mechanical Inexplicability in Kant and Aristotle," 41. I take the matter to be more complex. Nowhere does Kant deny the possibility of a mechanical explanation for generation in 1755; he simply accepts that presenting such an explanation seems impossible in practice. The position I develop in this study is closer to Ferrini, who argues that the mechanical explanation of a simple organism "is not taken as theoretically impossible but as practically highly problematic." Ferrini, "Testing the Limits of Mechanical Explanation in Kant's Pre-Critical Writings," 302.

Kant and the Transformation of Natural History. Andrew Cooper, Oxford University Press. © Andrew Cooper 2023.
DOI: 10.1093/oso/9780192869784.003.0005

living natural products and, eventually, rational natural products, even to a degree beyond earth-bound humans.[2] Given the mechanical-teleological system advanced in *Universal Natural History*, Kant felt entitled to posit that the "purpose" of the planets is to generate life to the highest degree of complexity (NTH 1:352–4).

In Kant's view, we get stuck when it comes to explaining the generation of living natural products because we are ignorant of their inner nature. While the theory of matter presented in *Universal Natural History* makes it the case that to be a natural product is to feature within a single causal sequence, how organizations came to be nested in one another such as to give rise to beings capable of maintaining their organized state remains unexplained. The problem concerns the possibility of localized principles that coordinate the generation of specific kinds of living thing. If the laws of generation are in principle reducible to the general laws of nature, they would be on par with the emergent laws of vortices. One could examine the vortex structure of the celestial system as an educt that unfolds (*auswickelt*) according to a principle.[3] The system would be thus considered as a machine in which the pre-built parts cause the whole. When one grasps the properties of matter, however, such an account can be replaced with a material-mechanical explanation in which the vortex structure is generated (*erzeugt*) as a product within the causal sequence of nature. The problem raised by living things is that, if we were to consider them as educts, they would not feature in a *universal* natural history; there would be as many natural histories as there are things that have a nature. In what sense, then, can living things be considered as natural *products*?

While Kant did not speculate about the generation of living things in *Universal Natural History*, we gain an insight into his position from a new lecture course he developed for the summer term of 1756 entitled "Physical Geography," which he continued to teach without a break until his retirement forty years later.[4] In the spring of 1757, Kant wrote an advertisement for the lectures in which he presents physical geography as a young and developing field that, as yet, lacks a rigorous method and systematic structure (EACG 2:4). While he devised the course programme with the help of recent travelogues and natural histories, there was no available textbook for the series of lectures he wanted to develop, meaning that he had to apply for special permission from the Prussian Ministry of Education to

---

[2] Kant argues that "most of the planets are certainly inhabited and those that are not will be at some stage," and speculates about the varying levels of intelligence among rational beings on the different planets in proportion to their proximity to the sun (NTH 1:354).

[3] In his lectures on metaphysics, Kant distinguishes educts from products in the following way: "A substance is 1) an educt, that is what was once in another substance but is not presented separately [; or] 2) A product, what before was not yet present, but now is generated [*erzeugt*] for the first time" (V-Met/Mron 29:760).

[4] Adickes, *Untersuchungen zu Kants physischer Geographie*, 9.

offer the course.[5] Werner Stark suggests that Kant's programme for a physical geography originally came from Karl Rappolt, who announced a course entitled *Geographicam Physicam, Verenio, Woodwardo, Scheuchzero ac Jurino ducibus* at Königsberg in 1750. Rappolt himself derived the idea from Bernhard Varenius, a former student at Königsberg, who had proposed a study of physical geography in 1650 in the Netherlands. Others including John Woodward had pioneered similar programmes in the early eighteenth century in Britain. Stark contends that Kant would have encountered Woodward's *Essay toward a Natural History of the Earth* during his undergraduate studies, which was published in English in 1695, Latin in 1704, and German in 1744.[6] Noting Kant's ongoing concern with physicotheology in the lectures, he counts "John Ray (1627–1705) and William Derham (1657–1735) among the intellectual forefathers of the course."[7]

Yet as we saw in Section 3.2, Kant's conception of physicotheology was radically at odds with Woodward's *Essay*. In this chapter, I argue that while Kant draws from Woodward, Ray, and Derham in his lectures, the structure of his physical geography course follows the lead of Linnaeus and Buffon by identifying the role of place in constraining the dynamics by which natural products arise. Yet in contrast to Linnaeus, who considered place as a static concept that occasions accidental modifications in substances, Kant sides with Buffon to examine the co-emergence of place *and* natural products in a universal system. Kant lists Buffon as one of the three authorities for physical geography in the announcement he wrote for the course in 1757 (EACG 2:4), and yet he refers to Buffon only on occasion throughout the lectures.[8] Nevertheless, I argue that there is evidence to suggest that Kant worked more closely with the German translation of the first three volumes of *Histoire naturelle* than his offhanded references to Buffon convey.[9] The structural impact of Buffon's work is especially clear in the concept of race that appears in Kant's lectures from 1774, which, I argue, was developed in conversation with Buffon's article "On the Degeneration of Animals" (1766).

---

[5] Church, "Immanuel Kant and the Emergence of Modern Geography," 40. In October 1778, Karl Abraham von Zeldlitz, the minister of education, exempted Kant from the normal requirements: "professors may improve upon the author as much as they can, but lecturing from one's own notes must absolutely be stopped. However, from this Professor Kant and his lectures on physical geography are exempted, because it is known that no entirely suitable textbook is yet available." Cited in Adickes, *Untersuchungen zu Kants physischer Geographie*, 10. While Kant had plans to publish a textbook on physical geography in the 1790s, by the time he wrote the preface to *Anthropology* in 1798 he states that he is now too old to do the same for his physical geography lectures, and that he is the only person capable of deciphering his lecture notes (Anth 7:122).

[6] Stark, "Kant's Lectures on 'Physical Geography'," 71.

[7] Stark, "Kant's Lectures on 'Physical Geography'," 72.

[8] See Jahn, *Grundzüge der Biologiegeschichte*, 229–33. Jahn traces the significance of Buffon's identification of a general and particular part of natural history for the following generation of German natural historians. For a discussion of Buffon's influence on Kant's early conception of natural history, see Sloan, "Kant on the History of Nature," 633.

[9] Here I agree with Düsing, who argues that Kant draws from Buffon's "presentation of a universal natural history" to differentiate natural history from mere description. Düsing, *Die Teleologie in Kant's Weltbegriff*, 134.

Before we begin, it is essential to note the interpretive difficulties associated with Kant's lectures on physical geography. The published Rink (1805) edition is often taken as the definitive representation of the lectures, for Kant publicly endorsed it over the earlier Vollmer (1801) publication.[10] Yet this view is problematic, for a close reading shows that the first volume of the Rink edition is based on lectures dated to 1774 (PG 9:156–273), and the second volume (PG 9:273–436) is based on lectures given during the late 1750s.[11] In response to the exponential growth of travel writings during the second half of the eighteenth century, Kant significantly changed material for the course between 1756 and 1796. To make matters even more complicated, none of the lecture notes include text written by Kant himself. We have instead a collection of seventeen sets of notes that aim to capture Professor Kant's spoken words, providing a genre altogether different from his published works.

To mitigate some of these difficulties, I complement the Rink edition with a selection of lecture notes chosen from various periods leading up to and including the critical period: Ms Holstein (1757/9), Ms Hesse (1770), Ms Kaehler (1774), and Ms Dönhoff (1781/2), along with Erich Adickes' comprehensive analysis of the twenty-two sets of lecture notes that were available in 1911. In Section 4.1, I examine Kant's conception of physical geography in the general part of the lectures, along with some of Kant's early course announcements. In Section 4.2, I turn to the particular part of the lectures, where I identify several connections between Kant's classificatory method and Buffon's physical concept of race. In Section 4.3, I depart from the lectures to consider Kant's theoretical writings during the 1760s, in which he calls on the problem of generation to illustrate a fundamental tendency in reason to overstep the limits of hypothetical inquiry. In Section 4.4, I examine the effect of Kant's growing critique of metaphysics on his engagement with the popular debate concerning human origins in the mid-1770s.

4.1 The Idea of a Physical Geography

In what sense is a geography *physical*? In this opening section, I suggest that Kant's physical geography can be understood as a second, pragmatic level of inquiry that

---

[10] Kant wrote a "public declaration" in 1801, which established Rink as the official editor: "At the last trade fair, the bookdealer Vollmer published a physical geography under my name, based, as he himself says, on student notes; I do not recognize this text as mine, neither in the subject matter nor in form. I have assigned the legitimate publication of my physical geography to Prof. Dr Rinck." Kant, "Nachricht an das Publicum," translated in Stark, "Kant's Lectures on 'Physical Geography'," 82.

[11] Adickes dates the first fifty-two sections to summer 1775, and remaining sections to sometime before 1760. Adickes, *Untersuchungen zu Kants physischer Geographie*, 278. I follow Stark's more recent analysis, which dates the first section to 1774, and the second to 1757/9. Stark, "Kant's Lectures on 'Physical Geography'," 83. To assist readers to follow the historical development of Kant's understanding of physical geography, references to the lectures include the year in which the notes were recorded.

seeks to fill in the formal relations presented in *Universal Natural History* from a human standpoint. In his announcement for the lecture course of spring 1757, Kant stated that his goal is to introduce his students to the various sources of geographical knowledge (EACG 2:4). By the time he wrote an announcement for the winter semester of 1765/6, however, he had come to view physical geography as the preparation for philosophy in general. Knowledge of the world transforms the vague and general information gathered from piecemeal observations and travel writings into clear and particular concepts by means of concrete examples. Kant's involvement in the physical influx debate during the 1750s, and his development of a physical monadology during the 1760s, pointed towards the fundamental role of nature acting on the body in all acts of cognition. The physical origins of knowledge entail that a proper philosophical education must be furnished with natural history. Kant explains that while his students were being taught the "art of subtle argumentation," they nevertheless "lacked any adequate knowledge of historical maters which could make good their lack of *experience*. Accordingly, I conceived the project of making the history of the present state of the earth, in other words, a geography in the widest sense of the term" (NEV 2:312). Kant transposes the physical account of truth he developed in the 1750s into a pedagogy for his new lecture course. His aim is not to train budding natural philosophers but rather to provide students destined for other careers with a historical foundation by which they can orient themselves in the world. In his announcement for the 1775 lectures, Kant describes his course as "more of a useful entertainment than a laborious business," more like a "game" than "deep inquiry" (VvRM75 2:429/6:3).[12] Towards the end of the announcement he describes the knowledge that his students will attain from the lectures as "world knowledge [*Weltkenntnis*]" (VvRM75 2:443/6:26).[13] In the student notes recorded that year, we find Kant stating that physical geography is "the first part of world knowledge"; the second part being "the knowledge of humankind" or "anthropology" (V-Geo/Kaehler 1775 26.2:300).

There has been extensive discussion of the meaning of *Weltkenntnis* in recent scholarship.[14] Here I want to focus on Kant's presentation of *Weltkenntnis* in the physical geography lectures as serving a "pragmatic" purpose (PG 1774 9:157), as this will shape our analysis of his concept of race in later sections. Robert Louden describes Kant's pragmatic purpose in terms of an "impure ethics," which is not

---

[12] References to Kant's announcement for physical geography lectures of 1775, entitled "Of the Different Races of Human Beings," refer to both the Akademie edition and Kant's *Werke*. See Introduction, footnote 21.

[13] Wilson renders *Weltkenntnis* as "cosmopolitan knowledge" to highlight the political nature of Kant's project. Wilson, *Kant's Pragmatic Anthropology*, 20.

[14] For a recent summary of the discussion, see Bianchi, "The Stage on which Our Ingenious Play Is Performed," 58–9.

about formulating action according to reason but cultivating a practical outlook.[15] Holly Wilson argues that in contrast to a general view, which explains a phenomenon by providing a causal hypothesis, a pragmatic view furthers our *ability* to provide an explanation.[16] The former is an account that satisfies the abstract intellect, the latter is limited to the sphere of nature that can have an effect on our actions. Thus, in contrast to the general outlook of *Universal Natural History*, a pragmatic inquiry orients the human being within the "setting [*Schauplatz*]" that is meaningful to them: the earth (PG 1774 9:160). Kant elaborates in dramatic terms (he was, after all, chasing student enrolments): the study of physical geography is "useful for life," for it introduces the student "to the stage of his vocation [*auf den Schauplatz seiner Bestimmung*], namely the *world*" (VvRM75 2:443/6:26).

Kant divides the lectures into a "general" and a "particular" part, which reflects Buffon's presentation of natural history as *générale et particulière* (PG 1774 9:183).[17] Like the articles that fall under Buffon's "History and theory of the Earth," including "Geography," "On the production of the layers or beds of the earth," and "On shells and other products of the sea, found in the interior of the earth," the general part of Kant's physical geography examines "the earth according to its parts and all that belongs to it" (PG 1774 9:183). This consists of a series of "histories [*Geschichten*]," including the history of seas, lands and islands, rivers, mountains, and great changes in the earth's surface. In the second part of the lectures, Kant examines "the particular products and creatures of the earth" (PG 1774 9:183), which mirrors the particular part of *Histoire naturelle*. In each section Kant accounts for the particular morphological characteristics of living natural products as the result of a dynamic interaction between an original stem (*ursprüngliche Stamm*) and the birthplace (*Geburtsort*) in which it develops (PG 1774 9:160). In contrast to general physical geography, which accounts of a natural product within the earth's system, particular physical geography examines a living natural product as a localized system, with various lines of descent that branch out as descendants from the original stem faced new climactic conditions and patterns of nutrition. This is why both parts of physical geography are pragmatic: how terrestrial formations or the original stem of a living being appear

---

[15] Louden, *Kant's Impure Ethics*, 21.

[16] It is the difference between "knowing how something happens and how to use it." Wilson, *Kant's Pragmatic Anthropology*, 29.

[17] As noted in Section 2.4, Zink and Kästner translated the first three volumes of *Histoire naturelle* as *Universal History of Nature, Dealt with According to All its Particular Parts*. Schmitt notes that while Buffon set the *générale* and *particulière* parts of natural history on equal epistemic footing, Zink and Kästner's translation introduces a conceptual hierarchy, implying that the particular part is nested within the general. The student lecture notes suggest that Kant at least read the text this way. In the general part, physical geography provides an account of time and space as an expanding causal sequence with conditions that are the same everywhere. In the particular part, physical geography seeks to orient the human being within a specific place, namely, the setting of the earth. See Schmitt, "From Paris to Moscow via Leipzig (1749–1787)," 249.

within the single causal nexus remains unknown. Nevertheless, geographers are entitled to trace physical connections as far as they can, for, given the general conditions of nature presented in *Universal Natural History*, to be a natural product is to feature within the single causal sequence. That geography must be physical is determined by nature understood as the regress of connections that constitute time and space.

Kant's description of his lectures on physical geography as a "history of the present state of the earth" has puzzled interpreters, for it seems to confuse diachronic with synchronic analysis. Max Marcuzzi suggests that there is a "vicious cycle" in the connection Kant draws between geography and history.[18] According to Marcuzzi, Kant states that geography can achieve "a systematic form insofar as its object is the entire earth," yet he then "affirms that it is only complete when it integrates becoming, and in moving into history, which is impossible." Yet Kant is clearly using "history" in the Buffonian sense, which consists of an account of how the present state of natural products arose according to natural causes. Many of the section titles recorded in the earliest remaining student notes indicate the historical basis of geography: "history of seas," "history of the continents and islands," "history of rivers," "history of the great changes that the earth has undergone and is still undergoing" (V-Geo/Holstein 1757/9 26.1:10, 21, 41, 66). In contrast to mathematical or political geography, a physical geography contains "a treatment of the natural relationship which holds between all the countries and seas of the world, and the reason for their connection" (PG 1757/9 9:312). This natural relation is, after all, "the real foundation of all history." A physical geography draws the "reports [*Nachrichten*]" documented by world travellers into a system that grounds the component parts within a physical process. While Kant certainly saw himself as a pioneer in physical geography, especially in later versions of the section "On Human Beings," his task was ultimately to operate as "a reporter of the research of others."[19] The guiding framework he presents enables the student of physical geography to anticipate possible future experience. The geographical works of Kant's time had so far failed to meet this practical demand.

In the section entitled "history of the great changes the earth has undergone and is still undergoing," which features in each of the Holstein, Hesse, Kaehler, Dönhoff, and Rink manuscripts, Kant gives an account of how the earth transforms itself through earthquakes, rivers, rain, wind, frost, and sea.[20] He even considers how human actions—the construction of dams, the draining of swamps, and the felling of forests—alter the local climates in which they are undertaken.

---

[18] Marcuzzi, "Writing Space," 120.   [19] Stark, "Kant's Lectures on 'Physical Geography'," 78.
[20] In Ms Kaehler, this section is entitled "Explanation of the changes of the deposits and mountains out of the chaotic conditions of the earth" (V-Geo/Kaehler 1775 26.2:488). In Ms Dönhoff, there is no title for this section, but Kant is recorded as speaking at length about the great changes in the earth through natural processes (V-Geo/Dönhoff 1781/2 26.2:849–74).

These changes happen on the level of the earth understood as an interrelated system, without reference to other celestial bodies. Kant's history of the earth's great changes is based on "proofs" that the sea formerly covered the whole earth, such as shells discovered on high mountains, the shapes of certain valleys, and the constellation of layers of the ground that give evidence to the constant movement of the earth's crust (V-Geo/Holstein 1757/9 26.1:69, PG 1757/9 9:298, V-Geo/Dönhoff 1781/2 26.2:864).

Kant's history of the "great changes" undergone by the earth offers a clear insight into the working relationship between *Universal Natural History* and physical geography. His universal account of nature sets the conditions in which physical geographers can search out the laws that govern particular processes and products. *Given* that natural processes and products are dynamically connected by virtue of featuring within a single chain of causes and effects, the proofs of dramatic changes in the earth lead physical geographers to project backwards from the present moment along a causal sequence that runs (via the proof) towards the initial dispersion of matter. Because physical geographers anticipate that the links in the chain of nature are causal, they are unsatisfied by the physicotheologians, including Burnet, Woodward, Whiston, and Linnaeus, who explain such proofs within a Mosaical timeframe (PG 1757/9 9:301–13). Even Simon de La Loubère, who manages to provide a physical account (in which monkeys carried the shells into the mountains!), is deemed "ridiculous," for he must reject a far simpler hypothesis (the recession of the sea) in order to remain consistent with a causal history of 6,000 years (PG 1757/9 9:298). The fundamental question of natural history, Kant states, is how we conceive of "the cause of all these changes" (PG 1757/9 9:301). His answer is that we must conceive of these changes as the result of the physical constitution of space and time.

Kant's attack on the physicotheologians closely resembles Buffon's critique of Whiston, Burnet, and Woodward in "Evidence for the Theory of the Earth," which ridicules their attempts to provide physical explanations for revealed truths (see Section 3.2).[21] Yet Kant also criticizes Buffon's account of the earth's formation for failing on its own terms. While Buffon rightly located the great alterations in the sphere of physical geography, he is unable to provide a causal explanation for the sea's retreat from the mountainous regions; he merely describes it as having retreated (PG 1757/9 9:303). What marks physical geography from mere fiction is that it accounts for past events according to physical connections, filling in the formal conditions of nature with physical content. For Kant, the proofs can only be understood through a process whereby the earth was originally a liquid mass that progressively hardened, taking the form of a sphere that is flatter at its poles. As the earth hardened, the heavier masses were moved to the centre of the

---

[21] Buffon, *Histoire naturelle*, I 168–88.

earth while lighter ones were moved to the surface. While this history involves speculation, the physical geographer is licensed to make it, for the connections follow the formal structure outlined in universal natural history.

What is crucial to note in the student lecture notes is the various levels from which nature can be understood as a dynamic system. Local systems including climate and geophysical formation are part of the global system, meaning that they are shaped by and give shape to their surrounds. Yet as we will see in the following section, living natural products are a special, localized kind of system. To examine the generation of plants and animals as a part of physical geography, we must assume that they are both fully resident in the physical order of nature *and* constrained by generative forces that are specific to a historical line of descent. In contrast to the passive earth, which is shaped by natural processes, living natural products *shape themselves* in response to environmental changes and, in turn, shape their environment.

4.2 Particular Physical Geography

In the particular part of the physical geography lectures, Kant draws many of his facts from the particular part of Buffon's *Histoire naturelle*.[22] Having outlined the general theory of the earth, Buffon opens the particular part of natural history with his theory of generation.[23] His theory is based on the acknowledgment that living natural products are underdetermined by the general conditions of nature outlined in the first part. While most natural historians conclude that generation is therefore a non-natural cause, Buffon affirms Maupertuis' claim that generation can be understood as a form of movement specific to an organic kind of matter.[24] He defends his speculations about organic matter pragmatically: we *must* speculate about organic matter, for it is the only alternative that navigates between two unacceptable positions. The first position is to appeal to a hyperphysical cause, which violates the material conditions of the natural system. The second position is to explain the animal economy by mechanisms such as levers, springs, and bellows, which is "vain and ineffectual," for the functions of the animal body, including the circulation of blood and the movement of muscles, cannot be captured by "any of the common laws of mechanism."[25] Thus a viable alternative must hold two seemingly contradictory claims together: (1) to be a natural product is to feature within the single causal nexus, and (2) in comparison to

[22] The footnotes in Stark's transcription of the lecture notes provide a detailed analysis of Kant's sources. While Kant draws extensively from a range of texts, including Maupertuis' *Die Naturlehre der Venus*, Stark's notes suggest that Buffon's *Allgemeine Historie der Natur* is the primary source of inspiration.

[23] Buffon, *Histoire naturelle*, II 20–62.   [24] Buffon, *Histoire naturelle*, II 20.

[25] Buffon, *Histoire naturelle*, II 23.

the universal law of gravity, impulsion, growth, and reproduction "are effects of laws of a different nature."[26] To walk this tightrope, Buffon proposed an analogy with Newton's gravitational force. If Newton is permitted to posit gravity as a force that unites the celestial sphere, despite the fact that its possibility remains unknown, natural historians are permitted to assume an analogous force "to collect the superfluous organic particles [*molecules organiques*], and bestow on them the figure of the body from which the proceed." Buffon was careful to maintain the hypothetical status of his theory of generation. Yet his claim is that, given the general conditions of nature, it is the best available hypothesis, for it can explain physiological effects according to natural causes.

Kant recognized that Buffon's general account of nature as a physical process transforms the practice of natural history from the logical procedure of division into a method of discovery, whereby natural historians seek to ground divisions in what Buffon terms a "natural cause." He begins the lectures with the Buffonian distinction between logical and physical knowledge: "Division of knowledge according to concepts is **logical**; according to time and space it is **physical**" (PG 1774 9:159). Kant began to distinguish between logical and physical knowledge in his lectures on metaphysics in the early 1760s. In the Herder notes (1762–4), for instance, he is recorded as separating logical from real grounds:

> A ground is thus something by which, having been posited, something else is posited.... Every *ground* is either logical, through which the consequence, which is identical to it, is posited as a predicate according to the rule of identity, or *real*, through which the consequence, which is not identical to it, is not posited according to the rule of identity. (V-Met/Herder 28:11)

A ground is logical, Kant explains, when the relata of a logical grounding relation are identical, that is, something is a logical ground of something else if the concept of the former contains the concept of the latter (giving birth to live young is a logical ground of membership within the genus *mammal*). Logical grounds are thus conceptually determining grounds (*ratio cognoscendi*). Yet Kant, having encountered David Hume's *Inquiry* in the late 1750s, recognized the incapacity of a logical relation to connect two distinct and self-sufficient entities.[27] The relata of a real grounding relation are not related by identity: "Every determination of things, however, which demands a real ground, is posited through something else, and the connection of a real ground with the real consequence is thus not comprehended from the rule of identity, also cannot be expressed through a judgement, but is rather a simple concept" (V-Met/Herder 28:24). Real grounds

---

[26] Buffon, *Histoire naturelle*, II 23.
[27] For an account of Kant's encounter with the German translation of Hume's *Inquiry*, see Watkins, *Kant and the Metaphysics of Causality*, 179.

capture an entirely different class of law-like claims. If a real ground is posited as a *cause*, for instance, a consequence follows as something non-identical, namely, an *effect*. Thus, a real consequence does not follow logically but existentially from its ground (reproduction in a line of descent in which members give birth to live young is a real ground of membership in the genus *mammal*). The relationship between the cause and the effect is not determined cognitively but metaphysically, for the real ground determines what it grounds.

The upshot of Kant's distinction between logical and real grounds is that, in a physical system, the connection between a real ground and its consequence cannot be known *a priori*; the relations between the objects themselves must be taken into account. Kant states that the "connection between the logical ground and the consequence is comprehensible, but not that between the real ground [and the consequence]" (V-Met/Herder 28:12). The natural philosopher cannot infer that an effect necessarily follows from its real ground, for "Only through experience can we have insight into the connection of the real ground, not logically" (V-Met/Herder 28:24). The distinction between logical and real grounds thus clarifies the epistemic status of the hypothesis presented in *Universal Natural History*, in which each causal link determines the following effect *a priori*. A universal natural history presents real grounding relations, and yet many of the effects it purports to explain (such as the surface of the earth hardening) are not given in experience. It thus remains a hypothesis that presents what is *possibly*, but not what is *actually*, true. Du Châtelet captured the asymmetry of possibility of actuality in *Foundations of Physics* when she noted that "all that does not imply contradiction is possible, but is not actual. ... all that exists being necessarily possible, one can conclude possibility from existence, but not existence from possibility."[28] As a hypothesis, the truth of a universal natural history cannot be determined by consistency alone.[29] The pragmatic standpoint of physical geography operates on a different epistemic plane. Physical geographers begin with the manifold of natural products, and seek their real grounds. Instead of cognizing the effect through the cause, as would a universal natural historian, the physical geographer works backwards from the effect *to* the cause, tracing an inference *within* a projected universal natural history.

The asymmetry of possibility and actuality entails that deduction is not by itself capable of arriving at truths of existing things. Because the consequence of a real ground does not follow logically but existentially, our only access to the ground is mediated by the consequence, which we encounter in experience. This entails that

---

[28] Du Châtelet, *Institutions de Physique*, 26/131.

[29] This places a serious check on Kant's argument in *Universal Natural History*. For instance, Kant concludes his chapter on the various densities of the planets "by adding an analogy which, all by itself, is able to raise the present theory of the mechanical formation of the heavenly bodies from the probability of a hypothesis to a certainty" (NTH 1:277).

the categories of the scholastic system, which are logically determined by a higher category through a relation of identity, yield merely artificial divisions: "Division of knowledge according to concepts is logical; according to time and space it is physical. By means of the former [logical division], we obtain a system of nature (*systema naturae*), as for example that of Linnaeus. With the latter [physical division] we obtain a geographical description of nature" (PG 1774 9:159). It is partly unfair to present the Linnaean system exclusively in terms of logical divisions. While Linnaeus accepted that the classificatory categories are logically related, he nevertheless treated the relata within the lowest category of variety to the higher level of species in terms of a causal relation, whereby a substance is the real ground of its accidents.[30] Yet Kant's separation of logical and physical division further demonstrates his commitment to Buffon's physical account of truth, which aspires to ground *all* classificatory distinctions in natural causes.[31] Buffon argued that by retaining the set of logical concepts as the fundamental concepts of classification, Linnaeus remained impervious to the enduring modifications undergone by a variety when faced with changed conditions, which are not captured by the logical concept of variety.[32] Kant agrees, claiming that Buffon transformed the scholastic divisions into physical divisions, meaning that the taxonomical categories themselves are grounded in natural causes:

> If, for example, I say that the species 'cattle' is one of the kinds of four-footed animals... then this is a division I make in my head: it is a logical division. The *systema naturae* is, as it were, a kind of register of the whole, wherein I situate all things, each in the class to which it belongs, even if on earth they are to be found in widely separated areas.
>
> In accordance with the physical division, however, things are considered in terms of the positions they occupy on earth. The system indicates their position in the classification. The physical geographical description of nature, on the other hand, seeks after the positions on earth where those things are actually found. Thus, for example, the lizard and the crocodile are basically the same animal. The crocodile is only an enormous lizard. But the places where the two are found are different. The crocodile lives on the Nile; the lizard on land, including in our area. In sum, we are concerned with the setting of nature, the earth itself, and those regions where things are actually encountered. But what matters in the system of nature is not birthplace, but similarity of form.   (PG 1774 9:159–60)

---

[30] In *Ratio operis* (1737), for example, Linnaeus speaks of originally created species that "afterwards produce more, but always similar forms according to inherent laws of generation." Müller-Wille and Reeds, "A translation of Carl Linnaeus's introduction to *Genera plantarum*," 565.

[31] For a comparison of Buffon and Kant's conception of physical truth, see Sloan, "Kant on the History of Nature," 630–3.

[32] Buffon, *Histoire naturelle*, I 51–2.

Kant contrasts Buffon's physical system with the scholastic system for it relates the extrinsic differences between living beings (their place and environment) according to a real ground. From the perspective of a physical system, the classification of the species *cattle* under the genus *four-footed animal* is arbitrary, for there may well be four-footed things all over the earth that bear no physical connection with cattle. Or take the crocodile. When considered purely according to common morphological characters, physical geographers could classify the crocodile under *lizard*, for the only qualitative difference is its size. But when they consider the crocodile's birthplace, and recognize that it lives on the Nile and not on the continent, they examine it within a projected lineage related by a causal sequence. By examining the crocodile within a projected physical lineage, physical geographers can then search for marks specific to this line of descent. A physical lineage gives rise to a class division that is not made in one's head but is anchored in nature. For this reason, geography is fundamental to history, for it provides the physical context for understanding living beings: "History and geography extend our knowledge in relation to time and space. History concerns the events that have taken place one after another in time. Geography concerns phenomena that occur simultaneously in space" (PG 1774 9:160). The combination of history and geography enables students of nature to extend their knowledge of natural products by identifying physical boundaries between natural groups that are not simply applied or learnt by habit but that are physically extended temporally and spatially. By combining spatial distribution with time, they can represent the location and ground of each species within a projected system of physical connections. What appears as the accidental alteration of a permanent or enduring locus of heredity in the Linnaean system becomes the essential characteristic of what Kant terms a "race," a physical network of historical filiation which "have sprung from a single stem" (PG 1774 9:162).[33]

Kant's nascent theory of race confronts us with one of the most controversial parts of his corpus. In the Holstein notes of 1757/9, we find Kant identifying varieties within the human species without the concept of race (V-Geo/Holstein 1757/9 26.1:85–7). In the Hesse notes of 1770, we find him using the concept of race to refer to groups that were produced in isolated geographical locations:

---

[33] In the section "On Human Beings," Kant states that a race "is a *degeneration* [Abartung], which stands in contrast to the other [kind of descendent] that cannot reproduce, which can be called a *variety* [Varietaet] or deviation [*Ausartung*]" (V-Geo/Kaehler 1775 26.2:506). On the assumption that Kant's classificatory concepts are constructed in conversation with Kästner's rendering of Buffon's taxonomical terms, my translations of Kant's classificatory terms differ from Zöller (Cambridge edition) and Mikkelson (SUNY edition). Zöller renders *Abartung* "subspecies" and Mikkelson "deviate forms," and both render *Ausartung* as "degeneration." In contrast, I render *Abartung* as "degeneration," following the German rendering of Buffon's "De la dégénération des animaux" as "Der Abartung der Thiere," and *Ausartung* as "deviation" (I explain this decision further in what follows). In translating *Stamm*, I follow Mikkelson's literal rendering as "stem" in contrast to Zöller's use of the nineteenth century neologism "phylum," which is historically misleading.

The more that travel and commerce have increased, the more the races have blended, and blends have arisen from two blended *races*, such as the Spaniards from the Goths and Moors, the English from the old Britons and Saxons. Only pure *races* are found in countries that have not been flooded by foreign peoples for many thousands of years.   (V-Geo/Hesse 1770 26.2:107–8)

This passage reveals Kant's assumption that a race captures a line of descent that developed over a long period of time in isolation, only recently disrupted by trade and migration. He goes on to list many different human "blends," and makes some attempt to discern the "stem races [*Stammracen*]" from which they derive. However, he does not tell us how to distinguish a pure race from a mere blend. It is not until the Rink edition of 1774, and the Kaehler student notes of 1775, that Kant is recorded as adopting the Linnaean schema in which four original races developed in isolation on each of the four continents. Yet in contrast to Linnaeus, Kant employs Buffon's physical notion of a "principle stem [*Hauptstämme*]" to argue that each of the four races derive from an original group that spread across the earth.[34] Variation is not the result of an external change (environment, nourishment, etc.) but the effect of internal, purposive forces, which triggered formal and structural adaptations when confronted with the environmental conditions particular to each continent. In the Kaehler notes, Kant is recorded as calling on Buffon to distinguish between two kinds of generation that can only be discerned if one assumes the existence of a "generative force":

Some living beings that are different can, through mating, produce offspring that are able to reproduce, and have several similar aspects from one to the other progeny [*Zeugenden*]. These are named *races*. In other living beings it is observed that, if they are the same, they still produce such products which self-propagate and are entirely similar from one to the other of the progeny. These are named variations by Buffon, because the difference between the animals does not have an influence on the generative force [*Zeugungskraft*].

(V-Geo/Kaehler 1775 26.2:503)

Here Kant draws on Buffon's 1766 article "On the Degeneration of Animals," which was translated by Kästner in 1772 as "Von der Abartung der Thiere." In this article, Buffon criticizes Linnaeus for adopting a static conception of geography, and thus for failing to consider the migration and subsequent interbreeding of the races. In contrast, he examines the fertility of some mules to argue that hybrids are not monsters composed of two natures but an intermediate kind of species, which

---

[34] Kästner translates *souches principals* as *Hauptstämme*, which Kant adopts in the taxonomy of human difference found in his lectures on physical geography and his essays on race. See, for instance, Buffon, "Von der Abartung der Thiere," 214.

he calls a race.[35] In Section 4.4, I will suggest that Buffon's article provides the background for Kant's 1775 course announcement and his 1777 published essay on race. Remaining with the student lecture notes for now, we can see that from the Rink edition and Kaehler notes onwards Kant follows Kästner's translation of *dégénération* as *Abartung* to refer to decedents that have hereditary morphological differences and yet belong to a common ancestor stem.[36] His use of *Racen*, we will see, is reserved for a distinct kind of *Abartung* that remains constant despite relocation to a new environment.

Kant recognized that Buffon's physical method identifies classificatory categories according to real grounds, enabling natural historians to construct a science of bodies in time and space. In the Rink edition, Kant is recorded as stating that by integrating history into geography, Buffon split the genuine practice of "natural history [*Naturgeschichte*]" from "natural description [*Naturbeschreibung*]" (PG 1774 9:161).[37] In contrast to natural description, which classifies varieties according to logical affinities, natural history combines temporal and spatial relations to examine variation as the result of a physical process. The problem, however, is that only if one were to "describe the events of the whole of nature as it has been through all time, then and only then would one write a real so-called natural history" (PG 1774 9:162). By a "real so-called natural history" Kant seems to be referring to a universal natural history that accounts not only for time and space but also for the generation of natural products and places. Such an account is only available to the mind of God, in which every effect is posited by its cause, for such a natural history "is not one whit shorter than history itself" (PG 1774 9:162; cf. V-Geo/Kaehler 1775 26.2:304–5). Here Kant explicitly acknowledges a structural feature of his system that, on my reading, was at least implicitly in place from the first series of lectures given in 1756: a universal natural history that includes particular natural products, while possible *in theory* (i.e. for a divine mind), lies beyond human cognition *in practice*.[38] This is why physical geography is pragmatic. The dynamic interactions of the compound parts over geological time are too multifaceted, and the alteration of organic form over biological time too

---

[35] Kästner translates Buffon's "Race" as "Rasse." Buffon, "Von der Abartung der Thiere," 191. Kant tends to use the French term.

[36] Sloan also translates *Abartung* as "degeneration." See Sloan, "Kant on the History of Nature," 635. For a discussion of the confusion introduced into the German translation of Buffon's use of *espèce* and *dégénération*, see Schmitt, "From Paris to Moscow via Leipzig (1749–1787)," 252.

[37] In the Kaehler notes we find Kant saying that all "foreign experience," that is, knowledge through "reports [*Nachrichten*] of foreign distant lands," is either "a *narrative* or a *description* [*eine Erzählung oder eine* Beschreibung]," where the first is a "history" and the second is a "graph" (V-Geo/Kaehler 1775 26.2:302). Kant's attempt to clarify the distinction may have been aimed at Kästner's decision to translate the *histoires* presented in the text as *Beschreibungen*, which fails to capture the temporal dimension of *Geschichte*.

[38] In Section 7.3, where I examine the role of the archetypal intellect in the resolution to the antinomy of the reflecting power of judgement, I suggest that Kant has a similar idea in mind. In his critical philosophy, Kant clarifies the problem not as one of complexity but of the discursive nature of cognition.

complex, to be cognized by a human intellect.[39] Nor would such a cognition be practically interesting to world citizens. The task confronting world citizens is to orient themselves within the spatial and temporal conditions of the earth by following the methodological ideal of the natural system, building up from their observations to a system of physical relations for pragmatic ends.

Before turning to Kant's essays on race, it is important to examine the broader role of generation in his growing awareness of the limits of metaphysics during the 1760s. So far, I have argued that Kant rejected the logical procedure of *Schulphilosophie*, which follows an *a priori* system of classification, and drew instead on Buffon's conception of natural history in which classificatory categories capture physical connections that project back from the present geographical distribution of a species to an original stem. In the following section, I turn to Kant's published work, where he identifies an error in Buffon's hypothetical account of generation. In the final section, I show how Kant's diagnosis of this error clarifies the epistemic parameters of natural history.

4.3 Generation and Reason's Limits

In *Universal Natural History*, Kant argued that the systematic order of nature can be explained as an effect of point-like centres of force. Armed only with a hypothetical determination of matter, he proceeded to explain how the system of natural things arises within a single, casual sequence. By the time he wrote *The Only Possible Argument in Support of a Demonstration of the Existence of God* (1763), however, Kant no longer held that the truth of a hypothesis can be established by intellectual coherence alone. In this essay, Kant employs the distinction between logical and real grounds to advance a new critique of the ontological argument. The ontological argument is supposed to prove the actual existence of God from the concept of the *ens realissimum*, the supremely real being. At its core, the argument deduces the property of existence from the analysis of the concept of perfection. Because it is logically contradictory to claim that the supremely real being does not exist, it must therefore exist. For Kant, the argument is sound only if one assumes that logical necessity entails real possibility. To say that "God is supremely perfect" is to think the logical relation between God and perfection. The laws of reason allow one to discern through analysis whether such a thought is logically possible. Existence, in contrast, is "the absolute positing of a thing" (BDG 2:73). While Kant notes that everyone can agree that possibility disappears "when an internal contradiction, as the logical

---

[39] For an important study of the problem of organic structure in the physical geography lectures, see Morris, "The Place of the Organism in Kantian Philosophy," 173–92.

element of impossibility, is present," he makes the further claim that possibility disappears "also when there exists no material element, no *datum*, to be thought" (BDG 2:78). When our concepts are empty, the real possibility of the objects to which they are supposed to refer is an "illusion [*Blendwerke*]" (BDG 2:80). The illusion tempts us to make determinate claims about those objects, and thus to conflate conceivability with real possibility.[40] Yet Kant insists that while an object might be conceivable—a perfect being or, indeed, a logically consistent natural history—its real possibility remains a problem.

Kant then turns to the physicotheological argument, which begins with the data of experience and attempts to work to a proof of God's existence. He notes that while real grounding relations enable us to think of effects through their cause, they do not give an interconnected *system* of causes, that is, they do not determine "whether the internal possibility of things is itself necessarily related to order and harmony" (BDG 2:92). This is why the physicotheologians, upon every appearance of contingent order in nature (beauty, usefulness, purposiveness, etc.), rashly conclude that it must be "an arrangement instituted by wisdom" (BDG 2:118). Yet Kant claims that the inference from contingency to design has been refuted by the remarkable progress made by natural philosophers over the past century. In cosmology, for instance, astronomers formerly called on teleological causes to explain the rising of some bodies and the falling of others. Because their conception of the world lacked physical unity, they appealed to agential properties to ensure that the objects cohere as parts of a whole. Yet Newton's discovery of gravity accounts for many different effects by a single force (BDG 2:113). Once the force of gravity is extended to the single world system, contingency vanishes. What had formerly been judged to be the work of design can now be considered as the product of a material process. The success of Newtonian science demonstrates that the appearance of contingency in nature merely indicates that something has not yet been understood.

Yet Kant once more acknowledges that living natural products pose a different kind of challenge to the Newtonian. In *Universal Natural History*, he implied that the contingent order of living natural products could be reduced to the necessary order of nature, just as the contingent order of the winds can be reduced to the general motions in the atmosphere. Now he acknowledges that while the technical features of living natural products can indeed be reduced to the necessary order of the system, it would be "absurd to regard the initial generation of a plant or animal as a mechanical effect incidentally arising from the universal laws of nature" (BDG 2:114). How then should we regard this initial generation, which appears to be contingent in regards to natural laws? Kant considers two available answers, and concludes that both end in failure:

[40] See Grier, *Kant's Doctrine of Transcendental Illusion*, 24.

Is each individual member of the plant- and animal-kingdoms directly formed by God, and thus of supernatural origin, with only propagation, that is to say, only the periodic transmission for the purposes of development, being entrusted to natural law? Or do some individual members of the plant- and animal-kingdoms, although immediately formed by God and thus of divine origin, possess the capacity, which we cannot understand, actually to generate [*erzeugen*] their own kind in accordance with a regular law of nature, and not merely to unfold [*auszuwickeln*] them?   (BDG 2:114)

Kant argues that, in the end, the mechanist and the materialist theories of generation both explain the possibility of generation by introducing a hyperphysical cause. Proponents of pre-existence attribute generation to God's creative act at the origin of the causal series. Their account of generation is "a futile method of evading the issue," for, by violating the causal principle, it brings natural science to an end (BDG 2:115). Proponents of epigenesis attempt to explain the possibility of generation according to organic particles endowed with secondary forces. While this account keeps the matter of generation within the physical system of nature, it nevertheless defers the explanation in an alternative manner.

Kant calls on Buffon's account of generation to illustrate the failure of epigenesis. As we saw earlier, Buffon denies that impulsion, growth, and reproduction cannot be accounted for by "the common laws of mechanism."[41] Yet instead of appealing to unknown mechanisms to explain organic processes, Buffon's commitment to materialism leads him to conclude that they must be "effects of laws of a different nature." On the assumption that organic processes are naturally caused, he proposes a physical hypothesis (interior moulds and organic particles) that supposedly provides "a satisfactory explanation of every species of reproduction."[42] Kant acknowledges that Buffon's mould hypothesis locates the generative process in the physical order of nature. Yet by introducing laws of a *different* nature, Buffon destroys the possibility of a *universal* natural history: "The internal forms proposed by *Buffon*, and the elements of organic matter which, in the opinion of *Maupertuis*, join together as their memories dictate and in accordance with the laws of desire and aversion, are either as incomprehensible as the thing itself, or they are entirely arbitrary inventions" (BDG 2:115). The non-material causes proposed by Buffon and Maupertuis exploit an analogy with human capacities (memory) or artefacts (moulds) to explain a process that seems to be non-mechanical, acquiring a determinate meaning when they are in fact empty. They neither extend our understanding of physical processes nor prompt further inquiry, but stand in for a process that is not yet understood.

---

[41] Buffon, *Histoire naturelle*, II 23.   [42] Buffon, *Histoire naturelle*, II 21.

Kant's contention is that the difference between the mechanist and the materialist accounts of generation is simply *when* a hyperphysical cause is used to explain physical phenomena. The mechanists assume an original act of creation, which explains the possibility of each kind of machine. The materialists posit internal forming causes to explain how organic matter is able to give form to itself. Neither takes us any closer to answering the question of the "natural manner of coming to be," by which Kant seems to mean the emergence of living natural products in nature conceived of as a single causal sequence (BDG 2:115). Kant's point is that, despite their differences, both attempts to explain the generative process fill a gap in our understanding and yet remain without a material element or *datum*. The natural philosopher can avoid this error by acknowledging that speculation alone cannot yield cognition of extant things. In contrast to a divine mind, which can determine an effect by positing its ground, finite human minds work back from effects to their grounds. Kant agrees with the materialist Newtonians that "one must concede to the things of nature a possibility, greater than that which is commonly conceded, of producing their effects in accordance with universal laws" (BDG 2:115). Yet he denies that one can move from this concession to a speculative claim about the condition of the possibility of generation. His position is closer to Haller's analogical Newtonianism, in which the natural philosopher refrains from speculating about the possibility of physiological movement and instead examines specific instances of such movement as effects of an unknown cause. When understood as a methodological requirement rather than an object of knowledge, the assumption that generation is law-governed enables the natural philosopher to search for physical connections between living natural products without positing a spurious cause. The standpoint of particular natural history is, once more, pragmatic. The goal is not one of completion but of discovery; in this case, the discovery of stable species lines behind the present variation.

In a bemusing text published in 1766, *Dreams of a Spirit Seer*, Kant develops this argument in a satirical response to the Swedish mystic Emanuel Swedenborg. One of Kant's aims is to assist his readers to distinguish between a genuine hypothesis and a spurious invention of the imagination (*ein Hirngespinst*). What, for instance, separates Newton's universal force of gravitation from the pneumatic forces postulated by the spirit seer? To answer the question, Kant distinguishes between two "advantages [*Vortheile*]" of metaphysics. The first advantage is that, to "solve the problems thrown up by the enquiring mind," metaphysics "uses reason to spy after the more hidden properties of things" (TG 2:367). Kant admits to having fallen in love with this advantage, for his ongoing reflection on features of reality led him to questions for which the answers transcend observation and experiment. Yet he acknowledges that it has hitherto failed to provide satisfactory answers. In fact, the use of reason to spy out hidden properties has led to all kinds of delusion, thereby inhibiting the progress of inquiry. The second advantage of metaphysics is "consonant with the nature of the human understanding" (TG 2:367). This advantage consists in "knowing whether the task has been determined by reference to what one can know, and in which all our judgments must at all times be used."

Here we see the consolidation of an immense turn in Kant's work, in which he reconceives metaphysics as a propaedeutic to positive inquiry rather than a positive inquiry itself. This second advantage of metaphysics is "the least known and the most important," and can be defined as "a science of the *limits of human reason*" (TG 2:368). To turn the unbridled use of metaphysics into a disciplined science is to take the questions that reason naturally raises about the inner nature of things and to determine whether such an inquiry lies within the limits of human knowledge. Kant affirms once more the separation between logical and real grounds, which shows that non-contradiction is insufficient to determine the reality of an intellectual idea. Human reason cannot, on its own, achieve determinate knowledge of intellectual objects, which means that it must be limited to the data given in experience. While he acknowledges that he has not yet sufficiently determined the boundary of human reason, Kant states that his provisional argument will at least "enable the reader ... to establish that he can spare himself the trouble of all futile research into a question, the answering of which demands *data* which are to be found in a world other than the one which he exists as a conscious being" (TG 2:368). To illustrate how the unreflective use of metaphysics can lead to "futile research," Kant returns to the problem of generation. The two main positions, he states, both fall prey to reason's deception: hylozoism, which "invests everything with life," and mechanism, which "deprives everything of life" (TG 2:330). Kant singles out Maupertuis as a representative of hylozoism, for he ascribes the lowest degree of life to the "organic particles of nourishment" that animals consume in order to explain the possibility of generation. Hofmann and Boerhaave represent mechanism, for they regard all particles as "nothing but dead masses" and use mechanical analogies (levers, pipes, etc.) to explain the possibility of generation. In Kant's view, both positions are deceived, for they attempt to satisfy reason's need for completion by applying an "illusion of one's imagination" outside of oneself such that "the figment of the imagination [*Hirngespinst*] is transposed as an object" (TG 2:344). For the hylozoist, the object is a living kind of matter subject to non-material laws. For the mechanist, it is a part of a functioning machine, the cause of which is unknown. Neither object takes us any further in understanding the generative process. Instead, the objective claims made by the materialist and the mechanist parade as knowledge and thus inhibit productive research. Swedenborg's claims about the spirit world thus serve as an allegory of the natural philosopher who postulates unknown forces to explain empirical effects. Such claims result from a "deception of reason," in which reason's drive for completion entices the natural philosopher to consider non-material forces as though they were objects.

Kant does not develop a positive view of hypothetical reasoning in *Dreams*. His primary goal is to alert the reader to the dangers of speculation. Newton is assumedly warranted to attribute attractive and repulsive forces to bodies due to extensive experimental support or "data" he is able to provide in *Principia*. We get some clue to what Kant has in mind when he praises Stahl for being "closer to the truth than *Hofmann* or *Boerhaave*" concerning the question of generation (TG 2:331). Hofmann and Boerhaave propose "mechanical causes" to explain the generative process, thereby locating hypothetical causes within the world of experience. Stahl, in contrast, employs "immaterial forces," which do not purport to complete inquiry but enable him to discern between various kinds of corporeal movement as effects of different forces. Kant proclaims that "this method alone...is of use in science," for it limits inquiry to the examination of effects, the data given in experience. Kant's point is once more that because reason is not directed at the world of sensation, it is incapable of discovering real grounds:

> It is impossible for reason ever to understand how something can be a cause, or have a force; such relations can only be derived from experience. For our rule of reason only governs the drawing of comparisons in respect of *identity* and *contradiction*. If something is a cause, then *something* is posited by something *else*; there is not, however, any connection between the two things here which is based on an agreement.   (TG 2:370)

Reason is directed at the world of cognition, which coordinates the data given in experience. Because causality is an existential relation, if the fundamental causes of things "are not derived from experience, then they are wholly arbitrary, and they admit of neither proof nor refutation." The only legitimate causal claims, Kant concludes, are those whose actuality can be confirmed in experience.

In his *Inaugural Dissertation* (1770), Kant clarifies the distinction between the world of sensation and the world of cognition by identifying a "fallacy of subreption" that occurs through the attempt to apply a concept proper to the intellect within the spatial and temporal conditions of sensibility (MSI 2:412).[43] The *Dissertation* marks a significant break from his earlier work, for it is the first time Kant explicitly separates sensation and understanding as two distinct cognitive faculties. Sensation is responsible for the "receptivity of a subject in virtue of which it is possible for the subject's own representative state to be affected in a definite way by the presence of some object" (MSI 2:392). The "definite way" in which the subject's representative state is affected is to bring to perception the forms of space and time. Here Kant integrates the pragmatic standpoint of

---

[43] In the student notes from Kant's lectures on logic given around the same time as the *Inaugural Dissertation*, Kant is reported to have identified the *vitium subreptionis* (the error of subreption) as the result of "mixing" concepts of experience and reason (V-Lo/Blomberg 24:255).

physical geography into his developing epistemology, from which time and place are not constituted by the relations between actual objects, as they are in *Universal Natural History*, but the forms in which it is possible for the human subject's representative state to be affected by things. The understanding, in contrast, is "the faculty of a subject in virtue of which it has the power to represent things which cannot by their own quality come before the senses of the subject" (MSI 3:392). This is to say that it represents objects in their "noumenal perfection," independent of the subjective conditions of sensibility. Each faculty has access to a distinct kind of object that is conditioned by its mode of cognition. Subject to the laws of sensibility, cognition is "sensible." Subject to the laws of the understanding, cognition is "intellectual."

Kant's distinction between sensible and intellectual cognition unearths a fundamental "lack of accord" between the two faculties, for they are directed at two different worlds (MSI 2:389). While the two worlds are connected, their relation is not as ground to consequent (subordination) but as parts to whole (coordination) (MSI 2:387–8).[44] The forms of intuition bring a non-conceptual order to perception, which assumedly serves to prepare the data of experience for conceptual coordination. The laws of the understanding then bring a conceptual order to the data of experience. The understanding's laws thus have what we might call a *normative superiority* over the laws of sensibility, for the relation between them is *prescriptive* and *asymmetrical*. Kant explains that whatever "*conflicts with* the laws of the understanding and the laws of reason is undoubtedly impossible," whereas "that which being an object of pure reason simply *does not come under* the laws of intuitive cognition, is not in the same position" (MSI 2:389). The normative superiority of the understanding means that it provides a "common measure" for things experienced in the sensible world, enabling one to coordinate the phenomena of sensation by drawing connections between sensible objects and bringing them under concepts. The objects of intellectual cognition, however, do not adhere to the forms of intuitive cognition.

While the lack of accord between the two worlds is mitigated by the coordinating role of the understanding, the result is a situation in which the very nature of the intellect disposes us to commit the fallacy of subreption. Because intellectual cognition is not intuitive but discursive, it is capable of conceiving of its object under conditions for which it is not suited. For instance, intellectual cognition can conceive of its object within the forms of intuitive cognition, as though it were an object of the sensible world. This move "rashly confers the conditions which are peculiar to the *subject*"—the conditions of sensibility—onto the object of thought (MSI 2:417). Such a confusion gives rise to "a counterfeit and erroneous axiom," for the conditions of sensibility do not legitimately apply to objects of thought but

---

[44] See Allison, *Kant's Transcendental Deduction*, 53.

only to objects of sense. For instance, if we take the sensible conditions of space and time as the conditions of the possibility of *any* object (either intellectual *or* sensible), we arrive at the axiom, "*Whatever is, is somewhere and somewhen*" (MSI 2:413). This axiom entails that the objects of thought, such as God, the world, and the soul, either exist somewhere in time and space or they do not exist at all. Yet the questions opened by such an axiom are "idle," Kant explains, for there are no possible data that could decide the matter. The subreptive axiom simply makes it *seem* like a compelling conclusion. Kant's claim is not that the axiom is false but that it is merely a subjectively valid principle. It does not present a necessary condition of *existence* but a necessary condition of *experience*. To be an object of sense is to be somewhere and somewhen. One of the basic tasks of metaphysics, understood as the science of the limits of human reason, is thus to prevent the application of sensible conditions to intellectual objects.

In the following section, I examine the implications of Kant's scientific conception of metaphysics for his account of natural history. If one conceives of the system of nature as a real causal sequence unfolding in space and time, two alternatives arise. The possibility of living natural products must be located either outside spatial and temporal conditions, thus removing generation from the physical system, or at a specific moment, thereby positing the existence of unexplained moulds or memories that unite various members within a line of descent.[45] Yet Kant's scientific metaphysics denies that the system of nature, conceived as an intellectual object, can be given in the conditions of sensibility. When time and space are understood as the forms in which it is possible for the subject's representative state to be affected by an object, and when the rational requirement for a complete series of conditions is understood as a prescription of the understanding, speculation about generation is strictly hypothetical. The upshot of Kant's scientific metaphysics, I argue, is that the conditions of particular physical geography—the conditions in which physical geographers reflect on the particular items they encounter—are no longer determined by nature conceived of as a self-creating process. They are determined by the conditions of sensibility combined with the understanding's coordinating function, which instruct physical geographers to seek physical-mechanical connections for the facts they encounter in the course of their experience. The pragmatic standpoint of physical geography thus becomes the starting point for natural history.

4.4 On Human Beings

The implications of Kant's scientific account of metaphysics for natural history can been seen in his response to the popular debate concerning human origins in

---

[45] See Sloan, "Buffon, German Biology, and the Historical Interpretation of Biological Species," 110.

the mid-1770s. Kant had included a section entitled "On Human Beings" in the second part of his physical geography lectures from the earliest recorded notes, in which he presents a history of human beings across the known world. The notes even record Kant speculating about the causes responsible for variation. He is recorded as explaining the darkness of skin as an effect of hot climatic conditions, which dries out the blood vessels, allowing light to harden the remaining blood (V-Geo/Holstein 1757/9 26.1:90–1). Further, he is recorded as claiming that once several generations have seen this effect, the acquired characteristics can become hereditary. Yet Kant's account of such alterations remains within the Linnaean framework. Acquired characteristics are "accidental," and their inheritance is "not easy to explain" (V-Geo/Holstein 1757/9 26.1:91). Proposing an analogy between humans and chickens (dark skin : humans = dark feathers : chickens), he suggests that it would be possible to select lighter children from darker parents to bring them back to their original colour. He echoes a widely accepted claim among natural historians that albinism provides evidence that white is the skin colour of the original race.[46] Variation in colour implies an accidental change from the original stem.

In 1775, Kant published an essay entitled "On the Different Races of Human Beings" as a new advertisement for his physical geography lectures.[47] The essay is a condensed version of "On Human Beings," and yet, as we saw in the Rink edition and Kaehler student notes, Kant updated his lectures with a physical concept of race in the academic year of 1774/5. Of course, Kant had already presented a hierarchical account of human variety without the concept of race (V-Geo/Holstein 1757/9 26.1:85–7). From as early as *Observations on the Feeling of the Beautiful and the Sublime* (1763), he publicly expressed a widely held view concerning the inferiority of non-white peoples, drawn from Father Labat's popular travel writings in America (BGSE 2:252–5).[48] Yet it is not until 1774 that Kant began to account for characteristics of varieties in the human species as the result of a physical process in which a localized generative force dynamically responds to particular geographical conditions. In this section, I argue that the key to Kant's account of race lies in his separation of Linnaean variation from

---

[46] See Maupertuis, *Venus physique*, 188–93; Buffon, *Historie naturelle*, III 502. For an analysis of Maupertuis' "scientific" account of albinism, see Terrall, *The Man Who Flattened the Earth*, 208, 338. In the following chapters we will see that Kant's assumption about the originality of whiteness shapes his historical reasoning about the characteristics of non-white races. In "Eurocentrism in Philosophy," Serequeberhan demonstrates that the use of albinism to justify the originality of whiteness is unsubstantiated by the evidence and reflects a thinly veiled prejudice of European superiority.

[47] The full title of the text is "Of the Different Races of Human Beings to Announce the Lectures on Physical Geography of Immanuel Kant, Professor Ordinarius of Logic and Metaphysics."

[48] Kant draws on Labat's writings to make several ungrounded assertions about the lack of aesthetic sense in non-white peoples. At one point he comments on a witticism attributed to an African carpenter: there "might be something here worth considering, except for the fact that this scoundrel was completely black from head to foot, a distinct poof that he was stupid" (BGSE 2:255).

Buffonian degeneration. However, while Kant emphasizes this separation to show his support for Buffon's explanatory system of natural history, I suggest that he goes beyond Buffon's tentative account of race in "On the Degeneration of Animals," which falls short of defining race as a real category. Because variation for Buffon is not produced by the inner mould, which remains constant, but is occasioned by changes in nutrition, climate, and mores, racial boundaries are not strictly enduring. When Kant decided to publish his 1775 announcement in the popular journal *Der Philosoph für die Welt* in 1777, the major contribution he sought to make to the human origins debate was to fix race as the physical sub-kind that fits under an original stem.[49] Kant's account of degeneration thus introduces a quasi-essentialist element to the concept of race that was absent in Buffon, giving rise to the first recorded version of what Michael Hardimon terms a *racialized* concept of race.[50]

Kant begins his essay by clarifying the role of "Buffon's rule" in his theory of classification, once more signalling his desire to replace Linnaeus' logical concept of variety with Buffon's physical concept of race (VvRM77 2:429). Buffon's rule, he states, is "that animals, which reproduce fertile young with one another (of whatever variety of form they may be), belong to one and the same physical species [*physisches Gattung*]." The concept of a physical species falls within a system that represents causal connections by which parents pass on adapted characteristics to their young. The Linnaean concept of variety had led many natural historians to adopt a polygenetic account of human origins, for, according to Linnaeus' theory of generation, enduring characteristics entail a distinct line of descent. Voltaire argued that the isolation of various people groups provides evidence for polygenesis.[51] Lord Kames proposed a history in which humankind

---

[49] For a telling examination of Kant's motivations for publishing the physical geography announcement in a popular *Aufklärung* journal, see Zammito, "Policing Polygeneticism in Germany."

[50] Hardimon states that a racialized concept of race "maintains that races have intrinsic biological essences, are distinguished by normatively important features such as intelligence and moral character, and can, on the basis of these features, be objectively ranked as superior and inferior." Hardimon, *Rethinking Race*, 2. That Kant was a pioneer of a racialized concept of race was first established by Eze and Serequeberhan in the 1990s. Their studies conclude that Kant's critical epistemology, on which his reasoning about racial difference is grounded, is therefore racist. While I agree that Kant was a pioneer of racialized race, in the remainder of this study, I argue that we must first identify the difference between the constitutive knowledge of experience and the empirical knowledge derived *through* experience before we can evaluate the effect of Kant's racism on the critical project. Bernasconi takes the fixity of Kant's race concept, and its reception over the following decade, as evidence for the claim that Kant "invented" the concept of race. On the interpretation I develop in this study, Bernasconi's narrative overdetermines Kant's role in the development of a racialized concept of race. Nevertheless, I agree that Kant was the first to provide the concept of race with a quasi-essentialist, physical grounding. See Bernasconi, "Who Invented the Concept of Race?," 15.

[51] "Thus it seems to me that I am justified in believing that it is with humans as it is with trees; that pear, pine, oak and apricot trees do not come from the same tree, and that white bearded men, that black woolly haired men, yellow men with manes and men without beards do not come from the same man." Voltaire, "Traité de métaphysique," 492.

was originally divided into several small tribes.[52] In contrast, Buffon contended that some physiological variations *become* enduring as a new sub-kind breaks away from the original stem. In *The Epochs of Nature*, the fifth supplement to *Histoire naturelle* (published in 1778 and translated into German in 1781), Buffon re-entered the human origins debate, arguing that the "races in each species of animal are only constant varieties which perpetuate themselves by generation."[53] This definition reinforced the physical dimension of the human origins debate, enabling natural historians to move from the present distribution of natural products to a science of bodies in time and space. Yet as Haller had pointed out in his preface to the second volume of *Allgemeine Historie der Natur*, Buffon's theory of generation could not in fact explain the mechanism for variation any more than it could account for the inheritance of acquired traits.[54]

Kant had already rejected Buffon's theory of generation on the grounds that it confused hypothetical reasoning with explanation. The formal conditions of nature presented in a universal natural history provides no reason to anticipate the existence of purposive forces in the system of nature. It is the actual encounter with *living* natural products, which exist as localized systems within the system of the earth, that leads natural historians to speculate about laws of a different nature. While Kant had affirmed Buffon's view that analogical reasoning about the causality of natural products can reach a level of probability equal to certainty, he now recasts analogical reasoning within the boundaries of human knowledge determined by scientific metaphysics. His diagnosis of logical subreption in the *Inaugural Dissertation* demonstrated that speculation about the cause of an effect is strictly hypothetical, for a cause cannot be given in sensation. The normative superiority of the understanding means that its concepts have a coordinating role, instructing us to examine the data given in sensation as effects of a force. In his essay on race, Kant applies this insight by showing that while the cause of a hypothetical generative force remains unknown, *assuming* such a force enables natural historians to present the variety of human form as natural history in his technical sense of the term.

Kant's basic move in the essay is to separate two kinds of variation: accidental variation, which occurs in a single natural product due to the contingencies of an environment, and variation that becomes necessary, for it is passed on without fail despite environmental change. The first kind of variation can be seen in birds that have the capacity to develop a moderate layer of feathers in mild climates or an additional layer if they migrate to a cold climate (VvRM77 2:434). Such birds

---

[52] In *Sketches of the History of Man* (1774), which was translated into German in 1775, Kames argued that the variation we find today, and the relative isolation of each group, indicates that "these original tribes were different races of men, placed in proper climates, and left to form their own language." Home [Kames], *Sketches of the History of Man*, I. I 75.

[53] Buffon, *Les Époques de la nature*, 252.

[54] Haller, "Reflections on the Theory of Generation of Mr. Buffon," 320.

invariably pass on the *capacity* to produce the appropriate layering of feathers, and yet the *expression* of that capacity is contingent on climatic factors. The second kind of variation entails that some acquired characteristics are passed on invariably, which can be seen in cases where populations have been artificially relocated. The enduring quality of skin colour was a case that caused particular difficulty for the Linnaean natural historians. Why is it that the African climate can darken the skin of its original inhabitants, and yet the Portuguese, who have lived in tropical Africa for several generations, remain as white as their compatriots in Lisbon?[55] Kant argues that we can derive the African and Portuguese populations from a common stem only if we assume a force that does not only pass on the *capacity* to alter its form, but also *the altered form itself.*

To account for such phenomena, Kant speculates that *two* forces, germs (*Keime*) and dispositions (*Anlagen*), were present in the original stem.[56] Germs were of course the hallmark of pre-existence, for they were used to explain the generation of organic structure according to a capacity already planted within the living natural product. Yet in practice they were an extremely mutable concept. Haller added his physiological faculties to explain how the essential parts of a foetus develop independently of one another, and become something quite different to what they were at first.[57] Charles Bonnet called on pre-existing germs as mechanical centres of organization that dynamically respond to environmental conditions.[58] Kant's account is different again, for germs are not posited as objects but as placeholders for an unknown cause of observed effects. Germs regulate the development or unfolding (*Auswickelung*) of a "particular part" of an organic body, and dispositions direct the "the size or the relationship of the parts among one another" (VvRM77 2:434). Kant's novel combination of two forces explains how a structuring power (a predisposition) acts upon specific pre-existing capacities (germs), such that an inner purpose is expressed in dynamic interaction with external conditions.[59]

---

[55] We find Kant raising this question in the earliest remaining lecture notes (see V-Geo/Holstein 1757/9 26.1:88). However, it is not until 1775 that he provides a physical explanation for the phenomenon.

[56] Here I follow Sloan's translations of *Keime* and *Anlagen*. Sloan explains that *Keime* was regularly used as the German translation for the French "germs," and *Anlagen*, which derives from the German *legen* meaning "to lay out," refers to an "organizational layout" or "disposition." Sloan, "Preforming the Categories," 240. See also Sloan, "The Essence of Race," 192–3. Kant is the first to use *Keime* and *Anlagen* together in this technical usage, combining the pre-existence idea of original germs with the epigenetic idea of unfolding development.

[57] Haller, *Sur la formation du coeur dans le poulet*, II 172. This was Haller's solution to the problems he identified in Buffon's theory of generation in the preface to the third volume of *Historie der Natur* in 1752.

[58] The cause of variation, according to Bonnet, is the fact that "all the germs of a single species are not developed in the same womb, at the same time, in the same place, in the same climate; in short, in the same circumstances." Bonnet, *Considérations sur les corps organisés*, 293.

[59] Sloan argues that Kant's addition of predispositions to the Haller-Bonnet theory of germs is Kant's "own coherent theoretical solution to the problem [of generation]." Sloan, "Preforming the Categories," 239.

Kant's account of generation enables him to clearly distinguish two kinds of cause that are often confused in Buffon's article on human variation: the "occasioning cause [*Gelegenheitsursache*]," which acts *on* a living body (air, sun, nutrition, etc.), and the "producing cause [*hervorbringende Ursache*]," which effects a change in a part (germs) or in the relation between the parts (dispositions). The conjunction of external conditions and inner generative forces shows that accidental variation is insufficient to determine a race. A race, on Kant's definition, is a line of descent that branches out from an original stem in which some adaptations, over long periods of time, are passed on invariably if both parents possess the acquired property.[60] To explain this phenomenon, Kant speculates that different germs are triggered to make a group "fitted [*anpassend*]" or "suited [*angemessen*]" to its environment as determined by the need to "preserve [*erhalten*]" the species (VvRM77 2:434–5). The agreement of form and environment cannot, Kant attests, be the result of "chance or the universal mechanical laws." Air, sun, and nutrition can modify the shape of the body and the relation of the parts, but they cannot explain how this change could be reproduced in subsequent generations. To account for the inheritance of acquired characteristics, Kant argues that the producing cause must have the capacity to solidify in a certain state, such that the "purposive adaptations" become fixed. The unity of isolated groups occurs because the expressed germs shut the others off, such that alternative forms that *were* possible in the beginning are now "turned off" or "held back."[61] The invariable inheritance of such adaptations become the "mark [*Merkmale*]" and "distinguishing feature [*Kennzeichen*]" of their "generative origination [*Erzeugung*]" as a distinct racial group. Acquired characteristics can change only through interbreeding, which, according to Buffon's rule, marks the boundary of a species. To bring the manifold variety of human form into a physical system, Kant identifies four "base races [*Grundracen*]" that have derived from a single "stem species [*Stammgattung*]."

Kant's conjectures about human origins are pragmatic. He was well aware that Linnaeus did not intend the fourfold system to describe the empirical phenomena

---

[60] Kant uses the term "race" to refer to a particular kind of "degeneration [*Abartung*]" that persistently reproduce themselves despite relocation to a new environment. The Wilson and Zöller translation of the relevant passage is misleading, even if one considers the German footnotes provided in the text. My rendering is as follows: "An animal species [*Thiergattung*] which at the same time has a common stem [*gemeinschaftlichen Stamm*] contains under itself not different kinds [*Arten*] (since the latter signify precisely the differences of the original stem [*Abstammung*]); rather, their divergences [*Abweichungen*] from one another are called degenerations [*Abartungen*] if they are hereditary [*erblich*].... Among the degenerations [*Abartungen*], i.e., the hereditary differences of the animals which belong to a single stem [*Stamm*], those which persistently preserve themselves in all transplantings (transpositions to other regions) over prolonged generations among themselves and which also always beget half-breed [*halbschlächtige*] young in the mixing with other degenerations [*Abartungen*] of the same stem [*Stamme*] are called *races* [*Racen*]" (VvRM77 2:430).

[61] For an account of Kant's reasons for emphasizing the enduring quality of adaptation, see McLaughlin, "Kant on Heredity and Adaptation," 284–6.

but rather to provide natural historians with a practical tool with which to make evaluations of the present diversity of human form. Indeed, when Buffon attempted to capture the actual diversity of human form in "Varieties in the Human Species," the reader is confronted with so many different races that they are left in a state of wonderment and yet with little understanding.[62] Kant's argument is that his "conjectures...have at least sufficient grounds to counterbalance other conjectures which find the differences in the human species so incompatible that they rather assume on that account many local creations" (VvRM77 2:440). His conjectures merit the confidence of his readers, for, in contrast to his opponents, they offer a *history* of nature:

> The description of nature [*Naturbeschreibung*] (condition of nature at the present time) is far from sufficient to indicate the ground for the manifold variations. No matter how much one opposes, and rightly so, the boldness of opinions, one must venture a *history* of nature [*eine* Geschichte *der Natur*], which is a separate science and which could gradually advance from opinions to insights.   (VvRM77 2:443)

Kant's argument is that one *must* venture a history of nature, for it is the only way to develop a physical system that consistently follows the understanding's instruction. Here Kant strains to find a vocabulary capable of expressing the need for historical reflection and yet the impossibility of such a programme taking on the completion to which the understanding aspires. Natural history does not produce a complete system made up of deductive inferences in which every material thing is logically necessary. Rather, it seeks the physical connections manifest through the continuous reproduction of particular natural products with certain observed capacities. Natural history is therefore genealogical, carving up nature according to "natural divisions" in time and space "from the standpoint of generation" (VvRM77 2:429). The key to classification is not the synchronic affinities between external marks but the diachronic unity of a stem that connects varieties in a line of descent, thereby transforming "scholastic species [*Schulgattungen*]" into "natural species [*Naturgattungen*]." From the standpoint of generation, natural history will "lead us back from the great number of seemingly different kinds [*Arten*] to races of the same species [*Gattung*] and transform the presently overly detailed system [*weitläuftige Schulsystem*] for the description of nature into a physical system for the understanding" (VvRM77 2:435n).

---

[62] Buffon, *Histoire naturelle*, III 371–530. For an English translation of the article, see chapter IX of the fourth volume of *Barr's Buffon* (1792). However, the reader of Barr's translation should be aware that it omits the extensive citations to colonial and missionary travelogues in the original, giving the false impression that the extensive observations were made by Buffon himself. The citations are retained in the second volume of Kästner's German translation.

When applied to the question of human origins, Kant's scientific account of metaphysics has a double effect. On the one hand, it diagnoses the human tendency to postulate immaterial forces and places strict limits on the epistemic status of natural history. Kant presents his history of the human races in language appropriate to hypothetical inquiry: "one is only compelled to *assume* four races of the human species in order to be able to derive from these all the easily distinguishable and self-perpetuating differences" (VvRM77 2:432; my emphasis). This fourfold schema is not meant to be a descriptive account of actual human variation but rather a working assumption with which natural historians can make further physical divisions. On the other hand, scientific metaphysics identifies a practical standard by which a system can move from opinion to insight (one is *compelled* to assume). While his system is based on hypothetical forces, Kant claims that he can defend his position against opponents, for it is best equipped to unify the manifold of human form under laws, and thereby satisfy the understanding.

Yet Kant's system is only best equipped to unify the manifold if one shares at least three of his assumptions: (1) that the physical, moral, and temperamental characteristics described in the travelogues are the effects of *natural* causes (physical geohumoralism), (2) that those characteristics are the markers of distinct communities that developed in isolation on the four continents of the earth (racial purity), and (3) that white is the original and superior race (white superiority). While Kant believes that he has evidence for (3) (Mauperuis and Buffon's study of albinism), however spurious it might be, (1) and (2) reveal his near complete reliance on the "reports" documented by world travellers. Kant seems to be wholly impervious to the fact that his selected travelogues do not exclusively describe the effects of nature. Many of the travel writings he calls upon—indeed, many of those that provide the foundation for Linnaeus' and Buffon's classificatory schemes, which form the empirical basis for Kant's own account—describe local systems of social stratification produced by the purity of blood laws enforced under colonial administration in the early sixteenth century.[63] These laws were used to separate colonial subjects by what the colonists took to be isolated lines of descent marked by skin colour, thereby constructing the allegedly "natural" characteristics depicted in the travelogues through human laws. Others describe the communities of indentured labourers and former slaves in the colonies and Americas, and were explicitly written to shape colonial policy. Kant is blind to what Michel Foucault would later call the "biopolitics" of racialized groups, according to which human laws and power relations construct the supposedly "natural"

---

[63] Mazzolini for instance documents the travel writings from Latin America available to Linnaeus, Buffon, and Kant. These writings describe stratified social systems (*las castas*), which result from the transcription of late Medieval Iberian purity laws to the colonies. Mazzolini, "Inter-Racial Crossing and Social Structure (1770–1835)," 349–74.

order. Kant's racialized concept of race is thus co-determined by the understanding's prescription to seek physical conditions *and* the human laws established to satisfy the European obsession with racial purity, thereby providing that obsession with scientific grounding.[64]

With the general readers of the popular journal *Der Philosoph für die Welt* in mind, Kant defends his physical system of classification by showing how it provides a more sophisticated account of the well-known Linnaean schema than his opponents.[65] The result is a physical rendering of geohumoralism in which exterior form, interior constitution, temperament, and moral characteristics are not the accidental effects of environmental conditions but the productive effects of a generative force. Several comments in a letter to Johann Jacob Engel in 1779 indicate that Kant was aware that public interest tracked accounts that could combine physical classifications with moral and temperamental markers. He informs Engel that his "principles of a moral characterization of the different human races will serve to satisfy the taste of those who do not particularly pay attention to the physical aspects" (Br 10:256). In his 1777 essay, Kant attempts to explain both the physical and moral aspects of the human races by appealing to the four elements of Galenic medicine (hot, wet, cold, and dry), following the Linnaean tradition of deriving human qualities from various elemental combinations.[66] Yet in contrast to Linnaeus, Kant does not think that the properties of the elements are the producing cause of qualitative human change. The preponderance of a particular element in an environmental niche is merely the occasioning cause, prompting a dynamic response in human bodies from the interplay of germs and their dispositions. For instance, the hot and wet conditions of Africa (the occasioning cause) trigger the germ responsible for black skin and a strong and supple body (the producing cause) to degenerate from the original stem. Alternatively, the abundant conditions produced in warm, humid environments result in a race that is "lazy, soft and trifling" (VvRM77 2:438).[67] The upshot of Kant's physical system of classification is that Africans are not

---

[64] There is evidence to suggest that Kant's essays on race, by providing scientific legitimacy to travelogues and colonial reports, aided pro-slavery arguments in the 1790s. See Bernasconi, "Defining Race Scientifically," 144–5.

[65] Larrimore suggests that Kant's strategy is to demonstrate the power of his physical system of classification by demonstrating how it provides a scientific foundation for a schema that would "look familiar" to his readers. Larrimore, "Race, Freedom and the Fall in Steffens and Kant," 112. Linnaeus was not the first to connect physical and temperamental variation; it was commonplace in early modern travelogues. Nevertheless, he gave experimental credence to geohumoralism by offering causal reasons for the preponderance of one humour over the others, which Kant then transcribes onto a physical plane. See Müller-Wille, "Linnaeus and the Four Corners of the World," 192.

[66] For an analysis of Kant's use of the Socratic elements, see McLaughlin, "Kant on Heredity and Adaptation," 285. Note, however, that McLaughlin overlooks the Galenic tradition of medicine that Kant, following Haller's conception of life forces, aims to subvert.

[67] For an analysis of Kant's description of Africans and Amerindians as "lazy," see Lu-Adler, "Kant on Lazy Savagery, Racialized."

phlegmatic, as Linnaeus had proposed, but sanguine; and it is this temperamental profile, Kant extrapolates, that explains their reported inability to discriminate value.

Kant does not interrogate the connection between temperamental and physical characteristics he encountered in the travelogues. This is not because he was a passive adherent to the assumptions of his time. Several experimental philosophers challenged the geohumoralist connection between temperamental and physical characteristics long before Kant dabbled in medical science. Locke for instance described the Galenic humours as "learned empty sounds," which parade as knowledge but are mere inventions of the mind.[68] The humours are "suppositions taken up gratis," Locke claims, hypotheses that guide the mind of the physician but do not explain medical phenomena. Kant also recognized the explanatory deficiencies of humoralism. Yet instead of challenging the geohumoralist assumption that physical, temperamental, and moral characteristics are causally contiguous, he transcribes it into the framework of physical geography such that the diversity of human life can be explained as the effect of occasioning *and* producing causes. The pernicious results of this transcription are particularly evident in Kant's history of the Amerindian race. While he affirms the Linnaean classification of Amerindians as "reddish [*rubescens*]," Kant follows Buffon by offering a physical explanation of this phenomenon.[69] He infers that the Amerindians must have originally migrated from northern Asia, for the "red-brown color" of their skin ("an effect the aerial acid [*Luftsäure*]") is suited to a cold climate, while the "olive-brown color" ("an effect of the alkaline-bilious [*Laugenhaft-Galligten*] nature of the fluids") is suited to the newer, hot climate. Yet in contrast to Buffon's account, Kant's hypothetical germs ensure that this skin colour, along with the temperamental chrematistics that have co-developed with it, is now fixed. And because their migration to America supposedly occurred after some of the germs became fixed, Amerindians are deemed to be an "incompletely adapted race," a condition that is betrayed by their "half extinguished life force" (VvRM77 2:438). They are not choleric, as the Linnaean schema would have it, but have a mixed and unstable temperament, unsuited for the development of culture.

Kant's scientific conception of metaphysics is unable to prevent the proliferation of hypotheses we see in his essay on race. In fact, it motivates his unsavoury claims. Scientific metaphysics denies that an effect can be posited through its

[68] Locke to Dr. Thomas Molyneux, 20 January 1693, in Locke, *The Correspondence of John Locke*, 629.

[69] In "Varieties in the Human Species," Buffon accounts for the small number of Amerindians, along with their "ignorance and the little progress the most civilized among them have made in the arts," as follows: "All the Americans have sprung from the same stem, and they have, with little variation, retained the characteristics of their race…because, their climate, with respect to heat and cold, is not so unequal as that of the old continent, and because, being newly established in the country, the causes by which varieties are produced have not had time to manifest their effects." Buffon, *Histoire naturelle*, III 510–1.

cause. However, the normative superiority of the understanding instructs us to seek a cause for adaptive changes ("we *must* venture a history of nature"), prescribing a mandate to fill in the gaps in the system projected by the understanding. When faced with the descriptions recorded in the travelogues, which capture the physical, moral, and temperamental characteristics of isolated people groups as natural effects, Kant infers that reason is compelled to postulate occasioning and producing causes and thereby to transform natural description into natural history. His derogatory remarks about the enduring temperaments of non-white peoples betray an enthusiasm to fill in the causal template projected by the understanding with claims that reflect his ungrounded assumptions. The social, political, and economic implications of his race concept are not accidental. As a work of physical geography, Kant's aim is to orient his students within the diversity of humankind by giving them a concept that captures differences in genealogical descent, social standing, and moral character. The task of *Weltkenntnis* is to enable budding world citizens, whose cultural progress will empower them to overcome the naturally defined boundaries of their race, to understand *why* non-white races have not developed states that promote universal ideals, and thereby to know how to behave towards members of those races in the course of their global endeavours. Kant's physical geography reveals a profound failure to see that the prejudice of white superiority actively prevents social progress and extends inequality. Indeed, it cloaks the malicious effects of white prejudice in the guise of nature.

One of the questions to be considered in the remaining part of this study is whether Kant's critical philosophy, which solves several problems remaining in his nascent science of metaphysics, bolsters or resists the hypotheses defended in his essays on race. In the following chapters, I argue that Kant's concept of race can be seen as an important application of the methodological rules outlined in the Transcendental Dialectic, for it gives expression to the contradictory demands of reason to seek ultimate explanations and yet to restrict scientific inquiry to appearances. Yet I also argue that as Kant worked out the implications of his critique, it became increasingly difficult to defend the fixity of racial boundaries and the corresponding natural-humoral explanation of racial characteristics. I argue that by the time he published *Critique of the Power of Judgment* in 1790, Kant recognized that his racialized concept of race could not be supported on rational grounds. While this does not prevent him from continuing to hold racist views, it opens his physical system of classification to empirical scrutiny. The impact of Kant's critical philosophy on his account of natural history will occupy us in the final part of this study.

PART III
CRITICAL PHILOSOPHY AND SCIENTIFIC METHOD

5

Seeking Order in Nature

Scholars generally consider Kant's motivation for undertaking a critique of pure reason in the context of debates unfolding at the Berlin Academy concerning the scientific status of metaphysics[1] and the concerns raised by his early reviewers.[2] In this chapter, I suggest that Kant's critical philosophy can also be understood against the background of methodological questions concerning the use of hypotheses in natural history, in which the problem of unifying phenomena under concepts, and locating those concepts within a system of knowledge, was an ongoing matter of dispute. Recall Haller's preface to the first volume of Kästner's translation of *Histoire naturelle*, in which he criticizes two kinds of natural philosophers: those who search exclusively for certainty, and thus restrict inquiry to what can be demonstrated mathematically, and those who build fictitious sky castles, in which every hypothesis depends on a further hypothesis. Claiming that both kinds of philosophers stifle genuine progress, Haller proposes an alternative, which he dubs a "theoretician of nature":

A theoretician of Nature acts like a land surveyor, who begins a map on which he has determined some locations, but lacks the positions of other places in between. [He] nevertheless makes an outline [*Umriss*], and according to half-certain reports, indicates the remaining towns, of which he still has no mathematical knowledge. If he had made absolutely no sketch [*Entwurf*] in which he combined the certain and uncertain [components] in one composition, then his work of determining more exactly the locations and boundaries which still remained

---

[1] I have in mind here Kant's engagement with Mendelssohn, Lambert, and Tetens concerning the prize question of the Berlin Academy in 1764, which asked whether metaphysics could receive the same standard of proof as geometry, and, if not, what kind of certainty it could achieve. While Kant's argument in the *Critique* certainly engages at length with a local set of questions concerning the grounding of cognition, I argue that it also engages with broader questions concerning human understanding in natural history, which are summarized in Haller's preface to Buffon's *Histoire naturelle*. In "Kant on Empirical Schemata," Williams makes a similar case in regard to the schematism chapter. My focus here will be on the Transcendental Dialectic and Doctrine of Method.

[2] For instance, the first review of the *Critique*, appearing via Feder in the *Göttingischen Anzeigen von gelehrten Sachen* in January 1782, focuses on the nature of Kant's idealism, which supposedly "transforms the world and ourselves into representations." Anon., "The Göttingen Review," in Sassen, *Kant's Early Critics*, 53.

Kant and the Transformation of Natural History. Andrew Cooper, Oxford University Press. © Andrew Cooper 2023.
DOI: 10.1093/oso/9780192869784.003.0006

would be much more difficult and almost impossible. Indeed, it would not have been possible, because [the work] would have no coherence, and would constitute no whole.[3]

Haller's theoretician provides a model for Buffon's German readers to critically examine the histories presented in *Histoire naturelle*. While these histories clearly involve speculation (think of Buffon's mechanical hypothesis regarding the origin of the solar system), the theoretician *must* begin with a provisional sketch if they are to seek beyond their familiar horizon for unknown or half-certain towns. Haller calls on Kepler's unfounded conjecture that the sun has an attractive virtue, which enabled him to uncover the laws of celestial motion, and Linnaeus' "arbitrary ruling principles," which led to his discovery of the generative unity of species according to their sexual organs.[4] In every major advancement in natural history, he claims, a system "poses an innumerable quantity of questions which we can pose to Nature, and which it very often answers."[5] Haller's point is that "if we did not fill in the missing parts with probabilities, and construct a building instead of a ruin," then the distinct parts of human knowledge would be nothing but "fragments and independent pieces without connection and unification."[6] Yet his theoretician also serves to warn Buffon's German readers, for it implies that a conjectural history, no matter how consistent, cannot verify itself. Hypotheses are "still not the truth," Haller attests. Yet they can "lead to it."

My interpretive claim in this chapter is that Kant's critical epistemology can be read in continuity with the set of issues Haller evokes in his cautious endorsement of hypotheses in natural history.[7] Like Haller, Kant affirms Buffon's conviction that natural history does not progress by collecting more and more facts. As he notes in the B Preface, the great breakthroughs in our understanding of nature occur when reason formulates a design by which it can "compel nature to answer its questions" (Bxiii). Yet Kant's scientific method begins one step prior to Buffon's general sketch of the earth's formation, which simply assumes that nature is amenable to our cartographical endeavours. By determining the limits of possible experience, Kant's goal is to ensure that our hypotheses do not merely "grope about [*herumtappen*]" in search of answers to reason's questions, but adhere to a method by which progress can be expected (Bvii). Consider the following passage from the Doctrine of Method, where Kant provides a similar

---

[3] Haller, "Preface to the German Translation of *Histoire Naturelle*," 304.
[4] Haller, "Preface to the German Translation of *Histoire Naturelle*," 301.
[5] Haller, "Preface to the German Translation of *Histoire Naturelle*," 304.
[6] Haller, "Preface to the German Translation of *Histoire Naturelle*," 301.
[7] This is not a causal claim. While in previous chapters, I have presented evidence that Kant read Haller's preface (see especially Section 3.2), Haller gives voice to a set of issues that can also be found in the work of several of Kant's interlocutors, including Linnaeus, Du Châtelet, Buffon, and Maupertuis.

account of hypotheses to that which we saw in *Dreams* and the *Inaugural Dissertation*, yet with one important difference:

> If the imagination is not simply **to enthuse** but is, under the strict oversight of reason, **to invent**, something must always first be fully certain and not invented, or a mere opinion, and that is the **possibility** of the object itself. In that case it is permissible to take refuge in opinion concerning the actuality of the object, which opinion, however, in order not to be groundless, must be connected as a ground of explanation with that which is actually given and consequently certain, and it is then called an **hypothesis**. (A770/B798)

The worry Kant shared with practically every experimental philosopher following Bacon is that the imagination, untethered from experience, is liable to produce spurious inventions that have no legitimate object of reference. While he joined the chorus of philosophers who were convinced that Newton's rules for reasoning held the key to scientific progress, Kant recognized that Newton's interpreters had hitherto been unable to agree on a method to define which hypotheses—if any— are acceptable in a programme of research. Building on the argument presented in *Dreams*, Kant once more seeks to distinguish between spurious fictions and genuine hypotheses. However, while in *Dreams* he had asserted that a legitimate hypothesis is one that can be confirmed by the data of experience, Kant now introduces an additional constraint on legitimate hypothesizing. A hypothesis is legitimate if the *possibility* of its object is certain.[8] This possibility does not simply refer to logical possibility, which tells us that contradictory things (round squares, warm-blooded reptiles, etc.) cannot exist. It includes the sphere of *real* possibility, understood as conformity to the conditions of possible experience.

Before we proceed, it is important to recall that scholars generally interpret Kant's critical philosophy as a deliberate retreat from his earlier work on natural history.[9] On this interpretation, Kant's critical turn removes the hope of a genuine history of nature and affords a thin conception of natural history much closer to his earlier conception of natural description. In Part III of this study, I present an alternative account of the implications of Kant's critical turn for natural history. In Part II, I argued that Kant, in his pre-critical writings, was already alive to the disparity between the study of particular natural products and universal natural

---

[8] For an analysis on the modal constraint Kant places on legitimate hypothesizing, see Allison, *Kant's Transcendental Deduction*, 41.

[9] Sloan argues that Kant's critical philosophy provides "grounds for rejecting a historical science of nature." Sloan, "Kant on the History of Nature," 629. Lagier accounts for this transition as the outworking of the narrow conception of proper science outlined in *Metaphysical Foundations*, arguing that the "principles that materialized in this period are in fact the result of a process of *purification* of the possible sciences." Lagier, *Les Races humaines selon Kant*, 140. Zammito takes a stronger line still, describing Kant's work on human origins during the 1780s as a "*historical* retreat." Zammito, "Teleology Then and Now," 749.

history. I suggested that his physical geography was not in tension with the general conditions of nature determined by his dynamic account of matter, but featured as a pragmatic level of inquiry concerned with particular natural products. Furthermore, I showed that in the 1760s Kant began to develop a scientific metaphysics in which the conditions of empirical inquiry are not determined by matter understood as extended substance but by the formal conditions of sensibility and the intellect, which instructs us to build a physical system consisting of real connections between objects in time and space. The claim that Kant's critical philosophy stages a retreat overlooks two key concerns in his pre-critical work, which, I argue in what follows, are refined during the critical period: (1) to distinguish between mere conjecture and legitimate hypotheses, and (2) to determine the rules for reasoning in natural philosophy that enable genuine disagreement about historical claims.

In Section 5.1, I begin with Kant's account of synthetic *a priori* knowledge of objects in general, which constrains legitimate hypothesizing to the form of possible experience. While this constraint determines how hypotheses ought to relate to appearances, it does not tell us how they ought to relate to other laws and observed phenomena. To reconstruct Kant's positive account of hypotheses, we must turn to his examination of reason's regulative use in the Transcendental Dialectic. In Sections 5.2 and 5.3, I propose a normative interpretation of reason's regulative use, according to which the empirical use of ideas is both legitimate, for ideas merely prescribe the relations between appearances and their conditions, and necessary, for they indicate the context of intelligibility in which the understanding can be coherently deployed. In Section 5.4, I examine the disciplinary rules Kant presents in the Doctrine of Method to ensure that scientific knowledge is kept free from transcendental illusion. I argue that these disciplinary rules serve to ensure that natural history is scientific in the sense that it presents a physical-mechanical (and thus explanatory) system. While Kant denies natural history the status of a proper science, in which every part would be cognized *a priori* from the objective grounds of the understanding, this restriction directs us to evaluate our reasons for assenting to hypotheses. The success of this restriction will be determined by the extent to which Kant can convince us that, without it, there can be no touchstone against which we can come to agreement in matters of historical reasoning.

5.1 The Objective Validity of the Understanding's Concepts

In Section 4.3, we saw that, during the 1760s, Kant became increasingly aware that natural philosophy was shot through with speculative metaphysics. In *Dreams* he argued that both the mechanical and materialist Newtonians commit an error that occurs when an intellectual concept (such as God or the world) is applied to the spatial and temporal conditions of sensibility. His solution was to separate sensibility and the understanding as two distinct cognitive faculties, each directed at a different world; the first world populated by sensible objects in space and time, the second by intelligible objects connected as consequents and grounds. While the concepts of the understanding have a coordinating role, for they arrange the sensibly given phenomena in the form of a system, Kant denied that the concepts of the understanding have a legitimate application to sensibility, for they cannot be the source of the principles that govern the interaction between sensible objects.[10] This left a problem that Kant raised in a letter to Marcus Herz in 1772. How do the concepts of the intellect "agree with" what is given in the conditions of sensibility (Br 10:130)? The missing element in his treatment of sensible cognition is an account of how we come to know (through the understanding) the object we are affected by in sensibility.[11] Kant illustrates the problem with the concept of causation.[12] The connection between cause and effect is such that the effect does not merely "come along with" the cause, as one representation follows another in time. Rather, an effect is posited *through* its cause, and follows necessarily from it. If sensible objects are simply given one after the other, how could we know that one *causes* another?

In *Critique of Pure Reason*, Kant proposes a radically different account of the mind's faculties according to which sensibility and the understanding are *both* involved in cognition. His proposal is motivated by a threat that arises due to the problem of agreement. If we maintain a separation between sensible and intellectual representations, then the former "might very well be so constituted that the understanding should not find them to be in accordance with" its own conditions (A90/B123). If such were the case, our cognitive faculties would lie in "confusion," for the succession of sensible representations tells us nothing "that would furnish a rule of synthesis and thus correspond to the concept of cause and effect." The understanding's concepts (such as causation) would be "empty, nugatory, and without significance [*Bedeutung*]," for they would be heterogeneous to the conditions of sensibility. Kant's aim in the *Critique* is to demonstrate that the intellect's concepts can only agree with what is given in sensation if space and time are not transcendentally real objects but the forms of human sensibility. If

---

[10] This is Lambert's important feedback on Kant's argument in *Inaugural Dissertation*. Lambert claims that Kant's twofold account of cognition raises "the question of *generality*: namely, to what extent these two ways of knowing [sensibility and the understanding] are so completely *separated* that they *never* come together" (Br 10:105).

[11] For an account of how Kant's letter to Herz identifies the fundamental problem motivating the *Critique*, see Schulting, *Kant's Deduction and Apperception*, 15–19.

[12] In *Prolegomena*, Kant explains that Hume originally led him to raise this question by showing that the causal connection we habitually make between two different things takes a constant conjunction given in sensibility for a metaphysical relation whereby one thing determines another thing by necessity. Hume's critique, Kant recounts, prompted him to recognize that when an intellectual concept is considered in isolation from the conditions of sensibility, it is "nothing but a bastard of the imagination" (Prol 4:258). See Hume, *An Enquiry Concerning Human Understanding*, IV II 16, 43.

space and time are not real objects but merely the forms in which objects are given to us, then the understanding would not apply its concepts to things "*as they are*," as Kant had claimed in the *Inaugural Dissertation* (MSI 2:392; cf. A258/B313–4). It would apply its concepts to things *as they appear*, that is, as they are given in the spatial and temporal conditions of sensibility. Such judgements would be synthetic, requiring that the manifold given in intuition "first be gone though, taken up, and combined in a certain way in order for a cognition to be made out of it" (A77/B102). The synthetic use of judgement would place different representations together to comprehend their manifoldness in one cognition. While the act of synthesis would be pure, for "the manifold is given not empirically but *a priori*" (A77/B103), cognition would be discursive, that is, the appearance of spatio-temporal objects.

Kant's claim is that if we assume that objects are not mere aggregates of perceptions but *a priori* determined entities, a new procedure becomes available that can provide "satisfactory proofs of the laws that are the *a priori* ground of nature, as the sum total of objects of experience" (Bxix). These proofs consist of the transcendental deduction of the understanding's concepts, which, by explaining how these concepts relate to objects *a priori*, demonstrates their validity for every object of possible experience (A85/B117). Concepts relate to objects *a priori* to the extent that the understanding applies them to appearances through transcendental schemata, procedural rules by which the imagination provides a concept with its image (A179/B140). In the Analogies of Experience, for instance, Kant examines the concepts that enable the understanding to reflect on the relations among appearances. The Analogies "compare" logical relations (including substance-accident, cause-effect, and agent-patient) with the relations found in intuition, and thereby generate *a priori* cognition of "dependence" or "conditioning" relations among appearances.[13] Cognitions are "conditioned" in the sense that they have dependence relations prescribed by the understanding's relational concepts.[14] For example, the schematized concept of substance provides a procedural rule for finding something in intuition that persists, and for distinguishing it from its accidents. The schematized concept of causality provides the procedural rule for finding the necessary connection of determinate features in time, either as cause to its effect or as parts to their whole. And the schematized concept of community provides the procedural rule for finding the necessary connection of determinate features in space, as coexisting in mutual interaction. Kant's claim is that for substance, causality, and community to belong to appearances, despite not being found among them, the relational categories must be *a priori* and

---

[13] For an account of the analogical character of the relational categories, see Kraus, *Kant on Self-Knowledge and Self-Formation*, 203.

[14] For an account of the various relations captured by Kant's generic notion of a condition, see Stang, *Kant's Modal Metaphysics*, 289.

synthetically connected to perception. Such categories are "objectively valid," that is, the necessary conditioning relations for objects of possible experience (A89–90/B122).

Kant's contention is that objects are not independently existing things to which we have only limited access. This is the view of the transcendental realist, who considers the objects to which our knowledge must conform as things in themselves, and thus for whom the grounding of cognition remains a problem. The transcendental idealist considers objects as appearances (*Erscheinungen*), things as they appear to a representing subject.[15] Experience is governed by synthetic *a priori* laws that are dependent on knowing minds and yet necessary for possible objects. This places a serious constraint on what we can legitimately hypothesize about them. Minimally, a hypothesis is legitimate if it is not simply *logically* possible but also *really* possible, where "real" things are those that are given in the conditions of sensibility (see A19/B33). Because we can know *a priori* that sensible objects are spatio-temporal and that they adhere to the structure of objecthood determined by the categories, we are justified on the appearance of a conditioned object to assume that there is a condition.

Real possibility places a negative constraint on legitimate hypotheses: legitimate hypotheses are propositions that conform to the conditions of possible experience. However, it does not inform us how hypotheses should relate to other hypotheses and observed phenomena. To use Haller's terms, it does not tell us how the theoretician is justified in making an "outline" to connect known towns with those for which we have only half-certain reports, and in explaining how those parts feature within the whole. For instance, the understanding does not anticipate that conditioned cognitions appear within a totality of conditions, such as an empirical regress of causes and effects. The totality of conditions cannot be given as an object of cognition, for it corresponds to a completeness that extends beyond the conditions of sensibility. In Kant's critical account of the cognitive faculties, the idea of explanatory completeness lies not with the understanding but with reason, a distinct faculty that instructs the understanding to seek the "unconditioned" for whatever "conditioned" thing it encounters (Bxx). In some cases, reason's demand for the unconditioned takes the form of an unconditioned object that lies outside any particular series of conditions, such as God (the ground of all grounds), the soul (the unity of inner appearances), or the world (the totality of empirical conditions). Because such objects cannot be given in the conditions of sensibility, they are not *real* in the sense that they can appear in sensible form. Rather, they are *ideas*, logically consistent concepts of objects that require a

---

[15] The implications of this claim are, of course, an ongoing matter of debate. Here I build on Allais' account, according to which an object is a mind-dependent appearance of things that we cannot know apart from their appearance. Allais, *Manifest Reality*, 35. For an overview of the various positions, see Oberst, "Two Worlds *and* Two Aspects," 53–75; Gardner, *Kant and the Critique of Pure Reason*, 271–9.

completeness that cannot be given in experience (A313/B369–70).[16] The Transcendental Analytic thus solves the problem of agreement inasmuch as it demonstrates the objective validity of the understanding's concepts, which can be applied to appearances via transcendental schemata. It does not, however, vindicate the agreement of reason's ideas with conditioned objects.

In the Transcendental Dialectic, Kant identifies a way that we can legitimately think of the objects of experience as conditioned by conditions that are not given by the understanding. This is to think of them as appearing within a totality of empirical conditions—to think of them as *empirical objects*, whose conditions lie beyond what is immediately given—which is made possible by the regulative use of reason's ideas.[17] So far we have seen that, in the Transcendental Analytic, Kant demonstrates that we cannot cognize the way that things are in themselves; human cognition is cognition of spatio-temporal objects as appearances.[18] For the main part of the Transcendental Dialectic, Kant is concerned with the errors that occur when reason's ideas create a deception that tempts us to hypostasize them as transcendent objects. Yet this negative task has a positive result. By limiting cognition to the conditions of sensibility, Kant transforms the spurious objects of metaphysics into legitimate and "indispensably necessary" rules that guide the understanding beyond that which is immediately given to it (A644/ B672). Or so I will argue.

5.2 The Transcendental Dialectic

The main part of the Transcendental Dialectic is dedicated to exposing a tendency in human reason to assume that reality corresponds with the form of rational thought (A297/B353). Kant diagnoses this assumption as a "transcendental illusion," which comes about when "the subjective necessity of a certain connection of our concepts on behalf of the understanding is taken for an objective necessity, the determination of things in themselves" (A297/B354). To take a connection of the understanding's concepts as an objective necessity would purport to *a priori* cognition of things in themselves, which Kant denied in the Transcendental Analytic by limiting cognition to appearances. This mistake is not exclusive to metaphysicians, who make explicit claims about transcendent objects. Kant insists that human reason has a "natural and unavoidable" tendency to make claims about things in themselves, including the empirical qualities of objects and the

---

[16] For an account of Kant's use of ideas in the Appendix to the Transcendental Dialectic, see Stang, *Kant's Modal Metaphysics*, 289.

[17] Kant states that the regulative use of reason prescribes that "we ought to **seek after** the constitution and connection of objects of experience in general" (A671/B699).

[18] As Allais puts it, Kant's claim is that "we can cognize *only* essentially manifest features of reality." Allais, *Manifest Reality*, 125.

process of their generation. While the first task of critique is to expose this tendency and to render it harmless, Kant also seeks to show that it has a legitimate "immanent" or "regulative" use, and, moreover, that this regulative use is in some sense "necessary" (A644/B672).

Kant's account of reason's regulative use raises serious interpretive difficulties, leading commentators to radically different views concerning the role of reason in empirical inquiry.[19] The debate has served to reinforce the negative view of Kant's account of natural history, for it implies that Kant's critical examination of reason's principles (procedural rules that contain ideas as concepts, and thereby organize the manifold of cognitions) either reduces the classification of the understanding's cognitions to a merely logical procedure, rendering his account of empirical knowledge as something akin to Locke's associationism, or blatantly contradicts the teaching of the Transcendental Analytic. In this section, I examine a central issue in the debate—the role of illusion in reason's empirical use—by considering two influential readings of the Transcendental Dialectic: Michelle Grier's "strong" or "illusory" reading, and Marcus Willaschek "weak" or "methodological" reading.[20] While both readings seek to vindicate a positive use of reason's ideas, I suggest that neither fully succeeds in showing how this use is both legitimate and necessary. This is because Grier and Willaschek share the assumption that reason's ideas, if they are to guide the understanding, must be adopted *as hypotheses*, which purportedly describe the connections between conditioned cognitions and their conditions. Rejecting this assumption, I propose a normative reading that separates the hypothetical use of reason from the formulation of explanatory hypotheses, such that reason's ideas do not *describe* the connections between objects and their grounds, which lie beyond the reach of the understanding, but merely *prescribe* the relations between appearances and their conditions, for which the understanding must seek.[21]

Let us begin with Grier's reading of reason's regulative use, which ascribes a positive role to the illusion Kant identifies in the Transcendental Dialectic. Grier's reading centres on the so-called "transition passage" in the introduction, where Kant presents two formulations of reason's law. Kant begins by stating that because reason does not legitimately apply to objects but rather seeks to unify

---

[19] Key points of dispute include the lawfulness of empirical laws, the transcendental status of reason's principles, and the role of illusion in reason's empirical use.

[20] Ypi describes the two readings as "weak" and "strong," emphasizing their metaphysical implications. Ypi, *The Architectonic of Reason*, 103. Kraus and Spagnesi characterize the narrower debate concerning the role of illusion in empirical inquiry according to "illusory" and "methodological" accounts. Kraus, *Kant on Self-Knowledge and Self-Formation*, 190–3; Spagnesi, "A Rule-Based Account of the Regulative Use of Reason in Kant's *Critique of Pure Reason*," 3–5.

[21] My account builds on several recent normative readings of reason's regulative use, including Massimi, "Grounds, Modality, and Nomic Necessity in the Critical Kant"; Breitenbach, "Laws and Ideal Unity"; Kraus, *Kant on Self-Knowledge and Self-Formation*; Spagnesi, "The Idea of God and the Empirical Investigation of Nature."

the laws of the understanding, it is "prescriptive" and "subjective" (A306/B362). The subjective law can be defined as reason's "logical maxim":

Logical Maxim: find the unconditioned for conditioned cognitions of the understanding, with which its unity will be completed.   (A307/B364)

The Logical Maxim is subjective in the sense that it expresses a conceptual requirement that does not apply directly to objects but governs the use of the cognitive faculties. It instructs the understanding to unite its conditioned cognitions in a series of rational inferences, bringing "the great manifold of cognitions of the understanding to the smallest number of principles (universal conditions), and thereby to effect the highest unity of the manifold" (A305/B361).[22] The structure of the system is *a priori*—what Kant terms "the form of a whole of cognition"[23]—and yet, because it is not applied to objects, it is metaphysically innocent (see A832/B860).[24] The Logical Maxim is simply a "subjective law of the economy for the provision of our understanding" (A306/B362), telling us not about the constitution of objects but about the structure of thought.

However, Kant then claims that the Logical Maxim can only operate as a principle of pure reason if one "assumes [*annimmt*]" that it possesses objective validity, that is, if one assumes that appearances *are* arranged according to real connections (A307/B364). This step is clearly taken by Buffon, for his general natural history presupposes that objects are physically connected in time and space. Yet Kant contends that it is also taken by Locke and Linnaeus, who take classificatory divisions to be artificial precisely because they stand in contrast to real connections in the system of nature.[25] Kant's point seems to be that for the understanding to act on reason's demand, reason's subjective law must be transformed into a synthetic principle that connects conditioned cognitions with a complete series of conditions. Kant describes this formulation of reason's law the "supreme principle of pure reason," "supreme" in the sense that it cannot be derived from other principles that are independently certain:

Supreme Principle: when the conditioned is given, then so is the whole series of conditions subordinated one to the other, which is itself unconditioned, also given (i.e., contained in the object and its connection).   (A308/B364)

---

[22] Allison, *Kant's Transcendental Idealism*, 311.

[23] The "**systematic** in cognition . . . presupposes an idea . . . of the form of a whole of cognition, which precedes the determinate knowledge of the parts and contains the conditions for determining *a priori* the position of each part and its relation to the others" (A645/B673).

[24] Walden, "Reason Unbound," 575.

[25] In the Appendix to the Transcendental Dialectic, Kant states that natural philosophers who search for species, genera, and families within the manifold of cognition presuppose reason's principles (specification, homogeneity, and continuity) as *transcendental* principles (A652/B681). I discuss this presupposition in Section 5.3.

The Supreme Principle is "obviously **synthetic**," Kant explains, for it relates the conditioned object of experience to the unconditioned. If we take Kant's use of "given" to refer to the way that objects are given by intuition—intuition allows us to represent and think about real or existent objects (A19/B33)—then the Supreme Principle carries serious ontological implications.[26] It would require that if the conditioned *exists*, then the unconditioned also *exists*.

Scholars have struggled to understand Kant's claim that following reason's requirement to order the manifold of cognitions means that we must assume that the whole series is "given." Many readers of the Transcendental Dialectic have concluded with Norm Kemp-Smith that the "teaching of this section is extremely self-contradictory," for it seems to endorse the transcendental use of reason's ideas.[27] Yet Grier contends that the illusion generated by the transcendental use of reason's ideas has a legitimate, even necessary function in Kant's account of empirical knowledge. On her reading, the inference from the logical to the real use of reason is a "slide from a principle expressing a subjective necessity to a 'transcendental' principle asserting an objective necessity."[28] This seems to be implied by Kant's insistence that the errors arise through a "misunderstanding," whereby reason's logical law is "taken for a transcendental principle of reason, which overhastily postulates such an unlimited completeness in the series of conditions in objects themselves" (A309/B366). While the misunderstanding is indeed a form of transcendental illusion, Grier claims that it is nonetheless legitimate, for it does not promote transcendent metaphysics but merely the empirical use of the understanding. In fact, Grier stresses that the Supreme Principle *must* be adopted as a constitutive principle if the understanding is to search for the particular qualities of empirical objects. The Supreme Principle, she states, serves as the "application condition" of the Logical Maxim, implying that the transcendental principle must be synthetically applied to what is given in intuition if the understanding is to seek the empirical conditions of its conditioned cognitions.[29] Kant's position is thus "tantamount to claiming that the regulative function of the principle of systematic unity is itself parasitic upon the transcendental and illusory postulation that nature, as an object of our knowledge, is

---

[26] This is how Stang and Willaschek interpret the Supreme Principle. Stang, *Kant's Modal Metaphysics*, 290; Willaschek, *Kant on the Sources of Metaphysics*, 72–3. Alternatively, I suggest that this is one step in Kant's move towards a *regulative* formulation of the Supreme Principle.

[27] Kemp-Smith, *A Commentary to Kant's Critique of Pure Reason*, 547. For similar conclusions, see Strawson, *The Bounds of Sense*, 229; Pippin, *Kant's Theory of Form*, 211; Horstmann, "Why Must There Be a Transcendental Deduction in Kant's *Critique of Judgment*?," 166.

[28] Grier, *Kant's Doctrine of Transcendental Illusion*, 122. This interpretation implies that the dialectical errors that lead reason into transcendental illusion are ultimately grounded in the Supreme Principle. For instance, Grier states that the Supreme Principle is the "projection" of the Logical Maxim, meaning that the latter is "objective because it is presented as holding of 'objects themselves'." Grier, *Kant's Doctrine of Transcendental Illusion*, 277.

[29] Grier, *Kant's Doctrine of Transcendental Illusion*, 126. Similar accounts can be found in Allison, *Kant's Transcendental Idealism*, 330; Boehm, "Kant's Regulative Spinozism," 314.

already given as a complete whole."[30] This is to say that reason's principles are, like the understanding's concepts, descriptive, and purport to relate to things. Their use is indispensably necessary, for, by describing the real conditions of objects, which lie beyond the remit of possible experience, they bind the understanding to follow its lead.

While Grier's reading explains how reason's ideas can be binding on the understanding, it has difficulty telling us how the empirical use of transcendental principles is legitimate. A central implication of her reading is that reason's ideas apply to things in themselves, thus endorsing a positive use of the transcendental illusion Kant unambiguously seeks to diagnose and diffuse (A297/B354). Willaschek criticizes Grier for advocating a legitimate use of transcendental illusion, and argues instead that a transcendental principle, used regulatively, need not be illusory. On his reading, the Supreme Principle does not result from a mistaken "slide" but consists rather of the "regulative use of a transcendental principle," which, while presenting the understanding with an illusion, carries no metaphysical implications.[31] Willaschek stresses Kant's distinction between the constitutive and the regulative use of reason, such that a transcendental principle need not refer to a real series if it is to guide reflection on the manifold. In the Appendix to the Transcendental Dialectic, Kant explains that an idea is used constitutively when a universal rule assumed as a hypothesis is judged to be true, such that the consequents of the rule necessarily follow. An idea is used regulatively, in contrast, when it is used to bring unity to the cognitions of the understanding by "approximating" a universal rule (A647/B675). Consider an example from Kant's discussion of reason's cosmological ideas in the Antinomies, where he identifies a legitimate regulative use of the principle of totality in which the complete series of conditions is not given "as a thing in itself" but is "merely **given as a problem** in the regress of this series" (A508/B536). When the complete series of conditions is given not as a thing in itself but merely as a problem, the principle of totality operates as "a **rule**, prescribing a regress in the series of conditions for given appearances, in which regress it is never allowed to stop with an absolutely unconditioned." It is not a "**constitutive principle**," which would extend the concept of the sensory world beyond possible experience, but "a **regulative** principle of reason," for it is not "given in itself in the object (in the appearances)" (A509/B537). Willaschek claims that the difference between *mere* illusion and *transcendental* illusion turns on how the universal is taken—as certain and given, or assumed as a problem—such that illusion is merely the "enticement" to error, not the error itself (A293/B350).[32] A transcendental illusion is a particular species of illusion that occurs when we mistake the subjective principles of

[30] Grier, *Kant's Doctrine of Transcendental Illusion*, 275.
[31] Willaschek, *Kant on the Sources of Metaphysics*, 112.
[32] Willaschek, *Kant on the Sources of Metaphysics*, 136.

reason for constitutive principles of nature, which are supposed to be true descriptive statements about objects. Yet Kant never says that a transcendental law must be constitutive.[33] Deployed regulatively, reason's descriptive principles operate as hypotheses that guide the understanding to seek further connections within a series that is given. Yet for all we know, those principles may be false; nature may not be amenable to reason's needs.[34]

Willaschek rightly demonstrates that a transcendental principle need not be constitutive if it is to guide the understanding. However, I am not convinced that his account adequately distinguishes the use of reason that leads to transcendent metaphysics from the legitimate and necessary use of reason in empirical inquiry.[35] Willaschek's reading implies that the Supreme Principle *purports* to be objectively valid, thereby instructing us to consider appearances *as* appearing in an empirical regress.[36] Thus, while it avoids the transcendental illusion evoked by Grier, for it maintains that transcendental principles, used regulatively, are only hypothetically descriptive of nature, Willaschek's reading nevertheless entails that we must adopt transcendental realism *as a hypothesis*.[37] This is to say that for the understanding to investigate empirical nature, we must *consider* the empirical regress as given.[38] Thus Willaschek's reading does not satisfactorily explain why reason's ideas are legitimate, for a legitimate hypothesis, according to Kant, consists of an opinion that is "connected as a ground of explanation with that which is actually given and is consequently certain" (A770/B789; see Section 5.4).[39] Indeed, Kant clearly states that reason's ideas cannot be legitimately formulated as hypotheses, for they "have no object of any sort of experience" (A771/B800).[40] If an idea were to be used as a hypothesis, it would have to be *possibly* true of nature, and adhere to the model of causality anticipated by the

---

[33] Willaschek, *Kant on the Sources of Metaphysics*, 112.

[34] Geiger describes such readings as "methodological," for they operate conditionally in the context of a research project. Geiger, "The Assumption of a Systematic Whole," 274. For prominent examples, see Horstmann, "Why Must There Be a Transcendental Deduction in Kant's *Critique of Judgment*," 165–8; Guyer, "Reason and Reflective Judgment," 21–34.

[35] I came to this view while reading Spagnesi, "A Rule-Based Account of the Regulative Use of Reason in Kant's *Critique of Pure Reason*," 5.

[36] Willaschek, *Kant on the Sources of Metaphysics*, 107; cf. Grier, *Kant's Doctrine of Transcendental Illusion*, 275.

[37] "If we use them [reason's principles] regulatively, we do not accept them as true (nor, of course, do we reject them as false) but rather hypothetically employ them in order to generate hypotheses about objects in nature." Willaschek, *Kant on the Sources of Metaphysics*, 116.

[38] It thus matches Kant's description of the transcendental realist, who "makes **mere appearances** into things in themselves" (A491/B519).

[39] As Spagnesi argues, it is not clear how a prescription based on an illusory presumption is less deceptive than a prescription based on a transcendent claim. Spagnesi, "A Rule-Based Account of the Regulative Use of Reason in Kant's *Critique of Pure Reason*," 4.

[40] Indeed, at several points in the Dialectic Kant clearly states that reason's ideas can never be used in direct relation to objects, for the totality of conditions thought in ideas cannot be given in experience. For instance: "Reason never relates directly to an object, but solely to the understanding and by means of it to reason's own empirical use, hence it does not create any concepts (of objects) but only orders them and gives them that unity which they can have in their greatest possible extension, i.e., in relation

understanding. To use an idea of reason to explain a conditioned cognition would bypass the understanding, and "thus be no explanation at all" (A772/B800). And even if reason's principles could be used as hypotheses, it is unclear how a proposition that is potentially false could rationally bind us. It may be beneficial for a particular project of inquiry to find out whether a hypothesis is correct, but it is hardly rationally binding that we do so.

The question confronting interpreters of the transition passage is whether it is possible to assume that when the conditioned is given, so the whole series of conditions is also given, without succumbing to transcendental illusion. In the next section, I follow Willaschek's lead by interpreting the transition from the Logical Maxim to the Supreme Principle through Kant's notion of "presupposing [voraussetzen] a transcendental principle" in the Appendix (A651/B679). Yet in contrast to Willaschek's methodological interpretation, I argue that to presuppose a transcendental principle is not to present an object beyond the conditions of sensibility, such as an empirical regress. Kant is clear that reason's ideas "cannot say **what the object is**, but only **how the empirical regress is to be instituted** so as to attain to the complete concept of the object" (A510/B538).[41] I interpret this passage to mean that reason's ideas prescribe how the empirical regress is to be instituted, not in the sense that they give a particular concept of the object that the understanding must find, but in the sense that they give the relation of an appearance to a condition as "a **problem** for the understanding" (A508/B536). This is to say that the relation of an appearance to a condition is not given *as an illusion* that the understanding must seek to determine. Rather, it is given "for the subject in initiating and continuing, in accordance with the completeness of the idea, the regress in the series of conditions for a given conditioned."[42] Reason thus guides the empirical use of the understanding without positing an empirical regress by instructing the understanding to "seek such disclosures and to keep on assuming them even when they do not immediately reveal themselves to the senses" (A657/B685).

5.3 The Indirect Objective Validity of Reason's Ideas

In the Transcendental Analytic, Kant demonstrated that the concepts of the understanding, though mere forms of thought, validly apply to objects to the

---

to the totality of series" (A643/B671; see also A670/B698). For a similar criticism of Willaschek's argument, see Spagnesi, "A Rule-Based Account of the Regulative Use of Reason in Kant's *Critique of Pure Reason*," 5.

[41] Here I have in mind something akin to Massimi's distinction between *I-Archetype* and *I-Rule*, where *I-Archetype* is "illusory" in the sense that it presents an object, and an *I-Rule* is a projected point that enables us to achieve the greatest unity of the understanding's cognitions. Massimi, "What Is This Thing Called 'Scientific Knowledge,'" 66.

[42] Spagnesi calls this the "Regulative Supreme Principle," which clarifies that the Supreme Principle is not valid for appearances but simply for the actions of the understanding. Spagnesi, "A Rule-Based Account of the Regulative Use of Reason in Kant's *Critique of Pure Reason*," 8.

extent that they relate to appearances through transcendental schemata. In the Transcendental Dialectic, he explains that in contrast to the understanding's concepts, reason's ideas cannot be schematized, for no empirical representation can possibly correspond to them (A567/B595). Yet if reason's ideas cannot be schematized, there is no way they could validly apply to objects in the manner Kant describes in the Transcendental Analytic. Nevertheless, in the Appendix to the Transcendental Dialectic he argues that ideas can have an "indirect" objective validity (A665/B693), which can be understood in contrast to the way in which reason relates to that which is given "directly" in intuition. In the Transcendental Aesthetic, Kant claimed that "all thought, whether straightaway (directe) or through a detour (indirecte), must ultimately be related to intuitions,…since there is no other way in which objects can be given to us" (A19/B33). In contrast to the concepts of the understanding, which are *directly* valid for objects, reason's ideas are *indirectly* valid, for they show "not how an object is constituted but how, under the guidance of that concept, we ought to seek after the constitution [*Beschaffenheit*] and connection [*Verknüpfung*] of objects of experience in general" (A671/B699). This is to say that ideas instruct the understanding to examine sensible objects as *empirical objects*, whose conditions lie beyond what is immediately given to it.

Kant's argument in the Appendix shares the ambiguity of the transition passage, yet he makes no mention of the Logical Maxim or Supreme Principle. Instead, he claims that there is a "**logical** principle" that requires that we strive to unify our cognitions "as far as this can be done," even though we cannot legitimately claim that objects themselves are rationally unified (A648/B676). Such a claim would be "a **transcendental** principle of reason, which would make systematic unity not merely something subjectively and logically necessary, as method, but objectively necessary." At first glance, the logical and transcendental principles seem to map onto the regulative and constitutive uses of reason's ideas.[43] This would suggest that if a principle of reason were used transcendentally, it would be a condition of the possibility of experience, synthetically applied

---

[43] Willaschek terms this the "identification reading," which suggests that a principle of reason can be transcendental, and thus have objective validity, only if it is used constitutively. Willaschek, *Kant on the Sources of Metaphysics*, 111. The identification reading has driven many commentators to argue that reason can have no legitimate transcendental use: Kant's claim that we must presuppose the Supreme Principle relapses into transcendental realism (see footnote 27). It has also led commentators to the opposite conclusion: Kant's notion of presupposing a constitutive principle is a genuine condition for the application of empirical concepts, anticipating the reflecting use of judgement in *Critique of the Power of Judgment*. For examples, see Geiger, "The Assumption of a Systematic Whole," 278; and Allison, *Kant's Transcendental Idealism*, 436. I have sympathies for the latter reading, as it places Kant's argument in greater continuity with the transcendental principle of the third *Critique* (see Section 7.1). However, it is problematic as an interpretation of the Appendix, for it contradicts Kant's account of experience in the Transcendental Analytic. Unlike the categories of the understanding, the ideas of reason have no sensible schema that would allow us to apply them directly to empirical objects (A670/B698). Ideas cannot be directly applied to objects, but rather prescribe the empirical actions of the understanding.

to appearances.[44] A transcendental principle would thus be a descriptive constitutive principle, and to "presuppose" or "assume" it would be to take it as a true claim about the objects of experience. Yet as Willaschek has shown, Kant does not think that a transcendental principle needs to be constitutive. I propose that neither does he think that a transcendental principle needs to be determinate and descriptive; it can be *indeterminate* and *prescriptive*.

We can get a clearer sense of what it means to presuppose a transcendental principle—and why it is both legitimate and necessary to do so—by examining Kant's notion of the "indeterminate" objective validity of the three logical principles of reason: specification, homogeneity, and continuity (A663/B691). Kant explains that the three logical principles stand above the distributive unity of concepts required by the understanding, so as to guide the understanding's actions (A651–4/B679–82). Specification states that "every **genus** [*Gattung*] requires different **kinds** [*Arten*], and these **sub-kinds** [*Unterarten*]" (A655/B683). This law requires that we always divide higher classifications into more specific ones. Yet Kant then states that if the law is to guide the actions of the understanding, we must presuppose that there are always further "disclosures and to keep on assuming them even when they do not immediately reveal themselves to the senses" (A656/B684). This is the "transcendental **law of specification**," which does not demand an "actual **infinity**" of sub-kinds but rather "impose[s] on the understanding the demand to seek under every kind that comes before us a sub-kind, and for every variety smaller varieties." The law of specification is transcendental in the sense that, by assuming it, we are instructed to *seek* sub-kinds under every kind; it "demands a ceaseless continuing specification of its concepts."

To place a limit to our search for ever greater specification, reason issues the principle of homogeneity: "several kinds must be treated only as various determinations of fewer **genera**" (A652/B680). Homogeneity is akin to the law of parsimony, and "guards against excess in the manifold variety" by recommending the "sameness of kind" (A660/B688). It pertains to reason's interest in universality and explains why we continue to search for fundamental properties despite the apparently infinite variety we encounter (A652/B680). Yet if the understanding is to examine the manifold of phenomena in search of higher concepts, up to the limit of a single power underlying all phenomena, it must presuppose that nature holds together as a single material substance (cf. A582/B610). There could not be a logical principle of homogeneity "unless a transcendental principle is presupposed, through which such a systematic unity . . . is assumed *a priori* as necessary" (A650–1/B678–9). The transcendental assumption does not describe objects

---

[44] Kant seems to imply this in two important passages, where he states that without assuming the unity of nature as a transcendental principle, "no empirical concepts and hence no experience would be possible" (A654/B682; A651/B679). See Guyer, "Reason and Reflective Judgment," 28–9.

understood as things in themselves. It simply "limits in turn this inclination to unanimity, and demands that one distinguish sub-kinds before one turns to the individuals with one's universal concepts" (A660/B688).

The principles of homogeneity and specification pertain to reason's two interests that are in conflict with each other: "on the one side, an interest in the **domain** (universality) in regard to genera, on the other an interest in **content** (determinacy) in respect to the manifold of kinds" (A654/B682). If one were to take the two principles as constitutive principles that describe what is the case, they would form an antinomy. If one were to take them as hypothetical principles that potentially describe what is the case, they would *still* form an antinomy, for both could not be true. As maxims that guide the understanding's actions, however, homogeneity and specification refer merely to reason's divergent interests, and can thus be united under a third principle: "there is a continuous transition from every kind to every other through a graduated increase of varieties" (A657–8/B685–6). Again, Kant insists that continuity must be presupposed as a transcendental principle if reason is to reach any one concept from any other by ascending from a lower concept to another that is high enough to then descend back to the other via a different route. Assumed transcendentally, continuity prescribes "even in the case of the highest manifoldness a sameness of kind through the graduated transition from one species [*Spezies*] to others, which shows a kind of affinity of various branches, insofar as they have all sprouted from the same stem" (A660/B688). If we suppose that there is an infinite and yet continuous variation among natural forms, then we find that any variety we distinguish can nevertheless be subsumed under a higher concept due to a property they share.[45]

Taken together, the three principles serve to "make systematic the unity of all possible empirical actions of the understanding" (A664/B692). Notice that the referent of reason's principles are not objects themselves but rather the empirical actions of the understanding. Used regulatively, the principles do not describe a systematic unity that the understanding must seek. If so, then homogeneity and specification would contradict each other, and the empirical actions of the understanding would lie in confusion. Rather, the principles coordinate the empirical deployment of the understanding by acting as the "**analogue** of a schema" (A665/B693). In the Transcendental Analytic, the schemata of sensibility serve to allow the understanding to unify the sensory manifold under concepts (A141/B180). While there can be no schema of an idea, for no representation can ever correspond with them, the principles of reason operate *analogously* to schemata by demanding the "**maximum** of division and unification of the understanding's cognition in one principle" (A665/B693). Here Kant strains to find a vocabulary to

---

[45] See Guyer, *Kant's System of Nature and Freedom*, 19.

articulate how judgement can operate without determining that something *is* the case, and, instead, provide the form of reflection that corresponds to the idea.[46] Ideas act schematically insofar as they offer procedural rules that aid the understanding to maximally unify appearances according to an empirical regress or homogeneity of kinds. This is what Kant means when he states that ideas are "indeterminate": in its empirical use, reason's ideas "seem to be transcendental," even though the understanding can follow them "only asymptotically, as it were, i.e., merely by approximation, without ever reaching them" (A653/B681).

In the broader context of this study, Kant's argument in the Appendix can be viewed as an attempt to determine a legitimate and necessary use of reason in natural philosophy, which had hitherto evaded experimental philosophers in the eighteenth century. Kant achieves this not by establishing that things *are* arranged purposively—indeed, he emphatically states that we must not mistake reason's principles for descriptions of reality—but by demonstrating that the understanding must *presuppose* a purposive unity of things, lest it fail to bring the sensory manifold into maximal unity. Kant explains that the ideas of reason are "grounded only as analogues of real things, but not as things in themselves" (A674/B702). This is to say that the ideas give only the relation of an appearance to something that remains unknown, not the thing itself.[47]

Kant calls on Newton's method in *Principia* to exemplify the legitimate use of reason in natural philosophy. On Kant's reconstruction, Newton follows the principle of homogeneity by proposing a "fundamental force [*Grundkraft*]" behind every particular bodily motion to unify the distribution of forces. This is not to issue a descriptive claim but rather to present "the problem" of whether, by assuming a single *kind* of force (Newton's second rule), the understanding might be able to unify "the manifoldness of forces" (A649/B677).[48] Newton's analogy opened a series of hypotheses against which consequences that *are* given can be tested. While it is the understanding that provides the idea of a force, for it requires that appearances are given causal explanations, reason adds the

---

[46] In the third *Critique*, Kant settles on a new conceptual vocabulary to explain this form of reflection, namely, the "symbolic" use of judgement. He explains that there are two modes of presentation by which judgement uses concepts sensibly: "either **schematic**, where to a concept grasped by the understanding the corresponding intuition is given *a priori*; or **symbolic**, where to a concept that only reason can think, and to which no sensible intuition can be adequate, an intuition is attributed with which the power of judgment proceeds in a way merely analogous to that which it observes in schematization" (KU 5:351).

[47] See Spagnesi, "A Rule-Based Account of the Regulative Use of Reason in Kant's *Critique of Pure Reason*," 10–1.

[48] In his lectures on logic, Kant is recorded as describing this move as an analogical form of reasoning, which seeks to infer "from some predicates of the things to all the remaining ones" (V-Lo/Dohna 24:777). The inference is made "*ob paritatem rationis* [because of the equality of the ground]." For an account of the logical and aesthetic functions of judgement in Kant's lectures on logic, see Nassar, "Analogy, Natural History and the Philosophy of Nature," 248–9.

constraint of unity, requiring the minimization of pure forces. No matter how many moving objects Newton could have experienced, without the transcendental presupposition of reason's principles there could be no coherent use of the understanding with respect to empirical laws (A653–4/B681–2). If, through comparison, the understanding is able to find contingent affinities—for instance, that different effects are compared and found to be instances of the same kind of force—then we can provisionally infer the "universality of the rule" (Newton's third rule). The systematic unity of reason, deployed as the principles of specification, homogeneity, and continuity, is thus not a hypothesis, from which we seek to derive additional hypotheses. It is the condition of the possibility of the understanding's coherent use. The principles are indispensably necessary, for, without their indeterminate objective use, the understanding would be unable to seek the conditions of its conditioned cognitions.

So far we have seen that reason's ideas, deployed as transcendental principles, coordinate the activities of the understanding such that it can search for the conditions of its cognitions within a system of conditions. In the second part of the Appendix, Kant returns to his critique of physicotheology to show that the greatest harmony that reason and the understanding can achieve is to conceive of this system of conditions as a *physical-mechanical* system. He begins by explaining that the highest formal unity that reason can achieve is "the **purposive** unity of things" (A686/B714). Purposiveness refers to a species of causality whereby a concept is said to cause an object; in a machine, for instance, the arrangement of the parts is caused by a concept of the whole. As logical principles, the purposive unity prescribed by specification, homogeneity, and continuity is a structural feature of our knowledge; they instruct us to place cognitions in a system in which every part is a member of the whole. Yet once more Kant undertakes the transition we have been tracing in the Appendix, by which reason's ideas must be assumed as transcendental principles if the understanding is to bring its cognitions into maximal unity and extension. To seek a purposive unity of *things*, we must presuppose that the universal laws of nature (i.e. the material-mechanical laws of the understanding) are arranged according to a schema of the whole, *as if* that unity "had sprouted from the intention of a highest reason."

Kant is clearly aware that this transition, if not checked by critique, leads to transcendental illusion. The first task he undertakes is to diagnose the errors that occur if one mistakes purposive unity as a constitutive principle. If the idea of the purposive unity of things is adopted constitutively, reason is led to the fallacious inferences made by the physicotheologians, who consider "the shape of the earth, . . . its mountains, seas, etc., to be wise intentions of a world-author" (A687/B715). The constitutive use of the principle is "lazy," for reason thinks that it "can take a rest, as though it had fully accomplished its business" (A689–90/B717–8). Reason obviously has *not* accomplished its business, for the constitutive use of purposiveness would entail that the shape of the earth is contingent in relation to the understanding's laws.[49] If the systematic unity of nature is taken to be the product of design, then the order of appearances is "entirely foreign and contingent in relation to the nature of things and it cannot even be cognized from the universal laws thereof" (A693/B720). A vicious circle arises when the principle of purposiveness is used constitutively, for one "presupposes what really ought to have been proved" (A693/B721).

Kant's strategy is once more to transform the spurious objects of metaphysics into legitimate and necessary rules that expand the empirical use of the understanding. Transformed into a regulative principle, the purposive unity of things instructs the understanding to view appearances as empirical objects that arise within the constraints of the world system, such that the shape of the earth and the formation of mountains and seas "are designated only in a way that is more or less discernible by us" (A692/B720). Assuming the purposive unity of things does not explain the existence of mountains and seas as parts of a whole. Rather, it instructs the understanding to find out *how* mountains and seas feature as parts of a whole, that is, it instructs the understanding to view mountains and seas not simply as empirical objects, whose conditions lie beyond what is immediately given to it, but also as *natural products*, whose conditions are generated within nature understood as a self-producing system. In contrast to the understanding's laws, which are descriptive and constitutive, the purposive unity of things does not "determine beforehand" but is something that we "expect while pursuing the physical-mechanical connection according to universal laws" (A691–2/B719–20).

What Kant means by a "physical-mechanical connection" is underdeveloped in the Appendix; a problem he will seek to amend in the third *Critique* (see Section 7.1). Remaining with the Appendix for now, what I take Kant to mean by "physical-mechanical connection" is a causal relation within nature understood as a physical-mechanical system in which the particular laws that govern certain kinds of objects are admixtures of pure laws that arise within the empirical regress, even though many, if not most of the inferences between the pure laws and the empirical laws are unknown. In this sense, Buffon's "History and Theory of the Earth" provides a better example of the regulative use of purposive unity than Newton's *Principia*, for it seeks to determine the physical conditions of planetary motion. By rejecting design as a legitimate cause, and by assuming that the world system has been autonomous since the initial diffusion of matter, Buffon refuses to conflate the idea of purposive unity with the concept of a complete object. He is thus driven to formulate a series of physical hypotheses, according to which a comet collided with the sun, breaking into pieces that, over a long period of time, became spherical objects in a system that generates its own particular conditions from the smallest number of original conditions. The idea of purposive unity of

---

[49] For an analysis of the tension between external and internal purposiveness that arises in this section, see Ypi, *The Architectonic of Reason*, 123–8.

things thus does no explanatory work in Buffon's natural history, for each conditioned cognition is explained only by a real condition within the empirical regress. Of course, each condition in Buffon's conjectural history is hypothetical, for it cannot be deduced from the highest idea of a purposive unity (see A646/B674). Experience is required before Buffon could postulate a natural history of the earth. Yet such a history nevertheless presents a *possible* object that can grow in probability, and, if it successfully guides the understanding to new observations and experiments against which it *can* be tested, can even rise to a "formal certainty."[50]

Without assuming a system of physical-mechanical relations, the understanding could not anticipate that its material-mechanical laws feature within an interconnected system of laws.[51] Under the idea of the purposive unity of things, the principles of reason instruct the understanding not to be satisfied with logically ordered cognitions arranged according to contingent affinities but to seek a determinate location for each thing within a physical-mechanical system. Kant thus transforms the mechanical-teleological system of *Universal Natural History*, which presents a hypothetical series of conditions tracing back to a material cause, into "a certain goal respecting which the lines and direction of all its rules converge at one point" (A644/B672). The idea of a completed system is not a transcendent object but an "outline" or "sketch" that instructs the understanding to reflect on appearances not simply as consequences of a rule but as products of a physical-mechanical process. The conception of empirical inquiry we find in the Appendix is thus akin to the pragmatic stance of Kant's physical geography: the regulative use of reason orients the understanding within the empirical manifold by "point[ing] the way toward systematic unity" (A668/B696). When constrained to the form of possible objects, reason relinquishes all pretentions to knowledge. The idea of nature as a physical-mechanical system is

---

[50] In Section 5.4, I examine the transition from hypothesis to knowledge. We find a clue to the transition in the abridged version of *Universal Natural History* published as an appendix to Herschel's *Über den Bau des Himmels* in 1791. In preparing the manuscript, Kant made several changes to reflect the epistemic register of his critical philosophy. For instance, he states that the "present theory of the mechanical formation of celestial bodies can, on the probability of the hypothesis alone, be raised to a formal certainty by the following remark." Kant, in Herschel, *Über den Bau des Himmels*, 184. As Ferrini notes, Kant's use of the adjective "formal" (which he inserts in the abridged version) does not imply certainty about the *content* of the hypothesis, but about the *logical connection* of the hypothesis with the observable consequences. Ferrini, "Heavenly Bodies, Crystals and Organisms," 312. The "following remark" (which replaces a phrase from the original, "I conclude this chapter by adding an analogy which, all by itself...."; NTH 1:277) refers to his cosmological theory, in which a density must arise in the mixture of all planets that is almost equal to the density of the sun's body. This, Kant states, was established by Buffon, who demonstrated that the densities of the entire planetary matter are nearly identical to that of the sun.

[51] By "material-mechanical" I refer to causality by means of interaction between moving particles in space, that is, the science of mechanics as presented in *Metaphysical Foundations* (MAN 4:543). This can easily be confused with Kant's notion of a "physical-mechanical" connection at A692/B720, which concerns the connection between things in nature understood as a physical-teleological mechanism. I elaborate the distinction between these two kinds of connection in Section 7.1.

not given but serves as the highest formal unity, instructing the understanding to extend its empirical investigations without limit.

Kant's examination of reason's logical principles in the Appendix assists us to see how the transition from the Logical Maxim to the Supreme Principle is both legitimate and necessary, for it demonstrates how the prescription to search for the inferential and epistemic conditions of conditioned cognitions requires the regulative use of transcendental principles. To use a transcendental principle regulatively is not to "**anticipate** what is given in itself **in the object**" but rather to have a capacity for *action*, to be able to form hypotheses about conditioned objects and their conditions that direct the understanding *to* the consequences given in experience, to find out whether they follow from the rule (A509/B537). This is how Kant can claim that the regulative use of reason's principles is "valid, albeit only indirectly" (A665/B693), and that reason's ideas have "objective, but indeterminate validity" (A663/B691). The objective validity of reason's principles is indirect, for they cannot be applied to cognitions "so as to **determine** something in it, but only to indicate the procedure in accordance with which the empirical and determinate use of the understanding in experience can be brought into thoroughgoing agreement in itself" (A665/B693). And their objective validity is indeterminate, for "reason does not beg but commands, though without being able to determine the bounds of this unity" (A653/B681). For example, reason does not describe how many subspecies there are under a species but simply instructs the understanding to seek further subspecies under every species. Reason's principles are metaphysically innocent; they do not commit us to any claims about the world. They are indirectly and indeterminately valid, for, by assuming them, we can formulate hypotheses that *can* come into accordance with the understanding's legitimate use.

5.4 Legitimate Hypotheses

In *Prolegomena to Any Future Metaphysics* (1783), Kant states that the account of reason's principles in the Appendix to the Transcendental Dialectic could be used for "making natural history generally systematic" (Prol 4:364). Natural history is an important expression of reason's regulative use, he explains, for it raises the question of how reason's principles can be bought into harmony with the understanding's laws. Yet Kant concedes that he has "not attempted its solution" in the *Critique*. In *Metaphysical Foundations*, he explains that while natural history does not have the status of a proper science, it nevertheless aspires towards the completion that reason prescribes. In "accordance with the demands of reason, every doctrine of nature must finally lead to natural science and conclude there" (MAN 4:469). This is to say that the goal of natural history is that its subject matter will be "thoroughly comprehended," driving natural historians to seek connections that are not given in experience. If unchecked, the goal of thorough comprehension leads to transcendental illusion, for it drives natural historians to postulate spurious objects that complete the inquiry but do not adhere to the conditions of sensibility, such as originally organized seeds or organic particles governed by non-material laws. If checked, however, the goal of thorough comprehension can serve as a regulative idea that instructs natural historians to continue searching for the empirical conditions of sensible objects, even if there are many blank spaces remaining on the map.

In this final section, I suggest that while Kant does not solve the problem of making natural history generally systematic in the *Critique*, the disciplinary rules outlined in the Doctrine of Method nevertheless demonstrate how natural historians can seek physical-mechanical (i.e. explanatory) connections without falling into transcendental illusion. In the following chapter, I then examine how Kant applies these rules in his confrontation with Herder and Forster during the mid-1780s. In the opening section of the Doctrine of Method, Kant states that where "neither experience nor pure intuition keeps reason in a visible track," reason can only be checked by self-discipline, the active limitation of the "compulsion through which the constant propensity to stray from certain rules" (A709/B737).[52] While the highest formal unity of reason sets the understanding a goal that is, practically speaking, incompletable, discipline enables natural historians to stay their ambitions before determining which hypotheses are worth assuming.

One of the basic components of discipline in the Doctrine of Method is an awareness of the epistemological register appropriate for reason's empirical use, which Kant describes as "assent" or "holding-for-true" (*Fürwahrhalten*).[53] In contrast to cognition, understood in the strict sense of our awareness of the existence and distinctive features of objects, assent is an epistemic attitude one adopts towards a judgement that requires an awareness of the grounds one has for holding it to be true.[54] The strength of the epistemic attitude is determined by the kinds of ground one can cite to justify one's assent (A822/B850). Subjective grounds typically refer to the state of the subject, including a particular experience, the testimony one receives from someone else, or reason's need for systematic coherence. A subjective ground is "sufficient" if one judges that it is convincing for oneself. The "touchstone" of subjective sufficiency is thus the bets one would be willing to make on a judgement; a "subjective conviction" or "firm belief" is

---

[52] Kant's account of discipline has striking parallels in Bacon's project in *Novum organum*, which have recently come to scholarly attention. See Kim, *Bacon und Kant*, ch. 2; Lu-Adler, *Kant and the Science of Logic*, 71–7. Ferrini argues that Kant is not directly interacting with Bacon, but rather with the way Bacon's disciplinary method was taken up by his contemporaries such as Georg Forster. See Ferrini, "Illusions of Imagination and Adventures of Reason in Kant's first *Critique*," 172–5.

[53] This section has gained recent attention in Kant scholarship, for it has several important similarities with contemporary literature on credence. See Chignell, "Belief in Kant"; Gava, "Kant and Crusius on Belief and Practical Justification"; Pasternack, "Kant on Opinion."

[54] Willaschek and Watkins, "Kant on Cognition and Knowledge," 3197.

evident in the actions one is willing to take on the assumption that the judgement is true (A824/B825). Objective grounds, in contrast, are based on the conditions that make a proposition true.[55] This includes reliable information about "the constitution of the object," which indicates that the ground has an objective probability of being true (A821/B849). Because the constitution of the object extends beyond the limits of possible experience, the sufficiency of an objective ground is not restricted to cognition. It is also a matter of universal assent. The "touchstone" of objective sufficiency, Kant states, is "the possibility of communicating it and finding it to be valid for the reason of every human being to take it to be true" (A820–1/B849). A judgement is objectively sufficient when it is based on grounds that one discovers are also grounds for other epistemic agents.[56] Objectivity in the Doctrine of Method is thus not entirely coterminous with the "objective validity" of the Transcendental Deduction, for it does not spontaneously follow the judgement. A ground is objective if we *judge* that it has "the same effect on the reason of others" (A820/B848).[57]

Kant identifies three epistemic attitudes that an act of judging can have: opinion (*Meinung*), belief (*Glaube*), and knowledge (*Wissen*) (A820/B848). An opinion is marked by an attitude we take towards a proposition when we judge that its ground is subjectively and objectively insufficient. A hypothesis, for instance, is a particular kind of opinion about the condition of a conditioned cognition, when we lack sufficient grounds to hold it for true. In contrast to opinion, a belief is marked by an attitude we take to a proposition when we judge that its ground is subjectively sufficient and yet objectively insufficient (A822/B850). And in contrast to both opinion and belief, knowledge is marked by an attitude that naturally follows when we judge that the ground of a proposition is both subjectively and objectively sufficient, that is, "valid for all human reason" (A820/B848). While our opinions and beliefs require ongoing assessment as our knowledge develops, opinions must be held more lightly, and wherever possible should not be used to ground further opinions (though in some situations, such as natural history, this is unavoidable; see A774–5/B802–3).

In the section entitled "The discipline of pure reason with regard to hypotheses," Kant sets out to determine which hypotheses are "worthy of assuming [*Annehmungswürdig*]" in a programme of research by formulating two

---

[55] Kant is operating with a fairly conventional definition of truth here, which "rests upon agreement with the object" (A820/B848).

[56] As Chignell puts it, in addition to adhering to the conditions of possible experience, objective sufficiency requires further grounds that render the proposition "objectively probable to a moderate-to-high degree." Chignell, "Belief in Kant," 44.

[57] This does not imply a form of doxastic voluntarism, such that we have direct control over our assents. Kant's aim in the Doctrine of Method to show that we have control over the *maxims* that guide the acquisition of assents, meaning that we have indirect control over the assents we actually acquire. See Cohen, "Kant on the Ethics of Belief," 318–20.

disciplinary rules.[58] The first rule states that while a hypothesis extends beyond the field of experience, "something must always first be fully certain and not invented, or a mere opinion, and that is the **possibility** of the object itself" (A770/B798).[59] Call this rule *Real Possibility*:

Real Possibility: A hypothesis is *really possible* iff it agrees with the formal conditions of experience (forms of intuition and the categories).[60]

Real Possibility entails that legitimate hypotheses are *physical* hypotheses, which account for consequences according to the "constitution and connection of objects of experience in general" (A771/B799).[61] While we cannot prove Newton's gravitational force through repeated experience, for it seeks to account for every possible bodily motion, it stands as a legitimate hypothesis, for it adheres to the form of causality anticipated by the understanding. In contrast, Newton's claim that the planetary system is the product of design is an illegitimate hypothesis, for it violates Real Possibility. Newton proposes what Kant terms a "transcendental" or "hyperphysical" hypothesis, for it bypasses the understanding and employs an idea of reason to explain the possibility of an object (A772/B800). As Kant demonstrated in his critique of physicotheology, to explain the possibility of an object by deriving it from an idea of reason "would thus be no explanation at all, since that which one does not adequately understand on the basis of known empirical principles would be explained by means of something about which one understands nothing at all." Such an inquiry might be free of contradiction, yet it would be without a possible object. In the Canon, Kant explains that a hypothesis is legitimate when "there is at least a presumption that the ground of the agreement of all judgments, regardless of the difference among the subjects, rests on the common ground, namely, the object, with which they therefore all agree and through which the truth of the judgment is proved" (A821/B849).

While Real Possibility defines a narrower field than what is logically possible, its field is far greater than what is actually possible. Kant provides further definition to the first rule by explaining that legitimate hypotheses must be "connected to the given appearances by already known laws of appearances" (A772/B800). By

---

[58] Drawing primarily from Kant's lectures on logic, Vanzo identifies three rules for legitimate hypotheses: they must (1) offer an explanation for phenomena that actually take place, (2) be testable against the consequences, and (3) be sufficient to explain a set of phenomena without requiring further hypotheses. The rules I identify in the following are drawn primarily from the *Critique*, and thus give greater weight to Kant's modal metaphysics. See Vanzo, "Kant on Experiment," 83–4.

[59] For an alternative account of the two rules, see Butts, "Hypothesis and Explanation in Kant's Philosophy of Science," 166.

[60] My formulation of Kant's modal requirements draws from Stang, *Kant's Modal Metaphysics*, ch. 7, and the application of those requirements to Kant's doctrine of assent by Chignell, "Knowledge, Discipline, System, Hope," 269–75.

[61] My characterization of legitimate hypotheses as "physical" hypotheses draws from Leduc, "Les Critères kantiens de validité de l'hypothèse physique," 126.

"already known laws of appearances" I take Kant to mean not simply the under-standing's laws, which apply universally and necessarily to any possible object, but also the empirical laws discovered in the course of experience.[62] To define what is possible in regard to actual objects, experience is required. The formation of opinions must be restricted to what is *empirically* possible, which is thicker than the formal conditions of possibility.[63] Empirical Possibility includes Real Possibility *and* the already known empirical laws:

Empirical Possibility: A hypothesis is *empirically possible* iff its existence agrees with the universal conditions of experience plus the already known empirical laws.

This version of the first rule places non-logical constraints on possibility. When we seek the ground of an effect, a hypothesis must be assessed in relation to other pieces of a subject's background knowledge. The coherence of a hypothesis with that background knowledge does not determine the necessity of a regular occur-rence we discern in experience, as some commentators have claimed.[64] The necessity conveyed by a force can originate only in the understanding, which requires that appearances are given causal explanations. Reason's instruction to minimize the number of forces by seeking a "sameness of kind" presupposes that there *are* laws; it cannot legitimately produce them. Alberto Vanzo illustrates the rule with an example from the lectures on physical geography.[65] To explain the phenomena of earthquakes and volcanoes we could formulate the proposition, "there are flames at the centre of the earth," which does not fail the first rule (PG 1774 9:259–60). A possible world in which the earth consists of a fiery centre is thinkable (e.g. the world of Dante's *Commedia*). Given the laws of combustion discovered by Hales, however, we know that the existence of flames at the earth's centre is impossible, for combustion requires air. A world in which flames could burn without air would require a very different causal history to that of our own. Given the preceding actual events of *our* world, and the resultant empirical laws we have already adopted, the proposition fails the second rule. Within the unique field of empirical possibility, a hypothesis we *can* entertain is that the centre of the world is composed of heated matter (PG 1774 9:260).

The first rule of hypothesizing indicates just how different Kant's method is from other eighteenth-century experimental philosophers. Before Kant, most

---

[62] Here I disagree with Butts, who assumes that Real Possibility can be established with the relational categories of the understanding alone. See Butts, "Hypothesis and Explanation in Kant's Philosophy of Science," 166.

[63] See Chignell, "Knowledge, Discipline, System, Hope," 272.

[64] Proponents of the "best system" account of empirical laws argue that the necessity of a law-like proposition is granted by the location it takes in our best system of scientific knowledge. Buchdahl, "Causality, Causal Law, and Scientific Theory," 201–2; Kitcher, "Projecting the Order of Nature," 204–15; Butts, "The Methodological Structure of Kant's Metaphysics of Science," 179–87; Guyer, "Reason and Reflective Judgment," 39–43.

[65] Vanzo, "Kant on Experiment," 83.

philosophers held that to determine given appearances *a priori* is either impossible, for sensibility is distinct from the intellect, or a proposition describing such appearances as logically implied by a law. The former implies that empirical science is merely inductive, for causal connections cannot be established *a priori*. The latter provides a deductive model for explanations. Kant's alternative is that a hypothesis is legitimate when the *relation* between an appearance and its condition, which the hypothesis seeks to determine, is certain. A hypothesis ascribes a rule to all members of a class, despite having only experienced some of them, on the assumption that they share a common condition.[66] It thereby directs the understanding to undertake observations and experiments to test the appearance against the rule, to find out whether the hypothesis correctly picks out the condition.[67] The key is that while the hypothesis may or may not be true, we are entitled to make it because *a priori* it stands as a possible condition of the given conditioned.

I assume here that many of the already known laws have not (yet) been demonstrated mathematically, and are thus held for true with various strengths of credence. In the introduction to the Transcendental Dialectic, Kant states that if one holds a proposition as probable, one does not succumb to illusion. Probability, he explains, is "truth, but cognized through insufficient grounds, so that the cognition of it is defective, but not therefore deceptive" (A293/B349). Probable propositions are not deceptive but defective, for they are revisable and prone to error as we increase our experience and bring greater unity to the understanding's cognitions. This entails that a hypothesis that fails Empirical Possibility is not categorically illegitimate. Our current body of knowledge may imply that the hypothesis is not worth assuming, yet Kant was well aware that the history of natural philosophy is littered with examples in which new observations exposed false hypotheses or a new hypothesis accounted for the consequences so powerfully that one or several accepted hypotheses were cast aside. The fact that the connections within a science *are* explanatory is precisely why the consequences given in experience can be tested against them.[68] Their explanatory character is why we must carefully evaluate our grounds for assuming them.

---

[66] In *Jäsche Logik*, Kant describes induction as an analogical form of inference that moves "from *many* determinations and properties, in which things of one kind agree, *to the remaining ones, insofar as they belong to the same principle*" (Log 9:132; cf. V-Lo/Blomberg 24:287; V-Lo/Hechsel 109–10; V-Lo/Dohna 24:771–2). See Vanzo, "Kant on Experiment," 82.

[67] For an insightful reconstruction of this procedure, see McNulty's ideational interpretation of empirical laws, according to which the systematization of principles allows us to determine which principle is the ground of a particular judgement. McNulty, "Rehabilitating the Regulative Use of Reason," 9.

[68] In this sense Kant presages Nelson Goodman's account of counterfactual conditionals, which demonstrates that "Only a statement that is lawlike—regardless of its truth or falsity or its scientific importance—is capable of receiving confirmation from an instance of it; accidental statements are not." Goodman, *Fact, Fiction, and Forecast*, 73.

The danger is that a physical hypothesis can very quickly become enmeshed in a network of hypotheses. If we must call on further auxiliary hypotheses to defend an initial hypothesis, the network begins to "arouse the suspicion of being a mere invention" (A774/B802). To block the proliferation of hypotheses, Kant proposes a second disciplinary rule:

Adequacy: A hypothesis is worth assuming when it is adequate for determining *a priori* the consequences that are given.

To erase the suspicion of mere invention, we must strive to avoid auxiliary hypotheses and limit our assent to those that are adequate to determine something that *is* given. Such hypotheses are at least anchored to something objective. Kant tells us very little about how we might move from a hypothesis that is adequate for determining *a priori* the given consequence to judging that it *actually* determines the consequence *a priori*.[69] Several hints can be found in his lectures on logic. In *Blomberg Logic*, for instance, he explains that "when the ground suffices for *all* the determinations but also *not* for more determinations than are contained in the consequence, then there is a true ground, and then *hypothesis* ceases. The ground becomes a *theory*. A certainty" (V-Lo/Blomberg 24:221–2). Here Kant implies that a confirmed hypothesis ceases to be a hypothesis and becomes a theory.[70] By "true ground" I take Kant to mean the ground whose truth is probable to a degree that surpasses any practical level of doubt for a rational being, where several possibilities were available. In the Doctrine of Method, Kant does not describe the transition from opinion to knowledge. He is less concerned with the actual context of discovery—how the objects of experience can be tested against a rule—than he is with the prior question of legitimate hypotheses. Andrew Chignell suggests that the move from opinion to knowledge is a matter of degree, met when one judges that a hypothesis has sufficient subjective grounds to merit one's commitment but insufficient objective grounds to gain the agreement of all others.[71] Of course, the only way to remove the possibility of doubt would be to grasp the system in its entirety, such that the ideas that guide our inquiry become determinate concepts in a system of proper science. While such a system is beyond our reach, the *idea* of a completed system instructs us to expect that the laws discovered through our

---

[69] For a brief discussion of this transition, see Cooper, "Hypotheses in Kant's Philosophy of Science." While several studies are emerging on Kant's account of hypotheses, there is still much work to be done to clarify how a hypothesis "becomes a theory," or even if such a transition is coherent within the constraints of Kantian science.

[70] For a discussion of Kant's odd use of theory in this passage, see Pasternack, "Kant on Opinion," 68.

[71] Chignell, "Belief in Kant," 42–4. The problem of degree—when exactly we deem a ground to reach objective sufficiency—is debated in the literature. All I want to establish here is that Kant changes the empirical question of probabilistic knowledge we saw in Newton, Locke, du Châtelet, and Buffon, for he demonstrates that *something* in the cognition must be certain for the hypothesis to get up and running in the first place.

empirical investigation will be the laws under ideal conditions.[72] This, I take it, is why Kant thinks that probability, while deficient, is nevertheless a species of truth.

The implications of Kant's account of reason's regulative use for natural history are significant. While I explore these implications in greater detail in the following chapters, here I want to make the provisional conclusion that, in contrast to commentators who insist that the shift in Kant's natural history is from "explanatory to heuristic," the restriction Kant places on knowledge serves only to establish the criteria against which we can distinguish mere fiction from legitimate hypotheses. The danger is that the physical connections in a system of natural history *are* explanatory, which is precisely why we must carefully evaluate the strength of our grounds for assenting to them; their actuality remains a problem. Consider a Kantian reconstruction of Buffon's study of hares in "On the Degeneration of Animals." From the hypothetically employed transcendental principle of homogeneity, combined with the observation of two populations of hares on separate continents, Buffon assumes that there is "a kind of affinity of various branches, insofar as they have all sprouted from the same stem" (A660/B688). Under the highest idea of purposive unity, he reflects on this affinity as the product of a regress of physical-mechanical connections, which directs him to seek a shared condition of the two branches. To do so, he formulates a hypothesis: an original group, which, endowed with an adaptive force, migrated to two different locations, such that the size and colour altered to ensure the propagation of each group in new environmental conditions. This hypothesis stands as a possible ground of the affinity between the two groups, thereby guiding the understanding to seek other sub-kinds that may also be conjoined according to the rule. The understanding is thus able to bring greater unity to the manifold of its cognitions by grouping members of the two populations according to real connections in space and time, without taking those groups, and their logical connection, as given.

The difference between Buffon's physical system and Linnaeus' artificial system is thus that Buffon follows the highest formal unity of reason with greater consistency, for Linnaeus continued to assume that, despite physical alterations in time and space, an original logical order is simply given. In Buffon's study, the transcendental principle of homogeneity enables him to generate hypotheses about higher genera, such that reason's speculative interest in completion directs him to seek the genera that are problematically assumed. If Buffon did not assume that there was a common stem endowed with an adaptive force, that is, if he had not proposed a common stem as a physical hypothesis, he would not have attempted to find out which characteristics are accidental and which are necessary. As Haller suggests in his methodological preface, Buffon shows us that, to work towards a complete system, we *must* go beyond our current cognitions and

---

[72] Breitenbach, "Laws and Ideal Unity," 119.

concepts by sketching a map that directs us to new and half-certain towns. In Kant's terms, the logical principals *must* presuppose the transcendental principles (the imperative is practical), lest they remain without "sense and application [*Sinn und Anwendung*]" (A656/B684).[73] The key to Kant's account of reason's regulative use is that while the *whole* is not empirically given, in which case it would be "**possible** to go back **to infinity** in the series of its inner conditions," the *first* is given through an empirical regress, meaning that "it is **possible** to progress to still higher conditions in the series **to infinity**" (A514/B543). The difference between the possibility *of* an infinite empirical regress and the possibility of making progress to still higher conditions *in* the regress is the difference between the transcendental use of a *descriptive* principle and the transcendental use of an *indeterminate* and *prescriptive* principle.[74]

Kant's defence of the indeterminate objective validity of reason's principles does not restrict the scope of historical reasoning but rather ensures that "we do not stop with any answer to its [reason's] questions except that which is appropriate to the object" (A516/B544). Thus it is more accurate to describe Kant's critical philosophy as determining the disciplinary rules to ensure that natural history does not stop with spurious answers to the questions generated by reason's empirical use, but continues to make genuine progress, than as restricting its explanatory power. As I have argued, one of Kant's aims in the *Critique* is to defend the legitimate and necessary rules for reasoning in natural philosophy that can (a) protect reason from lazy conclusions and (b) lead to defensible opinions, even well-founded theories. The key is the form of possible objects combined with the regulative use of reason's ideas, which, under the stimulation of experience, generates the highest formal unity of a physical-mechanical system according to which sensible objects are viewed as natural products.

Yet this is only a provisional conclusion. In the following chapters we will see that Kant's engagement with the question of human origins in the mid-1780s returned his attention to a question that dogged his earlier writings and lectures on natural history. While the hypothetical use of reason can be legitimately used to unify appearances by seeking their physical-mechanical grounds, during the mid-1780s Kant realized that living natural products present a deeper problem to the physical-mechanical system of nature than he had previously acknowledged.

---

[73] Kant states the case more strongly at A651/B679: without presupposing "the systematic unity of nature as objectively valid and necessary" there would be "no coherent use of the understanding, and in the absence of this no adequate criterion of empirical truth."

[74] For an illustration of this difference, see the final paragraph of "On the Volcanoes on the Moon," where Kant criticizes Buffon's explanation of the volcanic activity as a residue of the sun's heat (given that the earth is a former fragment of the sun), for it fails to explain the origin of that heat. Yet Kant insists that Buffon's failure should not cause us to "invoke an immediate divine decree as an explanation." Despite the failure of every attempt to identify an initial cause of the cosmos, "we are not relieved of the obligation to search among the causes of things as far as is possible for us, and follow the causal chain in accordance with known laws as far as it extends" (VM 8:76). Kant can disagree with Buffon precisely because he provides a *physical* hypothesis that can be judged against reason's rules.

His hypothesis of germs and dispositions, which enabled him to unify sub-kinds under a higher kind according to physical-mechanical connections, does not strictly follow Real Possibility. There is a contingent connection between the parts of a living natural product, such that the parts do not simply determine the whole, as they do in a physical-mechanical body, but the whole, in response to external changes, determines the arrangement of the parts. In the Architectonic, Kant calls on an analogy with the development of a living being from gestation to adulthood to explain the development of a system of reason on its path to maturity. He states that "The systems seem to have been formed, like maggots, by a *generatio aequivoca* from the mere confluence of aggregated concepts, garbled at first but compete in time, although they all had their schema, as the original germ, in the mere self-development of reason" (A835/B863). In 1781, Kant could already see that an original germ is not a physical-mechanical force, by which the parts determine the whole, but an organizing force, by which the parts are generated according to a schema.[75] Yet to assume that the germ of a maggot is a schematizing force that organizes diffuse parts into a whole would violate Real Possibility, for it postulates a connection that is inadequate to explain the consequences *a priori*. While Kant established in the Appendix that reason legitimately commands the understanding to search for a condition for every conditioned cognition, he denied that reason can bypass the understanding and concoct new kinds of possible connection to unify the manifold (see A771/B799). This problem comes to the fore in his confrontation with Herder and Forster, forcing him to reconsider the role of analogy in natural history. Kant's recognition of the problem, and his solution, will be the subject of the remaining chapters.

---

[75] See also A688/B716, where Kant explains that we can achieve the highest systematic unity of our knowledge in physiology if we presuppose that the parts of an organic body are arranged *as if* they are the product of the highest intelligence.

6

From Natural Products to Organized Beings

In a letter to Moses Mendelssohn on 16 August 1783, Kant expresses a growing concern that the revolution staged in his critical philosophy had not been understood (Br 10:345).[1] The early reviews of *Critique of Pure Reason* criticized Kant for advocating Humean scepticism, for defending Berkeleyan idealism, and for simply reproducing Leibniz.[2] His essay on race, which appeared in the popular journal *Der Philosoph für die Welt*, was also read in the wrong light. The essay defended a biblically orthodox view of monogenism against the polygenism advanced by Voltaire and Kames.[3] Yet Kant's position was far from conventional. It presented a revised version of Buffon's physical concept of race. Indeed, several of Kant's readers viewed his conception of natural history in continuity with *The Epochs of Nature* (1778), the latest volume of *Histoire naturelle* in which Buffon proposed a genetic history of the earth in seven epochs, which included the generation of living beings from unformed matter. Johann Gottfried Herder, one of Kant's former students (1762–4), called on Kant's early work *Universal Natural History* to complete Buffon's epochal theory of the earth. Georg Forster, who accompanied Captain James Cook to the Pacific on HMS *Resolution* (1772–5), interpreted Kant's theory of race as a Buffonian history of origins.

Kant was clearly unsettled. Could his readers not see that Buffon's speculative history was indistinguishable from fiction, and that his critical philosophy had established the criteria by which historical claims could warrant our assent? Despite the immense body of writing he was undertaking in the mid-1780s, Kant somehow found time to respond with a two-part review of Herder's *Outlines of a Philosophy of the History of Man* (January and November 1785)

---

[1] Mendelssohn refused to engage with *Critique of Pure Reason* at all, for he was repelled by the metaphysical nature of its contents. Kant attempts to alleviate Mendelssohn's concerns by insisting that the book deals only with "the formal condition of a possible (inner or outer) experience" (Br 10:346). In the 1787 edition of the *Critique*, Kant prefaces his revisions by stating that he fears "not that I will be refuted, but that I will not be understood" (Bxliii).

[2] The reviews can be found in translation in Sassen, *Kant's Early Critics*.

[3] In *The Philosophy of History* (1765), Voltaire criticizes philosophers for discarding their rigorous experimental method when it comes to the origins of organic form. He claims that the available experimental evidence points to polygenesis, and even to the extinction of several races. See Voltaire, "Of the Different Races of Men," 5–7.

Kant and the Transformation of Natural History. Andrew Cooper, Oxford University Press. © Andrew Cooper 2023.
DOI: 10.1093/oso/9780192869784.003.0007

and a reply to Forster entitled "On the Use of Teleological Principles in Philosophy" (January and February 1788). In these essays, Kant drops the playfulness of physical geography and, with sobriety, sets out to confront a problem that he considered indirectly in the *Critique*: how reason's principles could "make natural history generally systematic" (Prol 4:364). The issue at stake was not simply conjecture on human origins but the very status of scientific knowledge.[4]

Kant's response to Herder and Forster has been interpreted as a reactionary attempt to reign in the development of a genuine history of nature.[5] Hein van den Berg argues that Kant "strictly limit[s] the epistemic pretensions of natural history in the 1780s and 1790s."[6] Phillip Sloan contends that the controversy associated with Herder and Forster forced Kant "to weaken the claims of *Naturgeschichte*, and to elevate those of *Naturbeschreibung*."[7] On Sloan's reconstruction, Kant subjected the knowledge claims of natural history to "the limitations of the critical philosophy," which inverts the deductive model of *Universal Natural History* and proceeds instead via an inference from known objects to the past. John Zammito argues that Kant was motivated by a "*metaphysical* agenda" to save human reason from collapsing into the natural order.[8] He thus set out to develop a strict conception of science that would place "severe limits" on the dreams sketched by his opponents.[9]

Kant's response to Herder and Forster certainly was provocative, perhaps even reactionary. However, my aim in this chapter is to show that his motivations were not *first* metaphysical. In contrast to Zammito's depiction of Kant's motivations, I argue that Kant was primarily concerned with clarifying the epistemological implications of the *Critique*, which established a legitimate and necessary use of hypotheses in natural science.[10] And in contrast to van den Berg and Sloan's portrait of Kant's deflated ambitions, I propose that this clarification did not weaken the claims of natural history but in fact strengthened the distinction between history and description, which Kant had, from his earliest work, sought

---

[4] I take it that Kant's ironic tone in "Conjectural beginning of human history" (1786) serves to make this exact point. See especially MAM 8:109–15.

[5] Zammito, *The Genesis of the Critique of Judgment*, 180–213; Sloan, "Preforming the Categories," 242–3; Lagier, *Les Races humaines selon Kant*, 140; Swift, "Kant, Herder and the Question of Philosophical Anthropology," 222.

[6] van den Berg, "Kant and the Scope of Analogy in the Life Sciences," 75.

[7] Sloan, "Kant on the History of Nature," 640.

[8] Zammito, "The Lenoir Thesis Revisited," 121–2.

[9] See Zammito, *Genesis of the Critique of Judgment*, 178.

[10] Here I agree with commentators who argue that Kant's debate with Herder must be framed within an epistemological register. See Zuckert, "Organisms and Metaphysics," 62; Zuckert, "History, Biology, and Philosophical Anthropology in Kant and Herder," 36; Waldow, "Natural History and the Formation of the Human Being," 68.

to establish. As we saw in his lectures on physical geography, Kant began to place the claims of natural history in a practical register in the late 1750s. Indeed, he criticized the use of God as the explanatory ground of systematic order—an assumption in the argument of *Universal Natural History*—from at least 1763.[11] In what follows, I examine Kant's response to Herder and Forster as a case study of how reason's principles, under the discipline of critique, can be used to "make natural history generally systematic." I argue that in the course of responding to the two young naturalists, Kant recognized that the concept of a living natural product bears a tension that threatens the unity of nature as a physical-mechanical system. *Qua* product, a living being is produced within the physical-mechanical conditions of nature. *Qua* living, it is the producer of itself. Kant's solution required modifications to the conception of judgement presented in the *Critique*. These modifications will be important for our broader analysis of Kant's concept of race, for they undermine the fixity he had formerly attributed to sub-kinds, opening a wider scope for morphological change than his earlier conception of natural history had allowed.

In Section 6.1, I lay out Kant's concept of a race as presented in his 1785 essay "Determination of the Concept of a Human Race." In defence of monogenism, Kant deploys his account of reason's regulative use to show that the hypothesis of germs and dispositions enables the understanding's greatest extension and reach. In Sections 6.2 and 6.3, I examine Kant's response to Herder and Forster's respective attacks on his concept of race. I argue that the question at the heart of the dispute is epistemological: how the observation of "unfailing *hereditary* peculiarity" (ÜGTP 8:165)—the acquisition of a property that *becomes* necessary—can be used to identify a stable subspecies. Kant's answer is that heredity is a legitimate marker of class divisions in natural history only when considered as the consequence of a rule. In Section 6.4, I provide evidence to show that, in responding to Herder and Forster, Kant was alerted to the need for a critical examination of our reflection on the causal structure of living natural products, which he begins to call "organized beings" and "natural purposes." While he was critical of Herder's speculative natural history and Forster's neo-Linnaean description, Kant's engagement with their work led him to clarify and expand the role of analogy in his critical philosophy. The implications of this expansion will be examined in the final chapter.

---

[11] The implications of critical philosophy for Kant's argument in *Universal Natural History* can be seen in the abridged version of the essay included as an appendix in Herschel's *Über den Bau des Himmels* in 1791. In the initial version, Kant argued that the systematicity of empirical nature is grounded in the essential properties of matter as designed by God's infinite understanding. In the abridged version, Kant describes the "tendency" of matter to self-formation, which has a chemical rather than a theological ground. While Ferrini characterizes Kant's revisions as a "descriptive" rather than "genetic" cosmogony, Kant nevertheless continued to view his theory of the heavens as an explanation of sorts. See Ferrini, "Heavenly Bodies, Crystals and Organisms," 282–3.

6.1 The Concept of a Human Race

Before turning to Kant's debate with Herder and Forster, let us begin with his first essay on natural history following the *Critique*, "Determination of the Concept of a Human Race," published in the popular *Aufklärung* periodical *Berlinische Monatsschift* in 1785.[12] In this essay, Kant repeats the defence of monogenism presented in his 1775/7 essay. His goal, however, is not simply to uphold his former position in the midst of ongoing public debate but also to define the scope of historical speculation according to the methodological rules outlined in the *Critique*. To allay any fears that his earlier essay presented a speculative history of origins, Kant argues that natural history, which aspires to provide a physical-mechanical account of the present manifold of appearances, must be disciplined to parameters about which we can be certain.

In the Appendix to the Transcendental Dialectic, Kant argued that the maximal unity of appearances is achieved by presupposing a set of principles that instruct the understanding to seek a continuous (though indeterminate) gradient of forms (see Section 5.3). To guide the understanding in its empirical use, reason projects a genus as the "object in the idea," prescribing the formal relations that the understanding must seek to fill (A692/B720). While the content of the genus is different in physics (gravity; A649/B677), chemistry (earth, water, air, etc.; A646/B674), and natural history (a single stem; A660/B689), the formal relations are the same: the understanding determines the conditions of possible objects, thereby requiring that appearances are given material explanations, and reason requires the minimization of kinds, instructing the understanding to consider empirical kinds and particular laws as admixtures of fundamental kinds and general laws. With this procedure in view, consider the student notes taken from the 1781/2 physical geography, where Kant is recorded as suggesting that concepts can be considered as determining grounds:

> The first question is whether the human race should be initially conceived of under a single title, and whether all humans are of a single kind, or whether it contains different humans who could not have arisen from a single stem, but must have come from different stems. Whether they have all arisen from a single stem cannot be determined by reason; it [reason] can only ask about the possibility of such a proposition. If it is possible, then reason has a basis to accept it. The question can be reduced to the following: do all humans of the earth belong to a single species of animal? This can also be phrased, have they all arisen from a single stem?   (V-Geo/Dönhoff 1781/2 26.2:878–9)

---

[12] "Determination of the Concept of a Human Race" and Kant's first review of Herder's *Outlines* were both published in November 1785, so we can assume that Kant was aware of Herder's critique of his concept of race as he sought to clarify the argument of his previous essays.

In this passage, Kant applies the first disciplinary rule to the study of human diversity. Reason cannot generate legitimate hypotheses on its own, yet it can direct the understanding to seek subspecies connected to an original stem by a physical line of descent. Because a single stem is possible (it adheres to Real Possibility), we have grounds to accept it as a hypothesis.

In "Determination of the Concept of a Human Race," Kant applies his account of reason's regulative use to the public debate on human origins. He begins by stressing the youth and vibrancy of natural history, which has not yet acquired a scientific status. "The knowledge which the new travels have disseminated about the manifoldness in the human species," he states, "so far have contributed more to exciting the understanding to investigation on this point than to satisfying it" (BBMR 8:91). Kant's provocation is that in contrast to the Linnaean natural historians, who base their classificatory concepts on affinities between phenomena, it "is of great consequence to have previously determined the concept that one wants to elucidate through observation before questioning experience about it" (BBMR 8:91). This is for the reason that, as in all Newtonian science, "one finds in experience what one needs only if one knows in advance what to look for." In the context of natural history, reason instructs the understanding to search for a species under which to subsume every conditioned thing, and then a higher genus under which to subsume every species. Following the direction of reason's highest formal unity—the purposive unity of things—the understanding is instructed to seek physical-mechanical connections, which define membership within a species according to real grounds in space and time. Confronted with the empirical data, reason formulates the hypothesis of an original stem, a common ancestor imbued with a "germ" or "generative force" that explains how the contingent variations within the species are in fact necessary adaptations in response to changes in environment. The original stem—what one knows to look for "in advance"—guides reflection on the manifold to discern which variations are accidental and which are unfailingly hereditary.

Consider a natural historian who discovers a population of birds in Aotearoa New Zealand, which, apart from their wingspan and a slight variation in colouring, are similar to a population found in Australia. By discerning an affinity between members of both populations, the natural historian abstracts from all members to form a schema, such that the two populations can be classified as varieties of a common species. Following the Linnaean binomial system of nomenclature, our natural historian names the first *Diomedea sanfordi* (Northern Royal Albatross) and the second *Diomedea epomophora* (Southern Royal Albatross). Because affinity is merely a logical relation, she is not warranted to assume that this artificial division tracks a natural division. Yet the highest formal unity of things, combined with the form of causality given by the understanding, drives her to seek a physical-mechanical connection between the two varieties. To do so, she projects a hypothetical stem behind the two actual populations ("an object lying outside the field of possible empirical cognition"; A644/B672), members of which, at some point in the past, settled in two distinct climates. To account for the marks that distinguish the two varieties, she postulates a hypothetical adaptive force that causes a slight alteration in wingspan and colouring of the feathers to fit new environmental demands. Only as the consequents of a rule can the acquired traits be considered necessary, such that the connections in the natural system are physical-mechanical connections.

Kant's account of reason's regulative use in the Appendix sheds light on his central claim in "Determination of the Concept of a Human Race" that only that which is "unfailingly hereditary" can justify the designation of a race (BBMR 8:99). The structure of the connection is, once more, Kant's modified version of Buffonian degeneration, which captures a purposive adaptation that *becomes* necessary for a future generation. Kant's contention is that we can only search for defining marks, understood as acquired characteristics that are passed on to future generations without fail, if we assume that certain adaptive dispositions lie "in the germs of the to us unknown original stem" (BBMR 8:98). While these germs are still preformed (Kant describes them as "created germs [*anerschaffene Keime*]"; BBMR 8:103), he now employs them to account for a broader range of phenomena than the on/off function they served in his 1775/7 essay. In "Determination of the Concept of a Human Race," germs serve to explain (a) generation and self-maintenance, including embryonic development, growth, and repair; (b) response to stimuli, such as change in appearance to better suit changed environmental conditions; and (c) inheritance, that is, the capacity to pass both the *capacities* (a) and (b), and the *properties acquired by (b)*, unfailingly to the next generation (BBMR 8:98).

Kant's germs are, in several ways, akin to Haller's life forces; they do not provide a mechanical explanation of the cause, as do Buffon's moulds, but merely stand as placeholders for unknown causes.[13] Yet in contrast to sensibility and irritability, which determine the functionality of a part (e.g. the response of muscle fibres to irritation), Kant is interested in how the germs are coordinated by dispositions, which trigger an alteration in order to produce and then maintain the whole in a state of equilibrium (BBMR 8:97).[14] All natural historians have to work with are the present variety of specimens and fossilized remains, which

---

[13] This is at least true to Haller's presentation of his method (see Section 2.4). While Haller referred to irritability and sensibility as the "properties [*Eigenschaften*]" of various fibres, during the latter part of the eighteenth century they came to be described as "living forces [*Lebenskräfte*]." The term "*Lebenskraft*" was introduced by the doctor and botanist Friedrich Cassimir Medicus in *Von der Lebenskraft* (1774) to emphasize the fact that irritability and sensibility are not merely properties of unknown faculties but independent forces that can be investigated in their own right. See Noll, *Die "Lebenskraft" in den Schriften der Vitalisten und ihrer Gegner*, 6; Engles, *Die Teleologie des Lebendigen*, 93n–95n.

[14] In *On the Formation of the Heart in the Chicken*, Haller assumes the pre-existence of miniature parts, which are then irritated by spermatozoa in such a way that they expand to meet the conditions within the egg (see Section 2.4).

provide hints of the previous form that a present variety may have taken. The "proof" of germs and dispositions is that, once assumed, natural historians can arrange the present variety of a species in a physical line of descent that branched out over long periods of time as the forces caused different effects due to alterations in climate and birthplace. The projected system classifies variations according to physical-mechanical connections, kept in check by Buffon's rule, which takes the physical capacity for reproduction as a marker for the boundary of a stem species.

While Kant maintains the fourfold account of race originally presented in his 1775/7 essay, he is much more cautious to frame his case in the grammar of hypotheses. Moreover, he does not make any hierarchical classifications, at least in regards to intellectual capacity or moral character.[15] "I have assumed only four races of the human species," he explains,

> not as if I were completely certain that there is nowhere a trace of still more, but because what I require for the character of a race, namely the generation of half-breeds [die halbschlächtige Zeugung], has been made out only in those and has been sufficiently established in no other class of human beings.   (BBMR 8:100–1)

Kant's argument is that a fourfold account is worth assuming in a programme of research, for, in contrast to its competitors, it (1) adheres to Real Possibility, (2) explains the relevant observations (unfailing heredity of acquired characteristics, reproductive capacity between varieties, etc.), and (3) brings the greatest unity to the available phenomena. The polygenism defended by Kames and Voltaire works from the observation of the varieties of human form to the claim that different kinds of human being spontaneously sprouted in various regions of the earth with qualities predisposed to flourish in a certain climate. For Kant, this hypothesis fails on two counts. First, it fails to explain the capacity of the various kinds to reproduce fertile young. Second, it fails to differentiate between accidental and necessary characteristics. Kant contends that variation in the human species must be grounded in "one single stem, because without the latter the necessity of the heredity would not be comprehensible" (BBMR 8:99). The necessary inheritance of acquired traits is the physical anchor to which Kant ties his determination of a race. The notion of a single stem excludes "any explanation which maintains that the transmission [of inheritable characteristics]—even that which is only acciden-tal, which is not always successful—could ever be the effect of a cause other than that which lies in the germs and dispositions of the species [Gattung] itself" (BBMR 8:97).

---

[15] We should not, however, jump the conclusion that Kant no longer subscribed to a racial hierarchy. As we will see shortly, Kant's racial hierarchy reappears in his response to Forster. See Kleingeld, "Kant's Second Thoughts on Race," 578.

Kant is certainly right to argue that, without proposing an inner force responsible for adaptation, the conjectures of his opponents rely on spontaneous causes and fail to explain the empirically salient phenomena. Yet do his hypothetical forces conform to the disciplinary rules presented in the Doctrine of Method? While Kant evidently believes that his germs and dispositions hypothesis can account for (a), (b), and (c), he concedes that "it is an awkward undertaking to make out *a priori* what brings it about that something which does not belong to the essence of the species [*Gattung*] can be hereditary" (BBMR 8:96). The question is whether a "generative force" strictly adheres to the understanding's model of causality or whether it is in fact a "ghost story [*Gespenstergeschichte*]" fabricated by the mind to satisfy reason's need for completion (BBMR 8:97).[16] In one sense, it is only by reflecting on the connections between species as physical-mechanical connections in an empirical regress that natural historians can coherently follow reason's instruction. Yet in another sense, the temporal structure of an adaptive capacity is different to the linear succession given in intuition and determined by the schematized concept of causality, which is either adjacent in space or sequential in time. Kant's Third Analogy identified the necessary community of objects as a *compostium reale*, which means that each object must be considered within a single causal sequence (A215/B262). Yet the relation between the whole (the world) and the parts (the objects) is not causal, for composition is predicated on causal relations between *the parts*, which determine the whole. The causality of a living natural product, in contrast, moves from parts to whole *and* from whole to parts. This is to say that it is not simply a natural product but also the producer of itself. Natural historians must assume this whole-to-part causality if they are to propose a dispositional force that coordinates the germs, for, while the germs operate like Haller's irritability and sensibility to the extent that they react to various stimuli, the dispositional force is purposive. Kant states that "the *purposiveness* [*das Zweckmäßige*] in an organization is surely the general reason for inferring a preparation that is originally placed in nature with this intent, and for inferring created germs," for the alteration is produced *for the sake of* maintaining its state of functionality (BBMR 8:102–3). Morphological change is intelligible only if one assumes a causality that moves from whole to parts, such that a part is altered for the sake of the whole—either for its own propagation or the propagation of the species of which it is a member.

Kant's critical philosophy clarifies the epistemic status of germs and dispositions in the following way. By restricting speculation to the conditions of possible experience, it rejects the possibility of unconditioned conditions in nature's causal history. The original stem is not given as an object of knowledge but is rather an indeterminate formal relation prescribed by reason to guide reflection on the

---

[16] See Zuckert, "Organisms and Metaphysics," 70.

manifold as the understanding seeks the empirical conditions of living natural products. This is why natural history belongs to the historical doctrine of nature: it is organized under an idea that has been postulated but not (yet) demonstrated. Yet Kant nevertheless contends that the highest formal unity of cognitions—the purposive unity of things—requires that we think of objects not as educts of a hyperphysical cause but as products of physical-mechanical causes. As reason instructs the understanding to attain greater unity and extension, natural historians seek to bring the contingent features of empirical objects into determinate relations. To do so, they propose hypothetical forces on the assumption that they are admixtures of pure forces. Germs and dispositions stand in extreme tension, for they cannot be educts implanted by the Creator, and nor can they be the products of a causal history. They are placeholders for unknown causes, enabling natural historians to classify varieties under races, and races under a higher stem, in a physical-mechanical system of nature.

6.2 Herder and the Unifying Force

If Kant was not aware that the hypothesis of germs and dispositions did not strictly adhere to Real Possibility as he wrote "Determination of the Concept of a Human Race," it became apparent as he reviewed Herder's *Outlines of a Philosophy of the History of Man* for the *Allgemeine Literaturzeitung* later that year. Herder opens with a glowing commendation of Kant's *Universal Natural History* ("a work much less known, than it deserves"), and sets out, following the structure of Kant's book, to sketch a developmental history of nature that begins with the formation of the earth as "a star among stars" and culminates in the cultivation of human capacities.[17] He locates Kant within a great host of natural philosophers who paved the way for a physical account of celestial dynamics: Copernicus, Kepler, Newton, Huygens, and Kant. Moreover, he praises those who have extended this project to the classification of living beings, and directed inquiry along materialist lines: Varenius, Buffon, Maupertuis, Wolff, and Blumenbach.

Herder recognized that his predecessors had all used analogies to achieve their breakthroughs. In an earlier essay, "On the Cognition and Sensation of the Human Soul" (1778), he stated that "*Newton* in his system of the world became a poet contrary to his wishes," as did "*Buffon* in his cosmology."[18] In Newton's *Principia* and Buffon's *Histoire naturelle*, a "single analogy gave birth to the brightest and boldest of theories." However, while each natural philosopher used the analogy to venture boldly into *terra incognita*, none has succeeded in

---

[17] Herder, *Outlines of a Philosophy of the History of Man*, 1.
[18] Herder, "On the Cognition and Sensation of the Human Soul," 186.

realizing the "fine words" offered in hope of a complete account of natural development based on a single, unifying force.[19] In *Universal Natural History*, Kant had gone a step further to grant that the generation of a worm from matter's attractive and repulsive forces is thinkable in principle. Yet the inner complexity of even the simplest living being entails that comprehending this process according to the laws of matter lies beyond our reach. Herder proposes to complete the task by means of the "*analogy of Nature*."[20] While we "cannot penetrate the inmost recesses of her powers," he exclaims, "the modes and effects of her forces lie before us."

Herder draws the analogy of nature from *Universal Natural History*, where Kant argued that analogical reasoning is the proper method for investigating real causes that lie beyond the remit of experience.[21] Yet where Kant refrained from speculating about the generation of living beings within the universal natural system, Herder seeks to present nature as a single, unbroken, continuous process. Herderian nature encompasses the development of animals from plants, the original differentiation of the sexes, the capacity of cold-blooded animals to absorb warmth and warm-blooded animals to create it, the external production of young in birds of flight, and the internal generation of heavy land-dwelling animals.[22] "How much has nature thus contributed to the perfection of the species," Herder extols, as it works incessantly towards higher levels of being.[23]

Disregarding Kant's transcendental notion of analogy, by which the understanding connects every appearance with a material cause through the schematized concept of causality, Herder proposes a naturalized analogy as the basis of cognition. He recasts Kant's legislative understanding as the "terrestrial understanding," which does not spontaneously schematize the appearances given in intuition but is "gradually fashioned by the things around us, that make themselves perceptible to our senses."[24] The terrestrial understanding is not the ground of nature, but a part of it. It does not constitute the causal nexus, but exists within it. At the most basic level, the understanding consists of irritations and sensations, and only then extends to the higher capacity to transform the lesser sensations into structured and meaningful experience. Living beings create images for themselves that transform the manifold of sense data into a unity that has meaning for the particular form of life they bear. The capacity to create an image is a matter of pairing sensations with thoughts, thereby transforming the image into a concept,

[19] Herder, *Outlines of a Philosophy of the History of Man*, 106.
[20] Herder, *Outlines of a Philosophy of the History of Man*, 106.
[21] Kant presented his argument in *Universal Natural History* in continuity with the analogical method he discerned in the work of Kepler, Newton, and Buffon. He states that we may "use the analogy of what has been observed in the orbits of our solar system, namely that the same cause that has imparted centrifugal force to the planets as a result of which they describe their orbits, has also arranged them in such a way that they all relate to one plane, which is therefore also the cause" (NTH 1:250).
[22] Herder, *Outlines of a Philosophy of the History of Man*, 112.
[23] Herder, *Outlines of a Philosophy of the History of Man*, 47.
[24] Herder, *Outlines of a Philosophy of the History of Man*, 6.

such that cognition bears "the stamp of *analogy*." Cognition is analogical all the way down, for it allows the human being to conceive of things through other things, to anticipate what is to come, and to reflect on what has already been experienced. Analogy enables a unified experience what otherwise would be an infinite manifold of particulars.

Herder's goal in *Outlines* is to push analogical reasoning to its supreme limit by unifying the manifold of living nature under a single principle, just as his predecessors had done for cosmology. Newton's physics was made possible by the principle of analogy: "*where effect is, there must be a force.*"[25] The empirical description of the formation of organic bodies by William Harvey and Casper Friedrich Wolff were made possibly by a corresponding "natural analogy": "*where new life is, a principle of new life must exist.*" The natural analogy identifies a law for the organic sphere as a counterpart to the law that Newton had assumed in his mathematical demonstration of the inverse square law of gravity. The representation of an object as living carries with it, by power of the natural analogy, a principle of lawfulness that *becomes* transcendental:

> How must the man have been astonished, who first saw the wonders of the creation of a living being! Globules, with fluids shooting between them, become a living point; and from this point an animal forms itself. The heart soon becomes visible, and, weak and imperfect as it is, begins to beat.... What would he who saw this wonder for the first time call it? There, he would say, is a *living organic force* [lebendige, organische Kraft]: I know not whence it came, or what it intrinsically is: but that it is there, that it lives, that it has acquired itself organic parts out of the chaos of homogeneal matter, I see: it is incontestable.[26]

Herder argues that the manifest effects of a living organic force renders Kant's account of pre-existing germs redundant. "The theory of germs," he declares, "which has been taken to explain vegetation, explains in reality nothing: for the germ is already a form; and where a form is, there must be an organic power, that formed it."[27] And Herder recognized that his critique of the germ hypothesis also demonstrates that Kant's race concept is arbitrary. If one thinks too broadly, then all humans come from a single race. If one thinks too narrowly, then there is an indeterminate number of races, many having the same colour. "I see no reason for

[25] Herder, *Outlines of a Philosophy of the History of Man*, 51. I have modified Churchill's translation of *Kraft* from "power" to "force" to remain consistent with my translations of Kant. Herder also states the principle in terms of physiology: "*Wherever an effect exists in nature, there must be an operating force: where irritability displays itself in effort, or in spasm, a stimulus must be felt within.*"

[26] Herder, *Outlines of a Philosophy of the History of Man*, 319.

[27] Herder, *Outlines of a Philosophy of the History of Man*, 51.

this appellation," Herder concludes, for "race refers to a difference in origin, which in this case does not exist."[28]

It must have been a shock for Kant, now in the spotlight of the Prussian academy for defending transcendental idealism as the proper foundation of natural science, to find his early essay re-entering the human origins debate. Herder dismisses Kant's cautious argument in "Determination of the Concept of a Human Race" only to extend his universal conception of natural history to include the production of life in all of its gradients. In his review of the first volume of *Outlines*, Kant scrutinizes Herder's call for a universal natural history with the methodology of the *Critique*. Scholars tend to interpret Kant as accusing Herder of speculation, based on his charge that Herder's unifying force "lies wholly outside the field of the observational doctrine of nature and belongs merely to speculative philosophy" (RezHerder 8:54).[29] Yet here I agree with Rachel Zuckert, who argues that this interpretation places the debate in the wrong epistemic key.[30] Not only did Herder claim to reject metaphysics in favour of an observational and physiological basis, but Kant also praises Herder's hypothetical starting point (RezHerder 8:54). Kant recognized that Herder's account of the part-whole relation of living beings makes some headway in grounding classification in a physiological basis. Indeed, in Section 6.4, I suggest that Herder's *Outlines* pushed Kant to provide greater conceptual clarity to the use of analogy in his account of living natural products. Yet Kant rejects the parity Herder grants to the mechanical analogy (*where effect is, there must be a force*) and the organic analogy (*where new life is, a principle of new life must exist*). Herder's empiricism cannot explain why there *must* be a force where there is an effect any more than it can explain how the most primitive organization arose from mere matter. The analogy does all the work, leaving Herder unable to explain how *nature* determines an effect through its cause, or life through its principle. Recall Kant's restriction of physical hypotheses in the Doctrine of Method:

It is only possible for our reason to use the conditions of possible experience as conditions of the possibility of things; but it is by no means possible for reason as it were to create new ones, independent of those conditions, for concepts of this sought, although free of contradiction, would nevertheless also be without any object. (A771/B799)

---

[28] Herder, *Outlines of a Philosophy of the History of Man*, 298.
[29] For example, Sloan interprets Kant's criticism as an epistemological restriction that denies Herder's ontological commitment to the principle of life. Sloan, "Preforming the Categories," 249. Zammito argues that Kant's criticism is motivated by a metaphysical commitment to the distinctness of human beings in respect to the animal genus and, correspondingly, to the fixity of species. Zammito, *The Genesis of Kant's Critique of Judgment*, 185–6.
[30] Zuckert, "Organisms and Metaphysics," 70. See also Waldow, "Natural History and the Formation of the Human Being," 67.

The disciplinary rules outlined in the Doctrine of Method state that a hypothesis is only worth assuming if the connection between the consequent and the ground is certain. Without this certainty, we have no reason to assume that an idealization tracks anything real. Thus, even if Herder's hypothetical force could unite the manifold without contradiction, it would remain without an object. The problem with Herder's *Outlines*, then, is not that it presents a system that is false but rather that it presents a system without a truth value.

Here we begin to see a distinction between two kinds of analogy in Kant's review, which will become important for his later account of judgement's power of reflection. The first kind of analogy is grounded in the understanding, which synthetically and *a priori* determines the time ordering of a series given in intuition, resulting in the cognition of an object. Reason's principles introduce an additional layer to this analogy, for they instruct the understanding to seek physical-mechanical conditions of the object, and an economy of the total conditions, on the assumption that like effects have like causes. The second kind of analogy is not grounded in the understanding, which unites a conditioned with its condition, but in reason, which guides reflection on the arrangement of the parts—an arrangement that is contingent on the first analogy—by transposing the schematizing function of an idea to the empirical level of experience. Herder's analogy of nature conflates the two kinds of analogy, and thus directs him to seek a single force that could ground nature as a whole. Kant states that the "reviewer must admit that he does not understand this inference from the analogy of nature, even if he were to concede that continuous gradation of its creatures, together with the rule of governing it" (RezHerder 8:52–3). The reviewer does not understand this inference, for "they are *different* beings that occupy the many stages of the ever more perfect organization" (RezHerder 8:53).

Herein lies the crux of Kant's argument. The use of analogy sets a limit on what speculation can achieve in natural history. Even if one accepts Herder's claim that continuous gradation occurs in nature, the continuity of this gradation can only be represented as real by subsuming every connection under a rule. By analogy, natural historians can connect varieties according to affinities between their manifest properties. Yet these connections do not *explain* those affinities (i.e. they do not ground variation in a higher principle), but identify a *possible* relation that requires careful empirical study to find out whether two natural products can indeed be brought under a higher principle. In this sense, natural history is always striving to become universal, for reason's idea of systematicity, in which every condition can be deduced from a higher condition, is the ideal to which natural historians aspire (recall MAN 4:468). Yet given the limitations of discursive cognition, natural historians must discipline their minds to the rules outlined in the Doctrine of Method to ensure that they do not overrun the scope of legitimate hypothesizing and return to reason's lazy state of false completion. To examine affinities as the result of a rule, natural historians must assume that every natural product appears in an empirical regress. Herder does not provide a causal rule that could link a new kind of offspring to its parents, or an alteration in a single natural product over time that altered its kind, but simply an analogy between organizations in a gradient of increasing complexity:

> as to the ladder of the organizations . . . its use in regard to the realms of nature here on earth . . . leads to nothing. The smallness of the distinctions, if one places the species one after another in accordance with their *similarities*, is, given so huge a manifoldness, a necessary consequence of this manifoldness. Only an *affinity* among them, where either one species would have arisen from the other and all from a single original species or perhaps from a single procreative maternal womb, would lead to *ideas* which, however, are so monstrous that reason recoils before them.   (RezHerder 8:54)

Affinity, Kant contends, is not a physical-mechanical relation. It is a logical relation that establishes a possible physical-mechanical connection in a projected history, thus directing the understanding to *seek* indications of this connection. Herder's natural history grounds variation in an unknown cause that supposedly determines the connections between different kinds of natural product in a single empirical regress. By doing so, it removes the necessity of hereditary peculiarities. That is, it accepts that like can give birth to *un*like, for the "animating forces that organize everything" somehow change themselves in a purposive manner (RezHerder 8:52). Reason recoils from such an idea, Kant protests, for it entails that the laws of nature can be broken and remade. Without the lawfulness of a particular variety, it is impossible for natural historians to search for marks that could indicate a line of descent, for the causal chain would include discontinuous ruptures and nature could potentially be a mosaic of particular things. By removing the original stem, Herder simply replaces physical-mechanical connections with "spiritual forces" that purportedly cause non-physical purposes (RezHerder 8:52). Without such a hypothesis, physical lines of descent fall apart and we find ourselves back in the realm of ghost stories.

Kant's charge is that Herder's hypothesis of a unifying force is futile, for it attempts to "explain *what one does not comprehend* from *what one comprehends even less*" (RezHerder 8:54). Here Kant redeploys the grammar used against Maupertuis and Buffon in *Only Possible Argument*, where he criticized the postulation of mechanical causes to explain the self-organizing capacity of living matter (see Section 4.3). Herder's unifying force is supposed to "constitute the entire distinctiveness of its many genera and species" (RezHerder 8:54). Yet it fails to explain nature's variety—it fails to "clearly determine the concept of a race" (RezHerder 8:62)—for it attributes the diversity of form according to a force that is unbound to a law. Herder's *Outlines* presents a speculative philosophy only to the extent that it cannot anchor a line of development in nature. While Kant "fully concurs" with Herder on account of the need for a force to explain the invariable transference of acquired traits, Herder's force fails to shed light on the *natural* connections manifest in the unfailing hereditary peculiarity manifest in lines of descent. One cannot dispute the hypotheses in Herder's sweeping cosmological history, for there is no touchstone against which they can be tested.

Kant focuses on the question of lawfulness in his review of the second volume of *Outlines*. He begins by repeating his argument that Herder's analogy, which permits one kind of lawfulness emerging from another, denies a historical narrative the status of *natural* history. To provide an alternative, Kant reframes his account of generation as a hypothesis. His account endorses Herder's call for a force that "appropriately modifies *itself* internally in accordance with differences of the external circumstances," yet it entails that the force must be "limited by its nature" (RezHerder 8:62). One could equally define this generative force as "germs" or "original dispositions," Kant contends, without having to regard them "as primordially implanted machines and buds that unfold themselves only when occasioned (as in the system of evolution [i.e. pre-existence])" (RezHerder 8:62–3). They would serve "merely as limitations, not further explicable, of a self-forming faculty." Here Kant revises his germs and dispositions hypothesis in a way that avoids Herder's empirical attack on pre-existence. Germs and dispositions are simply the natural limits of a self-forming faculty, the possibility of which remains unknown. Kant's point is that without assuming a faculty that possesses original unity, the increasing differentiation of matter would be unintelligible, for we would be unable to represent continuity within the empirical regress.

Kant fashions his review as the worry of a natural philosopher who esteems Herder's project, for it is "natural" given the "drive for inquiry" to extend natural history beyond cognitive limits, and yet humbly restricts his hypotheses to the public and contestable domain of natural philosophy (RezHerder 8:55). As Karl Ameriks puts it, Kant's main concern is "more a matter of philosophical method than of final conclusions."[31] Philosophy, Kant ruminates, is concerned "more with pruning abundant saplings than with making them sprout" (RezHerder 8:55). It should guide our reasoning in natural science "not through conjectured but observed laws, not by means of a force of imagination given wings whether through metaphysics or through feelings, but through a reason which is expansive in its design but cautious in the execution."

6.3 Forster and Observation

By the time Kant sketched his 1788 essay "On the Use of Teleological Principles in Philosophy," his account of natural history had developed in light of his reviews of

---

[31] Ameriks, *Kant's Elliptical Path*, 226.

the first two volumes of Herder's *Outlines*. Analogy plays a much more distinctive role than it did in "Determination of the Concept of a Human Race," particularly in the extended account of what he now terms "organic" and "organized beings." Before we turn to his account of organized beings in Section 6.4, it is important to consider Kant's occasion for writing the essay: an article by Georg Forster published in the *Teutsche Merkur* in 1786, entitled "Something More about the Human Races." In this article, Forster attacks Kant's distinction between natural history and the description of nature (and thus his distinction between race and variety), criticizing Kant for requiring natural historians to project structural features onto nature that are far more arbitrary than the physiological markers established by Linnaeus.

Forster's primary concern is that Kant provides subjective grounds for what ought to be grounded in the objects themselves. His attack picks out the guiding principle Kant presented in "Determination of the Concept of a Human Race," that one "finds in experience what one needs only if one knows in advance what to look for." On Forster's reading, Kant's principle derives an original condition of the human species that no one has ever encountered.[32] Far from leading natural historians to the true conception of heredity, Forster charges Kant with being guilty of "the most common of all illusions, namely, that we, in the appointed search for that which we need, often also believe that we have found it there, where it does not really exist."[33] As a fictional postulation in the mind of the historian, Kant's projected focal point is "not sufficient for the differentiation of species."[34] In opposition to Kantian natural history, Forster proposes to differentiate race from species "simply through the inconstancy of its characteristic features."[35] Gradations of skin colour are not fixed but merely accidental qualities caused by alterations in climate, and thus cannot serve to determine a race.

To update the Linnaean schema with the observations accrued during his voyage on the *Resolution*, Forster turns to a "physiological and anatomical basis," which supposedly yields the true invariably heritable characteristics.[36] This criterion identifies *two* races: "*Africa* produced its human beings (the Negroes), *Asia* its human beings (all others), the affinity of all derived from there."[37] While Forster states that he refrains from collapsing race into species, he does so in practice, for the invariable inheritance of anatomy renders the two races distinct kinds by virtue of their separate lineage.[38] His point is that Kant's monogenism, because it appeals to a single line of descent that can never be

---

[32] Forster, "Something More about the Human Races," 153.

[33] Forster, "Something More about the Human Races," 148.

[34] Forster, "Something More about the Human Races," 153.

[35] Forster, "Something More about the Human Races," 159.

[36] Forster, "Something More about the Human Races," 155.

[37] This is Kant's paraphrase of Forster's argument (ÜGTP 8:179–80).

[38] Forster, "Something More about the Human Races," 156.

experienced, is "a science for gods and not for human beings." "Who has the means of making known the ancestral tree of even a single variety up to its species," Forster asks, "if that variety did not first come into being from another before our very own eyes?"[39] If the invariable differences characteristic of a race

> can no longer be traced historically back to their point of origination, then the least that we can do is regard the descent as underdetermined; and the distinction that Kant wants to make between the concepts of the description of nature and the knowledge of natural history must become altogether void.[40]

Thus Kant found himself attacked from both sides (see ÜGTP 8:160). Herder *and* Forster viewed his proposal for natural history as a radical historical narrative. Herder appraised it. Forster condemned it. In "Teleological Principles," Kant sets out to show that Forster's objections to his race concept "derive only from the misunderstanding of the principle from which I start" (ÜGTP 8:161). In Kant's view, Forster had accused him of "wanting to answer a question of the *physical* investigation of nature through documents of religion," that is, of replacing natural history with a "science of the gods" (ÜGTP 8:160). This accusation betrays a fundamental misunderstanding of critical philosophy, Kant laments, for it mistakes the hypothetical connections within a system of history for nature itself. He thus begins by clarifying the starting principle for natural history in light of the *Critique*. Nature, he states, "is the sum-total of all that exists as determined by laws," which includes the world and its "supreme cause" (ÜGTP 8:157). When it comes to investigating nature, we can pursue two paths: physics, which takes a theoretical path, and metaphysics, which takes a teleological path. In "all examination of nature reason rightly calls for theory first," which seeks causal connections within the physical-mechanical system of experimental science.

Yet "where theory abandons us"—where we encounter empirical phenomena whose form is mechanically contingent—Kant insists that we "need to start from a teleological principle" (ÜGTP 8:157). Experience alone cannot yield a theory of invariable inheritance. The understanding simply would not be able to discern which characteristics were significant for classification unless judgement, the faculty responsible for bringing objects under concepts, had already presupposed that the parts were arranged according to a purpose. Forster is right to the extent that, in terms of nature as a physical-mechanical system, varieties are underdetermined. Without proposing the hypothetical dispositions, which coordinate the expression of the germs, variations would be utterly contingent in regards to nature's universal laws. However, Kant then claims that something *in nature* summons reason to devise such a hypothesis. When "reason on the theoretical

---

[39] Forster, "Something More about the Human Races," 156.
[40] Forster, "Something More about the Human Races," 164.

path of nature ... is not able to achieve its *entire* intention as wished"—to bring the understanding's cognitions into maximal unity and extension—we *must* proceed teleologically, that is, we *must* presuppose a purposive unity that coordinates the forces for which the understanding seeks. Reason is compelled to "establish a *principle* in advance ... to guide the investigator of nature even *in searching* and observing, and especially a principle that would orient observation towards a *natural history* to be furthered by this procedure, in contrast to a mere *description of nature*" (ÜGTP 8:161).

On Sloan's reconstruction, Kant's response to Forster is to weaken the claims of natural history and to advocate something closer to natural description. To prove that his critical philosophy does not advance a science for the gods, Kant concedes that it is a "systematic description, not a history of nature, that is able to achieve the desired unity of nature as a system."[41] Yet Sloan's reconstruction cannot be right. Kant's aim is not simply to clarify his separation between history and description, but to demonstrate that we *must* seek a history of nature if the understanding is to harmonize with reason when confronted with the demands of empirical nature. The problem Kant identifies with Forster's essay is that it claims to ground lower level concepts in the distinction between invariable characteristics and accidental modifications with exclusive reference to marks found in experience. Kant agrees with Forster that "a *narrative* of events in nature [cannot] be reached by any human reason," for such would be, as Forster duly noted, a science of the gods. Yet a purely descriptive account is equally untenable, for "nothing of a purposive nature could ever be found through mere empirical groping without a guiding principle of what to search for." To steer between mere description and rational projection, Kant proposes the method of "observation [*Beobachtung*]."[42] Observation is more expansive than the notion of experience Kant examined in the Transcendental Analytic, for it refers to a kind of "*meth-odologically* conducted experience." To observe is to be "guided by a determinate principle," such that one can "pay attention to that which could indicate the original stem, not just the resemblance of characters" (ÜGTP 8:164).

Kant defends the superiority of methodologically conducted experience over Forster's supposedly bare description by showing how it affords the greatest unity and extension of the understanding's cognitions. Forster's Linnaean conception of variation attributes the variety of skin colour to external effects in the environment. He thus considers skin colour to be an accidental, non-hereditary characteristic that could change back to its original state given the right environmental conditions.[43] Yet by attending only to accidental causes, Forster is faced with an

---

[41] Sloan, "Kant on the History of Nature," 640.

[42] For an account of observation as a precursor to reflecting judgement, see Cooper, "Kant on Observation," 947–9.

[43] See Forster, "Something More about the Human Races," 153.

empirical problem. To explain the coexistence of peoples of different skin colour in the same environment, he must "assume two original stems in order to explain these characters" (ÜGTP 8:169). Yet what justification can he provide for differentiating the accidental variation of skin colour from what has been inherited necessarily from the original stems? Forster's "rash reasoning" simply "follows the lead of *Linné's* principle of the persistence of the character," *claiming* unmediated observation but in fact imposing an arbitrary logic onto the phenomena (ÜGTP 8:161).

Kant argues that natural history will have greater success if Linnaeus' arbitrary principle is abandoned in favour of a rational principle. The coexistence of peoples with different skin colour in the same climate confirms "the conjection of an entirely consistent generative affinity [*Zeugungsverwandtschaft*] through the unity of an original stem, while simultaneously confirming the conjection of a *cause* of their classificatory difference residing in the human beings themselves, not merely in the climate" (ÜGTP 8:177). Here Kant acknowledges that the notion of an inner force is merely hypothetical. Yet he contends that it is a hypothesis summoned by reason when confronted with the demands of empirical nature. What Forster viewed as the "*deviation from an original stem* [Ausartung]" (an accidental variety) is in fact a "*degeneration* [Abartung]" (a self-reproducing variety) (ÜGTP 8:163–4). By rejecting the distinction between natural description and natural history, Forster removes the capacity of natural historians to distinguish accidental deviations from rule-governed degenerations, and thus the possibility of reflecting on variation as governed by a law.

Kant's separation of natural description from natural history is informed by his critical philosophy in the following way. As established in the Transcendental Analytic, the schematized concept of causation serves as the analogical frame in which the understanding can represent any succession in outer sense. Yet to unify its conditioned cognitions, reason must instruct the understanding to seek physical-mechanical connections within an empirical regress of causes and effects that autonomously produces itself from the smallest number of fundamental forces. Following reason's instruction, the understanding seeks the material conditions of appearances as products of a physical-mechanical process. Yet Kant now identifies a further problem for the understanding as it moves deeper into the demands of empirical nature. While many of the affinities between natural products remain contingent on the mechanical analogy, something *in experience* arises that exceeds understanding and invites reflection; namely, characteristics that are both acquired and "propagated unfailingly." The experience of necessity in the face of physical-mechanical contingency could only be possible if one were to follow a principle that enabled one to reflect on the forces that govern an object's functionality as coordinated by a concept. Such a principle is teleological, for it guides reflection on the object as a "natural purpose [*Naturzweck*]," as something that cannot be grasped according to physical-mechanical relations, whereby wholes are caused by their parts, but according to teleological relations, whereby parts are caused by the whole (ÜGTP 8:162).

When natural historians experience an object as a natural purpose—as a purpose *in* nature—they examine its seemingly contingent characteristics as necessary effects of a generative force. A race captures a line of descent by which certain characteristics, acquired for the purpose of maintaining its state of organization, are passed on without fail. Thus understood, race is not an artificial concept that captures mere affinities that connect subspecies under a species. Kant contends that race, as an empirically conditioned concept, "is well grounded in the reason of each observer of nature who infers from a hereditary particularity of different interbreeding animals that does not at all lie in the concept of their genus a common cause, namely a cause that lies originally in the stem of the species [*Gattung*]" (ÜGTP 8:163). The concept of race is thus necessary "in respect to natural history," for it allows "the greatest degree of manifoldness in the generation can be united by reason with the greatest unity of original stem [*Abstammung*]" (ÜGTP 8:164). Kant's contention is that reason generates the concept of race in response to the hereditary particularity of organized beings, which pass on certain acquired characteristics to members of the following generation. The use of reason does not entail that racial boundaries lack objective grounds. The concept of race, Kant declares, is solicited by and stands to be confirmed though experience: "Whether there really is such an affinity in the human species must be decided through the observations that make known the unity of the original stem" (ÜGTP 8:164).

Kant's discovery of a new way that reason coordinates the activities of the understanding marks an important development in his critical philosophy that we will examine further in the following section. Before doing so, however, it is vital to note that the observations Kant calls on to "make known the unity of the human species" are, once more, deeply problematic, indicating that his critical turn has done little to resist his racist views. Kant was well aware that the available travel writings fell profoundly short of achieving a scientific status ("I do not care for the mere empirical traveler and his narrative," ÜGTP 8:161). Yet it is not the accuracy of their descriptions that attract his scorn him but rather their ability to follow the demands reason. Kant's aim is to demonstrate that the descriptions recorded in the available travel writings can—or rather, *must*—be transformed into natural history. In one of the most damming moments of his entire corpus, Kant defends the fixity of racial boundaries by citing a German paraphrase of an anonymous pro-slavery text published in the fifth volume of Matthias Christian Sprengel's *Beiträge zur Völker- und Länderkunde*, originally titled "Cursory Remarks upon the Reverend Mr Ramsay's Essay on the Treatment and Conversion of African Slaves in the Sugar Colonies." The essay, now known to be written by the anti-abolitionist merchant James Tobin, presents a sustained attack on Reverend James Ramsay's *An Essay on the Treatment and Conversion of*

African Slaves in the British Sugar Colonies (1784), in which Ramsay defends abolition by calling on personal observations from his missionary activities in the colonies. In a chapter entitled "Natural Capacity of African Slaves Vindicated," Ramsay argues that if a lack of intellectual capacity or ingenuity were truly found among African slaves, it should be attributed to environmental factors, and balanced with the abundant evidence of learning and innovation *despite* the inhumane conditions of slavery. Yet the available travel writings do not accurately document the facts, Ramsay contends, but reflect a prejudice held by European colonizers. As soon as Africans are "allowed to be a *distinct* race," he observes, "European pride immediately concludes them an *inferior* race, and then it allows, of course, that nature formed them to be slaves to their superiors."[44] Ramsay claims that only one who is blinded by prejudice could deny that if an African slave were "properly educated," "taught his importance as a member of society," and "accustomed to weigh his claim to, and enjoy the possession of the unalienable rights of humanity," he would match the European in learning and art.[45] There is "no difference between the intellects of whites and blacks," he concludes, "but such as circumstances and education naturally produce."[46]

In his reply to Ramsay, Tobin provides evidence to establish that racial temperament persists despite changes in environment. Kant summarizes the relevant section of Tobin's argument in a footnote:

> The same author notes on this matter that it is not the northern climate that makes the Negroes disinclined for labor. For they would rather endure waiting behind the coaches of their masters or, during the worst winter nights, in the cold entrances of the theatres (in England) than to be threshing, diffing, carrying loads, etc.   (ÜGTP 8:174n)

Kant infers from Tobin's description of freed slaves that the incapacity for "industrious" labour is not environmental but can only be derived from the "natural predisposition" of the African race (ÜGTP 8:174n). The "drive to activity," a capacity that lay unrealized in the original stem, has been indelibly lost. This inference does not appear to Kant as a hypothesis that *could* explain the inactivity of freed slaves. It shares the epistemic status of monogenism (it is well grounded in the reason of each observer of nature when confronted with the empirical data), thereby transforming Tobin's description into natural history,

---

[44] Ramsay, *An Essay on the Treatment and Conversion of African Slaves in the British Sugar Colonies*, 231. Ramsay calls on Hume's "Of National Characters" as both an example of and a key source of inspiration for this conclusion—a text that Kant uses to justify hierarchical racial divisions in his physical geography lectures (V-Geo/Dohna 1792 26.2.2:1131).

[45] Ramsay, *An Essay on the Treatment and Conversion of African Slaves in the British Sugar Colonies*, 253.

[46] Ramsay, *An Essay on the Treatment and Conversion of African Slaves in the British Sugar Colonies*, 203.

even when Ramsay's contradictory observations were published alongside it in Sprengel's *Beiträge*.[47] Huaping Lu-Adler observes that Kant is "eager to use Tobin's testimony to corroborate his hypothesis that, if a people exhibit a characteristic that appears unalterable in a new environment, this heredity can only be explained in the same manner that he has explained the heredity of skin color."[48] Kant's eagerness is betrayed by the fact that, despite assuring his audience that natural history deals only in "fragments" and "hypotheses," he is sufficiently confident with his explanation to extend it to his own observations of the gypsies in Königsberg, who "bring with them and pass on to their offspring no more of this impulse [to work] when living in other climates than what they had needed in their old mother land" (ÜGTP 8:174n). Here Kant's "opinion" about racial profiles is better described as "persuasion", a species of assent that obtains when one holds a proposition to be true on account of a cognitive illusion. In Kant's terms, persuasion "is really a kind of delusion; for one always considers only the one side, without in the least reflecting on the opposite side" (V-Lo/Blomberg 24:144). It appears that Kant's critical philosophy does not protect him from this kind of delusion, and the proliferation of hypotheses he builds upon it.

It is important to note, however, that Kant's conjectures do not follow directly from the disciplinary rules outlined in his critical philosophy. His attempt to apply the critical method in the context of the human origins debate operates in collusion with the assumptions we identified in Section 4.4, and betray (at least) two serious failings as a *Naturforscher*. First, the fact that Kant feels no need to consult additional observations, even when Ramsay's essay (the subject of Tobin's cursory remarks) lay in his hands, betrays a reckless disregard for the disciplined procedure sketched in the Doctrine of Method. Judged against his own rules, Kant's conjectures are *un*disciplined, for he has insufficient grounds to merit the level of credence he bestows on them. The inference he draws from Tobin's description of freed slaves does not follow from reason when confronted with the documented observations, as he would have his readers think. Kant's inference follows from reason when deployed with the prior assumption that temperamental characteristics are (1) physical-mechanical (physical geohumoralism), (2) enduring (racial purity), and (3) measurable against a European standard (white superiority). What we see is a disturbing selection bias, as Kant appeals to observations that, in his view, capture the natural temperament of African slaves, and brushes aside those that do not. Second, Kant's inability to define and actively seek the kind of evidence that *could* corroborate (or refute) his hypothesis betrays an ineptitude to determine what counts as epistemic grounds when it comes to

---

[47] Bernasconi stresses the significance of this neglect in "Kant as an Unfamiliar Source of Racism," 148.

[48] Lu-Adler insightfully asks, "how often do we see [Kant] so unreservedly trusting another man's testimony?" Lu-Adler, "Kant's Use of Travel Reports in Theorizing about Race," 18.

evidential confirmation. Nowhere does he consider the available counterevidence, and nowhere does he consider alternative hypotheses (such as Ramsay's). While Kant acknowledges that natural history "can only point to fragments or shaky hypotheses" (ÜGTP 8:163), he nevertheless claims that any observer of nature, under the stimulation of a narrative expressly written to refute an abolitionist argument, ought to accept his physical explanation of why African slaves fail to express the moral characteristics of Europeans. Given the practical risk he is willing to take by publicly defending his rational principle against Forster's attack, Kant clearly adopted these shaky hypotheses as opinions that, in his judgement, have sufficient justification to merit the assent of his readers.

6.4 Natural Products and Organized Beings

So far we have seen that the opinions defended in "Teleological Principles" demonstrate that, in 1788, Kant continued to hold a racialized concept of race. It is thus interesting to note that in *Critique of the Power of Judgment*, published just two years later, Kant makes no mention of race. This is partly due to the fact that an empirical concept does not strictly belong to a critique of judgement, which seeks to discern the *a priori* principles of reflection. However, in the following chapter, I argue that the absence of race in the third *Critique* neverthe- less reflects a shift in Kant's thought that occurs between 1788 and 1790, after which he no longer holds that reason requires us to assume that the boundaries between subspecies are fixed. In this final section, I anticipate this argument by showing that while the observations cited in "Teleological Principles" corroborate Kant's racialized concept of race, his *critique* of observation—his attempt to determine the legitimate use of teleological principles in natural science— undermines his claim that a racialized concept of race is necessary in respect to natural history. This will help us to understand why, in 1790, Kant concedes that it is not contrary to reason to entertain a hypothesis according to which subspecies are in a state of becoming.

Having defended his account of the human races in the main part of the essay, Kant concludes "Teleological Principles" by determining what can and cannot feature in a scientific natural history. Because the understanding requires that empirical objects are explained according to its model of causation, which, under the guidance of reason's highest formal unity, takes the form of physical- mechanical causation, a hypothesis in which original human beings were created at some point in the earth's development, or spontaneously arose from seeds that were scattered across the earth, is illegitimate. Yet Kant nevertheless seeks to determine a legitimate use of teleology in scientific research. If there are things in nature that require us to assume an alternative part-to-whole relation in order to understand them, it must be possible to represent a kind of being whose parts are internally coordinated by a generative force. While beings of such a kind must be judged as products of physical-mechanical causes, they must also be judged as purposive structures that produce *themselves* by modifying, maintaining, and reproducing their form within that system. We find ourselves at the extreme boundaries of natural science, for it seems that we *must* introduce "self-concocted forces of matter following unheard-of and unverifiable laws" (ÜGTP 8:179). In other words, to bring the maximal extension and unity to the understanding's cognitions, reason is compelled to introduce a causality according to ends *to* the investigation of nature, thereby invoking an additional order of determinacy to that provided by the understanding. While the forces that govern living natural products are "natural" to the extent that they are entirely resident in the physical-mechanical system, we must assume a coordinating force "the existence of which cannot be proven through anything, or even the very possibility of which can hardly be reconciled with reason" (ÜGTP 8:179).

How can such forces be attributed to natural purposes without evoking Herder's spiritual force, which strips natural history of objectivity? Kant's solution is to propose an analogical kind of reflection by which natural historians are able to examine one thing *through* another, thereby turning that thing into an item that the understanding *can* investigate. This account of analogy has clear resonances with Herder's argument in *Outlines*, and yet it denies the parity Herder attributed to the mechanical and organizational analogies. In the student notes taken from Kant's lectures on logic, Kant is recorded as defining analogy as an aesthetic mode of judging. In *Jäsche Logic* (1800), for instance, Kant separates "logical distinctness" from "aesthetic distinctness," where the former "rests on objective clarity of marks" and the latter on "subjective clarity" (Log 9:62). Logical distinctness is clarity through concepts. Aesthetic distinctness does not pertain to cognition but rather to judgement as it searches for a ground, and thus involves "clarity through examples *in concreto*" (Log 9:62). Examples that manifest similar marks point to a concept, or suggest that the discovery of a unifying concept is possible, but do so without schematizing the intuition. This mode of presentation is analogical, for the intuition and the supposed concept "do not fit exactly." The use of analogy allows us to extend beyond the marks given in experience by exhibiting like intuitions alongside each other for comparison. This kind of analogy does not produce an object in thought but enables reflection on an actual object's form. A natural purpose, then, is a quasi-object that we reflect on as (a) a product that is fully resident within the causal sequence of nature and (b) a self-organizing whole. While the persistence of a natural purpose is represented *through* time by virtue of a specific generative force, its self-organizing structure is represented *in* time, whereby the whole accounts for the existence of the parts and the parts account for the existence of the whole. Yet how could such a structure be found in experience, if the faculty of sensibility necessarily places perceptions in a linear sequence and the schematized concept of causality provides the procedural rule for finding the necessary connection of determinate features in time? The unity of cognition is always composed of externally related parts that are independent of one another and distinct from the whole. The understanding cannot grasp parts that are internally related according to a part-whole structure that works forwards *and* backwards in time.

While objects *qua* objects of the understanding cannot be purposive, it is nevertheless clear that the possibility of exhibiting and then thinking an alternative part-whole relation lies in the power of judgement. Kant infers that judgement must be able to operate independently of the understanding by reflecting on a particular natural product as purposive. An organized being, he explains, "is a material being which is possible only though the relation of everything contained in it to each other as end and means" (ÜGTP 8:181). Like Herder, Kant was influenced by a growing body of research that investigated the form of living beings in the hope of discovering new classificatory marks that are not external but structural. It was obvious to him to say that "every anatomist as well as every physiologist actually starts from this concept [of an organized being]." Yet in contrast to Herder, Kant denies that the whole-to-parts relation of organized beings is analogous to the parts-to-whole relation of Newtonian mechanics, for the grounds of the two judgements are not equal. While we think of the basic force that governs organization as "a cause effective according to *purposes*," we know of such forces "*in terms of their ground of determination* only *in ourselves*, namely in our understanding and will, as a cause of the possibility of certain products that are arranged entirely according to purposes, namely that of *works of art*" (ÜGTP 8:181). To cause an artefact is a matter of efficient, physical-mechanical causes; the artist moves her arm to spread paint on the canvas. To cause the *possibility* of an artwork, however, requires a rational power, "a faculty to produce something *according to an idea*, which is called purpose" (ÜGTP 8:181). An artwork *qua* artwork (rather than a canvas covered with paint) is thus conceived not as the effect of a cause but as the product of an action. Applied to natural products, to observe an appearance as an organized being enables natural historians to search for the physical-mechanical forces that produce its parts. Yet to do so, they must presuppose a concept that coordinates those forces, just as reason's ideas coordinate the material laws of the understanding. This presupposing is the result of analogy, which places the artistic causality we know in ourselves alongside a certain natural product, such that we *think* the idea of a subjective cause as the condition for the possibility of its functional parts. We reflect on the unknown cause aesthetically by observing an item through the marks of another causality we know, but does not exactly fit.

Kant's subjective determination of a natural purpose entails that natural historians are not entitled to take purposiveness as an explanatory ground. To claim that effects are governed by a different kind of purpose, one that is "effective from itself *purposively* but *without a purpose*" (ÜGTP 8:181), one would have to "*make up* a basic force—something to which reason is not at all entitled, because otherwise it would take no effect for reason to explain *whatever* and *however* it wants" (ÜGTP 8:182). Yet to reflect on the arrangement of the parts *as* purposive—to "think an *intelligent being* along with them"—enables the understanding to search for the physical-mechanical properties that it *can* find. This use of analogy is incommensurate with Newton's deduction of gravity, for it is not an analogy with the understanding's determination of an effect through a cause but an analogy with reason's organization of the cognitive faculties. Kant concludes that while we "can very well know a priori that there must be a connection of causes and effects in nature," we cannot "know a priori that there must be ends in nature." The use of the teleological principle with respect to nature "is always empirically conditioned"; it is discovered through reflection on the peculiar contingency of some natural products.

If purposiveness cannot serve as an explanatory ground, then the inference Kant made in "Determination of the Concept of a Human Race" from purposiveness to "a preparation that is originally placed in the nature of a creature" is illegitimate (BBMR 8:102–3). Purposiveness is a principle by which natural historians observe the parts of a creature as members of a whole. Kant's account of observation thus resolves the tension between the understanding's conception of a force and the purposive unity of living natural products, for it identifies an additional kind of experience that is not governed by the understanding but guided by analogy. The analogy enables natural historians to reflect on the parts of a natural product as members of an organized whole, but it does not licence them to attribute functionality to a part in isolation of the whole's activity. If one were to hypothesize about *created* germs in the physical-mechanical order of nature, as Kant had done in "Determination of the Concept of a Human Race" (BBMR 8:103), one would place the understanding at odds with itself. On the one hand, created germs enable reflection on hereditary peculiarities as the product of a rule that satisfies the understanding. On the other hand, they locate the causality of design within the physical-mechanical system of nature, and thereby block the understanding from finding determinate conditions for its cognitions. Germs, if they can feature as a legitimate hypothesis at all, must be stripped of teleological qualities and reconceived as material forces that determine observed effects. Kant began to strip the germs of teleological qualities in the Herder review, where he qualified germs as natural limits of an unknown formative faculty. In the following chapter, I suggest that, by 1790, he had abandoned the germ hypothesis altogether.

Kant's critique of observation opens the conceptual space he will develop in *Critique of the Power of Judgment*, where the capacity to reflect on items in nature as the product of a concept is understood as an expression of the reflecting power of judgement. In the Transcendental Dialectic, the regulative principles that guide our reflection on nature as a system are available in advance and are "admitted as problematic only" (A646/B674). They instruct natural historians to seek the physical-mechanical conditions of their conditioned cognitions, and to continue searching for higher and lower divisions among them. In contrast, observation is methodologically conducted *experience*, allowing natural historians to examine certain *natural products* as purposive, even though the principle that grounds that judgement does not strictly belong to nature. It is thus Kant's attempt to defend a scientific account of natural history that leads him to assign analogical reasoning, formerly a matter of reason's regulative use, to the faculty of judgement, thereby opening a field of experience wherein we reflect on appearances through an analogy with ends.

In the following chapter, I suggest that Kant's critique of judgement's power of reflection opens a more expansive programme of classification in which a sub-species may be an incipient version of a higher division as natural historians push further back in their historical investigations. Kant recognized that Herder had something right when he attacked his preformed germs and claimed instead that specification is not simply a subjective principle but also an objective process. While a line of descent might be real to the extent that it can be represented within a physical-mechanical system, where one draws the line—four races, forty races, or as many races as there are individuals—could only be determined if one were to view germs as created for a purpose rather than as functions of a purposive whole. Of course, Kant's critique of judgement's power of reflection does not prevent him from defending racist opinions after 1790.[49] What it reveals is that those opinions were not dependent on the standard of scientificity defined by critique, but on prior assumptions that Kant was unable—or unwilling—to bring to critical reflection.

[49] For instance, in the section "On Human Beings" in the student notes from the physical geography lectures of 1792, Kant is recorded as making hierarchical divisions within humankind (V-Geo/Dohna 1792 26.2.2:1131), though without the explanatory detail he offers in "Teleological Principles." He continues to use race as the proper classificatory marker for documenting human difference, but refers to many more races than the four defined in the Dönhoff notes (cf. V-Geo/Dönhoff 1781/2 26.2.2:887–8). In a subsection entitled "A special note on Negroes," Kant cites Hume's essay "Of National Characters," which states that "among then many thousands of Negroes who are gradually being freed, there is not a single example of one who has distinguished himself," and takes Hume's observation as empirical evidence that there are natural levels of ingenuity among the races (V-Geo/Dohna 1792 26.2.2:1132). Furthermore, Kant's endorsement of Girtanner's *Über das kantische Prinzip für die Naturgeschichte* in 1798 seems to indicate his approval of Girtanner's appropriation of his racial hierarchy (Anth 7:320). See Gorkom, "Immanuel Kant's Racism in Context," 170–1.

7

The Method of Natural History

From his earliest work, Kant attempted to lay metaphysical foundations for a Newtonian mechanics capable of explaining the apparently contingent features of nature according to physical causes. Yet he also acknowledged that the further natural historians progress in their capacity to explain the generation of each empirical object within the system of nature, the clearer it becomes that some natural products are contingent in a particular sense. The attempts made by Hales, Buffon, and Haller to graft physiology into Newtonian science demonstrate that to explain physiological movement according to mechanical laws requires one to assume either some initial state of organization or the existence of organic particles capable of producing it. In either case, the appearance of organization in the mechanism of nature is contingent in regard to the universal laws of Newtonian physics, posing a threat to nature's physical unity.

While Kant was fully cognizant of the particular contingency of living natural products from at least the mid-1760s, his dispute with Herder and Forster prompted him to define and present an "unavoidable illusion" raised by the concept of a living natural product that, if left undiagnosed, deceives the natural historian (KU 5:386). In *Critique of the Power of Judgment* (1790), he claims that the illusion arises due to things in nature that summon us to employ two kinds of causality to understand them, both of which purport to explain their possibility. As a natural product, we reflect on the whole as generated by the mechanical interaction of the parts. As a *living* natural product—what Kant termed a "natural purpose" or "organized being" in "On the Use of Teleological Principles in Philosophy"—we also reflect on the parts according to a concept of the whole.[1] Kant presents the conflict in the form of two maxims of the reflecting power of judgement, which, in contrast to the understanding, is not given its principles in advance but finds them in the course of experience:

M_1: All generation of material things and their forms must be judged as possible in accordance with merely mechanical laws.

---

[1] The tension contained within the idea of a "living natural product" can also be seen in Kant's use of the term "organic products [*organischen Produkten*]" in *Critique of the Power of Judgment* (KU 5:379, 413, 414). An "organized product of nature," he explains, "is that in which everything is an end and reciprocally a means as well" (KU 5:376).

Kant and the Transformation of Natural History. Andrew Cooper, Oxford University Press. © Andrew Cooper 2023.
DOI: 10.1093/oso/9780192869784.003.0008

M₂: Some products of material nature cannot be judged as possible according to merely mechanical laws (judging them requires an entirely different law of causality, namely that of final causes).   (KU 5:387)

The two maxims of reflecting judgement are not evenly weighted. M_1 is a universal methodological maxim, instructing us to seek the conditions of material things in accordance with merely mechanical laws. "Merely" here denotes that M_1 is not simply necessary for our judging the generation of material things but also sufficient for the task.[2] M_2 does not challenge the necessity of judging natural products according to mechanical laws, and neither does it propose an alternative kind of generation. It simply denies the sufficiency of M_1 for judging some natural products. Despite the disparity in scope, Kant contends that the two maxims form an antinomy that threatens to deceive natural historians as they attempt to bring their observations into greater unity and extension.

The antinomy of reflecting judgement is riddled with interpretive difficulties.[3] There is disagreement whether reflecting judgement can have a genuine antinomy at all, and, even if it could, whether Kant would be able to resolve it. In this final chapter, I argue that Kant's presentation of the antinomy can be seen as a culminating moment in his career-long engagement with natural history, for it demonstrates that the problems persisting in the extant natural histories are entirely natural for discursive cognition as it enters more deeply into the demands of empirical nature. Commentators regularly overlook the fact that the conflict between M_1 and M_2 does not arise from the empirical underdetermination of organized form, as if there were causal processes in nature that could not be judged mechanistically.[4] That we must always judge the origins of material things mechanistically is never in question for Kant. Rather, the conflict arises when we discover that, when investigating the "generation of material things and their form," it is necessary to adopt an *additional* principle for judging the causal histories that gave rise to them.[5] This is to say that the antinomy arises from the way that reflecting judgement governs determining judgement when examining the "products of material nature," that is, when natural historians seek to classify natural products under concepts that capture physical descent.[6] I argue that when

---

[2] See Teufel, "What Is the Problem of Teleology," 215.

[3] For overviews of the primary difficulties, see Watkins, "The Antinomy of Teleological Judgment"; Quarfood, "The Antinomy of Teleological Judgment."

[4] This oversight is made by commentators who base M_2 on the "mechanical inexplicability" of a natural purpose, and thus suggest that the antinomy is generated from an empirical underdetermination experienced in nature. See Ginsborg, "Kant on Understanding Organisms as Natural Purposes," 238; Ginsborg, "Two Kinds of Mechanical Inexplicability," 33; Zammito, "Teleology Then and Now," 759.

[5] By "generation" I take Kant to refer to the kind of motion presented in *Universal Natural History*, whereby the physical relations that bind matter in a single world, over time, give rise to the manifold variety of natural products (see KU 5:408).

[6] Here I agree with Teufel, who contends that the antinomy must be understood as a conflict that arises within reflecting judgement's governance of determining judgement in the context of natural

viewed as a conflict between two maxims that arise in the attempt to classify natural products according to material generation, it becomes clear that there *is* an antinomy of reflecting judgement, and, moreover, that the antinomy requires a different kind of resolution to the Antinomies of the first *Critique*, where an appeal to the distinction between appearances and things in themselves either diffuses the proofs, as in the First and Second Antinomies, or restricts the scope of the principles such that they no longer conflict, as in the Third and Fourth. The thrust of Kant's resolution, I argue, is to show that if we refrain from locating the conflict in nature and consider it instead as one that arises from the peculiar character of discursive cognition when it attends to the demands of empirical nature, we can develop a logically consistent method for natural history that *retains* the conflict between M_1 and M_2 while removing its power to deceive.

Of course, Kant's primary concern in the Critique of the Teleological Power of Judgment is not to refine the method of natural history. In the context of his broader project in the third *Critique*, Kant's aim is to establish that our need to judge some natural products teleologically can be extended to guide the investigation of "the whole of nature as a system in accordance with the rule of ends" (KU 5:378), thereby opening a bridge between the practical and the theoretical domains (see KU 5:176). This aim is reflected in the Methodology, where Kant devotes just two sections to the method of natural history and the remaining ten sections to our presumption that nature is hospitable to the highest good. Nevertheless, Kant is clear that a critique of teleological judging "can and must provide the method for how nature must be judged in accordance with the principle of final causes" (KU 5:417), and it is to this restricted provision that we will attend.[7]

In the first two sections, I reconstruct the proofs for M_1 and M_2, which are notoriously unclear. In Section 7.1, I argue that Kant's transcendental argument for reflecting judgement's principle of purposiveness can also be seen as a proof of the more specific principle of the purposiveness of nature as a physical-mechanical system (M_1). In Section 7.2, I explicate Kant's argument for the necessity of judging some natural products as purposive in the Analytic of the Teleological Power of Judgment (M_2). Having established what I take to be the strongest and most plausible arguments for M_1 and M_2, I then consider the presentation and resolution of the antinomy in Section 7.3. Kant's resolution, I argue, entails that teleological judgement does not suspend the necessity of judging mechanistically but simply demonstrates that mechanical laws are insufficient to explain the form of living natural products. In Section 7.4, I turn to the

history. Yet in contrast to Teufel, I argue that the imperative is not hypothetical but practical, for, as we saw in Section 5.2, a legitimate hypothesis must be *possibly* true of nature. See Teufel, "What Is the Problem of Teleology," 205–6.

[7] For a study of the Critique of the Teleological Power of Judgment that gives equal weighting to both projects, see Geiger, *Kant and the Claims of the Empirical World*, 49–97.

opening sections of the Methodology, where Kant reformulates the two maxims as rules for the practice of natural history. I argue that natural history—or "the archaeology of nature," as Kant also describes it—is not curtailed by critique but, rightly understood, the research programme to which nature summons us. An upshot of my argument is that Kant longer holds his racialized concept of race as necessary in respect to natural history. The existence of stable subspecies in natural history is not a requirement of reason but a matter of empirical testing.

7.1 The Principle of Mechanism

In §70, Kant states that there can be an antinomy of reflecting judgement if its maxims (a) are necessary, (b) have their ground in the nature of the cognitive faculties, and (c) conflict with each other. While his criteria are clear enough, it is the frustration of every commentator that, unlike the Antinomies of the first *Critique*, which are each followed by a section that presents the argument for the thesis and antithesis, Kant does not provide an obvious argument for either maxim of reflecting judgement.[8] This lacuna has led to extensive debate, especially in regards to the global necessity of M_1.[9] In older scholarship, commentators tend to assume that Kant's argument for judging the generation of material things according to merely mechanical laws was established in *Metaphysical Foundations*, where he applies the relational categories to the empirical concept of matter to determine its mechanical principles.[10] While this view accounts for Kant's claim that the principle of mechanism is both universal and necessary (it shares the transcendental necessity of the categories), it comes with the rather blaring caveat that the concept of causality, now presented as a maxim of reflecting judgement, has been lowered "from its originally constitutive, categorial dignity to a regulative principle."[11] This view has been rejected in the more recent literature, not least because it strips the transcendental justification of the causal principle but also because it leaves the necessity of M_1 in a precarious state. Recent

---

[8] The closest Kant comes to providing such arguments occurs in the opening paragraphs of §78, where he provides arguments for the indispensability of mechanical and teleological reflection on nature. Whether or not these count as arguments for M_1 and M_2, however, is far from clear.

[9] For instance, in his major study of the second part of the third *Critique*, McLaughlin states that "Kant merely postulates the mechanical peculiarity of our understanding and makes no attempt to explain what it consists in and why it is justified." McLaughlin, *Kant's Critique of Teleology*, 174. For an overview of the debate, see Watkins, "The Antinomy of Teleological Judgment", 204–7; Teufel, "What Is the Problem of Teleology," 216–26.

[10] Cassirer asks "How can Kant treat the mechanical and teleological principles as reflective principles? Such an assertion is obviously contrary to the fundamental principles of his philosophy." Cassirer, *A Commentary on Kant's Critique of Judgment*, 345. See also Butts, "Teleology and Scientific Method," 4–5.

[11] Ernst, *Der Zweckbegriff bei Kant und sein Verhältnis zu den Kategorien*, 64.

commentary tends to stress the subjective character of the principle of mechanism, which operates as a "heuristic principle" or "methodological commitment" to guide the application of the concept of causality in our search for laws that are more specific than the universal natural laws.[12] Yet this reading is not without difficulties of its own. In particular, it does not strictly explain how M_1 could be both universal and necessary, which is required for there to be a genuine conflict.

In this section, I present a proof for the thesis of the antinomy by connecting the need for mechanism with the task of unifying particular laws under general laws, which we examined in Section 5.3 in terms of reason's highest formal unity: the purposive unity of things, which, when harmonized with the understanding, takes the form of a physical-mechanical system.[13] While M_1 does not partake in the transcendental necessity of the categories, I argue that it nevertheless shares the force of Kant's transcendental argument for reflecting judgement's principle of purposiveness, and thus can be said to *govern* the application of determining judgement in the context of natural history.

The defining feature of the third *Critique* is the introduction of a new faculty, the reflecting power of judgement, which operates free from the understanding by ascribing a principle to itself.[14] In the first *Critique*, Kant often uses judgement and understanding interchangeably. In acts of judging (understanding), the subject synthesizes the manifold according to rules that are given in advance to produce a unified cognition (A69/B94). In the third *Critique*, Kant distinguishes between two forms of judging: determining judgement, which refers to the use of judgement by the understanding, and reflecting judgement, which "compares" and "holds together" given representations in relation to "a concept that is thereby made possible" (EEKU 20:211). If the rule "is given," and a particular is subsumed underneath it, then judgement is determining (KU 5:179). If only the particular is given "for which the universal is to be found," judgement is reflecting. In contrast to determining judgement, which is bound to the laws given by the understanding, reflecting judgement is autonomous, meaning that it must prescribe laws "to itself...for reflection on nature" (KU 5:185–6).

As Rachel Zuckert observes, Kant motivates the need for judgement's reflecting power by presenting a "threat" posed to the understanding that was not fully

---

[12] McLaughlin, *Kant's Critique of Teleology*, 141–4; Allison, "Kant's Antinomy," 26; Zuckert, *Kant on Beauty and Biology*, 102; Ginsborg, "Two Kinds of Mechanical Inexplicability," 37; Breitenbach, *Die Analogie von Vernunft und Natur*, 39–41.

[13] Here I follow Watkins' suggestion that one way to prove the thesis of the antinomy might be to connect the normative strength of M_1 with the unification of particular laws under pure laws. Watkins, "The Antinomy of Teleological Judgment," 206–7. This line of argument follows Kant's assertion in §70 that both maxims have their "ground in the nature of our cognitive faculties" and that M_1 is "provided by the mere understanding a priori" (KU 5:386).

[14] For an interpretation of the third *Critique* as a critique of judgement's power of reflection, see Teufel, "What does Kant Mean by 'Power of Judgment,'" 313–24. See also Cooper, *The Tragedy of Philosophy*, 56–9.

resolved in his account of judgement in the first *Critique*.[15] The threat is that while the cognitions of the understanding are produced in accordance with transcendental laws, "there is still such an **infinite multiplicity** of empirical laws and such a **great heterogeneity of forms** of nature…that the concept of a system in accordance with these (empirical) laws must be entirely alien to the understanding" (EEKU 20:203). The understanding prescribes the rules that require that material objects can be described in terms of laws and classified under concepts. Yet it does not require that those laws might apply to other material objects, or that there are certain kinds of material objects that can be grouped under empirical concepts. It thus remains possible that empirical nature is underdetermined, posing a threat to the understanding's mandate to bring maximal order to the manifold of its cognitions. Given that the understanding's rules leave the manifold underdetermined, and that this underdetermination threatens the execution of its mandate, Kant claims that judgement requires an independent presupposition about the lawfulness of empirical nature. He terms this presupposition the "**law of the specification of nature**," which is "a subjectively necessary transcendental **presupposition** that such a disturbingly unbounded diversity of empirical laws and heterogeneity of natural forms does not pertain to nature, rather that nature itself, through the affinity of particular laws under more general ones, qualifies for an experience, as an empirical system" (EEKU 20:209). The notion of a law of specification evokes Kant's discussion of reason's principles in the Appendix to the Transcendental Dialectic, where the law of specification, used regulatively, instructs the understanding to specify its cognitions under concepts. There Kant argued that the transcendental law of specification has an indeterminate objective validity, for, if it were not presupposed as a principle, we would not be able to form empirical concepts under which to classify material objects (see Section 5.3). In the third *Critique*, the ideal of systematicity now lies with the faculty of judgement, at least in part. The threat of underdetermination serves to show that even if reason presents the ideal of systematicity, it would remain the role of judgement to discover and display it through the formation and application of empirical concepts.[16] The law of specification, then, is the presupposition that empirical concepts can be discovered and applied, and thus it underwrites the understanding's mandate to achieve the maximal unity and extension of its cognitions. Kant goes as far as to say that the law of specification, understood as a transcendental principle of reflecting judgement, enables an *experience* of nature as an empirical system.

---

[15] Zuckert, *Kant on Beauty and Biology*, 35. Allison presents this threat as the possibility of "empirical chaos" or "disorder at the empirical level." Allison, "Reflective Judgment and the Application of Logic to Nature," 184.

[16] Guyer, "Reason and Reflective Judgment," 34.

Kant describes judgement's principle as the principle of "the purposiveness of nature for our faculty of cognition" (KU 5:184). A purpose (*Zweck*), he explains, is "the object of a concept, insofar as the concept is seen as the cause of the object" (KU 5:222). Purposiveness (*Zweckmässigkeit*) thus refers to "the causality that a **concept** has with regard to its **object**." Kant presents the principle of the purposiveness of nature as follows:

> Now we call purposive that the existence of which seems to presuppose a representation of the same thing; natural laws, however, which are so constituted and related to each other as if they had been designed by the power of judgment for its own need, have a similarity with the possibility of things that presuppose a representation of themselves as their ground. Thus through its principle the power of judgment thinks of a purposiveness of nature in the specification of its forms through empirical laws.   (EEKU 20:216)

Kant states that the arrangement of natural laws is similar to the possibility of purposive things to the extent that they conveniently hold together as the power of judgement would require them. To acknowledge this similarity is not to describe natural laws as purposive, for we do not have to "place the cause of this form in a will" (KU 5:220). Purposiveness can pertain "without a purpose" insofar as we "make the explanation of its possibility conceivable to ourselves only by deriving it from a will." This is to say that the reflecting power of judgement is able to judge an object *as if* it were the object of a concept. Kant's claim is that the subsuming activity of determining judgement is underwritten by a subjective presupposition of reflecting judgement that nature takes the form of an empirical system, for without supposing that in the multiplicity of things there is "sufficient kinship among them to enable them to be brought under empirical concepts (classes) and these in turn under more general laws (higher genera)," determining judgement could neither form nor apply its concepts (EEKU 20:215).[17]

Having established that the power of judgement reflects on the contingent manifold as purposive, Kant then identifies two distinct ways that judgement reflects on objects as purposive:

> if empirical concepts and even empirical laws are already given in accordance with the mechanism of nature and the power of judgment compares such a concept of the understanding with reason and its principle of the possibility of a system, then, if this form is found in the object, the purposiveness is judged **objectively** and the thing is called a **natural purpose**, whereas previously things were judged as indeterminately purposive **natural forms**.   (EEKU 20:221)

---

[17] For a discussion of judgement's transcendental presupposition, see Geiger, *Kant and the Claims of the Empirical World*, 131–4.

In this dense passage, Kant contrasts two ways of reflecting on the form of an object as purposive. The first way, which he terms the "mechanism of nature," is to reflect on nature as a whole as the product of a concept, so that the natural forms and particular laws are arranged in such a way that an understanding like ours can discover them. The second way, which he terms "objective," is to reflect on a particular object as a purpose *in* nature, that is, as a natural purpose. Both ways of reflecting seek the "lawfulness of the contingent," an order that holds among contingent parts and explains why they belong together (KU 5:404).

We will consider Kant's account of a natural purpose in the following section. For now, let us consider the first way of reflecting on the form of an object as purposive: the mechanism of nature. To understand how the mechanism of nature can be a principle of reflecting judgement, it is vital to distinguish between two conceptions of mechanism in Kant's critical philosophy.[18] Both conceptions can be discerned in the first *Critique*, yet in a less developed form. In Section 5.3, we saw that, in the Appendix to the Transcendental Dialectic, Kant criticizes the use of purposes to account for features of nature that are useful for human beings. Physicotheology appeals to "the inscrutable degree of the highest wisdom," and blocks reason from "seeking them [explanations] in the mechanism of matter" (A691/B719). Here the "mechanism of matter" refers to causality by means of interaction between moving particles in space. It concerns the science of mechanics as presented in *Metaphysical Foundations*, which establishes that all change necessarily has an external cause (MAN 4:543). The status of mechanism in this sense is equivalent to the transcendental principle of causality, and is properly contrasted with transcendental freedom. If we appeal to the highest wisdom to account for useful features of nature, we "regard the toil of reason as completed when in fact the use of reason has been completely dispensed with" (A691/B719). Kant then states that

> This mistake can be avoided if we do not consider from the viewpoint of ends merely a few parts of nature, e.g., the distribution of dry land, its structure and the constitution and situation of mountains, or even only the organization of the vegetable and animal kingdoms, but if we rather make the systematic unity of nature **entirely universal** in relation to the idea of a highest intelligence. For then we make a purposiveness in accordance with universal laws of nature the ground, from which no particular arrangement is excepted, but arrangements are designated only in a way that is more or less discernible by us; then we have a regulative principle of the systematic unity of a teleological connection, which, however, we do not determine beforehand, but may only expect while pursing the physical-mechanical connection according to universal laws.   (A691–2/B719–20)

---

[18] I should say *at least* two; Ginsborg identifies five distinct uses of mechanism in Kant's work. Ginsborg, "Kant on Understanding Organisms as Natural Purposes," 238. The two noted here will be sufficient for understanding the force of M_1.

Here Kant mentions a "physical-mechanical" connection that is not determined beforehand but is something that we pursue by following a regulative principle. The regulative principle concerns the systematic unity of nature, which prescribes the relations between the understanding's cognitions and their conditions within a nested hierarchy that is "entirely universal" (i.e. "from which no particular arrangement is excepted") and "more or less discernible by us." As a regulative principle, mechanism in its physical sense does not simply refer to a material explanation, as it does in *Metaphysical Foundations*, but more specifically "to the explanation of wholes solely in terms of the causal interaction of their component parts."[19] While material-mechanical explanations can explain the movement of a part, it cannot explain its existence *as* a part. The mechanism of nature, then, is a principle that instructs the understanding to explain the generation of natural products according to physical-mechanical connections. Physical-mechanical explanations thus presuppose the regulative principle of the systematic unity of a teleological connection, which prescribes how the material-mechanical connections hold together.

In the third *Critique*, Kant is more explicit about the two kinds of mechanism:

> If one regards the parts for such a possible whole as already completely given, then the division proceeds **mechanically**, as the consequence of mere comparison, and the whole becomes an **aggregate**... But if one can and should presuppose the idea of a whole in accordance with a certain principle prior to the determination of the parts, then the division must proceed **scientifically**, and only in this way does the whole become a system.   (EEKU 20:247)

The first kind of division corresponds to what Kant termed the "mechanism of matter" in the first *Critique*, whereby one examines a part by comparing it to other parts in the aggregate. Kant terms this kind of comparison an "affinity," which is a logical relation. An affinity does not warrant a physical explanation, for it does not connect the real possibility of one part to that of another (there could be an infinite multiplicity of empirical laws). The second kind of division corresponds to physical-mechanical nature, in which judgement presupposes that appearances are parts of a system, such that it can reflect on any one part as physically connected to the other parts, despite having no determinate knowledge of those connections. Kant terms this second conception of mechanism the "**technique** of nature" (EEKU 20:204–5). Because the Second Analogy does not require explanations to be mechanistic in this sense, reflecting judgement must adopt the technique of nature as a principle to guide the application of determining judgement: "Now if we consider a material whole, as far as its form is concerned, as a

---

[19] Allison, "Kant's Antinomy," 27.

product of the parts and their forces and their capacity to combine by themselves (including as parts other material that they add to themselves), we represent a mechanical kind of generation" (KU 5:408). The representation of a mechanical kind of generation, in which the parts and their forces cause the whole, is not a constitutive principle of the understanding. The peculiarity of the understanding lies in the fact that it must proceed "from the **analytical universal** (of concepts) to the particular (of the given empirical intuition), in which it determines nothing with regard to the manifoldness of the latter" (KU 5:407). As the effect of material-mechanical forces, the manifold is merely an aggregate. To introduce systematic order to the manifold—which, Kant contends, we *must* do, on pain of failing the understanding's mandate to bring maximal unity and extension to its cognitions—reflecting judgement must find and then give the principle of mechanism to itself (through analogy with the causality of a will), thereby enabling reflection on the aggregate as a physical-mechanical system. The force of Kant's argument for the principle of the purposiveness of nature is practical. It *commands* us to judge all effects in nature according to merely mechanical laws, lest we fail to unify the understanding's cognitions according to material connections. In the context of natural history, where natural historians are concerned with a specific use of reflecting judgement's principle (judging the generation of material things), the principle is formulated as M_1: the generation of material things and their forms must be judged as possible in accordance with merely mechanical laws. The universal force of the maxim stems from the understanding's principle of causality *and* reflecting judgement's principle of purposiveness, for the principle of causality can only be applied to empirical nature (as opposed to the sequence of representations in time) by presupposing that nature takes the form of a physical-mechanical system.[20] Reflecting judgement's principle is thus the command to seek particular laws that are specified applications of the universal and necessary laws of nature, and thereby to seek the greatest unity and extension of cognition (see KU 5:488).

The second way that reflecting judgement seeks to discover the lawfulness of the contingent is to reflect on particular things as objects of a concept. In the two parts of the third *Critique*, Kant examines the formal and material purposiveness of individual objects. The paradigm case is a work of art, which we judge to be the object of a concept in a particular sense. Yet judging an object as a work of art does not (directly) conflict with M_1, for it carries no implications for the sufficiency of M_1 for judging natural products. As we will see in the following section, judging an object as a purpose *in* nature does conflict with M_1, for it denies the universal sufficiency of the physical-mechanical principle.

---

[20] Here I agree with Quarfood, who claims that mechanism, "as discussed in the 'Dialectic' of the third *Critique*, is subservient to reflecting judgement's principle of the purposiveness of nature." Quarfood, "The Antinomy of Teleological Judgment," 180n.

7.2 The Teleological Principle

Having reconstructed Kant's argument for M_1 in the strongest possible way, I now turn to his argument for M_2, which is presented in a convoluted manner in the Analytic of the Teleological Power of Judgment. The challenge of reconstructing Kant's argument in the Analytic is to discern how judging a natural purpose can be dependent on experience without making any determinate claims about the object of that experience. This requires that we avoid a common assumption in the literature that *natural purpose* is an empirical concept, like the concepts *tree*, *mammal*, or *living being*, and can thus be abstracted from experience and then applied to objects by determining judgement.[21] If such were the case, the Analytic would consist of the analysis of a concept in order to determine what a natural purpose *is*, which is precisely what Kant wants to avoid. Kant explains that the concept of a thing as a natural purpose is "an empirically conditioned concept, i.e., one that is possible only under conditions given in experience, but it is still not a concept that can be abstracted from experience, but one that is possible only in accordance with a principle of reason in the judging of an object" (KU 5:396). We can consider many things in nature as purposive if we view them as the means to a purpose that is external to them. For instance, we can consider snow in cold lands as purposive in that it protects seeds from frost and facilitates communication among humans (KU 5:396). The concept of a *natural* purpose, however, is legitimately applied only if certain conditions are met in experience. In such cases we *must* introduce a rational principle to our investigation of material generation, lest we succumb once more to the threat of underdetermination. The Analytic thus consists of an analysis of (1) how experience leads to the concept of a natural purpose, and (2) the conditions that must be met such that it is necessary to judge some natural products as purposive.

Kant begins the Analytic with an investigation of (1), a certain kind of experience that presupposes the concept of purposiveness in nature. His argument is not that we *should* judge some things as natural purposes. He simply assumes, without argument, that we *do* so judge some things.[22] The task, then, is to discern the principle that makes such judgements possible. In the opening section of the Analytic (§62), Kant identifies two distinct moments in the judgement of an object as a natural purpose, each marked by a particular feeling. The first moment is marked by the feeling of "astonishment [*Verwunderung*]," which occurs when we

---

[21] The assumption can be discerned wherever empirical concepts such as "living being" or "organism" are used interchangeably with "natural purpose." For just a few examples, see McFarland, *Kant's Concept of Teleology*, 102; Zumbach, *The Transcendental Science*, 19; Guyer, *Kant's System of Nature and Freedom*, 352–3; Geiger, *Kant and the Claims of the Empirical World*, 51–6. For a critique of this assumption, see Kreines, "The Inexplicability of Kant's *Naturzweck*," 275.

[22] "No one has doubted the correctness of the fundamental principle that certain things in nature (organized beings) and their possibility must be judged in accordance with the concept of final causes" (KU 5:389).

are shocked "at the incompatibility of a representation and the rule that is given through it with the principles already grounded in the mind" (KU 5:365). Kant does not give an example of the kind of experience he has in mind, but Abraham Tembley's discovery of the polyp's capacity to regenerate after an artificial cut provides an obvious case.[23] To represent the appearance of the severed part as a regeneration is to introduce a rule that is foreign to the causal principle "grounded in the mind." The rule is foreign to the causal principle, for it connects the effect to the causality of an idea, such that an idea of the whole causes the replacement of the lost part. We say that the polyp seeks to maintain its state of organization, even if that organization is disrupted by an external force. Because the movement from whole to parts is at odds with the parts-to-whole movement of physical-mechanical generation, it "produces doubt as to whether one has seen or judged correctly." When we have seen the experiment many times, and our doubt has been removed, the first moment of astonishment turns into the second: "admiration [*Bewunderung*]" (KU 5:365). Admiration, Kant explains, is "an entirely natural effect of that purposiveness observed in the essence of things (as appearances)." Because admiration stays with the apparent contradiction between the principles already in the mind and the rule that governs a non-mechanical connection, it enables the mind to make "profound investigations" into its representation of the causality of the recalcitrant item.

Kant undertakes these profound investigations in §§63–5. To show that it is necessary to judge some things in nature teleologically, he begins with a general examination of our everyday use of teleology to understand processes and things. "Experience leads our power of judgement to the concept of an objective and material purposiveness," he states, if there is a relation between a cause and effect that we can understand as lawful only insofar as we can subsume "the idea of the effect under the causality of its cause as the underlying condition of the possibility of the former" (KU 5:366–7). We can subsume the idea of the effect as the condition of the possibility of the cause in two ways: as a product of art (e.g. a watch: KU 5:374), or as an end or means for the purposive use of other causes (e.g. a sea that shrinks from its shores, leaving rich and sandy soil in which pine trees can flourish; KU 5:367). The purposiveness of a product of art is "technical," for its possibility lies in an intelligent mind (KU 5:368). The purposiveness of a product of material causes is "relative" or "accidental," for it is contingent on the presence and constitution of another object.

---

[23] On two occasions that Kant refers to the regenerative capacities of living beings to illustrate the operation of reflecting judgment, he calls on Trembley's polyp as an example (KU 5:371, 419). His critique of astonishment (*Verwunderung*) closely resembles Herder's description of astonishment (*Erstaunen*) in *Outlines of a Philosophy of the History of Man* (see Section 6.2). Yet in contrast to Herder, Kant's critique of astonishment seeks to show that the formative force is not analogous with the principle of causality. It can thus be read as an alternative to Herder's interpretation of the polyp experiment. Cf. Herder, *Outlines of a Philosophy of the History of Man*, 319.

With this general view of teleological judging in hand, Kant then examines the conditions by which it is *necessary* to judge some things teleologically, which is task (2) of the Analytic. While judging the retreating sea as purposive for the pine trees is necessary for embarking on a certain research project, for without it we would not begin to view the sea and the trees within an ecological system, it is not necessary to posit any purposive causality in the causal sequence of nature. The use of teleology in this case is subjective; the discursive nature of our cognition entails that we must begin this way, yet no causal claims about nature need be implied. To show that we *must* judge some things as objectively purposive, Kant needs to identify a condition that requires us to judge the *possibility* of a thing according to a purpose. To judge the possibility of a thing according to a purpose is to judge that "the causality of its origin . . . [is] not possible in accordance with mere natural laws, i.e., ones that can be cognized by us through the understanding" (KU 5:370). This condition separates the causality of the watch from the causality of the presence of pine trees on a river bank, for the possibility of the latter can be explained by merely mechanical laws. To judge that a thing is possible only as a purpose is to judge that the possibility of its form lies "in a cause whose productive capacity is determined by concepts" (KU 5:370). For such things, the "empirical cognition of their cause and effect presupposes concepts of reason." The watch is judged as possible according to the causality of a watchmaker. It is an artificial purpose, the product of technique.

To show that it is necessary to judge some things as a purpose *and* as a product of nature—as a natural purpose—Kant needs to identify a further condition. He offers a "provisional" account of this condition to guide his inquiry: a thing exists as a natural purpose "**if it is cause and effect of itself** (in a twofold sense)" (KU 5:370–1). The twofold sense of the cause-effect relation is that we reflect on a thing as a work of art (the effect of an idea) *and* as the artificer (the cause of the effect), which supposedly places the purposiveness in nature to the extent that the artificer is a natural product. To judge a thing as a natural purpose, then, is to be interested in how that thing produces itself. Kant tests this provisional definition by considering a tree's lifecycle, in which we can reflect on the generative process in (at least) three different ways: a tree is self-producing (trees come from trees), self-realizing (a tree grows by selecting and transforming its own supply of energy), and self-dependent (each part of the tree depends for its continued existence on the contributions of the other parts) (KU 5:371).

Extrapolating from the tree example, Kant formalizes his provisional definition of a natural purpose by identifying two conditions that must be met for it to be necessary to judge a thing as both a purpose and a product of nature. Call these the *design condition* and the *self-organization condition*.[24] An item fulfils the design

---

[24] Zumbach describes the two criteria as "design-like" and "designer-like." In the case of a watch, we judge it to be design-like but not designer-like. In the case of a tree, we judge it through both analogies:

condition if "its parts (as far as their existence and their form is concerned) are possible only through their relation to the whole" (KU 5:373).[25] This condition is met in both artefacts and organized beings: each part of a machine is there only on account of the whole in which it has a function. For an item to be judged as a natural purpose, it must meet a further condition: it must also have parts "combined into a whole by being reciprocally the cause and effect of their form" (KU 5:373). The self-organization condition separates artefacts from natural purposes, for the former are produced by an external cause while the latter produce themselves. This is clear in Kant's watch example: "one part is the instrument for the motion of another, but one wheel is not the efficient cause for the production of the other" (KU 5:374). A watch meets the design condition, for one part exists "for the sake of the other." Yet it does not meet the self-organization condition, for the parts do not exist "because of it." This is to say that a watch, unlike an organized being, "cannot by itself replace its parts," "make good defects in its original construction," or "repair itself when it has fallen into disorder." It manifests merely descending dependency, for the end is the result of an exterior, efficient cause (the designer). In contrast, natural purposes have "descending as well as ascending dependency," which is to say that they deserve "the name of a cause of the same thing of which it is an effect" (KU 5:372).

A thing that *can* replace its parts, make good its defects, and repair itself is "not a mere machine," Kant states, for machines possess only a "motive force" (KU 5:374). Such a thing is an "organized being," which possesses in itself a "**formative** force" to the extent that it communicates its form to matter that is unformed.[26] Here it is important to stress once more that the concept of a natural purpose is not an empirical concept—it is not abstracted from experience—yet neither is it given to judgement by the understanding. This is evident in the fact that we can never be sure that the concept actually fits (KU 5:397). Kant states that one captures *something* about the capacity of nature in organized products if we call it an "**analogue of art**" (KU 5:374). On its own, however, the artefact analogy says far too little about nature's capacity in organized products. The only causality we know in which the parts can be understood to produce each other, and the whole to produce the parts, is the causality of reason (recall the maggot analogy at A835/B863), not the technical capacity of reason to realize an idea but the systematizing

---

to the extent that its parts are arranged according to an idea of the whole, it is design-like, but to the extent to which the parts of a tree function to maintain it in a state of organization, it is designer-like. Zumbach, *The Transcendent Science*, 4.

[25] In part I of *Critique of the Power of Judgment*, Kant states that a purposive object is one whose structure we can understand only if we conceive of its possibility by assuming that it was produced intelligently: "an object or a state of mind or even an action ... is called purposive merely because its possibility can only be explained and conceived by us insofar as we assume as its ground a causality in accordance with ends, i.e. a will that has arranged it so in accordance with the representation of a certain rule" (KU 5:220).

[26] An organized being, Kant explains, is a thing that is possible only as a natural purpose (KU 5:375).

capacity of reason to organize its parts according to a concept of the whole, and to maintain that state of organization despite and in response to external changes.[27] Yet one would say far too much about the capacity of nature in organized products if one called it an **"analogue of life,"** for to do so would be to introduce a formative force (either living matter or an animating soul) to nature, which contradicts the part-to-whole movement of physical-mechanical causation (KU 5:375–6). We place the form of life alongside the relation between parts and whole to reflect on their form, and yet the capacity of nature in organized products—the coincidence of mechanism and teleology—is "not analogous with any causality we know."

We can summarize Kant's argument in the Analytic as follows. Astonishment and admiration are two moments that alert us to an experience that presupposes the concept of purposiveness in nature. Astonishment alerts us to the representation of an effect through a cause that is foreign to the understanding, which, once we accept what we are experiencing (and come to admire it), allows us to discern a principle that reflecting judgement has given to itself (not to the object) to find lawfulness in the contingent. What we learn about the thing that occasions the experience is not that it *is* a natural purpose, but rather that its form is such that, if we are to explain the manner in which it generates itself, minds like ours must judge the relation between part and whole according to the causality of an idea. While the principle of inner purposiveness is a "merely subjective principle," its use is nonetheless *necessary*, for without it the material generation and form of some natural products would remain contingent. Given this necessity, we question the sufficiency of M_1 by formulating M_2: some products of material nature cannot be judged as possible according to merely mechanical laws. This is to say that while M_1 is universally necessary for judging the generation of material things and their forms, it is not universally sufficient.[28]

7.3 The Antinomy of Reflecting Judgement

So far, we have established Kant's arguments for (a) the necessity of M_1 and M_2, which required an account of (b) how reflecting judgement takes the form of the understanding and the form of reason for its reflection on nature and some objects within it as purposive. We are now in a position to consider (c): whether the maxims of reflecting judgement genuinely conflict. In the opening section of the Dialectic, "What is an antinomy of the power of judgment?" (§69), Kant presents the two maxims as follows:

---

[27] Breitenbach puts it as follows: "Causality according to purposes, the practical capacity of reason in us, which is supposed to elucidate the organization of nature though analogy, can be understood as the general capacity of reason to govern itself according to a self-legislated purpose: the purpose of its own self-determined unity." Breitenbach, *Die Analogie von Vernunft und Natur*, 101.

[28] See Teufel, "What Is the Problem of Teleology," 203.

Now in the case of this contingent unity of particular laws the power of judgment can set out from two maxims in its reflection, one of which is provided [*an die Hand gegeben*] to it by the mere understanding a priori, the other of which, however, is suggested [*veranlasst*] by particular experiences that bring reason into play in order to conduct the judging of corporeal nature and its laws in accordance with a special principle.   (KU 5:386)

If one were to understand the first maxim in this passage as the material concep- tion of mechanism, it would seem that Kant had indeed lowered the concept of causality to the status of a regulative principle. Yet it should now be clear that Kant's use of mechanism in the antinomy refers to its physical-mechanical sense, which is necessary precisely because without it we could not seek particular instantiations of the material-mechanical principles of the understanding. Physical-mechanism does not follow analytically from the principle of causation but is rather "provided" or "proposed" by the understanding in the course of experience, such that judgement can reflect on the laws and forms of objects as the product of technique. Similarly, the maxim of teleology is "suggested" or "prompted" by things in nature that require us to introduce purposiveness to represent their form according to a rule. Given that one principle is provided by the understanding and the other is suggested by reason, it "may then seem that these two sorts of maxims are not consistent with each other, such that a dialectic will result that will make the power of judgment go astray in the principle of its reflection" (KU 5:387).

Commentators who deny the existence of an antinomy of reflecting judgement tend to take the Antinomies of the first *Critique* as the benchmark for a genuine conflict.[29] There Kant stated that only the transcendent use of reason can generate an antinomy, for judgement does not make claims about objects understood as things in themselves but merely applies the concepts of the understanding to intuition or regulates empirical investigation (see Section 5.3). Used regulatively, the principles of reason do not generate "a true conflict" but simply capture "a different interest of reason that causes a divorce between ways of thinking" (A666/B694).[30] For instance, specification and homogeneity "prepare the field for the understanding" by giving contrasting advice: to search for higher concepts and lower specifications (A658/B686). The two principles are "united" in the principle

---

[29] Adickes, *Kant als Naturforscher*, II 473–5; Cassirer, *Kant's Life and Thought*, 345. See also Walsh, *Reason and Experience*, 233; Ewing, *A Short Commentary of Kant's Critique of Pure Reason*, 260; McFarland, *Kant's Concept of Teleology*, 118.

[30] Kant notes that if reason's maxims were formulated as objective principles, then a genuine conflict would occur. Yet as Guyer observes, it is not clear how the constitutive use of reason's principles would in fact contradict each other, for there seems to be no obvious reason why the two principles could not be balanced, depending on the research programme adopted. Guyer, "Reason and Reflective Judgment," 32. See also Zuckert, *Kant on Beauty and Biology*, 150. The maxims of reflecting judgement must operate in a different manner if they are to genuinely conflict.

of continuity, which says that the higher and lower manifolds "are akin to one another, because they are all collectively descended ... from a single highest genus" (A568/B686). Together, the three principles instruct the understanding to seek the conditions of its cognitions within a system of conditions, where every particular can be subsumed under a universal.

If a true conflict requires that the maxims of reflecting judgement conflict in the same manner as the transcendent use of reason's ideas, then clearly there can be no antinomy. This has led commentators to conclude that it is Kant's *second* presentation of the antinomy that presents a true conflict. After presenting the conflict between M_1 and M_2, Kant warns that if one were to transform the regulative principles into constitutive principles, and thus "slide" from the logical to the ontological level (to use Grier's term), the antinomy would run as follows:

C_1: All generation of material things is possible in accordance with merely mechanical laws.

C_2: Some generation of such things is not possible in accordance with merely mechanical laws.

While the first presentation of the antinomy concerns how natural bodies must be judged, the second concerns how objects must *be*, thus "transforming" the first pair of maxims into constitutive principles that make a claim regarding "the possibility of the objects themselves" (KU 5:387). Yet as Kant clearly states, the second formulation would not be an antinomy of reflecting judgement but rather "a conflict in the legislation of reason." Indeed, commentators who suggest that only the second presentation of the antinomy captures the true conflict argue that Kant explicitly denies that reflecting judgement can have an antinomy.[31] On this reading, Kant's supposed resolution occurs in §71 (even though its title is "Preparation for the resolution of the above antinomy"), where he states that the appearance of the antinomy rests on "confusing a fundamental principle of the reflecting with that of the determining power of judgment" (KU 5:389).[32] The Dialectic can thus be forced into the mould of the Third and Fourth Antinomies of

---

[31] This line of argument is normally defended by Kant's cryptic sentence at 5:387, which has caused ongoing problems for English translators. The Cambridge translation reads: "By contrast, the maxims of a reflecting power of judgment that were initially expounded do not in fact contain any contradiction." Yet the original is clear that only one maxim is being referred to here ("Was dagegen *die zuerst vorgetragene Maxime* einer reflektierenden Urteilskraft..."), so Kant seems to be claiming that the first maxim is in fact true. See McLaughlin, *Kant's Critique of Teleology*, 149; Watkins, "The Antinomy of Teleological Judgment," 201–2.

[32] Cassirer presents the resolution as follows: "The antinomy between the concepts of finality and causality thus disappears, as soon as we think of the two of them as different *modes of ordering*, through which we try to unify the manifold of phenomena." Cassirer, *Kant's Life and Thought*, 345. Ewing offers a similar analysis: "the antinomy between mechanism and teleology is ... solved by declaring both principles regulative." Ewing, *A Short Commentary of Kant's Critique of Pure Reason*, 260.

the first *Critique*, where the appearance of an antinomy is resolved by demoting the constitutive use of reason's principles to their legitimate regulative use.

This interpretation is no longer accepted in the literature.[33] Not only does it overlook the following seven sections of the Dialectic, which culminate in the "resolution to the above antinomy" (§§75–8), it also contradicts Kant's explicit claim that "there can be a conflict, hence an antinomy" of the reflecting power of judgement (KU 5:386).[34] It is certainly true that there cannot be a conflict between the regulative use of reason's ideas, which, as we have seen, can be united under an additional principle to form a single, interconnected system. The maxims of reflecting judgement, however, cannot be united in this way. M_1 is concerned with the physical-mechanical system of nature in which we judge natural products to be *generated* according to merely mechanical laws. M_2 is not a principle about generation (as is C_2) but simply places a limit on the sufficiency of M_1 to account for the generation of *all* material objects and their forms according to merely mechanical laws.[35] There can thus be no third maxim that could unite the two, no higher genus under which the parts of a thing considered as a natural product and the form of a thing considered as a natural purpose could be classified. Even if we were to realize that C_1 and C_2 are based on a confusion, and return to M_1 and M_2, we nevertheless find that the two maxims, both natural and necessary, "exclude one another."[36] For instance, when classifying plants and animals, natural historians

> could just as little dispense with this teleological principle as they could do without the universal physical principle, since, just as in the case of the abandonment of the latter there would remain no experience at all, so in the case of the abandonment of the former principle there would remain no guideline for the observation of a kind of natural thing that we have conceived of teleologically under the concept of a natural purpose.   (KU 5:376)

---

[33] Cohen, "Kant's Antinomy of Reflective Judgment," 187–8; Breitenbach, "Two Views on Nature," 352–5; Watkins, "The Antinomy of Teleological Judgment," 199–200.

[34] One could, of course, take Kant's claim to be disingenuous. Adickes argues that Kant includes the antinomy merely for "systematic" reasons. See Adickes, *Kant's Systematik als systembildender Faktor*, 171. McFarland challenges this view, yet accepts that there is not strictly an antinomy of reflecting judgement. McFarland, *Kant's Concept of Teleology*, 121.

[35] Commentators regularly overlook the fact that M_2 does not mention generation, which means that they escape the interpretive task of explaining why the maxims of reflecting judgement conflict. For instance, see McLaughlin, *Kant's Critique of Teleology*, 134; Allison, "Reflective Judgment and the Application of Logic to Nature," 205. To correct this oversight, Geiger argues that the conflict in the antinomy is not genuine. While I am sympathetic to Geiger's reading, I argue that there *is* a genuine conflict, precisely because M_1 leaves the appearance of conceptual order in nature unexplained. See Geiger, *Kant and the Claims of the Empirical World*, 93–5.

[36] On my reading, M_1 and M_2 present an illusion that *threatens* to deceive us, whereas C_1 and C_2 present the claims that follow once the illusion *has* deceived us.

Kant's claim here is remarkably strong. Just as abandoning the "universal physical principle" would remove experience (presumably Kant means the experience under threat in the introductions: the experience of nature *as an empirical system*), abandoning the teleological principle would make it impossible to observe certain natural things, and thus to effectively deploy determining judgement when investigating the generation of their form. The two maxims thus provide conflicting instructions to determining judgement, and yet each is necessary for our research into nature's self-producing order.

So far we have established that M_1 and M_2 conflict. We have not, however, established that a conflict between two maxims of reflecting judgement forms an antinomy. Here I want to claim that the conflict between the maxims of reflecting judgement forms an antinomy to the extent that, by issuing conflicting instructions to determining judgement, it generates an illusion that threatens to deceive us.[37] In contrast to the regulative use of reason's principles, which instructs the understanding to seek the conditions of sensible objects that are given, reflecting judgement does not simply guide reflection but also operates as the condition of the possibility of certain kinds of experience, thereby enabling determining judgement to apply its concepts according to distinct sets of rules. In the opening paragraph of §77, Kant notes that reflecting judgement is structurally analogous to the regulative use of a transcendental principle. Yet he then states that in contrast to reason's ideas, which guide the actions of the understanding when its cognitions are already given, the principles of reflecting judgement enable certain kinds of objects to be "given in experience," even if they are not given "determinately" but merely to be "reflected upon" (KU 5:405).[38] For instance, while teleological judging does not constitute objects as purposive, "the consequence that answers to it (the product) is still given in nature [*ist doch in der Natur gegeben*]." The givenness of the object, Kant explains, "seems [*scheint*] to make the idea of a natural purpose into a constitutive principle"—and this "seeming" does not go away after critique. When an object *seems* to make a principle of reflecting judgement into a constitutive principle (note that the object *does not* do so, hence we are still concerned with M_1 and M_2 and not C_1 and C_2), we are tempted to resolve the conflict by positing an entirely mechanical order (idealism about

---

[37] My account thus shares the structure of Breitenbach's "two views" account. However, Breitenbach's "everyday" view is inadequate to characterize our reflection on objects as natural purposes. While judging things as purposive might be a mundane part of experience, judging things as *natural purposes* (i.e. as products of nature *and* as purposive) is the specialized and scientific activity of natural historians. This is to say that the antinomy arises as we enter more deeply into the demands of empirical nature. Breitenbach, "Two Views on Nature," 366.

[38] Here my interpretation is similar to Quarfood's "two-level" reading of the antinomy, in which each maxim can be considered on both a reflective ("philosophical") and a constitutive ("object-centred") level. Yet Quarfood's use of "constitutive" cannot be the right way to conceive of the lower level, for Kant is emphatic throughout the Dialectic that reflecting judgement is not constitutive (e.g. KU 5:361; cf. EEKU 20:220). Quarfood, "Kant on Biological Teleology," 736. My interpretation builds on the regulative use of transcendental principles identified in Section 5.3.

purposiveness, KU 5:393) or an order that is mechanical most of the time with occasional interventions (realism about purposiveness, KU 5:394). Yet to make either move is to depart the land of truth and step into the stormy sea of illusion:

> to exclude the teleological principle entirely, and always to stick with mere mechanism even where purposiveness... undeniably manifests itself as a relation to another kind of causality, must make reason fantastic and send it wandering about among figments of natural capacities that cannot even be conceived, just as a merely teleological mode of explanation which takes no regard of the mechanism of nature makes it into mere enthusiasm.   (KU 5:411)

Kant's point is that in contrast to reason's ideas, the principles of reflecting judgement each introduce a distinct "order of things" governed by certain rules that prescribe how determining judgement must apply its concepts (KU 5:377). In one order of things, we judge the generation of natural products as possible according to merely mechanical laws. Determining judgement must then apply its concepts on the assumption that natural products are materially related within a mechanical system. In the other order of things, we assume that some natural products, whose form is contingent with regard to mechanical principles, are originally organized. Determining judgement must then apply its concepts on the assumption that some natural products are materially *and* formally related (i.e. they are self-producing, self-realizing, and self-dependent). In our search for an undetermined genus of two species, formal similarities (e.g. they are both vertebrates) may indicate distant causal connections, for we must assume that the generation of form occurs within the mechanism of nature (see Section 7.4).

On this reading of the Dialectic, the antinomy poses a more demanding problem than commentators generally acknowledge.[39] The antinomy cannot be resolved simply by noting that we can coherently follow M_1 and M_2 if we accept that they are maxims of reflecting judgement (Kant seems to acknowledge this in §70, *before* the resolution), for the conflict it generates threatens the coherence of nature as a system. For a discursive cognition like ours, we can only bring determinate unity to some natural products if we judge their possibility according to a purpose, for otherwise their form would remain contingent ("nature, considered as mere mechanism, could have formed itself in a thousand different ways without hitting precisely upon the unity in accordance with a rule," KU 5:360). The teleological principle thus removes the contingency of some natural products by introducing *a different kind of contingency*, which opens a new kind of threat. If

---

[39] An exception is Cohen, who claims that the antinomy of reflecting judgement is "uniquely troubling" in the critical corpus. My reading of the resolution is more deflationary than Cohen's, which suggests that the antinomy requires a speculative solution. Cohen, "Kant's Antinomy of Reflective Judgment," 185.

judgement requires that we reflect on some natural products as if the arrangement of the parts were governed by a concept of the whole, then the appearance of conceptual order in nature would be mechanically contingent. The judgement of some natural products as organized introduces an additional kind of lawfulness that inexplicably coincides with the mechanical order.[40] The problem is not that some natural products are underdetermined by mechanism, but that the teleological principle, which is necessary for judging some natural products, introduces *too much* determinacy into nature, indeed, a whole other order of lawfulness, the relation of which to mechanism is impossible to determine. Put differently, even if the thing that we judge as a natural purpose can be reduced to mechanism—and Kant is clear that we cannot know whether a living being really is a natural purpose, which leaves the possibility entirely open that organized beings are simply natural products (see KU 5:400, 418)[41]—our need to judge them as natural purposes would not disappear. The conflict between the two principles would remain.

The threat posed by the contingent appearance of conceptual order in nature sheds light on Kant's reasons for evoking an intuitive intellect in the resolution to the antinomy.[42] To acknowledge the peculiar character of our understanding is to compare it to a possible understanding that does not operate discursively but with a "**complete spontaneity of intuition**" (KU 5:406). For an intuitive intellect, nature could *not* have formed itself "in a thousand different ways," for there is no contingency that results from discursivity.[43] The appearance of conceptual order in nature would be the necessary outcome of a sequence of mechanical causes, and thus would not arouse astonishment (KU 5:406). The resolution to the antinomy is not to show that the two maxims are unifiable under a higher principle of discursive cognition (as are the Third and Fourth Antinomies of the first *Critique*), such that both can be legitimately applied to objects. Rather, it is to show that they are unifiable for a non-discursive intellect, quite unlike our own:

> The two principles cannot be united in one and the same thing in nature as fundamental principles for the explanation (deduction) of one from the other, i.e., as dogmatic and constitutive principles of insight into nature for the determining power of judgment. If, e.g., I assume that a maggot can be regarded as a product of the mere mechanism of matter (a new formation that it produces for

---

[40] See Fisher, "Life, Lawfulness, and Contingency," 10–2.

[41] See Kreines, "The Inexplicability of Kant's *Naturzweck*," 282.

[42] For a study of the various ways in which Kant presents the ground of the antinomy's resolution (divine artisan, intuitive intellect, and the supersensible), see Goy, "The Antinomy of Teleological Judgment," 73–86. Here I limit my analysis to the intuitive intellect; like Goy, I take it that each way gives expression to Kant's critical subversion of the physicotheological argument as a regulative idea.

[43] Kant states that intuitive intellect "goes from the **synthetically universal** (of the intuition of a whole as such) to the particular, i.e., from the whole to the parts, in which, therefore, and in whose representation of the whole, there is no **contingency** in the combination of the parts, in order to make possible a determinate form of the whole" (KU 5:407).

itself when its elements are set free by putrefaction), I cannot derive the very same product from the very same matter as a causality acting according to ends. Conversely, if I assume that the same product is a natural purpose, I cannot count on a mechanical mode of generation for it and take that as a constitutive principle for the judging of its possibility, thus uniting both principles. For one kind of explanation excludes the other, even on the supposition that objectively both grounds of the possibly rest on a single one, but one of which we take no account. The principle which is to make possible the unifiability of both in the judging of nature in accordance with them must be placed in what lies outside of both (hence outside of the possible empirical representation of nature) but which still contains the ground of both, i.e., in the supersensible.   (KU 5:412)

Kant seems to be saying that if I follow the mechanical principle, and assume that a maggot can be judged as the product of the mere mechanism of nature (M_1), I cannot *also* derive it as a causality according to ends. The result would be an order of things much like that presented in *Universal Natural History*, in which the appearance of purposiveness in nature can be explained by merely mechanical laws. Objective purposiveness would disappear (or become consonant with mechanism), and the teleological principle would no longer govern a legitimate pro- gramme of research. Likewise, if I were to follow the teleological principle, and assume that mechanical laws are insufficient to explain the generation of a maggot (M_2), I cannot *also* derive it from merely mechanical laws.

   The antinomy is resolved when we recognize that the mechanical and teleo- logical principles do not determine discrete domains of objects but merely govern the empirical use of judgement. This resolution completes the metaphysical deflation of the mechanical-teleological system presented in *Universal Natural History*, which Kant began in his lectures on physical geography by adopting a pragmatic standpoint. The principles of reflecting judgement cannot be unified by subordinating teleology to mechanism, for they are not descriptive but regulative principles that govern our reflection on nature *from the inside*.[44] The unifiability of the mechanical and teleological principles requires a higher, supersensible ground as a practical necessity. We conclude that both principles "must cohere in a single higher principle and flow from it in common," for "otherwise they could not consist alongside one another in the consideration of nature" (KU 5:412). This higher principle "justifies the commonality of the maxims of natural research that depend upon it," meaning that we can "confidently research the law of nature… in accordance with both of these principles, without being troubled by the apparent conflict between the two principles" (KU 5:413). The resolution to the antinomy, then, is Kant's proof that unifying the mechanical and teleological

---

[44] See McLaughlin, *Kant's Critique of Teleology*, 137.

principles is possible for an intellect quite unlike ours. On the empirical level, however, the conflict remains: we must follow both principles. To this extent at least Kant's resolution follows the structure of his resolution of the antinomies presented in the first *Critique*: once we have gained critical insight into how the thesis and antithesis are formed, the illusion remains but no longer fools us (see KU 5:386).[45]

7.4 The Method of Natural History

In the Doctrine of Method, Kant formulated a set of rules to ensure that scientific knowledge remains free from the illusions exposed in the Transcendental Dialectic (see Section 5.4). In this final section, I suggest that a similar strategy can be found in the first part of the Methodology of the Teleological Power of Judgment (§§80–1): Kant presents a set of rules to ensure that natural historians are not deceived by the illusion exposed in the Dialectic.[46] The mechanical and teleological principles each open an order of things as species of an undetermined genus. In the physical-mechanical order of things, we assume that the highest genus is matter. However, we are unable to work analytically from matter's universal laws to the physical-material particular laws. The principle of purposiveness instructs the understanding to assume that particular laws are admixtures of universal laws that arise within nature as mechanism. The judgement of some things as natural purposes marks out a separate order within the mechanism of nature that we seek to arrange under a genus that is not provided by the understanding but suggested by reason. When pushed to its limit, the "archaeologist of nature" considers all living creatures as a "great family" by searching for a "unity of plan" or "common prototype" from which the various stem species derive (KU 5:419). Such a project would open a far more expansive conception of natural history than Kant had entertained in his essays on race, where he proposed that four human races could be arranged under a common species.

Commentators generally interpret Kant's portrayal of the archaeologist of nature as an example of reason's "daring adventure," which natural historians undertake when they adopt the hypothesis of an original "organisation

---

[45] In the *Critique*, Kant states that an antinomy is a "natural and unavoidable illusion, which even if one is no longer fooled by it, still deceives though it does not defraud and which thus can be rendered harmless but never destroyed" (A422/B449–50).

[46] In §79, Kant argues that teleology does not belong either to the doctrine of nature or to theology, but to the critique of the power of reflecting judgement. Yet he then notes that a critique of teleology (1) "can and must provide the method for how nature must be judged in accordance with the principle of final causes," and (2) have an important use in theology (KU 5:416–7). The second and longer part of the Methodology (§§82–91) presents an argument for the presumption of the highest good and the wise government of a benevolent God, based on Kant's transcendental argument for the principle of purposiveness. For a study of the Methodology as a whole, see Geiger, "The Methodology of the Teleological Power of Judgment."

purposively aimed at all these creatures" (KU 5:419n).[47] On this interpretation, the Methodology seeks to show that archaeology is a mere "figment of the imagination" (*Hirngespinst*) that begins when natural historians are deceived by the illusion generated by the antinomy.[48] Sloan for instance argues that Kant's caricature of the archaeologist is "only a restatement of his previous description of Herder's thesis of a general historical development of life from a common source under the action of a universal vital force."[49] The result of the presentation and resolution of the antinomy is that teleology is simply "a heuristic guiding principle of research" with "weak or regulative epistemic status only."[50]

In this final section, I argue that the undetermined genus Kant has in mind is not Herder's universal vital force but rather an idea that opens an order of things arranged according to the logic of organized beings. In the Methodology, Kant reformulates M_1 and M_2 as methodological rules that direct the application of the law of specification to conditioned cognitions. These rules do not simply guide but also command natural historians to judge the causal origins of cognitions mechanically, on pain of violating the causal principle. The archaeology of nature is thus the natural path for natural historians to take when faced with the demands of empirical nature, which is why they must practice discipline if they are to avoid the antinomy's tendency to deceive.[51] If natural historians were to adopt the unity of plan as a hypothesis that is adequate to explain the given consequences—that is, if they were to place the highest genus *in nature*, and thereby to treat teleology as part of the doctrine of nature—then they would, like Herder, be deceived. Yet if the unity of plan is held merely as a principle for reflecting on the material generation of natural things and their form, it can nevertheless guide natural historians to search for mechanical forces, fossilized remains of past ancestors, and interconnected subspecies on the empirical level. There is something daring about this project, for, at least in Kant's time, experience had not yielded evidence of genetic change. Yet Kant does not use "daring" to describe illegitimate projects (he describes illegitimate projects as "absurd," KU 5:419n) but simply those for which one does not yet have rational grounds to expect progress.[52] While Kant does not explicitly endorse archaeology as the formal structure of natural history, he clearly thinks that it is the natural path for reason to take. As a formal project, archaeology is not deceptive.

---

[47] van den Berg, "Kant and the Scope of Analogy in the Life Sciences," 75; Zammito, *The Genesis of Kant's Critique of Judgment*, 215–7.

[48] See Vanzo, "Kant on Experiment," 84.   [49] Sloan, "Kant on the History of Nature," 643.

[50] Sloan, "Kant on the History of Nature," 644.

[51] Here I agree with Mensch and Geiger, who read Kant as endorsing an archaeology of sorts. Mensch, *Kant's Organicism*, 146–54; Geiger, *Kant and the Claims of the Empirical World*, 73–4.

[52] "For even the most daring hypothesis can be authorized only if at least the **possibility** of that which is assumed to be its ground is **certain**, and one must be able to insure the objective reality of its concept" (KU 5:394).

The first methodological implication of the resolution to the antinomy is that the mechanical principle is not descriptive but prescriptive: mechanical explanations ought to be privileged over other ways of explaining phenomena. Because it is only by pursuing physical-mechanical connections that determining judgement can draw its conditioned cognitions under determinate principles, we can reformulate M_1 as a methodological rule:

R_1: Seek for a merely mechanical explanation of all natural products. (KU 5:417)

Note that R_1 says nothing about the possibility of natural products, as did M_1; it simply instructs determining judgement to consider its cognitions *as* natural products, that is, material objects whose properties are generated in nature as a physical-mechanical system. In theory, the principles of mechanical physics can be derived from the principle of causality (they "stand under" it, to use Kant's language from B165). The imperative to follow the mechanical principle means that if R_1 is not made the basis for research, there can be "no proper cognition of nature" (KU 5:387). Following R_1 enables the formulation of physical hypotheses to establish the empirical lawfulness of contingent cognitions, which can be arranged under the laws of mechanics. The mechanical principle directs us to seek the particular rule for an effect, which can be used in a determining judgement once it has been adopted in a system of knowledge (KU 5:466).

However, the antinomy revealed that while the authorization to seek mechanical explanations for natural products is unrestricted, our *capacity* to do so is "distinctly bounded" by the constitution of the understanding (KU 5:417). The discursive nature of our cognition requires us to introduce a different kind of causality, one opened through an analogy with reason, to make the contingent appearance of some natural products intelligible. The boundedness of discursive cognition results in a second methodological rule:

R_2: The explanation of things judged as natural purposes must be subordinated to a teleological principle. (KU 5:417)

Kant states that while it is "rational, indeed meritorious, to pursue the mechanism of nature, for the sake of an explanation of the products of nature, as far as can plausibly be done," it is nevertheless "impossible **in itself** to find the purposiveness of nature by this route" (KU 5:418). Only a non-sensible, intellectual intuition could "furnish the ground for the mechanism of the appearances in accordance with particular laws." Thus, even if natural historians were to examine the emergence of natural purposes from "a condition of chaos," they would nevertheless have to base their judgements "on some original organization, which uses that mechanism itself in order to produce other organized forms or to develop its own into new configurations" (KU 5:418). To base their judgements of natural purposes on some original organization is not to provide an explanation but simply to demonstrate reason's need to assume it for the generation of some natural products.[53]

The idea of an undetermined genus in a system of natural history cannot refer to a unifying force, for the disparity of the mechanical and teleological principles requires a strict separation of physical hypotheses and mere analogies. In §90, Kant explains that the teleological principle does not warrant the formulation of physical hypotheses (for example, a vital force capable of forming unformed matter), for it does not establish a connection through the schematized concept of causality but introduces a foreign causality through an analogy with reason. Judgement operates reflectively when we encounter a thing whose possibility is unknown. In such cases, reason must suggest a form of causality to assist judgement to reflect on a phenomenon as the effect of a law (KU 5:463–6). Teleological judgement enables us to seek the mechanisms responsible for the movement of the parts. It cannot, however, explain the appearance of conceptual order in nature. The original organization remains a problem.

There is textual evidence to suggest that Kant's argument in the Methodology is partly inspired by the second edition of Johann Friedrich Blumenbach's *On the Formative Drive*, which Blumenbach had sent to Kant in 1789 after reading "Teleological Principles."[54] Blumenbach endorsed a preformationist hypothesis of germs in the first edition, yet in the second edition he unambiguously alters his position: "no preformed germs exist, but only a special, lifelong, active drive [*Trieb*], which has been aroused in the previously crude, unshaped generative matter of organized bodies."[55] On Kant's interpretation of Blumenbach's revised position, Blumenbach begins with an original organization of matter and yet "leaves mechanism an indeterminable but at the same time also unmistakable role" (KU 5:424). Original organization thus remains a problem; the "formative drive [*Bildungstrieb*]" is not a teleological force (despite its name, and the manner in which Blumenbach seems to deploy it), but simply an "inscrutable **principle** of an original **organization**" (KU 5:424).[56] Nevertheless, *assuming* a formative drive

---

[53] Kant states that natural historians have not provided but "merely put off the explanation, and cannot presume to have made the generation of those two kingdoms independent from the condition of final causes" (KU 5:420).

[54] In a letter dated 5 August 1790, Kant thanks Blumenbach for sending him a copy of the book the previous year, and explains that it "has a close relationship to the ideas that occupy me: the union of two principles that people have believed to be irreconcilable, namely the physical-mechanistic and the merely teleological way of explaining organized nature" (Br 11:185). Sloan argues that §80 can be read "almost as a commentary on Blumenbach's second edition of *Über den Bildungstrieb*." Sloan, "Preforming the Categories," 249.

[55] Blumenbach, *Über den Bildungstrieb*, 24.

[56] There is significant divergence in the literature with regard to Kant's use of Blumenbach's *Bildungstrieb*. Larson argues that Kant's reading of the *Bildungstrieb* removes its lawful status and recasts it as "a maxim for judgment, a guide for investigation." Larson, *Interpreting Nature*, 178. Similarly, Richards argues that in contrast to Kant's understanding of the *Bildungstrieb* as a "heuristic

enables a "physical explanation" of the material generation and form of a living natural product according to the five vital forces Blumenbach presents in his study (sensibility, irritability, conception, nourishment, and reproduction). These forces explain the various functions of a living being and stand "under the guidance and direction of the former principle."[57]

Kant seeks to show that Blumenbach provides an account of generation that, in contrast to its competitors, consistently follows R_1 and R_2. Preformation, understood as the "system of generatings as mere educts," denies that living beings can be considered as natural products, and thus violates R_1 (KU 5:423). Hylozoism, understood as the system in which the "generation of an organized being through the mechanism of crude, unorganized matter," is an "absurd" hypothesis, for it violates R_2 (KU 5:419n). A legitimate hypothesis must be a form of *generatio univoca*, whereby "something organic would be generated out of something else that is also organic" (KU 5:419n). The only form of *generatio univoca* observed by natural historians is *generatio homonyma*, in which an organized being is generated from another organized being that is structurally homogeneous to it.[58] This is the kind of generation (or *degeneration*) Kant considers in his essays on race. Nevertheless, Kant acknowledges that natural historians can legitimately entertain the hypothesis of *generatio heteronyma*, whereby the product is structurally different from its producer. *Generatio heteronyma* would entail a "specific difference between these kinds of beings," such as "when certain aquatic animals are gradually transformed into amphibians and these, after some generations, into land animals."

Few commentators have noted that Kant accepts *generatio heteronyma* as a legitimate hypothesis ("there is no contradiction in this"), marking a considerable

concept, one that helped the naturalist seek out the mechanist causes assumed to be at work," Blumenbach saw it as "constitutive of nature" and as "a teleological cause fully resident in nature." Richards, "Kant and Blumenbach on the *Bildungstrieb*," 20. Larson and Richards rightly draw attention to the fact that Kant rejects the parity Blumenbach grants to gravity and the *Bildungstrieb*, and also to the fact that Blumenbach in his later physiological textbooks moved away from the experimental presentation of the *Bildungstrieb* to grant it an increasingly substantive meaning. Yet their presentation of Kant's account of the *Bildungstrieb* as a regulative principle or heuristic concept is misleading. The regulative principle at work is not the *Bildungstrieb* but the teleological principle, which enables natural historians to reflect on some natural products through the form of causality according to ends. They can then propose a hypothetical force responsible for organic effects without purporting to explain how organized beings originally came to possess organization. See also Sloan, "Preforming the Categories," 249–50; Richards, *The Romantic Conception of Life*, 229; Steigerwald, *Experimenting at the Boundaries of Life*, 92; Fisher, "Kant and Schelling on Blumenbach's Formative Drive," 395–9; Geiger, *Kant and the Claims of the Empirical World*, 67–9.

[57] Kant seems to read Blumenbach's vital forces as mechanical forces that are subordinated to an original organization. See Blumenbach, *Über den Bildungstrieb*, 25. Casper Friedrich Wolff's *vis essentialis* would not qualify as a mechanical force for Kant, for it is "that specific force which in vegetable bodies initiates all features that cause us to ascribe life to organic beings." Wolff, *Die Theorie der Generationen*, 160.

[58] See Lippmann, *Urzeugung und Lebenskraft*, 83.

concession to Herder.[59] Kant no longer claims that reason "shrinks back" from the monstrous proposal that a new species could be generated within the conditions of nature. It is now the natural path for reason to take in its search for a higher genus. This is not because Kant toys with non-mechanical causes in the system of nature. Rather, it is because he acknowledges (assumedly due to his encounter with Blumenbach) that one can coherently follow R_1 and R_2 by supposing that there is some mechanism of change residing in an original organization that traces back *further* than the original stem of a species. This is reflected in the fact that Kant seems to have abandoned the hypothesis of preformed germs in favour of "internally purposive dispositions [*inneren zweckmässige Anlagen*]," which no longer concern the structural relation between static parts but now operate as capacities for organization without predetermined constraints (KU 5:423).[60] This has serious implications for his account of natural history, for the fixity Kant had formerly attributed to the hypothetical germs is no longer a requirement of reason, as he had claimed in 1788 (see Section 6.3).[61] *Generatio heteronyma* cannot be ruled out *a priori*; its existence is a matter of empirical testing. Presently, there is no empirical evidence of the kind of structural change projected by the idea of a unity of plan, so it is not clear whether a research programme that connects two different species to a common ancestor could consistently follow Empirical Possibility. Such a research programme would certainly be daring, for there are no rational grounds to expect progress. But it does not, like the archaeologist who posits order from a condition of chaos, violate Real Possibility.[62]

The theory of generation natural historians *can* accept, then, is "generic preformationism," or what Kant takes to be epigenesis properly understood (KU 5:424). Like hylozoism, generic preformationism considers nature "as itself producing rather than as merely developing [organized beings]." Yet it is best understood as a subspecies of preformationism, for it does not view original organization as a natural product but rather as a form of judgement that enables us to consider how parts can emerge and function mechanically. However, in

---

[59] Exceptions include Zuckert, "Organisms and Metaphysics," 73; Huneman, "Naturalising Purpose," 663–4; Cohen, "Kant on Evolution," 131.

[60] Kant uses the same phrase when he speaks the "purposive disposition" of the imagination in regards to the understanding (KU 5:344), and the "internally purposive disposition of our cognitive faculties" (KU 5:359), implying that organized beings are judged to be structurally analogous to the purposiveness of the mind, as felt in aesthetic experience.

[61] Kant continues to call upon germs to explain the characteristics of peoples after 1790, and yet these references are found only in his moral writings. Here I agree with Sloan's claim that germs no longer have a legitimate theoretical application in Kant's natural philosophy, and thus have no pragmatic function. See Sloan, "Preforming the Categories," 250–1.

[62] At several points in his work Kant states that the idea of species transformation is contradictory, for a substance cannot be produced but rather persists (e.g. V-Met/Mron 29:760). Yet *species* for Kant is a logical concept, and thus concerns the arrangement of educts within a logical system. In contrast, a *Stammgattung* is a physical concept that refers to a line of descent connected through time despite alterations. Kant's recognition of the thinkability of *generatio heteronyma* permits the transformation of a *Stammgattung*, for physical concepts of natural history refer to products and not to educts.

contrast to both hylozoism and preformationism, generic preformationism is not a theoretical position but rather "a guideline for coming to know their constitution through observation without rising to the level of an investigation into their ultimate origin" (KU 5:389–90). It is concerned with drawing organized beings into basic unities and lower derivative variations by comparing building plans, allowing natural historians to find greater unity in the order of things than mere description could ever afford. While generic preformation does not explain the original production of organization, the progress we make in connecting stem species according to their structural form gives us a "weak ray of hope" that the mechanical principle can nevertheless make progress:

> The agreement of so many genera of animals [*Tiergattungen*] in a certain common schema, which seems to lie at the basis not only of their skeletal structure but also of the arrangement of their other parts, and by which a remarkable simplicity of plan [*Grundriss*] has been able to produce such a great variety of species by the shortening of one part and the elongation of another, by the involution of this part and the evolution of another, allows the mind at least a weak ray of hope that something may be accomplished here with the principle of the mechanism of nature, without which there can be no natural science at all. This analogy of forms, insofar as in spite of all the differences it seems to have been generated in accordance with a common prototype [*Urbild*] strengthens the suspicion of a real kinship among them in their generation from a common proto-mother [*Urmutter*] through the gradual approach of one animal genus to the other.   (KU 5:418–9)

Kant speaks not just of discovering a generative force behind different varieties which all trace back to a single stem, but also of an even more general plan that lies behind vertebrates, one that even extends to include polyps, enabling the archaeologist to unify the manifold of living natural products under the single idea of an organized being. Zammito contends that the developmental process depicted in this passage had, for Kant, "long since been *closed*, and that the world he contemplated was one of fixed species."[63] This is because Kant was "committed to preformation—even if 'generic' rather than individual—and this meant that there was an ineluctable *metaphysical* foundation for any consideration of organisms and life in the physical world." Yet once more this interpretation relies on the older reading of the antinomy, according to which the causality of ends contradicts the constitutive principle of mechanism. The limit Kant places on historical

---

[63] Zammito, *The Gestation of German Biology*, 232. Elsewhere Zammito argues that this passage "should be seen as a *counterfactual* exposition: a presentation of what one might wish could be done, but which Kant, from the outset and in principle, *denied* could be done." Zammito, "Should Kant have Abandoned the 'Daring Adventure of Reason'?," 136.

knowledge is simply that if we classify according to the analogy between forms, we are not (yet) in the business of mechanical explanation. Of course, in the above passage Kant is simply describing a potential programme of natural history; its viability remains to be seen. Yet nowhere does he say that it is illegitimate. The programme would entail a significant expansion of natural history from tracing lines of descent (variety, race, stem) to a comparative anatomy based on similarities between skeletal structures and building plans, allowing for a far more extensive historical analysis. The more the analogy of forms enables natural historians to unify individuals under stem species, and stem species under structural plans, the more reason they have to suspect a *real* kinship among them, that is, a physical-mechanical connection that excites the understanding and yet remains a mere possibility. This expansion can be seen as the outworking of Kant's claim in *Metaphysical Foundations* that, while natural history is not part of natural science but the historical doctrine of nature, "every doctrine of nature must finally lead to natural science and conclude there" (MAN 4:469). The Methodology of the third *Critique* seeks to show how natural historians are to proceed when so many connections within the system are yet unknown, and thus when the temptation to fill in the gaps is so great.

What limit, then, does the system of generic preformationism place on natural history? Natural historians unify groups of stem species using a method similar to that which Kant developed for classifying races under the same stem. Yet Kant does not mention race in *Critique of the Power of Judgment*, and the very idea of a fixed subspecies under an original stem is incompatible with the indeterminacy of the system of natural history he now describes. The Methodology of the third *Critique* opens a system of classification that is more sophisticated than anything we find in his writings and lectures on natural history, for the hypothesis of germs and predispositions is replaced with the causal relation between parts and wholes such that the groupings under *organized being* are united by a shared plan.[64] A genus such as *vertebrates* need not remain an arbitrary collection of organized beings that happen to have a backbone (a mere affinity between concepts). In a system of natural history, *vertebrates* can be viewed as an empirical concept that unities an enormous variety of organized beings according to a connection that could potentially find a determinate mechanical explanation. Natural history thus concerns the comparison of structure in animals of different species in search of a prototype to which different specimens can be compared. Of course, natural historians work with probabilities ("there can be no hope for certainty," KU 5:428n), as the structural changes that occurred long before cannot be experienced. Nevertheless, they can discern which classifications are better than others

---

[64] In the surviving notes from the physical geography lectures during the 1790s, Kant's interest seems to be far more wide-ranging as he attempts to capture the co-construction of human forms of life and the environment. See for instance V-Geo Dohna 1792 26.2.2:1131–41.

based on how well they follow R_1 and R_2 in the context of available observations ("there is reasonable grounds for making conjectures"). The strength of one's assent to empirical divisions lies in the careful archaeological observation of fossilized remains in comparison with the present variety and geographical distribution of organized beings.

Kant notes that there are few natural historians who have not occasionally entertained the radical idea that the entire field of organic form generated from a common proto-mother, for reason pushes inquiry back towards a single focal point in nature's causal series (KU 5:419n). This idea is not absurd, but rather the expression of reason's unrestricted command to seek higher genera: "I can always go still further in the regress, because no member is empirically given as absolutely unconditioned, and thus a higher member may be admitted as possible and hence the inquiry after it may be admitted as necessary" (A514/B542). To stipulate that there *is* a common ancestor would not open new avenues for the understanding but simply parade as knowledge of past events. The examination of some natural products according to the concept of a natural purpose *can* advance natural history, however, "since by means of it we have been able to discover many laws of nature which, given the limitation of our insights into the inner mechanisms of nature, would otherwise remain hidden from us" (KU 5:398). Natural history is strictly an empirical method for the discovery of material-mechanical connections through comparative anatomy. The task of natural history is to reflect on the enduring facts from past times in light of the present diversity of form and to derive the laws by which generative forces determine such effects:

> If the name **natural history** that has been adopted for the description of nature is to remain in use, then one can call that which it literally means, namely a representation of the **ancient** conditions of the earth—about which, even though there is no hope for certainty, there is reasonable ground for making conjectures—the **archaeology** of **nature**, in contrast to that of art. To the former belong fossils, just as to the latter belong carved stones, etc. For since we are really constantly if also, as is fitting, slowly working on such an archaeology (under the name of a theory of the earth), this name would not be given to a merely imaginary branch of research into nature, but to one to which nature itself invites and summons us.   (KU 5:428n)

Despite forty years of trying, Kant acknowledges that he has not yet been able to save the name "natural history" for a temporal project that does not present nature as art but as artisan. Understood as the archaeology of nature—as opposed to the *art* of nature—natural history seeks to maximize the unity and extension of the understanding by projecting back from the present to fossilized remains, bringing greater determinacy to the understanding's cognitions. While Kant remained critical of Buffon's speculative account of generation, which called on laws of another nature, he continues to employ Buffon's notion of a "theory of the earth" as the formal structure for the programme of research summoned by nature. A theory of the earth is mechanistic to the extent that we judge each thing as a part of a self-producing whole, such that the change undergone by any part can be determined by a higher part. Natural historians can claim with confidence that sudden volcanic eruptions and gradual alterations through rainfall altered the slope of the land, such that streams now flow in a manner that is suited to trees that grow along it, forming a habitat conducive to the flourishing of various organized beings (KU 5:428). They can even judge such organized beings as sorting themselves into kinds. However, while natural historians can trace the developmental history of organized beings back through the mechanism of nature, they cannot ground their initial generation in some moment of becoming, in which the peculiar character of organized form arose within the mechanical system. To examine natural products as self-organizing, natural historians must consider them as a local systems in which the parts do not simply determine the whole but the whole also determines the parts, even if the whole were, for a non-discursive intellect, conceivable according to mechanism. Natural history, pursued as archaeology, is thus the programme of research to which nature invites and even summons us. And yet, due to the peculiar and limited nature of our cognition, the demands of empirical nature evoke conflicting maxims that, if left uncriticized, lead us astray.

Conclusion

In this study, I have argued that if we desist from viewing natural history as an encyclopaedic obsession with taxonomy and conceive of it instead as a site of philosophical exploration as a gap opened between reason and nature, a new way of framing the epistemological and metaphysical problems of eighteenth-century natural philosophy becomes available. These problems centre on how the contingent regularities encountered in experience can find a determinate location in a physical-mechanical conception of the natural system. Experimental philosophy began in the seventeenth century with an attack on the essential qualities projected by the school philosophers, and a new system of learning in which human knowledge begins with natural history. Newton demonstrated how the natural philosopher can postulate hypothetical forces, and, through the application of mathematics to natural objects considered on a geometrical plane, work up from the facts of natural history to the laws that govern them. Yet the experimental turn resulted in a radical separation of reason from nature, such that any attempt to move from mathematical laws to the system of nature required natural philosophers to presuppose that the physical relation of facts coheres with the logical relation of ideas, thereby transgressing the sceptical impulse that initially gave rise to experimental philosophy. Even Newton's inverse square law presupposes an initial state of mechanical order, the possibility of which he attributes to a hyperphysical cause. By the mid-eighteenth century, the attempt to place Newtonian science on metaphysical foundations meant that the separation of nature and logic could be reconnected as a method of discovery. Natural philosophers could extend Newton's method by analogy on the assumption that the properties of material things are generated by physical-mechanical forces. The greater the success of this extension, the more firmly the assumption takes hold.

Kant's critical project can be seen as a culminating moment in his career-long engagement with the transformation of natural history, for it vindicates the human capacity to seek and find order in nature by grounding the context of discovery in metaphysics established as a science. To demonstrate how hypotheses can be more than mere fiction, Kant established a new foundation for natural science that redefines objectivity in terms of what can appear as an object of cognition. His critical philosophy, and the metaphysical foundations it lays for natural science, determines a sphere of real possibility and prescribes the relations for which the understanding must seek. To vindicate the extension of

Kant and the Transformation of Natural History. Andrew Cooper, Oxford University Press. © Andrew Cooper 2023.
DOI: 10.1093/oso/9780192869784.003.0009

Newtonian inquiry to regions of nature that are underdetermined by universal natural laws, Kant identifies an *a priori* principle that is objectively valid to the extent that it enables judgement to reflect on the manifold of objects as the products of a physical-mechanical system. Kant's ground-breaking achievement is to demonstrate that natural philosophers *must* withhold from explaining natural phenomena according to the ideas of reason and, instead, seek empirical regularities, formulate and test hypotheses, open new fields of inquiry, and strive for consensus in a community of scientific inquirers.

There are, of course, enormous gaps in Kant's conception of natural history. For instance, the mechanism by which descendants of an original stem altered their form as they encountered new environmental conditions remains unexplained. The search for a higher genus in a system of natural history is a daring adventure precisely because it requires natural historians to assume an adaptive capacity, the possibility of which is unknown. Yet these gaps are fundamentally different to the hypothetical connections in Descartes' fable, Buffon's epochal narrative, and Herder's history of humankind, in which speculative forces purportedly explain the changes that have occurred in organic form, and even the initial emergence of organization from mere matter. They are closer to the blank spaces left between the towns on Haller's map, for they await progress in other regions of inquiry that could assist natural historians to fill in the whole with the greatest depth and extension. Kant was adamant that while natural history remains in its infancy, natural historians must practise discipline if they are to maintain a productive programme of research that does not collapse into yet another ghost story. The hypothetical generative forces that connect structural affinities in natural history are placeholders for causes that potentially could, and therefore *should* (following R₁) be discovered.

There is one gap, however, that could never be traversed in a Kantian natural history. For discursive minds like our own, the appearance of purposiveness in the mechanism of nature remains contingent—an unceasing source of astonishment and admiration—not because organic change is underdetermined by mechanical forces but because discursive minds must judge the possibility of organized beings according to a causality that works from whole to parts, on pain of failing the understanding's task of bringing maximal unity to its cognitions. For Kant, this gap does not lie in nature but in the constitution of the human intellect, for which the constructive understanding is separated from speculative reason by an incalculable gulf (KU 5:175). While a new generation of natural philosophers—including Carl Friedrich Kielmeyer, Johann Wolfgang von Goethe, and Friedrich Wilhelm von Schelling—would be inspired by Kant's attempt to vindicate the necessity of both mechanical and teleological judgement in natural history, it is by rejecting this gap, and adopting a standpoint similar to the intuitive intellect Kant describes in §77 of the third *Critique*, that they began to determine the laws of structural adaptation.[1] The first task of a *philosophy* of nature would be to place Kant's dynamical concept of matter within a series of assent, where teleology does not introduce an additional order of determinacy but rather elevates or sublates (*hebt auf*) a previous level in nature grasped as a self-organizing process. Kant, however, remained committed to a critical conception of philosophy, which is concerned "more with pruning abundant saplings than with making them sprout" (RezHerder 8:55). The progress to be made in natural history, for Kant, is strictly empirical.

The transformation of the logical *scala naturae* in the work of Bacon, Boyle, and Locke, and the construction of a new programme of classification based on the generation of natural products, first suggested by Linnaeus and then realized in Buffon and Kant via the plant and animal physics developed by Hales and Haller, bestowed scientific credibility on the conception of nature as a self-producing order. Kant in many respects represents the supreme limit of this trajectory, for his discovery of judgement's power of reflection identifies how the principles of mechanism and teleology necessarily arise in response to the demands of empirical nature. The force of his transcendental argument for judgement's principle of purposiveness is that we *must* reflect on nature as a physical-mechanical system, on pain of failing determining judgement's mandate to bring the greatest extension and unity to cognition. Purposiveness, understood as judgement's *a priori* principle, holds to the idea of mechanism and follows it as far as possible, even though it denies that a causal explanation of the purpose is forthcoming. The shift in natural history from the logical classification of things to the experimental study of natural products is nothing less than a revolution in natural science, for it transforms the natural system from a given rational order into a condition of the possibility of empirical inquiry. Scientific knowledge is no longer understood exclusively in terms of a completed system; it includes a practical level on which natural scientists seek to extend experimental inquiry in the attempt to approximate systematic completion.

It is beyond the scope of this study to make any further claims about Kant's influence on the following generation of natural philosophers, who reimagined natural history as comparative anatomy and consolidated biology as the experimental science of organic structure. Nevertheless, the argument I have presented in this book raises serious questions for depictions of Kant in which his critical ideal of proper natural science stood to deny the study of natural history from achieving the status of a science. In contrast to readings of Kant's theory of science according to which critical philosophy restricts scientific knowledge to the ideal of completeness and certainty, I have argued that proper natural science determines

---

[1] For studies of Kielmeyer, Goethe, and Schelling's relation to Kant's account of natural history, see Cooper, "Force and Law in Kielmeyer's 1793 Speech"; Cooper, "The Economy of the *Bildungstrieb* in Goethe's Comparative Anatomy"; and Zammito, *The Gestation of German Biology*, ch. 10.

the formal conditions in which the experimental and historical sciences find their orientation in the midst of empirical diversity. It is thus a fundamental misreading of Kant's theory of science to conclude that he "despairs" of the scientific status of the experimental and historical sciences.[2] It is one of the basic achievements of Kant's theory of science to deny that empirical concepts and particular laws are part of proper science, even though proper science sets the ideal to which all sciences aspire.[3] Kant was convinced that it is only by establishing metaphysics as a science that we can determine the modal space in which hypotheses can be legitimately deployed, and thereby extend our empirical knowledge without falling prey to the illusions of speculation. He thus opened a broader conception of science as a research programme in which practitioners seek particular laws and empirical concepts, construct new fields of inquiry, and endlessly refine their knowledge.

That Kant deployed this broader conception of science to justify a quasi-essentialist hierarchy of human races in his *Racenschriften*, which helped consolidate the pernicious European fantasies of racial purity and white superiority with scientific credibility, demonstrates that scientificity is not immune to reason's tendency to mistake its subjective conditions for the conditions of objects. Here we encounter a failure that Kant partly unearthed and yet ultimately shared with many of his contemporaries. The critique of pure reason exposes an illusion that naturally occurs when we take reason's logical system as the ground of nature's order, tempting us to misconstrue hypothetical inferences as constitutive features of our knowledge. Kant's solution is not to operate without hypotheses but rather to practise the discipline of critique in order to discern *which* hypotheses are worthy of assuming in a body of knowledge. Hypotheses worthy of assuming can be entertained in a programme of research, directing us to seek observations and experiments that could be tested against them. The critical method enabled Kant to uncover several unwarranted assumptions that led his former thinking into error, including the confluence of sensibility and reason in the mid-1760s and the fixity of subspecies in the late 1780s.[4] While the latter discovery demotes any morally salient differences among human beings from natural determinations to

---

[2] Friedman, *Kant and the Exact Sciences*, xv.

[3] In the late 1790s, there is evidence to suggest that Kant attempts to traverse the gap. In the fragments collected as *Opus postumum*, he sketches a transition from the metaphysical foundations of natural science to physics. He is clear that the concept of a final cause contains the "concept of a causal relationship on the part of something which *precedes* (in the sequence of conditions), but which, nevertheless, is also to succeed its own self (in the sequence of causes and effects)." Yet he stresses that the contradiction internal to this concept means that it is "only a principle for the *investigation of nature*, which, as an *idea*, precedes empirical [investigation], and may {not} be lacking in the complete division of the transition from the metaphysical foundations of natural science to physics—despite the fact that it is merely problematic and takes [no] notice of the existence or nonexistence of such bodies [and their] forces" (OP 21:184–5). See van den Berg, *Kant on Proper Science*, 211ff.

[4] I thus agree with Kleingeld to the extent that I take Kant to have had second thoughts about his explanatory conception of germs, which provides the mechanics for his racialized concept of race. Yet

historically contingent facts, it did not prevent Kant from defending a hierarchical classification of human difference in the 1790s—one in which the white European, as classifier, enjoys a privileged status.[5] That Kant continued to make hierarchical distinctions between human races after 1790 betrays an inability, or unwillingness, to draw several closely held assumptions into the light of critique. Kant argued that reason is compelled to assume a monogenetic account of human origins, for without it we could not distinguish between accidental and self-perpetuating differences. Yet his prior assumption of a stable fourfold schema, and his attempt to transcribe the geohumoralism of his selected travelogues onto a physical plane, licensed the unbridled extension of historical reasoning to decide *which* differences are self-perpetuating, and thus derivable from natural properties.

Kant's inability to critically examine his presuppositions should unsettle us, and raise serious questions about his philosophy of science. Kant was clearly unfamiliar with the actual demands of experimental practice and shows little concern for the conditions of evidential reasoning by which we might find sufficient grounds to accept hypotheses in a programme of research. He did not simply confuse moral characteristics with physical and therefore biologically explainable traits, as if he somehow failed to read a distinction between cultural and natural phenomena off the facts. Rather, he inherited and indeed extended the geohumoral framework of colonial science, according to which exterior form, interior constitution, temperament, and moral characteristics are expressions of a generative force.

Kant's construction of racialized knowledge thus performs an ideological function: it both reflects and contributes to perpetuating illicit group privilege.[6] According to Kant's practical philosophy, to recognize a member of the human species as a person necessarily gives rise to a feeling of respect, which includes intentional content in regard to how that person is treated (see KpV 5:74–5). When it comes to non-Europeans, Kant's opinions about racial characteristics both reflect and contribute to perpetuating a constellation of power in which the colonizer's feeling of respect is withheld. For instance, his claim that Africans lack the natural drive to activity, and are thus destined to forced labour, reflects and

Bernasconi is right to reply that it does not prevent Kant from continuing to hold racist views. Kleingeld, "Kant's Second Thoughts on Race," 592; Bernasconi, "Kant's Third Thoughts on Race," 306–12.

[5] In the student notes from the 1792 physical geography lectures, for instance, Kant is recorded as offering a hierarchical account of the human races (V-Geo/Dohna 1792 26.2.2:1131–2). Yet his account lacks the detail of the Dönhoff notes, where Kant is recorded as explaining the superior intelligence and ingenuity of Europeans on physical grounds (the "character of race," Kant claims, can be explained according to the manner in which the original "organization" has expressed itself in different climactic and environmental conditions, V-Geo/Dönhoff 1781/2 26.2.2:892). In the 1802 version of the anthropology lectures, Kant no longer seems to believe that race is tied to matters that practically concern human beings on the stage of their destiny. Race is a matter of physiology, he states, with no "pragmatic" relevance (Anth 7:120).

[6] Mills, "'Ideal Theory' as Ideology," 166.

contributes to perpetuating the exploitative conditions of chattel slavery in which some human beings are treated as mere means (ÜGTP 8:174n). His claim that Amerindians are maladapted to their environment, and incapable of culture, reflects and contributes to perpetuating a system of colonial law in which the right to property of some human beings is violated (ÜGTP 8:176). Kant's history of the human species demonstrates why the moral progress of human beings as a species does not require moral respect for certain members of that class, allowing world citizens to endorse moral universalism *and* racist particularism without contradiction.[7]

If unwarranted opinions can negatively influence practical reasoning, it is possible that practical reasoning can play a positive role in natural science— provided that we acknowledge and destroy the prejudicial assumptions that led Kant to believe that the decontextualized vantage of physical geography could ever be disinterested. If Kant had read the accounts of indentured Indian labour, the mass displacement of indigenous Americans, or the dehumanizing impact of the slave trade with moral repugnance before using them to illustrate his racial schema, he may have paused to question whether "natural" properties can be derived from anecdotal evidence presented in defense of colonialism. The feeling of respect may have raised procedural questions regarding what we now call the "robustness" of experimental data, prompting Kant not only to interrogate the supposedly disinterested standpoint of the travel writer but also to seek alternative explanations that include the oppressive and unjust human laws under which physical, moral, and temperamental characteristics are observed. The challenge of natural science in the broad sense is to recognize that *all* knowledge is produced from somewhere; a fact that Reverend James Ramsay grasped when he sought to expose the workings of "European pride" in the construction of scientific concep- tions of race.[8] Kant's assumption of European superiority—which he took to be exhibited in and justified by the very practice of natural history—blocked the positive feedback that could occur between practical reasoning and scientific inquiry.

My aim in this study has not been to vindicate Kant's account of natural history but to enable readers to get a clearer grasp of its significance in the history of science. I argued that by removing the reconstruction of past events from the domain of cognition and placing it instead in an intersubjective sphere of histor- ical knowledge, Kant provides a framework in which historical claims can

---

[7] For a study of Kant as a "consistent inegalitarian," see Lu-Adler, *Kant, Race, and Racism*, 18. Lu-Adler emphasizes the fact that Kant developed his racialized concept of race in the classroom, with the aim of shaping his students' practical attitudes towards non-Europeans. As we saw in Section 4.1, a pedagogical goal of his lectures on physical geography was to explain to students lacking in worldly experience how the various players have enacted their part on the "world stage" (VvRM75 2:443/6:26), thereby aiding them to "discover an *aim of nature* in this nonsensical course of things human" (IaG 8:17).

[8] Ramsay, *An Essay on the Treatment and Conversion of African Slaves in the British Sugar Colonies*, 231.

genuinely be contested. This includes Kant's own historical claims, and the assumptions that make those claims seem reasonable to hold. Following Kant, the natural system is neither a given object with which our understanding is supposed to converge nor a spurious illusion that inevitably leads us astray. It is a shared project that unites the fields of scientific research, enabling a community of inquirers to give and receive reasons for why one should or should not assume a hypothesis. To grieve Kant's failure to expunge the ideal of the natural system is to overlook the challenge his philosophical project poses to us now. After Kant, the natural system no longer requires a divine author or a speculative programme of metaphysics but rather a growing attentiveness to the variety of natural things, an ever deepening search for the conditions of empirical phenomena, and a commitment to widening the range of voices participating in the intersubjective sphere in which we give and receive claims to scientific knowledge.

Bibliography

Adickes, Erich. *Kant's Systematik als systembildender Faktor* (Berlin, 1887).

Adickes, Erich. *Untersuchungen zu Kants physischer Geographie* (Tübingen: Mohr, 1911).

Adickes, Erich. *Kant als Naturforscher*, 2 vols (Berlin: De Gruyter, 1924).

Allais, Lucy. *Manifest Reality: Kant's Idealism and His Realism* (Oxford: Oxford University Press, 2015).

Allais, Lucy. "Kant's Racism." *Philosophical Papers* 45(1–2) (2016): 1–36.

Allison, Henry. "Kant's Antinomy of Teleological Judgment." *The Southern Journal of Philosophy* 30 (1991): 25–42.

Allison, Henry. "Causality and Causal Laws in Kant: A Critique of Michael Friedman." In *Kant and Contemporary Epistemology*, edited by P. Parrini (Dordrecht: Kluwer Academic, 1994), 291–307.

Allison, Henry. "Commentary on the Antinomy of Pure Reason Section 9." In *Immanuel Kant. Kritik der reinen Vernunft*, edited by Georg Mohr and Marcus Willaschek (Berlin: Akademie Verlag, 1998), 465–90.

Allison, Henry. *Kant's Transcendental Idealism: An Interpretation and Defence*, 2nd ed. (New Haven, CT: Yale University Press, 2004).

Allison, Henry. "Reflective Judgment and the Application of Logic to Nature: Kant's Deduction of the Principle of Purposiveness as an Answer to Hume." In *Essays on Kant* (Oxford: Oxford University Press, 2012), 177–88.

Allison, Henry. *Kant's Transcendental Deduction: An Analytical-Historical Commentary* (Oxford: Oxford University Press, 2015).

Ameriks, Karl. *Kant's Elliptical Path* (Oxford: Oxford University Press, 2012).

Anon. "Review of Buffon's *Histoire Naturelle*, January–March 1751." In *From Natural History to the History of Nature: Readings from Buffon and his Critics*, edited and translated by John Lyon and Phillip Sloan (Notre Dame, IN: University of Notre Dame Press, 1981), 269–82.

Anstey, Peter. *The Philosophy of Robert Boyle* (London: Routledge, 2000).

Anstey, Peter. "Experimental Versus Speculative Natural Philosophy." In *The Science of Nature in the Seventeenth Century*, edited by Peter Anstey and John Schuster. (Dordrecht: Springer, 2005), 215–42.

Anstey, Peter. *John Locke and Natural Philosophy* (Oxford: Oxford University Press, 2011).

Anstey, Peter. "Francis Bacon and the Classification of Natural History." *Early Science and Medicine* 17(1) (2012): 11–31.

Aristotle. *Posterior Analytics*. In *The Complete Works*, vol. 1, edited by Jonathan Barnes (Princeton, NJ: Princeton University Press, 1984), 114–66.

Aristotle. *Parts of Animals*. In *The Complete Works*, vol. 1, edited by Jonathan Barnes (Princeton, NJ: Princeton University Press, 1984), 994–1086.

Bacon, Francis. *The Works of Francis Bacon*, 14 vols, edited by James Spedding, Robert Leslie Ellis, and Douglas Benon Heath (London: Longman, 1857–74).

Bacon, Francis. *The Oxford Francis Bacon*, 15 vols, edited by Graham Rees et al. (Oxford: Oxford University Press, 1996–).

Ballauff, Theodor. *Die Wissenschaft vom Leben. Eine Geschichte der Biologie* (München: Freiburg, 1954).

Banton, Michael. "The Vertical and Horizontal Dimensions of the Word *Race*." *Ethnicities* 10(1) (2010): 127–40.

Bernasconi, Robert. "Who Invented the Concept of Race? Kant's Role in the Enlightenment Construction of Race." In *Race*, edited by Robert Bernasconi (Oxford: Blackwell, 2001), 11–36.

Bernasconi, Robert. "Kant as an Unfamiliar Source of Racism." In *Philosophers on Race: Critical Essays*, edited by Julie K. Ward and Tommy L. Lott (Malden, MA: Blackwell, 2002), 145–66.

Bernasconi, Robert. "Defining Race Scientifically: A Response to Michael Banton." *Ethnicities* 10(1) (2010): 141–48.

Bernasconi, Robert. "Kant's Third Thoughts on Race." In *Reading Kant's Geography*, edited by Stuart Elden and Eduardo Mendieta (Albany, NY: State University of New York Press, 2011), 291–318.

Berthier, Guillaume-François. "Review of Buffon's *Histoire naturelle*, October 1749." In *From Natural History to the History of Nature: Readings from Buffon and his Critics*, edited and translated by John Lyon and Phillip Sloan (Notre Dame, IN: University of Notre Dame Press, 1981), 223–26.

Berthier, Guillaume-François. "Review of Buffon's *Histoire naturelle*, March 1750." In *From Natural History to the History of Nature: Readings from Buffon and his Critics*, edited and translated by John Lyon and Phillip Sloan (Notre Dame, IN: University of Notre Dame Press, 1981), 227–30.

Bianchi, Silvia de. "The Stage on which Our Ingenious Play Is Performed: Kant's Epistemology of *Weltkenntnis*." *Studies in History and Philosophy of Science* 71 (2018): 58–66.

Blumenbach, Johann Friedrich. *Über den Bildungstrieb*, 2nd ed. (Göttingen: Johann Dieterich. 1789).

Boehm, Omri. "Kant's Regulative Spinozism." *Kant-Studien* 103(3) (2012): 292–317.

Boerhaave, Herman. *Dr. Boerhaave's Academical Lectures on the Theory of Physic, Being a Translation of His Institutes and Explanatory Comments*, 6 vols (London: W. Innys, 1751).

Bonnet, Charles. *Considérations sur les corps organisés*. In *Oeuvres d'histoire naturelle et de philosophie*, vol. 6 (Neuchâtel: Faulche, 1779–83).

Bowler, Peter. "Bonnet and Buffon: Theories of Generation and the Problem of Species." *Journal of the History of Biology* 6(2) (1973): 259–81.

Boyle, Robert. *The Works of the Honourable Robert Boyle*, 5 vols, edited by Thomas Birch (London: A. Millar, 1744).

Breitenbach, Angela. "Mechanical Explanation of Nature and Its Limits in Kant's *Critique of Judgment*." *Studies in History and Philosophy of Biological and Biomedical Sciences* 27 (2006): 694–711.

Breitenbach, Angela. "Two Views on Nature: A Solution to Kant's Antinomy of Mechanism and Teleology." *British Journal for the History of Philosophy* 16(2) (2008): 351–69.

Breitenbach, Angela. *Die Analogie von Vernunft und Natur. Eine Umweltphilosophie nach Kant* (Berlin: de Gruyter, 2009).

Breitenbach, Angela. "Biological Purposiveness and Analogical Reflection." In *Kant's Theory of Biology*, edited by Ina Goy and Eric Watkins (Berlin: de Gruyter, 2014), 131–48.

Breitenbach, Angela. "Laws and Ideal Unity." In *Laws of Nature*, edited by Walter Ott and Lydia Patton (Oxford: Oxford University Press, 2018), 108–22.

Breitenbach, Angela. "Kant's Normative Conception of Science." In *Cambridge Guide to the Metaphysical Foundations of Natural Science*, edited by Michael Bennett McNulty (Cambridge: Cambridge University Press, 2022), 36–54.

Brittan, Gordon. *Kant's Theory of Science* (Princeton, NJ: Princeton University Press, 1978).

Buchdahl, Gerd. "Causality, Causal Law, and Scientific Theory in the Philosophy of Kant." *British Journal for the Philosophy of Science* 16 (1965): 187–208.

Buchdahl, Gerd. *Metaphysics and the Philosophy of Science* (Oxford: Blackwell, 1969).

Buffon, Georges. "Preface du tradecteur." In *La Statique des végétaux, et l'analyse d l'air*, by Stephen Hales (Paris: Jacques Vincent, 1735), iii–vii.

Buffon, Georges. *Historie naturelle, générale et particulière, avec la description du Cabinet du Roy*, tome premier (Paris: Imprimerie Royale, 1749).

Buffon, Georges. *Historie naturelle, générale et particulière, avec la description du Cabinet du Roy*, tome deuxième (Paris: Imprimerie Royale, 1749).

Buffon, Georges. *Historie naturelle, générale et particulière, avec la description du Cabinet du Roy*, tome troisième (Paris: Imprimerie Royale, 1749).

Buffon, Georges. *Allgemeine Historie der Natur nach allen besondern Theilen abgehandelt*, 8 vols, edited and translated by Abraham Kästner (Hamburg: Grund und Holle, 1750–2).

Buffon, Georges. *Histoire naturelle générale et particulière, avec la description du Cabinet du Roy*, tome quatrième (Paris: Imprimerie Royale, 1753).

Buffon, Georges. *Histoire naturelle, générale et particulière, avec la description du Cabinet du Roy*, tome quatorzième (Paris: Imprimerie Royale, 1766).

Buffon, Georges. "Von der Abartung der Thiere." In *Allgemeine Historie der Natur*, vol. 7, translated by A. G. Kästner (Leipzig: H. H. Holle, 1772), 189–222.

Buffon, Georges. *Les Époques de la nature* (Paris: Imprimerie Royale, 1780).

Buffon, Georges. "Preface of the Translator." In *From Natural History to the History of Nature: Readings from Buffon and his Critics*, edited and translated by John Lyon and Phillip Sloan (Notre Dame, IN: University of Notre Dame Press, 1981), 37–40.

Buffon, Georges. "Response of M. de Buffon, to the Deputies and Syndic of the Faculty of Theology, March 12 1751." In *From Natural History to the History of Nature: Readings from Buffon and his Critics*, edited and translated by John Lyon and Phillip Sloan (Notre Dame, IN: University of Notre Dame Press, 1981), 289–91.

Butts, Robert. "Hypothesis and Explanation in Kant's Philosophy of Science." *Archiv für Geschichte der Philosophie* 43(2) (1961): 153–70.

Butts, Robert. "Kant on Hypotheses in the 'Doctrine of Method' and the *Logik*." *Archiv für Geschichte der Philosophie* 44(2) (1962): 185–203.

Butts, Robert. "The Methodological Structure of Kant's Metaphysics of Science." In *Kant's Philosophy of Physical Science*, edited by Robert Butts (Dordrecht: D. Reidel Publishing Company, 1986), 163–99.

Butts, Robert. "Teleology and Scientific Method in Kant's Critique of Judgment." *Noûs* 24(1) (1990): 1–16.

Cassirer, Ernst. *A Commentary on Kant's Critique of Judgment* (New York: Barnes and Noble, 1938).

Cassirer, Ernst. *Kant's Life and Thought*, translated by James Haden (New Haven, CT: Yale University Press, 1981).

Du Châtelet, Émilie. *Institutions de physique* (Paris: Prault, 1740).

Du Châtelet, Émilie. *Foundations of Physics*. In *Selected Philosophical and Scientific Writings*, edited by Judith Zinsser, translated by Isabelle Bour and Judith Zinsser (Chicago, IL: Chicago University Press, 2009), 105–200.

Chignell, Andrew. "Belief in Kant." *The Philosophical Review* 116(3) (2007): 323–60.

Chignell, Andrew. "Knowledge, Discipline, System, Hope: The Fate of Metaphysics in the Doctrine of Method." In *Kant's Critique of Pure Reason: A Critical Guide*, edited by James O'Shea (New York: Cambridge University Press, 2017), 259–79.

Church, Michael. "Immanuel Kant and the Emergence of Modern Geography." In *Reading Kant's Geography*, edited by Stuart Elden and Eduardo Mendieta (Albany, NY: State University of New York Press, 2011), 19–46.

Clewis, Robert. "Kant's Natural Teleology? The Case of Physical Geography." *Kant-Studien* 107(2) (2016), 314–42.

Cohen, Alix. "Kant's Antinomy of Reflective Judgment: A Re-evaluation." *Teorema* 23(1) (2004): 183–97.

Cohen, Alix. "Kant on Epigenesis, Monogenesis and Human Nature: The Biological Premises of Anthropology." *Studies in History and Philosophy of Biological and Biomedical Sciences* 37 (2006): 675–93.

Cohen, Alix. *Kant and the Human Sciences: Biology, Anthropology and History* (London: Palgrave Macmillan, 2009).

Cohen, Alix. *Kant's Lectures on Anthropology* (Cambridge: Cambridge University Press, 2014).

Cohen, Alix. "Kant on the Ethics of Belief." *Proceedings of the Aristotelian Society* CXIV (2014): 317–33.

Cohen, Alix. "Kant on Evolution: A Re-evaluation." In *Kant on Animals*, edited by John Callanan and Lucy Allais (Oxford: Oxford University Press, 2020), 122–35.

Cohen, Hermann. *Kants Theorie der Erfahrung* (Berlin: Dümmler, 1871).

Cohen, Morris. "The Myth about Francis Bacon and Inductive Method." *The Scientific Monthly* 23(6) (1926): 504–8.

Cohen, I. Bernard. *The Newtonian Revolution* (Cambridge: Cambridge University Press, 1980).

Coleridge, Samuel Taylor. *Collected Letters of Samuel Taylor Coleridge*, 6 vols, edited by E. L. Griggs (Oxford: Oxford University Press, 1957–71).

Cooper, Andrew. *The Tragedy of Philosophy: Kant's Critique of Judgment and the Project of Aesthetics* (Albany, NY: State University of New York Press, 2016).

Cooper, Andrew. "Kant and Experimental Philosophy." *British Journal for the History of Philosophy* 25(2) (2017): 256–86.

Cooper, Andrew. "Living Natural Products in Kant's Physical Geography." *Studies in History and Philosophy of Biological and Biomedical Sciences* 78(1) (December 2019, online publication): Doi:10.1016/j.shpsc.2019.101191.

Cooper, Andrew. "Force and Law in Kielmeyer's 1793 Speech." In *Kielmeyer and the Organic World*, edited by Daniel Whistler and Lydia Azadpour (London: Bloomsbury, 2020), 81–98.

Cooper, Andrew. "Kant's Universal Conception of Natural History." *Studies in History and Philosophy of Science* 79 (2020): 77–87.

Cooper, Andrew. "Kant on Observation." In *The Court of Reason: Proceedings for the 13th International Kant Congress*, edited by Camilla Serck-Hanssen and Beatrix Himmelmann (Berlin: de Gruyter, 2021), 941–50.

Cooper, Andrew. "The Economy of the *Bildungstrieb* in Goethe's Comparative Anatomy." In *The Concept of Drive in Classical German Philosophy*, edited by Manja Kisner and Jörg Noller (London: Palgrave MacMillan, 2022), 83–105.

Cooper, Andrew. "Hypotheses in Kant's Philosophy of Science." *Studies in History and Philosophy of Science* (May 2022, online publication): Doi:10.1016/j.shpsa.2022.04.007.

Deputies and Syndic of the Faculty of Theology of Paris, The. "Letter of the Deputies and Syndic of the Faculty of Theology of Paris to M. Buffon, January 17 1751." In *From*

Natural History to the History of Nature: Readings from Buffon and his Critics, edited and translated by John Lyon and Phillip Sloan (Notre Dame, IN: University of Notre Dame Press, 1981), 285–87.

Descartes, René. *Rules for the Direction of the Mind*. In *The Philosophical Writings of Descartes*, vol. 1, translated by John Cottingham, Robert Stoothoff, and Dugald Murdoch (Cambridge: Cambridge University Press, 1985), 9–78.

Descartes, René. *Discourse on Method*. In *The Philosophical Writings of Descartes*, vol. 1, translated by John Cottingham, Robert Stoothoff, and Dugald Murdoch (Cambridge: Cambridge University Press, 1985), 111–51.

Descartes, René. *The Principles of Philosophy*. In *The Philosophical Writings of Descartes*, vol. 1, translated by John Cottingham, Robert Stoothoff, and Dugald Murdoch (Cambridge: Cambridge University Press, 1985), 177–292.

Descartes, René. *The World and Other Writings*, edited and translated by Stephen Gaukroger (Cambridge: Cambridge University Press, 2004).

Düsing, Klaus. *Die Teleologie in Kants Weltbegriff* (Bonn: Bouvier, 1968).

Elden, Stuart, and Mendieta, Eduardo (eds.) *Reading Kant's Geography* (Albany, NY: State University of New York Press, 2011).

Ellis, Brian. *Scientific Essentialism* (Cambridge: Cambridge University Press, 2001).

Engelhard, Kristina. "The Problem of Grounding Natural Modality in Kant's Account of Empirical Laws of Nature." *Studies in History and Philosophy of Science* 71 (2018): 24–34.

Engles, Eve-Marie. *Die Teleologie des Lebendigen. Kritische Überlegungen zur Neuformulierung des Teleologie-problems in der angloamerikanischen Wissenschaftstheorie* (Berlin: Duncker and Humblot, 1982).

Ereshefsky, Marc. *The Poverty of the Linnaean Hierarchy: A Philosophical Study of Biological Taxonomy* (Cambridge: Cambridge University Press, 2009).

Ernst, Wilhelm. *Der Zweckbegriff bei Kant und sein Verhältnis zu den Kategorien* (Würzburg, 1909).

Ewing, A. C. *A Short Commentary of Kant's Critique of Pure Reason* (London: Methuen, 1938).

Eze, Emmanuel Chukwudi. "The Color of Reason: The Idea of 'Race' in Kant's Anthropology." *The Bucknell Review* 38(2) (1995): 201–41.

Farber, Paul. *Finding Order in Nature: The Naturalist Tradition from Linnaeus to E. O. Wilson* (Baltimore, MD: The Johns Hopkins University Press, 2000).

Ferrini, Cinzia. "Testing the Limits of Mechanical Explanation in Kant's Pre-Critical Writings." *Archiv für Geschichte der Philosophie* 82(3) (2000): 297–331.

Ferrini, Cinzia. "Heavenly Bodies, Crystals and Organisms: The Key Role of Chemical Affinity in Kant's Critical Cosmogony." In *Eredità kantiane (1804–2004). Questioni aperte e problemi irrisolti*, edited by Cinzia Ferrini (Napoli: Bibliopolis, 2004), 277–317.

Ferrini, Cinzia. "Illusions of Imagination and Adventures of Reason in Kant's first *Critique*." In *Philosophie nach Kant. Neue Wege zum Verständnis von Kants Transzendental- und Moralphilosophie*, edited by Mario Egger (Berlin: De Gruyter, 2014), 141–88.

Fichte, Johann. Gottlieb. *The Science of Knowledge*, translated and edited by Peter Heath and John Lachs (Cambridge: Cambridge University Press, 2008).

Findlen, Paula. "Francis Bacon and the Reform of Natural History in the Seventeenth Century." In *History and the Disciplines: The Reclassification of Knowledge in Early Modern Europe*, edited by Donald R. Kelley (New York: University of Rochester Press, 1997), 239–60.

Findlen, Paula. "Courting Nature." In *Cultures of Natural History*, edited by N. Jardine, A. Secord, and E. C. Spary (Cambridge: Cambridge University Press, 1996), 57–74.

Fisher, Mark. "Kant's Explanatory Natural History: Generation and Classification of Organisms in Kant's Natural Philosophy." In *Understanding Purpose: Kant and the Philosophy of Biology*, edited by Philippe Huneman (Rochester: University of Rochester Press, 2007), 101–22.

Fisher, Naomi. "Life, Lawfulness, and Contingency: Kant and Schelling on Organic Nature." *Archiv für Geschichte der Philosophie* (2021): 1–26.

Fisher, Naomi. "Kant and Schelling on Blumenbach's Formative Drive," *Intellectual History Review* 31(3) (2021): 391–409.

Floyd-Wilson, Mary. *English Ethnicity and Race in Early Modern Drama* (Cambridge: Cambridge University Press, 2003).

Forster, Georg. "Something More about the Human Races." In *Kant and the Concept of Race: Late Eighteenth-Century Writings*, edited and translated by Jon Mikkelsen (Albany, NY: State University of New York Press, 2013), 146–67.

Foucault, Michel. *Les Mots et les choses. Une archéologie des sciences humaines* (Paris: Gallimard, 1966).

Friedman, Michael. "Regulative and Constitutive." *Southern Journal of Philosophy* 30 (1992): 73–102.

Friedman, Michael. *Kant and the Exact Sciences* (Cambridge, MA: Harvard University Press, 1992).

Friedman, Michael. *Kant and the Construction of Nature* (Cambridge: Cambridge University Press, 2013).

Frierson, Patrick. *Freedom and Anthropology in Kant's Moral Philosophy* (Cambridge: Cambridge University Press, 2003).

Frierson, Patrick. *What Is the Human Being?* (London: Routledge, 2013).

Galen, Claudius. *De facultatibus naturalibus*, translated by A. J. Brock (Cambridge, MA: Harvard University Press, 1916).

Galen, Claudius. *On Temperaments: On Non-Uniform Distemperament. The Soul's Traits Depend on Bodily Temperament*, edited and translated by Ian Johnston (Cambridge, MA: Harvard University Press, 2020).

Gambarotto, Andrea. *Vital Forces, Teleology and Organization: Philosophy of Nature and the Rise of Biology in Germany* (Dordrecht: Springer, 2018).

Gardner, Sebastian. *Kant and the Critique of Pure Reason* (London: Routledge, 1999).

Gava, Gabriele. "Kant and Crusius on Belief and Practical Justification." *Kantian Review* 24(1) (2019): 53–75.

Geiger, Ido. "Is the Assumption of a Systematic Whole of Concepts a Necessary Condition of Knowledge?" *Kant-Studien* 94 (2003): 273–98.

Geiger, Ido. *Kant and the Claims of the Empirical World: A Transcendental Reading of the Critique of the Power of Judgment* (Cambridge: Cambridge University Press, 2022).

Geiger, Ido. "The Methodology of the Teleological Power of Judgment." In *The Kantian Mind*, edited by Sorin Baiasu and Mark Timmons (London: Routledge, forthcoming).

Gessner, Conrad. *Historia animalium*, 4 vols (Zurich, 1551–8).

Gibson, Francis. *De rachidite, sive morbo puerili tractatus*, 2nd ed. (London, 1660).

Ginsborg, Hannah. "Kant on Understanding Organisms as Natural Purposes." In *Kant and the Sciences*, edited by Eric Watkins (Oxford: Oxford University Press, 2001), 231–58.

Ginsborg, Hannah. "Two Kinds of Mechanical Inexplicability in Kant and Aristotle." *Journal of the History of Philosophy* 42(1) (2004): 33–65.

Goodman, Nelson. *Fact, Fiction, and Forecast* (Cambridge, MA: Harvard University Press, 1983).

Gorkom, Joris van. "The Reddish, Iron-Rust Color of the Native Americans: Immanuel Kant's Racism in Context." *Con-Textos Kantianos* 9 (2019): 154–77.

Gould, Stephen Jay. *Time's Arrow, Time's Cycle: Myth and Metaphor in the Discovery of Geological Time* (Cambridge, MA: Harvard University Press, 1987).

Goy, Ina. "The Antinomy of Teleological Judgment." *Studi Kantiani* 28 (2015): 65–88.

Goy, Ina. *Kants Theorie der Biologie. Ein Kommentar. Eine Lesart. Eine Historische Einordnung* (Berlin: De Gruyter, 2017).

Grier, Michelle. *Kant's Doctrine of Transcendental Illusion* (Cambridge: Cambridge University Press, 2004).

Guyer, Paul. *Kant and the Claims of Knowledge* (Cambridge: Cambridge University Press, 1987).

Guyer, Paul. "Reason and Reflective Judgment: Kant on the Significance of Systematicity." *Noûs* 24(1) (1990): 17–43.

Guyer, Paul. *Kant's System of Nature and Freedom: Selected Essays* (Oxford: Oxford University Press, 2005).

Hales, Stephen. *Vegetable staticks, or, An account of some statical experiments on the sap in vegetables* (London: W. and J. Innys, 1727).

Hales, Stephen. *Statical essays, or, An account of some hydraulick and hydrostatical experiments made on the blood and blood vessels of animals* (London: W. Innys and R. Manby, 1733).

Hales, Stephen. *La Statique des végétaux, et l'analyse d l'air*, translated by Georges Buffon (Paris: Jacques Vincent, 1735).

Hall, Thomas. "On Biological Analogs of Newtonian Paradigms." *Philosophy of Science* 35 (1) (1968): 6–27.

Hall, Thomas. *Ideas of Life and Matter: Studies in the History of General Physiology*, 2 vols (Chicago, IL: University of Chicago Press, 1969).

Hall, Rupert, and Hall, Marie Boas. *Unpublished Scientific Papers of Isaac Newton* (New York: Cambridge University Press, 1962).

Haller, Albrecht von. "Review of *Traité d'Insectologie*, by Charles Bonnet." In *Bibliothèque raisonnée des ouvrages des sevans de l'Europe*, vol. 36 (Amsterdam: J. Wetstein, 1746), 179–92.

Haller, Albrecht von. *Réflexions sur le systême de la gérération de M. de Buffon* (Geneva: Barrillot et Fils, 1751).

Haller, Albrecht von. *Elementa physiologiæ corporis humani*, vol. 1 (Lausanne: Marc-Michel Bousquet, 1757).

Haller, Albrecht von. *Sur la formation du coeur dans le poulet* (Lausanne: Bousquet, 1758).

Haller, Albrecht von. "A Dissertation on the Sensible and Irritable Parts of Animals." *Bulletin of the History of Medicine* 4 (1936): 651–91.

Haller, Albrecht von. "Preface to the German Translation of *Histoire Naturelle*." In *From Natural History to the History of Nature: Readings from Buffon and his Critics*, edited and translated by John Lyon and Phillip Sloan (Notre Dame, IN: University of Notre Dame Press, 1981), 297–310.

Haller, Albrecht von. "Reflections on the Theory of Generation of Mr. Buffon." In *From Natural History to the History of Nature: Readings from Buffon and his Critics*, edited and translated by John Lyon and Phillip Sloan (Notre Dame, IN: University of Notre Dame Press, 1981), 314–27.

Hardimon, Michael O. *Rethinking Race: The Case for Deflationary Realism* (Cambridge, MA: Harvard University Press, 2017).

Harvey, William. *The Works of William Harvey*, translated by Robert Willis (London: Sydenham Society, 1847).

Hegel, G. W. F. *The Science of Logic*, translated and edited by George Di Giovanni (Cambridge: Cambridge University Press, 2010).

Herder, Johann Friedrich. *Outlines of a Philosophy of the History of Man*, translated by T. Churchill (New York: Bergman Publishers, 1800).

Herder, Johann Friedrich. "On the Cognition and Sensation of the Human Soul." In *Philosophical Writings*, edited and translated by Michael Forster (Cambridge: University of Cambridge Press, 2004), 187–246.

Herschel, William. *Über den Bau des Himmels. Drei Abhandlungen aus dem Englischen übersezt. Nebst einem authentischen Auszug aus Kants allgemeiner Naturgeschichte und Theorie des Himmels* (Königsberg: Nicolovius, 1791).

Hill, Thomas E., and Boxill, Bernard. "Kant and Race." In *Race and Racism*, edited by Bernard Boxill (Oxford: Oxford University Press, 2001), 448–71.

Hippocrates. *Hippocratic Writings*, edited by G. E. R. Lloyd, translated by J. Chadwick and W. N. Mann (Harmondsworth: Penguin, 1983).

[Home, Henry], Lord Kames. *Versuche über die Geschichte des Menschen*, 2 vols (Leipzig: Johann Friedrich Junius, 1774–5).

Home, Henry, Lord Kames. *Sketches of the History of Man*, 4 vols (Edinburgh, 1778).

Hoquet, Thierry. "History without Time: Buffon's Natural History as a Nonmathematical Physique." *Isis* 101 (2010): 30–61.

Horstmann, Rolf-Peter. "Why Must There Be a Transcendental Deduction in Kant's *Critique of Judgment*?" In *Kant's Transcendental Deductions*, edited by Eckart Förster (Stanford, CA: Stanford University Press, 1989), 157–76.

Hume, David. *An Enquiry Concerning Human Understanding*, edited by Tom Beauchamp (Oxford: Oxford University Press, 1999).

Huneman, Philippe. "Naturalising Purpose: From Comparative Anatomy to the 'Adventure of Reason'." *Studies in History and Philosophy of Biology and the Biomedical Sciences* 37(4) (2006): 649–74.

Jahn, Ilse. *Grundzüge der Biologiegeschichte* (Jena: G. Fischer, 1990).

Jalobeanu, Dana. *The Art of Experimental Natural History: Francis Bacon in Context* (Bucharest: Zeta Books, 2015).

Kardel, Troels. "Willis and Steno on Muscles: Rediscovery of a 17th Century Biological Theory." *Journal of the History of the Neurosciences* 5 (1993): 100–7.

Kardel, Troels. "Function and Structure in Early Modern Muscular Mechanics." *Acta Anatomica* 159 (1997): 61–70.

Kemp-Smith, Norman. *A Commentary to Kant's Critique of Pure Reason* (New York: Humanities, 1962).

Kim, Shi-Hyong. *Bacon und Kant. Ein erkenntnistheoretischer Vergleich zwischen dem Novum Organum und der Kritik der reinen Vernunft* (Berlin: Walter de Gruyter, 2008).

Kitcher, Philip. "Projecting the Order of Nature." In *Kant's Philosophy of Physical Science*, edited by Robert Butts (Dordrecht: D. Reidel Publishing Company, 1986), 201–38.

Kleingeld, Pauline. "Kant's Second Thoughts on Race." *The Philosophical Quarterly* 57(229) (2007): 573–92.

Koselleck, Reinhart. "Vergangene Zukunft der frühen Neuzeit." In *Epirrhosis: Festgabe für Carl Schmitt*, edited by Hans Barion, E.-W. Böckenförde, E. Forsthoff, and W. Weber (Berlin, 1968), 546–66.

Koyré, Alexandre. *Newtonian Studies* (Cambridge, MA: Harvard University Press, 1965).

Krafft, Fritz. "Analogie—Theodizee—Akualismus: Wissenschaftshistorische Einführung in Kants Kosmogonie." In *Allgemeine Naturgeschichte und Theorie des Himmels*, edited by F. Kfrafft (München: Kindler, 2003), 179–95.

Kraus, Katharina. *Kant on Self-Knowledge and Self-Formation: The Nature of Inner Experience* (Cambridge: Cambridge University Press, 2020).

Kreines, James. "The Inexplicability of Kant's *Naturzweck*: Kant on Teleology, Explanation and Biology." *Archiv für Geschichte der Philosophie* 87(3) (2005): 270–311.

Kreines, James. "Kant on the Laws of Nature: Laws, Necessitation, and the Limitation of Our Knowledge." *European Journal of Philosophy* 17(4) (2009): 527–58.

Kuehn, Manfred. *Kant: A Biography* (Cambridge: Cambridge University Press, 2001).

La Mettrie, Julien Offray de. *Traité de l'âme*, vol. 1 (Reprinted Tours: Fayard, 1984).

La Mettrie, Julien Offray de. *Machine Man*. In *Machine Man and Other Writings*, edited by Ann Thomson (Cambridge: Cambridge University Press, 1996), 1–40.

Lagier, Raphaël. *Les Races humaines selon Kant* (Paris: Presses Universitaires de France, 2004).

Larrimore, Mark. "Race, Freedom and the Fall in Steffens and Kant." In *The German Invention of Race*, edited by Sara Eigen and Mark Larrimore (Albany, NY: State University of New York Press, 2006), 91–121.

Larson, James. *Interpreting Nature: The Science of Living Form from Linnaeus to Kant* (Baltimore, MD: Johns Hopkins University Press, 1994).

Leduc, Christian. "Les Critères kantiens de validité de l'hypothèse physique." In *Kant und die Philosophie in Weltbürglicher Absicht*, edited by S. Bacin, A. Ferrarin, C. La Rocca, and M. Ruffing (Berlin: De Gruyter, 2013), 125–38.

Leibniz, G. W. *The Human Body, Like that of an Animal, is a Sort of Machine*. In *Divine Machines: Leibniz and the Sciences of Life*, by Justin Smith (Princeton, NJ: Princeton University Press, 2011), 290–7.

Leibniz, G. W. "Mr. Leibniz's Third Paper being an Answer to Dr. Clarke's Second Reply." In *The Leibniz-Clarke Correspondence*, edited and translated by H. G. Alexander (Manchester: Manchester University Press, 1956), 25–30.

Leibniz, G. W. "Mr. Leibniz's Fourth Paper being an Answer to Dr. Clarke's Third Reply." In *The Leibniz-Clarke Correspondence*, edited and translated by H. G. Alexander (Manchester: Manchester University Press, 1956), 36–45.

Leibniz, G. W. "Mr. Leibniz's Fifth Paper being an Answer to Dr. Clarke's Fourth Reply." In *The Leibniz-Clarke Correspondence*, edited and translated by H. G. Alexander (Manchester: Manchester University Press, 1956), 55–96.

Leibniz, G. W. *The Monodology*. In *Discourse on Metaphysics and Other Essays*, edited and translated by Daniel Garber and Roger Ariew (Indianapolis, IN: Hackett, 1991), 68–81.

Leibniz, G. W. *New Essays on Human Understanding*, edited and translated by Peter Remnant and Jonathan Bennett (Cambridge: Cambridge University Press, 1996).

Lenoir, Timothy. *The Strategy of Life: Teleology and Mechanics in Nineteenth-Century Biology* (Dordrecht: D. Reidel, 1982).

Lepenies, Wolf. *Das Ende der Naturgeschichte. Wandel kultureller Selbstverständlichkeiten in den Wissenschaften des 18. und 19. Jahrhunderts* (Baden-Baden: Suhrkamp, 1978).

Linnaeus, Carl. *Fundamenta botanica* (Amsterdam: Schouten, 1736).

Linnaeus, Carl. *Philosophia botanica* (Stockholm: Kiesewetter, 1751).

Linnaeus, Carl. "Metamorphoses plantarum." In *Carli Linnaei Amoenitates academicae, seu Dissertationes variae physicae, medicae, botanicae antehac seorsim editae*, 10 vols, vol. 4 (Erlangen: Palm, 1788), 367–86.

Linnaeus, Carl. *A selection of the correspondence of Linnaeus and other naturalists, from the original manuscripts*, 2 vols, edited by J. E. Smith (London: Longmans, 1821).

Linnaeus, Carl. "Nya bevis för sexualitet hos växterna." In *Skrifter af Cal von Linné*, 4 vols (Upsala: Almqvist and Wiksell, 1905–8), 109–32.

Linnaeus, Carl. *Systema Naturae: Facsimile of the First Edition*, translated by M. Engel-Ledeboer and H. Engel (Nieuwkoop: B. DeGraaf, 1964).

Lippmann, Edmund. *Urzeugung und Lebenskraft: Zur Geschichte dieser Probleme von den ältesten Zeiten an bis zu den Angängen des 20. Jahrhundrets* (Berlin: Julius Springer, 1933).

Locke, John. *Elements of Natural Philosophy*. In *The Works of John Locke*, 7th ed., vol. 3 (London: C. and J. Rivington, 1768).

Locke, John. *The Correspondence of John Locke: In Eight Volumes, Vol. 4: Letters Nos. 1242–1701* (Oxford: Oxford University Press, 1978).

Locke, John. *An Essay Concerning Human Understanding*, edited by Pauline Phemister (Oxford: Oxford University Press, 2008).

Longuenesse, Béatrice. *Kant and the Capacity to Judge* (Princeton, NJ: Princeton University Press, 1998).

Longuenesse, Béatrice. *Kant on the Human Standpoint* (Cambridge: Cambridge University Press, 2005).

Louden, Robert. *Kant's Impure Ethics* (Oxford: Oxford University Press, 2002).

Lovejoy, Arthur. "Kant and Evolution I." *The Popular Science Monthly* 77 (1910), 538–53.

Lu-Adler, Huaping. *Kant and the Science of Logic: A Historical and Philosophical Reconstruction* (Oxford: Oxford University Press, 2018).

Lu-Adler, Huaping. "Kant's Use of Travel Reports in Theorizing about Race—A Case Study of How Testimony Features in Natural Philosophy." *Studies in History and Philosophy of Science* 91 (2022): 10–19.

Lu-Adler, Huaping. "Kant on Lazy Savagery, Racialized." *Journal of the History of Philosophy* 60 (2022): 253–75.

Lu-Adler, Huaping. *Kant, Race, and Racism: Views from Somewhere* (Oxford: Oxford University Press, 2023).

Lyon, John and Sloan, Phillip (eds. and trans.) *From Natural History to the History of Nature: Readings from Buffon and his Critics* (Notre Dame, IN: University of Notre Dame Press, 1981).

Marcuzzi, Max. "Writing Space: Historical Narrative and Geographical Description in Kant's *Physical Geography*." In *Reading Kant's Geography*, edited by Stuart Elden and Eduardo Mendieta (Albany, NY: State University of New York Press, 2011), 115–36.

Massimi, Michela. "Kant's Dynamical Theory of Matter in 1755, and Its Debt to Speculative Newtonian Experimentalism." *Studies in History and Philosophy of Science* 42 (2011): 525–43.

Massimi, Michela. "From Data to Phenomena: A Kantian Stance." *Synthese* 182 (2011): 101–16.

Massimi, Michela. "Grounds, Modality, and Nomic Necessity in the Critical Kant." In *Kant and the Laws of Nature*, edited by Michela Massimi and Angela Breitenbach (Cambridge: Cambridge University Press, 2017), 150–70.

Massimi, Michela. "What Is This Thing Called 'Scientific Knowledge'? Kant on Imaginary Standpoints and the Regulative Role of Reason." *Kant Yearbook* 9(1) (2017): 63–84.

Maupertuis, Pierre-Louis Moreau de. *Venus physique* (Paris: 1746).

Maupertuis, Pierre-Louis Moreau de. *Systéme de la nature*, vol. 2 of *Oeuvres*, 4 vols (Lyon: Bruyset, 1756).

Maupertuis, Pierre-Louis Moreau de. *The Earthly Venus*, translated by S. Boas (New York: Johnson Reprint, 1966).

May, J. A. *Kant's Concept of Geography and Its Relation to Recent Geographical Thought* (Toronto: University of Toronto Press, 1970).

Mayr, Ernst. *The Growth of Biological Thought: Diversity, Evolution and Inheritance* (Cambridge, MA: Belknap Press, 1982).

Mayr, Ernst. *This Is Biology: The Science of the Living World* (Cambridge, MA: Harvard University Press, 1997).

Mazzolini, Renato G. "Las Castas: Inter-Racial Crossing and Social Structure (1770–1835)." In *Heredity Produced: At the Crossroads of Biology, Politics and Culture, 1500–1870*, edited by Staffan Müller-Wille and Hans-Jörg Rheinberger (Cambridge, MA: The MIT Press, 2007), 349–74.

McFarland, John. *Kant's Concept of Teleology* (Edinburgh: Edinburgh University Press, 1970).

McLaughlin, Peter. *Kant's Critique of Teleology in Biological Explanation: Antinomy and Teleology* (Lewiston: Edwin Mellon Press, 1990).

McLaughlin, Peter. "Kants Organismusbegriff in der *Kritik der Urteilskraft*." In *Philosophy des organischen in der Goethezeit. Studien zu Werk und Wirkung des Naturforschers Carl Friedrich Kielmeyer*, edited by Kai Torsten Kanz (Stuttgart: Steiner, 1994), 100–10.

McLaughlin, Peter. "Kant on Heredity and Adaptation." In *Heredity Produced: At the Crossroads of Biology, Politics, and Culture, 1500–1870*, edited by Staffan Müller-Wille and Hans-Jörg Rheinberger (Cambridge, MA: The MIT Press, 2007), 277–92.

McLaughlin, Peter. "Transcendental Presuppositions and Ideas of Reason." *Kant-Studien* 105(4) (2014): 554–72.

McLaughlin, Peter. "The Impact of Newton on Biology on the Continent in the Eighteenth Century." In *The Reception of Isaac Newton in Europe*, vol. 2, edited by Helmut Pulte and Scott Mandelbrote (London: Bloomsbury, 2019), 515–31.

McNulty, Michael Bennett. "Rehabilitating the Regulative Use of Reason: Kant on Empirical and Chemical Laws." *Studies in History and Philosophy of Science* 54 (2015): 1–10.

McNulty, Michael Bennett. "A Science for Gods, a Science for Humans: Kant on Teleological Speculations in Natural History." *Studies in History and Philosophy of Science* 94 (2022): 47–55.

Medicus, Friedrich Casimir. *Von der Lebenskraft* (Mannheim, 1774).

Mensch, Jennifer. *Kant's Organicism* (Chicago, IL: Chicago University Press, 2013).

Messina, James. "Kant's Necessitation Account of Laws and the Nature of Natures." In *Kant and the Laws of Nature*, edited by Michela Massimi and Angela Breitenbach (Cambridge: Cambridge University Press, 2017), 131–49.

Mikkelsen, Jon (trans. and ed.) *Kant and the Concept of Race: Late Eighteenth-Century Writings* (Albany, NY: State University of New York Press, 2013).

Mikkelsen, Jon. "Recent Work on Kant's Race Theory." In *Kant and the Concept of Race: Late Eighteenth-Century Writings*, edited and translated by Jon Mikkelsen (Albany, NY: State University of New York Press, 2013), 1–40.

Mikkelsen, Jon (ed. and trans.) *Kant and the Concept of Race: Late Eighteenth-Century Writings* (Albany, NY: State University of New York Press, 2013).

Mills, Charles. "Kant's *Untermenschen*." In *Race and Racism in Modern Philosophy*, edited by Andrew Valls (Ithaca, NY: Cornell University Press, 2005), 169–93.

Mills, Charles. "'Ideal Theory' as Ideology." *Hypatia* 20(3) (2005): 165–84.

Mills, Charles. "Kant and Race, Redux." *Graduate Faculty Philosophy Journal* 35 (2014): 1–33.

Morris, David. "The Place of the Organism in Kantian Philosophy: Geography, Teleology, and the Limits of Philosophy." In *Reading Kant's Geography*, edited by Stuart Elden and Eduardo Mendieta (Albany, NY: State University of New York Press, 2011), 173–92.

Müller-Wille, Staffan. "Walnut-Trees at Hudson Bay, Coral Reefs in Gotland: Linnaean Botany and Its Relation to Colonialism." In *Colonial Botany: Science, Commerce, and Politics in the Early Modern World*, edited by L. Schiebinger and C. Swan (Philadelphia, PA: University of Pennsylvania Press, 2005), 34–48.

Müller-Wille, Staffan. "Collection and Collation: Theory and Practice of Linnaean Botany." *Studies in the History and Philosophy of Biology and Biomedical Science* 38 (2007): 541–62.

Müller-Wille, Staffan. "Linnaeus and the Four Corners of the World." In *The Cultural Politics of Blood, 1500–1900*, edited by K. A. Coles, R. Bauer, Z. Nunes, and C. L. Peterson (London: Palgrave Macmillan, 2014), 191–201.

Müller-Wille, Staffan, and Reeds, Karen. "A Translation of Carl Linnaeus's Introduction to *Genera Plantarum* (1737)." *Studies in the History and Philosophy of Biology and Biomedical Science* 38 (2007): 563–72.

Musschenbroek, Pieter van. *The Elements of Natural Philosophy*, translated by John Colson (London, 1734).

Nassar, Dalia. "Analogy, Natural History and the Philosophy of Nature: Kant, Herder and the Problem of Empirical Science." *Journal of the Philosophy of History* 9 (2015): 240–57.

Needham, John Turberville. "A Summary of Some Late Observations upon the Generation, Composition, and Decomposition of Animal and Vegetable Substances; Communicated in a Letter to Martin Folkes Esq.; President of the Royal Society, by Mr. Turbervill Needham, Fellow of the same Society." In *Philosophical Transactions* (London, 1749), 615–66.

Newton, Isaac. *Opticks: or, a treatise of the reflections, refractions, inflections and colours of light*, 3rd ed. (London, 1721).

Newton, Isaac. *Mathematical Principles of Natural Philosophy*, 2 vols, edited by Florian Cajori, translated by Andrew Motte (Berkeley, CA: University of California Press, 1973).

Newton, Isaac. *Newton's Philosophy of Nature: Selections from His Writings*, edited by H. S. Thayer (New York: Dover, 2005).

Noll, Alfred. *Die "Lebenskraft" in den Schriften der Vitalisten und ihrer Gegner* (Leipzig: Voigtländer, 1914).

Oberst, Michael. "Two Worlds *and* Two Aspects: on Kant's Distinction between Things in Themselves and Appearances." *Kantian Review* 20(1) (2015): 53–75.

Pasternack, Lawrence. "Kant on Opinion: Assent, Hypothesis, and the Norms of General Applied Logic." *Kant-Studien* 105(1) (2014): 41–82.

Pippin, Robert. *Kant's Theory of Form* (New Haven, CT: Yale University Press, 1982).

Pluche, Noël-Antoine. *The History of the Heavens Considered according to the Notions of the Poets and Philosophers compared with the Doctrines of Moses* (London, 1740).

Pratt, Vernon. "System-Building in the Eighteen Century." In *The Light of Nature*, edited by J. D. North and J. J. Roche (Dordrecht: Nijhoff, 1985), 421–32.

Quarfood, Marcel. "Kant on Biological Teleology: Towards a Two-Level Interpretation." *Studies in History and Philosophy of Biological and Biomedical Sciences* 37 (2006): 735–47.

Quarfood, Marcel. "The Antinomy of Teleological Judgment: What it is and How it is Solved." In *Kant's Theory of Biology*, edited by Ina Goy and Eric Watkins (Berlin: de Gruyter, 2014), 167–84.

Ramsay, James. *An Essay on the Treatment and Conversion of African Slaves in the British Sugar Colonies* (London: Phillips, 1784).

Raven, Charles. *John Ray, Naturalist: His Life and Works* (Cambridge: Cambridge University Press, 2009).

Richards, Richard. *The Species Problem: A Philosophical Analysis* (Cambridge: Cambridge University Press, 2010).

Richards, Robert. "Kant and Blumenbach on the *Bildungstrieb*: A Historical Misunderstanding." *Studies in History and Philosophy of Biology and Biomedical Sciences* 31 (2000): 11–32.

Richards, Robert. *The Romantic Conception of Life: Science and Philosophy in the Age of Goethe* (Chicago, IL: University of Chicago Press, 2002).

Ritzel, Wolfgang. *Immanuel Kant. Eine Biographie* (Berlin: de Gruyter, 1985).

Roche, Fontaine de la. "Review of Buffon's *Histoire Naturelle*, February 1750." In *From Natural History to the History of Nature: Readings from Buffon and His Critics*, edited and translated by John Lyon and Phillip Sloan (Notre Dame, IN: University of Notre Dame Press, 1981), 237–45.

Roe, Shirley. *Matter, Life, and Generation: 18th Century Embryology and the Haller-Wolff Debate* (Cambridge: Cambridge University Press, 1981).

Roe, Shirley. "John Turberville Needham and the Generation of Living Organisms." *Isis* 74(2) (1983): 158–84.

Roe, Shirley. "*Anatomia Animata*: The Newtonian Physiology of Albrecht von Haller." In *Transformation and Tradition in the Sciences: Essays in Honour of Bernard Cohen*, edited by Everett Mendelsohn (Cambridge: Cambridge University Press, 1984), 273–301.

Roger, Jacques. "The Living World." In *The Ferment of Knowledge: Studies in the Historiography of Eighteenth-Century Science*, edited by G. S. Rousseau and Guy Porter (Cambridge: Cambridge University Press, 1980), 255–84.

Roger, Jacques. *The Life Sciences in Eighteenth-Century French Thought*, translated by R. Ellrich (Stanford, CA: Stanford University Press, 1997).

Roose, Theodor Georg August. *Grundzüge der Lehre von Lehre von der Lebenskraft* (Braunschweig: Christian Friedrich Thomas, 1797).

Ross, Sydney. "*Scientist*: The Story of a Word." *Annals of Science* 18(2) (1962): 65–88.

Russo, François. "Théologie naturelle et secularisation de la science au XVIII siècle." *Recherches de Science Religieuse* 66 (1978): 27–62.

Sandford, Stela. "Kant, Race, and Natural History." *Philosophy and Social Criticism* 44(9) (2018): 950–77.

Sassen, Brigitte (ed.) *Kant's Early Critics: The Empiricist Critique of the Theoretical Philosophy* (Cambridge: Cambridge University Press, 2000).

Schaffer, Simon. "The Phoenix of Nature: Fire and Evolutionary Cosmology in Wright and Kant Schaffer." *Journal for the History of Astronomy* 9(3) (1978): 180–200.

Schlanger, Judith. *Les Metaphors de l'organisme* (Paris: L'Harmattan, 1995).

Schmitt, Stéphane. "From Paris to Moscow via Leipzig (1749–1787): Translational Metamorphoses of Buffon's *Histoire Naturelle*." *Erudition and the Republic of Letters* 4 (2019): 228–69.

Schmitt, Stéphane. "Buffon's Theories of Generation." In *Philosophy of Biology before Biology*, edited by Cécilia Bognon-Küss and Charles Wolfe (London: Routledge, 2019), 27–47.

Schofield, Robert. *Mechanism and Materialism: British Natural Philosophy in an Age of Reason* (Princeton, NJ: Princeton University Press, 1970).

Schönfeld, Martin. *The Philosophy of the Young Kant: The Precritical Project* (Oxford: Oxford University Press, 2000).

Schönfeld, Martin. "Kant's Early Dynamics." In *A Companion to Kant*, edited by Graham Bird (Oxford: Blackwell, 2006), 33–46.

Schönfeld, Martin. "Kant's Early Cosmology." In *A Companion to Kant*, edited by Graham Bird (Oxford: Blackwell, 2006), 47–62.

Schulting, Dennis. *Kant's Deduction and Apperception: Explaining the Categories* (London: Palgrave McMillan, 2013).

Serequeberhan, Tsenay. "Eurocentrism in Philosophy: The Case of Immanuel Kant." *Philosophical Forum* 27(4) (1996): 333–56.

Shrank, J. B. *The Newton Wars and the Beginning of the French Enlightenment* (Chicago, IL: University of Chicago Press, 2008).

Sloan, Phillip. "John Locke, John Ray, and the Problem of the Natural System." *Journal of the History of Biology* 5(1) (1972): 1–53.

Sloan, Phillip. "Buffon, German Biology, and the Historical Interpretation of Biological Species." *The British Journal for the History of Science* 12(41) (1979): 109–53.

Sloan, Phillip. "The 'Second Discourse' and 'Proofs of the Theory of the Earth' from Buffon's *Histoire naturelle* (1749)." In *From Natural History to the History of Nature: Readings from Buffon and his Critics*, edited and translated by John Lyon and Phillip Sloan (Notre Dame, IN: University of Notre Dame Press, 1981), 131–3.

Sloan, Phillip. "Natural History, 1670–1802." In *Companion to the History of Modern Science*, edited by R. C. Olby, G. N. Cantor, J. R. R. Christie, and M. J. S. Hodge (London: Routledge, 1990), 295–313.

Sloan, Phillip. "Preforming the Categories: Eighteenth-Century Generation Theory and the Biological Roots of Kant's A Priori." *Journal of the History of Philosophy* 40 (2002): 229–53.

Sloan, Phillip. "Kant on the History of Nature: The Ambiguous Heritage of the Critical Philosophy for Natural History." *Studies in History and Philosophy of Biological and Biomedical Sciences* 37 (2006): 627–48.

Sloan, Phillip. "The Essence of Race: Kant and Late Enlightenment Reflections." *Studies in History and Philosophy of Biological and Biomedical Sciences* 47 (2014): 191–5.

Sloan, Phillip. "Life Science and *Naturphilosophie*: Rethinking the Relationship." *Studies in History and Philosophy of Biological and Biomedical Sciences* 76 (2019): 98–100.

Sloan, Phillip. "Metaphysics and 'Vital' Materialism: Émile Du Châtelet and the Origins of French Vitalism." In *Philosophy of Biology before Biology*, edited by Cécilia Bognon-Küss and Charles T. Wolfe (Routledge: London, 2019), 48–65.

Sloan, Phillip, and Lyon, John. "Introduction." In *From Natural History to the History of Nature: Readings from Buffon and his Critics*, edited and translated by John Lyon and Phillip Sloan (Notre Dame, IN: University of Notre Dame Press, 1981), 1–32.

Smith, George. "The Methodology of the *Principia*." In *The Cambridge Companion to Newton*, edited by I. Bernard Cohen and George Smith (Cambridge: Cambridge University Press, 2002), 138–73.

Spagnesi, Lorenzo. "The Idea of God and the Empirical Investigation of Nature in Kant's *Critique of Pure Reason*." *Kantian Review* 27(2) (2022): 279–97.

Spagnesi, Lorenzo. "A Rule-Based Account of the Regulative Use of Reason in Kant's *Critique of Pure Reason*." *European Journal of Philosophy* forthcoming.

Stadler, August. *Kants Teleologie und ihre erkenntnisstheoretische Bedeutung. Eine Untersuchung* (Berlin: Dümmlers, 1874).

Stang, Nicholas. *Kant's Modal Metaphysics* (Oxford: Oxford University Press, 2016).

Stark, Werner. "Immanuel Kants physische Geographie—eine Herausforderung?" May 2001, https://www.online.uni-marburg.de/kant_old/webseitn/ws_lese4.htm

Stark, Werner. "Kant's Lectures on 'Physical Geography': A Brief Outline of Its Origins, Transmission, and Development: 1754–1805." In *Reading Kant's Geography*, edited by Stuart Elden and Eduardo Mendieta (Albany, NY: State University of New York Press, 2011), 69–86.

Stark, Werner. "La Géographie physique d'Immanuel Kant—avec une perspective sur les auteurs français." In *Kant et les sciences. Un dialogue philosophique avec la pluralité*, edited by Sophie Grapotte, Mai Lequan, and Margit Ruffing (Paris: Vrin, 2011), 171–90.

Steigerwald, Joan. *Experimenting at the Boundaries of Life: Organic Vitality in Germany Around 1800* (Pittsburgh, PA: University of Pittsburgh Press, 2019).

Strawson, Peter. *The Bounds of Sense* (London: Methuen, 1966).

Struik, Dirk. "Early colonial science in North America and Mexico." *Quipu* 1 (1984): 25–54.

Swabey, W. Curtis. "Kant's Analogies of Experience." *Philosophical Review* 31(1) (1922): 41–57.

Swift, Simon. "Kant, Herder and the Question of Philosophical Anthropology." *Textual Practice* 19(2) (2005): 219–38.

Terrall, Mary. *The Man Who Flattened the Earth: Maupertuis and the Sciences in the Enlightenment* (Chicago, IL: Chicago University Press, 2002).

Terrall, Mary. *Catching Nature in the Act: Réaumur and the Practice of Natural History in the Eighteenth Century* (Chicago, IL: Chicago University Pres, 2014).

Teufel, Thomas. "Wholes that Cause Their Parts: Organic *Self*-Reproduction and the Reality of Biological Teleology." *Studies in History and Philosophy of Biological and Biomedical Sciences* 42 (2011): 252–60.

Teufel, Thomas. "What Is the Problem of Teleology in Kant's *Critique of the Teleological Power of Judgment*?" *SATS* 12 (2011): 198–236.

Teufel, Thomas. "What Does Kant Mean by 'Power of Judgment' in His *Critique of the Power of Judgment*?" *Kantian Review* 17(2) (2012): 297–326.

Teufel, Thomas. "Kant's Transcendental Principle of Purposiveness and the 'Maxim of the Lawfulness of Empirical Laws'." In *Kant and the Laws of Nature*, edited by Michela Massimi and Angela Breitenbach (Cambridge: Cambridge University Press, 2017), 108–28.

Toulmin, Stephen, and Goodfield, June. *The Discovery of Time* (Harmondsworth: Penguin, 1965).

Ungerer, Emil. *Die Teleologie Kants und ihre Bedeutung für die Logik der Biologie* (Berlin: Borntraeger, 1922).

van den Berg, Hein. *Kant on Proper Science: Biology in the Critical Philosophy and the Opus Postumum* (Dordrecht: Springer, 2014).

van den Berg, Hein. "Kant and the Scope of Analogy in the Life Sciences." *Studies in the History and Philosophy of Science* 71 (2018): 67–76.

Vanzo, Alberto. "Kant on Experiment." *Rationis Defensor: Essays in Honour of Colin Cheyne*, edited by James Maclaurin (Dordrecht: Springer, 2012), 75–96.

Voltaire, Herbert François Gravelot. "Traité de métaphysique." In *Oeuvres Complettes de Mr. de Voltaire*, 4th ed., vol. 32 (Paris: Jean-François Bastien, 1771–6), 487–525.

Voltaire, Herbert François Gravelot. "Of the Different Races of Men." In *The* Idea *of Race*, edited by Robert Bernasconi and Tommy L. Lott (Indianapolis, IN: Hackett, 2000), 5–7.

Walden, Kenneth. "Reason Unbound: Kant's Theory of Regulative Principles." *European Journal of Philosophy* 27(3) (2009), 575–92.

Waldow, Anik. "Natural History and the Formation of the Human Being." *Studies in History and Philosophy of Science* 58 (2016): 67–76.

Walsh, W. H. *Reason and Experience* (Oxford: Oxford University Press, 1947).

Walsh, W. H. *Kant's Criticism of Metaphysics* (Edinburgh: Edinburgh University Press, 1975).

Watkins, Eric. *Kant and the Metaphysics of Causality* (Cambridge: Cambridge University Press, 2005).

Watkins, Eric. "The Antinomy of Teleological Judgment." *Kant Yearbook* 1 (2009): 197–222.

Watkins, Eric. "The Early Kant's (Anti-)Newtonianism." *Studies in History and Philosophy of Science* 44(3) (2013): 429–37.

Watkins, Eric. "Kant on Materialism." *British Journal for the History of Philosophy* 24 (2016): 1035–52.

Watkins, Eric. "Kant on Real Conditions." In *Akten des 12. Internationalen Kant-Kongresses, "Natur und Freiheit,"* edited by Violetta Waibel and Margit Ruffing (Berlin: de Gruyter, 2019), 1133–40.

Willaschek, Marcus. *Kant and the Sources of Metaphysics: The Dialectic of Pure Reason* (Cambridge: Cambridge University Press, 2018).

Willaschek, Marcus and Watkins, Eric. "Kant on Cognition and Knowledge." *Synthese* 197 (2020), 3195–3213.

Williams, Jessica. "'The Shape of a Four-Footed Animal in General': Kant on Empirical Schemata and the System of Nature." *HOPOS* 10 (2020): 1–23.

Wilson, Holly. *Kant's Pragmatic Anthropology: Its Origin, Meaning, and Critical Significance* (Albany, NY: State University of New York Press, 2006).

Wolfe, Charles. "Why Was There No Controversy Over Life in the Scientific Revolution?" In *Controversies in the Scientific Revolution*, edited by V. Boantza and M. Dascal (Amsterdam: John Benjamins, 2011), 187–219.

Wolfe, Charles. "On the Role of Newtonian Analogies in Eighteenth-Century Life Science." In Newton and *Empiricism*, edited by Zvi Biener and Eric Schliesser (Oxford: Oxford University Press, 2014), 223–61.

Wolff, Casper Friedrich. *Die Theorie der Generationen in zwei Abhandlungen erklärt und bewiesen* (Hildesheim: Georg Olms, 1966).

Wolff, Christian. *Vernünfftige Gedancken von den Absichten der natürlichen Dinge* (Halle im Magdeburg: Renger, 1724).

Woodward, John. *The Natural History of the Earth* (London, 1726).

Wotton, William. *Reflections upon Ancient and Modern Learning*, 3rd ed. (London, 1705).

Wright, Thomas. *The Universe and the Stars: Being an Original Theory of the Visible Creation, Founded on the Laws of Nature* (Philadelphia, PA: H. Probasco, 1837).

Wright, Thomas. *Second or Singular Thoughts upon the Theory of the Universe*, edited by M. A. Hoskin (London, 1968).

Ypi, Lea. *The Architectonic of Reason: Purposiveness and Systematic Unity in Kant's* Critique of Pure Reason (Oxford: Oxford University Press, 2021).

Zammito, John. *The Genesis of Kant's Critique of Judgment* (Chicago, IL: The University of Chicago Press, 1992).

Zammito, John. *Kant, Herder, and the Birth of Anthropology* (Chicago, IL: The University of Chicago Press, 2002).

Zammito, John. "'This Inscrutable *Principle* of an Original *Organization*': Epigenesis and 'Looseness of Fit' in Kant's Philosophy of Science." *Studies in History and Philosophy of Science* 34 (2003): 73–109.

Zammito, John. "Teleology Then and Now: The Question of Kant's Relevance for Contemporary Controversies over Function in Biology." *Studies in History and Philosophy of Biological and Biomedical Sciences* 37 (2006): 748–70.

Zammito, John. "Policing Polygeneticism in Germany, 1775: (Kames,) Kant, and Blumenbach." In *The German Invention of Race*, edited by Sara Eigen and Mark Larrimore (Albany, NY: State University of New York Press, 2006), 35–54.

Zammito, John. "The Lenoir Thesis Revisited: Blumenbach and Kant." In *Studies in History and Philosophy of Biological and Biomedical Sciences* 43 (2012): 120–32.

Zammito, John. "Should Kant Have Abandoned the 'Daring Adventure of Reason'? The Interest of Contemporary Naturalism in the Historicization of Nature in Kant and Idealist *Naturphilosophie*." *International Yearbook of German Idealism* 8 (2012): 130–64.

Zammito, John. "Epigenesis in Kant: Recent Reconsiderations." In *Studies in History and Philosophy of Biological and Biomedical Sciences* 58 (2016): 85–97.

Zammito, John. *The Gestation of German Biology: Philosophy and Physiology from Stahl to Schelling* (Chicago, IL: University of Chicago Press, 2018).

Zuckert, Rachel. *Kant on Beauty and Biology: An Interpretation of the* Critique of Judgment (Cambridge: Cambridge University Press, 2007).

Zuckert, Rachel. "History, Biology, and Philosophical Anthropology in Kant and Herder." *International Yearbook of German Idealism* 8 (2010): 38–59.

Zuckert, Rachel. "Organisms and Metaphysics: Kant's First Herder Review." In *Kant's Theory of Biology*, edited by Ina Goy and Eric Watkins (Berlin: de Gruyter, 2014), 61–77.

Zumbach, Clark. *The Transcendent Science: Kant's Conception of Biological Methodology* (The Hague: Nijhoff, 1984).

Index

For the benefit of digital users, indexed terms that span two pages (e.g., 52–53) may, on occasion, appear on only one of those pages.